Valley Forge

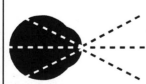

This Large Print Book carries the
Seal of Approval of N.A.V.H.

VALLEY FORGE

BOB DRURY
AND
TOM CLAVIN

THORNDIKE PRESS
A part of Gale, a Cengage Company

Farmington Hills, Mich • San Francisco • New York • Waterville, Maine
Meriden, Conn • Mason, Ohio • Chicago

**LIBRARY OF CONGRESS CIP DATA ON FILE.
CATALOGUING IN PUBLICATION FOR THIS BOOK
IS AVAILABLE FROM THE LIBRARY OF CONGRESS**

ISBN-13: 978-1-4328-5679-3 (hardcover)

Published in 2019 by arrangement with Simon & Schuster, Inc.

Printed in Mexico
2 3 4 5 6 7 23 22 21 20 19

For Ellen Drury Whitehurst
For Leslie Reingold

CONTENTS

A NOTE TO READERS

Eighteenth-century written English is notoriously cluttered with confounding punctuation, capitalized nouns erupting in the middle of sentences, and multiple spellings of the same word, all of which did not become standardized until comparatively recently.

Throughout the following text we have endeavored to present to readers the voluminous writings of our characters precisely as they themselves put those words to paper.

PROLOGUE

His troops had never seen George Washington so angry. His Excellency, as most of them called him, had always been the most composed soldier on the battlefield. But on this sweltering late June morning in 1778 the commander in chief of the Continental Army could not mask his fury.

He reined in his great white charger and trembled with rage. Rising in his stirrups, he towered over his second in command Gen. Charles Lee, the man he had charged with leading the attack. "What is the meaning of this, sir? I demand to know the meaning of this disorder and confusion!"

Nearly two years to the day since the signing of the Declaration of Independence, the fate of the American cause lay uncertain, all because the officer cowering before Washington had panicked and ordered a premature retreat. In a sense Washington blamed himself. General Lee had not wanted the assignment in the first place. He should have followed his instincts and left the Marquis de Lafayette in command. Lafayette had been by his side at Valley Forge, had witnessed and absorbed the *esprit* of the troops who had survived the horrors of that deadly winter. Valley Forge had been the crucible they had all come through together, the very reason the forces of the nascent United States were now poised to alter the course of the revolution. And was that same army now about to be destroyed because of one man's incompetence and lack of faith?

Charles Lee, dust-covered and dazed, gazed up at his superior. His eyes were dull, and his face wore the gray pallor of defeat. "Sir?" he stammered. "Sir?" The words were nearly unintelligible. He could find no others. Washington dismissed him and spurred his own horse forward.

As he'd approached the rolling green hills and swampy culverts surrounding the small New Jersey village of Monmouth Court House, an astonished Washington had demanded of each brigade and regimental commander he encountered to know why his unit was falling back. None could give a coherent answer, other than that Gen. Lee had ordered it. Now, as Washington galloped up and down the lines before his weary and bedraggled soldiery, the determination on his face was evident. Those who witnessed it would never forget it. "A gallant example animating his

14

forces," one veteran artillery officer later recalled.

Less than a mile to the east, 10,000 elite British troops had shed their packs, fixed bayonets, and were driving hard in counterattack. The British generals Henry Clinton and Charles Cornwallis could hardly believe their good fortune. After 12 months of a stalemated Philadelphia campaign, here was an opportunity to crush the colonial rebellion. If past was prologue, the mere sight of an endless wall of British "cold steel" would send the Continental rabble fleeing in disarray. A glorious rout would restore the transatlantic equilibrium. King George III would be ecstatic.

Washington knew otherwise. The hellish winter at Valley Forge had taught him so. He and his army had not endured the mud and blood of that winter encampment only to be turned back now. Half hidden in the smoke and cinders of battle, he ascended a rise and gathered about him the remnants of his exhausted army. It was the critical juncture of the war, and the tall Virginian exuded a sense of urgency and inspiration. Thirsty men who had wilted in the hundred-degree heat rose to their feet in anticipation.

"Will you fight?" Washington cried. "Will you fight?" The survivors of Valley Forge responded with three thunderous cheers that reverberated across the ridgeline. Lafayette, riding with Alexander Hamilton beside the commander in chief, was overwhelmed. "His presence," the young Frenchman wrote, "seemed to arrest fate with a single glance."

The skies darkened with cannon shot just as Washington raised his sword and pointed it toward the approaching sea of red. He was about to spur his horse again when Hamilton jumped from his own steed and shouted, "We are betrayed, and the moment has arrived when every true friend of America and her cause must be ready to die in their defense!"

Washington, his aristocratic reserve regained, replied in a calm voice. "Colonel Hamilton," he said, "get back on your horse."

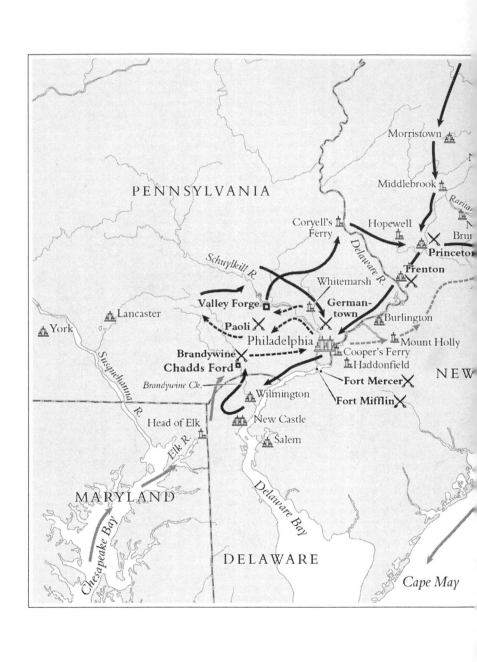

Morristown

Middlebrook

Raritan

PENNSYLVANIA

Coryell's
Ferry

Hopewell

Brun

Princeto

Delaware R.

Trenton

Schuylkill R.

Whitemarsh

Valley Forge

German-
town

Burlington

Lancaster

Paoli

Mount Holly

York

Philadelphia

Brandywine
Chadds Ford

Cooper's Ferry

Susquehanna R.

Haddonfield

NEW

Brandywine Ck.

Fort Mercer

Wilmington

Fort Mifflin

Head of Elk

New Castle

Salem

MARYLAND

Chesapeake Bay

Delaware Bay

Elk R.

DELAWARE

Cape May

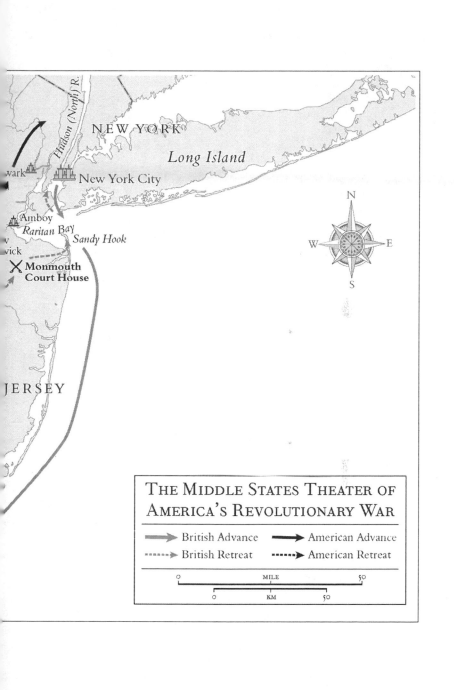

Hudson (North) R.

NEW YORK

Long Island

wark

New York City

Amboy
Raritan Bay
Sandy Hook

vick

✕ **Monmouth
Court House**

JERSEY

N

W ✦ E

S

THE MIDDLE STATES THEATER OF
AMERICA'S REVOLUTIONARY WAR

⟶ British Advance ⟶ American Advance
┈┈▸ British Retreat ┈┈▸ American Retreat

0   MILE   50

0   KM   50

■ ■ ■ ■

PART I

■ ■ ■ ■

The Enemy were routed in the greatest Confusion several Miles, we pass'd thro their Encampments & took some pieces of Cannon, in short we were flatter'd with every appearance of a most glorious & decisive Action when to my great surprize Our Men began to give way, which when the Line was once broke became pretty General & could not with our utmost Exertions be prevented & the only thing left was to draw them off in the best manner we could.

GEORGE WASHINGTON TO
GEN. ISRAEL PUTNAM,
OCTOBER 8, 1777

George Washington's experiences—both good and bad—as a young officer in the Virginia militia fighting alongside British forces in the French and Indian War served him well as commander of the American forces.

ONE:
A SPRIG OF GREEN

They marched in parade formation through the heart of Philadelphia, 12,000 strong. Down Front Street and up Chestnut Street they came, the heroes of Trenton and Princeton, the survivors of Long Island and Harlem Heights and White Plains, and they constituted a panoply foreshadowing the diversity that would define a future nation. The Grand Army, they were called: Irishmen, Germans, and Poles; French and disaffected Brits and Scots; a company of African American freemen, all now newly minted *Americans*. A "multiplicity of interests," as James Madison would call them, forging a distinct national identity. Every man wore a sprig of greenery affixed to his hat or woven through his hair. It was a symbol of hope and victory.

At their head, astride his white Arabian standing 16 hands high, rode the 45-year-old George Washington, his russet hair liberally powdered to look like a wig, pulled back into a queue and held in place by a black silk ribbon. In his elegant blue-and-buff uniform, the strapping Washington was a majestic and commanding figure, graceful to the point where contemporaries commented on his fluid dancing skills. But mounted, with his polished silver spurs girding knee-high black riding boots, he projected the powerful impression of martial virility itself. Six feet two inches tall, he had strong, narrow shoulders set atop a broad chest that flared out to a lifelong horseman's wide hips and muscled thighs. But it was his hands that caught one's attention — large and sinewy planter's hands strong enough to crack hickory nuts.

Washington was the centripetal force to which the soldiers parading through Philadelphia had each been drawn. Despite his imposing carriage, however, it was the general's melancholy blue eyes with their flecks of gray that hinted at the merest trace of self-doubt. Those eyes, set deep in his craggy, sunburned face, flashed the tale of a man who, to paraphrase one historian, had constructed his own fierce stoicism to mask his combustible emotions and insecurities.

The 19-year-old Marquis de Lafayette was given the honor of riding beside Washington. He was famously *soigné* in his signature blue cocked hat and matching greatcoat with red facing, and his gold-braided epaulets bounced to the rise and fall of his cantering sorrel over the river cobblestones. Hard on the duo's heels in their own long officers' coats, boots shined to a luster and spurs jangling, came the indispensable polymath Alexander Hamilton — who at 22 had already proved his mettle on battlefields from White Plains to Princeton — and the leonine John Laurens, also 22, the son of the South Carolina delegate Henry Laurens, soon to succeed John Hancock as president of the Continental Congress. These three adoring aides constituted what the childless Washington deemed a veritable troika of surrogate sons. They each returned his affection.

It was a feverish Sunday, August 24, 1777, almost 26 months since Washington had been culled from the Virginia delegation to the First Continental Congress and commissioned general and commander in chief of the army of the united colonies: a wealthy southern plantation owner tabbed to lead a revolution. Now, this morning, the flood tide of troops stepping smartly through Philadelphia's city center to the beat of fife and drum had been transformed from the "lower class" militiamen whom Washington once described as exhibiting "an unaccountable kind of stupidity" into a force for freedom. Most of the soldiers remained shabbily clad in motley vestments. Washington, never a man for spontaneity, had ordered the green sprigs in order to provide some uniformity to the Continentals' discrepant apparel. Despite their dishabille, they nonetheless awed the 40,000 inhabitants of the new nation's capital as they made for the floating bridge spanning the Schuylkill River that would carry them to their new camp across the water in Darby, Pennsylvania.

By 1777, Philadelphia stretched six blocks deep for two miles along the larger Delaware River, and for two solid hours the city's residents gaped from windows, verandas, and rooftops or crowded out of doorways to line the muddy wooden curbs to view the passing troops. The spectators included members of the Continental Congress, whose delegates packed the redbrick bell tower of the statehouse Lafayette would one day dub Independence Hall. With each passing regiment rose a great huzzah for the men from Delaware and New Jersey and New York, from Connecticut and Massachusetts and New Hampshire, from Maryland and North Carolina and Virginia. The crowd saved their loudest cheers for their fellow Pennsylvanians and, of course, for the commander in chief himself.

Washington had ordered the army's wagons and excess horses kept out of view during the promenade. The baggage train, which suggested the true nature of his ill-provisioned force, was to take a roundabout route to the new encampment. Given the hundreds of local soldiers under his command, Washington also warned of a punishment of 39 lashes to anyone who abandoned the parade route prematurely to visit with family and friends. Despite his efforts, he could not prevent the army's camp followers, perhaps 400 women and children, from pouring into the city behind the troops, "chattering and yelling in sluttish shrills as they went, and spitting in the gutters" below the rented rooms on Market Street where Thomas Jefferson had written the Declaration of Independence.

Still, the procession went off almost precisely as Washington had choreographed it, a splendid demonstration designed to plant seeds of doubt in the minds of the city's large Loyalist community. Although the commander in chief was not an overly religious man, even he may have felt the hand of divine intervention when the previous night's downpour had ceased abruptly at dawn and left the city's streets washed clean. Only his inner circle was aware that today's spic-and-span pageantry was mostly a bluff. For the British were coming. Soon. With a battle-tested force far greater than the number of Continental Army regulars. And they intended to take this city.

Since losing a series of battles and being driven from New York the previous summer, Washington and his closest advisers had been uncharacteristically flummoxed by General Sir William Howe, who led the 30,000-strong

British expeditionary force in North America. Throughout the spring and summer of 1777, Howe had orchestrated a series of feints that forced Washington into exaggerated counter-measures. He had dispatched companies of his exhausted Continentals from their camp in Morristown, New Jersey, through rain-storms and searing heat as far north as the Hudson Highlands and as far south as the lower Delaware River. Each expedition was for naught, as Howe always pulled his troops back to New York before the Americans ar-rived. This was all a part of the British com-mander's scheme; he was in no hurry to crush the rebels just yet. His superiors in Britain, particularly his friend King George III, hoped that the massive show of British force would bring the colonies to their senses and, subsequently, to the bargaining table.

In period paintings the 48-year-old Gen. Howe bore an eerie likeness to Washington, most notably in his erect bearing, high forehead, and aristocratic gaze, which was somewhat offset by a set of uneven and prob-ably false teeth that struck observers as similar to the perforations on a stamp. Con-temporary descriptions of the general were less kind than his portrait artists, with one young American who met him describing "a large portly man, of coarse features [who] appeared to have lost his teeth, as his mouth had fallen in." At least his similarity to the denture-wearing American commander in chief rings true.

Howe and his older brother Adm. Lord Richard "Black Dick" Howe, commander of the British fleet in America, were scions of an aristocratic family that had attained its peerage a century earlier under the Dutch-born "King Billy" III. Both had attended Eton. The admiral's taciturn demeanor and dusky complexion had earned him his nickname, and the general's skin tone was also of a darker hue than that of most contemporary Englishmen. The younger Howe was fond of both gambling and whoring — he compensated his American mistress's husband with a job as a prison commissioner. He had nonetheless earned his stars by showing valor on the front lines during the Seven Year's War — what the American colonists called the French and Indian War — and, later, during his costly victory at Bunker Hill. His energy and courage continued to endear him to his troops, who were the most highly trained in North America. Yet close observers also noted that the general "lacked the confidence, the sense of responsibility, and the professional dedication that distinguished" his older brother the admiral.

After the British general John Burgoyne's staggering recapture of upstate New York's Fort Ticonderoga in early July, Washington was nearly certain that Howe would move north to join Burgoyne to control the Hudson River and effectively cut off the more rebellious New England colonies from the rest of the country.* Since then, however, the Continental spy network in New York had increasingly reported that the Howe brothers were secretly mustering pilots familiar with the Delaware River. If these communiqués proved true, common sense dictated only one target — the British were aiming for Philadelphia, the largest city in North America and home to the Continental Congress. The morale-breaking display of the American delegates fleeing before a conquering enemy army was what Washington had come to prevent.

In late July Gen. Howe had teased Washington and his intelligence officers yet again when he loaded 17,000 of his British regulars and German mercenaries onto his brother's fleet of 228 ships — the largest flotilla to ever ply American waters — and sailed from Sandy Hook, New Jersey.† Their destination

---

* As certain as Burgoyne, whose plan for isolating New England from America's middle and southern colonies depended upon it.
† Though King George III had "rented" his foreign troops from the rulers of six German principalities, the vast majority of them — close to 19,000 — hailed from the Prussian landgraviate of Hesse-

was unclear. It was not lost on the Americans that Adm. Howe, so attuned to the world's tides that he was known as "the human sea chantey," had pioneered Britain's naval expertise in amphibious landings, and rumors abounded. One report had the Howes tacking toward occupied Rhode Island in an attempt to retake Boston, the city they had been driven from 17 months earlier. Another had them sailing south to open up a new front below Virginia. General George Weedon, Washington's fellow Virginian and longtime lieutenant, fretted that the Continentals were "in the dark with regard to [the enemy's] designs."

As a defense against the Royal Navy vessels advancing up the Delaware, Washington's volunteer French military engineers had constructed a series of underwater obstructions known as *chevaux-de-frise,* or "Frisian Horses," at various points along the river. These stockade-like rows of thick, iron-tipped wooden spears — employed during European wars since medieval times to impede cavalry charges — were weighted to the river bottom

---

Cassel. They combined with another 2,500 from Hesse-Hanau to lend the name Hessians to all German mercenaries. The second-largest contingent, just over 5,700 men, had come from the principality of Brunswick.

by heavy crates filled with rocks and designed to pierce the hulls of enemy craft. Washington did not have much faith in the contraptions. He wrote to a subordinate that "the idea of preventing ships from passing up & down rivers . . . has proved wrong . . . unless the water is narrow." He was more confident in the string of riverside forts the Continentals occupied, including two strong redoubts on opposite banks south of Philadelphia at just such a "narrow" point in the river. The Continentals hoped that taken together, all these obstacles would prove to be an impassable choke point.

Howe appeared to agree, and on August 23 — the day before the Continental Army's grand show of force in Philadelphia — reports reached Washington that the entire enemy squadron had reappeared and anchored off the capes of a northern inlet of Chesapeake Bay at the head of Maryland's Elk River. Within days, Gen. Howe's army had disembarked. This struck the Americans as an odd location from which to begin a march to capture a city over 50 miles away. But that is not what the Britisher had in mind. A week earlier a message had reached Howe, who was aboard his brother's command ship, from Lord George Germain, secretary of state for the Americas. In it, Germain suggested that after capturing Philadelphia and subduing the other Middle Atlantic colonies, Howe was to leave the conquered territories to be maintained by Loyalist militias while he drove north to join Burgoyne in upstate New York. Germain, a dour misanthrope with no patience for rebels of any stripe, strongly hinted that the Crown expected Gen. Howe to crush this bothersome uprising before 1777 was out. Thus Gen. Howe's primary intention was to lure Washington and his entire force into a major, warending confrontation. As it happened, this was what Washington also looked forward to — "One bold stroke [to] free the land from rapine, devastations, and burnings," he wrote to Gen. Benedict Arnold.

Meanwhile, the commander in chief was privately encountering a different kind of enemy, threefold, bureaucratic in nature, and wielding paper instead of guns: the Continental Congress, the civil government of Pennsylvania, and the Board of War. The third of these, officially titled the Board of War and Ordnance, had been established in June 1776 as a temporary liaison between the civil authorities and the military. Staffed by five congressional delegates and a skeleton crew of clerks, the board was charged with overseeing various functions of military administration from enlistments to promotions while remaining an arm's length from the physical army. But by April 1777 the original board members, burdened by mountains of organizational duties, reported to Congress that they could not keep pace with the workload. They suggested their own replacement by a permanent body of professional soldiers. Congress was deliberating just such a move, which Washington correctly viewed as a threat to his authority, even as he prepared to meet Gen. Howe's army.

Moreover, there were those in Congress, particularly among the New England contingent, whose confidence in Washington's leadership was eroding. Memories of the Continental Army's surprise Christmas victories of 1776 at Trenton and Princeton were fading, replaced by ennui over the lack of movement across the spring and summer of 1777. The fiery John Adams, one of the most influential members of the Continental Congress, feared handing Washington untrammeled power, and worried aloud that the country's growing devotion to the commander in chief was producing the very type of regal figure whose yoke America was fighting to throw off. More to the point: who was Washington to deserve this veneration if he remained unable to use the momentum of his victories in New Jersey to further the rebellion?

Finally, what was perhaps of most pressing, and distressing, importance to Washington was the Pennsylvania state government's apparent laissez-faire approach to the impending military clash. This attitude was most evident in the state's request that a portion of its militiamen be temporarily released from his command in order to return to their farms to plant winter corn. There was a precedent for this seeming indifference. The Continental Congress had always been wary of a standing national army, and the Pennsylvania state politicians followed suit. They were even, incredibly, under the impression that Washington's mixed force of regulars and militiamen was already "far too numerous." The absence of a few units, they reasoned, would not much be missed.

Washington knew better, no matter how far his host of raw recruits may have evolved since Bunker Hill. He understood perfectly that what seemed a formidable force to the throngs of cheering Philadelphians was in fact about to meet the most disciplined and confident armed force in the world. He had seen with his own eyes what could result.

Over two decades earlier, while fighting for the British during the French and Indian War as a 22-year-old lieutenant colonel, Washington had been charged with leading a ragtag unit of Virginia militiamen into the uncharted territory then called the Ohio Country — a vast area west of the Blue Ridge Mountains and south of the Great Lakes. His orders: to backstop a company of British regulars dispatched to drive the French from what is now western Pennsylvania. When the Redcoats and their colonial attendants found the French and their Indian allies, a murderous fight ensued. Though Washington's backwoodsmen had never seen action against trained soldiers, he was confident that their frontier wiles and experience would stand them well. Yet his green recruits withered under concerted and coordinated enemy fire, retreating and falling on their own rum supply in fright and despair. Washington had kept his composure and comported himself with dignity during what became a bloody slaughter, but the memory of his callow militiamen breaking against professional troops never left him.

So even as the huzzahs from Front and Chestnut Streets still echoed, he dispatched couriers west and south from his campsite at Darby with urgent requests for fresh regiments. He also took the opportunity to recross the Schuylkill and personally implore individual congressional delegates to pressure their states' recruiting officers to send more men as soon as possible. He reminded them that the hopes for independence so raised by his army on parade only a few days earlier were about to be sorely tested, and it would not be soaring rhetoric that beat back the enemy at the city's gates, but hard flint and steel. In response, the solons of the Continental Congress vowed to appoint a steering panel to explore the army's understaffing problem. And they did. It would be one of 114 committees they created that year.

TWO:
TO CROWN THE BRAVE

The distant echo of British boots had a sobering effect.

In late August, as news spread through Philadelphia of Gen. Howe's landing, the Pennsylvania state legislature rescinded its request to release soldiers for the summer planting season and instead ordered its militia commanders to station 5,000 men along the city's southwestern heights in a line of defense. The British army, no longer aboard a ghost fleet adrift somewhere on the Atlantic, was now a palpable threat, and a terrain that had previously seen little fighting suddenly pulsed in anticipation of battle. As the historian Wayne Bodle observes, "A summer of anxious maneuvering was finally about to culminate in combat."

It was with this sense of urgency that Congress ordered great stores of food, clothing, and military equipment heaped onto carts and hauled from Philadelphia into the western Pennsylvania towns of Lancaster and

York. A trickle of the city's citizens followed the juddering wagon trains, the same civilians who had cheered loudest during the Continental Army's parade through the city only days earlier. Now, in anticipation of Gen. Howe's arrival — and not a little apprehensive over Washington's ability to stop him — they, too, headed inland.

And then, in an anticlimax of a sort, a stillness fell over the city. Even as Washington directed his divisions south to head off the British, he and his staff remained confounded by the enemy's sluggish pace. The Americans had no way of knowing that, for the moment, Gen. Howe's Redcoats constituted a recovering army after having been battered by a series of ferocious storms during their month-long sea voyage. The British horses that hadn't been chucked overboard owing to a lack of fresh water were so malnourished as to be useless, and the cramped troopship quarters had turned the infantry into a shambolic mob less keen on fighting rebels than on looting Maryland's barns and grain sheds. Howe himself recognized that any movement toward Philadelphia would have to wait until his army regained its land legs, so he limited his forays to scouting parties sent north to report back on the most expeditious routes into Pennsylvania.

Earlier in the year there had been ephemeral hopes among England's war planners that

Howe would quickly dispose of Washington's ragtag regiments before leading his British and German forces north to join with Gen. John "Gentleman Johnny" Burgoyne's army marching south from Canada. This was the plan the satanically handsome Burgoyne had personally put forth the previous winter to King George in London. Burgoyne was renowned for his fondness for British gambling houses, German mistresses, and French champagne — the English Whig antiquarian Horace Walpole coined the phrase "all sail and no ballast" in his honor — and the *bon-viveur*'s horseback rides with the king through Hyde Park had inspired talk in Whitehall of putting an end to the American insurgency by Christmas. Now, Howe's leisurely pace rendered this timetable moot.

Unlike Burgoyne, Gen. Howe was by nature a cautious man. Upon landing in Maryland he wrote to George Germain that he was shocked to find patriotic passion running stronger than he anticipated among the inhabitants of the middle colonies of Pennsylvania, Maryland, Delaware, and New Jersey. He had issued a general order offering protection to all civilians who remained in their homes and turned over their arms. Yet along the roads he passed scores of abandoned farmsteads, their fields and orchards ready to be harvested, their fat cattle untended. At least his soldiers ate well. In his letter to

Whitehall he also grumbled that there was little hope of ending the war in 1777 "without the sizable addition of reinforcements from England."

This admission was eerily similar to his complaint of 18 months earlier, after he and his forces had been driven from Boston. Then he had written to Germain confessing apprehension about putting down the American rebellion as rapidly as London expected. Both justifications, of course, were fairly standard military tactics — underplay one's prospects for quick victory. Howe was also demonstrating a remarkable lack of self-awareness as to how he was being painted in London as a defeatist. In any event, after his abandonment of Boston and the humiliating defeat at Trenton, Howe's die was cast in Pennsylvania. When he was denied his request for 15,000 more troops, this was rationale enough for him to allow the Redcoats already under his command to halt intermittently to plunder local farmsteads while moving through Maryland and Delaware at a glacial pace. Oddly, with his insouciant strategy, Howe was matching Washington's own lagging pace.

Long before his civic virtues began to inspire comparisons to the selfless Roman citizen-soldier Cincinnatus, Washington was already known among his officer corps by another Roman epithet, "the Great Fabius." This was an homage to the general Quintus Fabius Maximus Verrucosus, whose tactics of side-slipping pitched battles with Hannibal's stronger Carthaginian invasion force in the third century BC eventually led to Rome's victory in the Second Punic War. However, Fabius's disposition toward eschewing direct assaults in favor of a guerrilla approach of ambush and harassment, particularly of the enemy's supply lines, did not come naturally to Washington. In fact, it went against everything in his aggressive temperament, as was noted by Hamilton: "The enemy will have Philadelphia . . . unless we fight them a pretty general action," he complained to the New York congressman Gouverneur Morris, a signer of the Declaration of Independence and the man destined to write the preamble to the United States Constitution. But to this point in the war, a Fabian strategy of bleeding not only the enemy force around its edges, but also the British taxpayers, had proved more efficacious for Washington. His was the weaker army, and if the fact of its simple survival mandated that the British spend their time and energy continually attempting to find and defeat it, he surmised that sooner or later King George and Parliament would decide that they were paying too steep a price to retain their American colonies.

Further, many of Washington's subordinates

carried in their rucksacks well-thumbed copies of *Caesar's Gallic Wars* to read aloud in Latin by firelight. What he and his officer corps were quick to recognize was that despite the invention of gunpowder and firearms, core military principles had not altered significantly since ancient times. Washington was fond of quoting key battle scenes from Shakespeare's *Julius Caesar* and *Henry V* at his war councils and, not surprisingly, his favorite play was Joseph Addison's *Cato, a Tragedy,* a drama in which he had performed some 25 years earlier. In its depiction of the stoic Marcus Portius Cato's republican resistance to the tyranny of Julius Caesar's dictatorship, the play served as a rather obvious metaphor. As Washington's biographer Ron Chernow notes, "The rhetoric of *Cato* saturated the American Revolution." Both Patrick Henry's famous appeal for liberty or death and the captured spy Nathan Hale's lament that he had but one life to give for his country were taken nearly word for word from two of the play's most famous lines.*

---

* "It is not now time to talk of aught, but chains or conquest, liberty or death," Cato tells his daughter's suitor Juba midway through Act Two. Later, when presented with the body of his slain son, he laments,

By early September, Continental scouts had located the British army plodding inexorably north through Delaware. Washington was forced to conclude that, sooner than later, his Fabian strategy could no longer abide. Yet true to the cautious nature he had adopted, over the next week he was content to merely shadow Howe while, with his farmer's instincts, he himself kept a close eye on the terrain for any battlefield advantage. A few units of Pennsylvania militiamen were pulled from their posts south of Philadelphia and ordered to harass Howe's rear. And forward pickets from the two maneuvering forces did sometimes skirmish, blundering into each other mostly by accident.* But as the days ground on the two generals were still marching their armies on parallel tracks in a generally

---

"Who would not be that youth? What pity is it that we can die but once to serve our country."

* It is sometimes difficult to comprehend how the era's commanders followed the delicate rules of war. During this cat-and-mouse harass-and-skirmish game, for example, Washington ordered one of his commanders to apologize to Gen. Howe "if there is any truth in report that an enemy flag was fired upon." ("George Washington to Brigadier General William Maxwell, 5 September 1777," *Founders Online,* National Archives; Original source: Syrett, *The Papers of Alexander Hamilton,* Vol. 1, p. 324.)

northwest direction, with Washington always positioning his main body of troops between the enemy and Philadelphia.

It frustrated Washington that the scores of prisoners his forward parties captured could provide no solid information as to Howe's intentions. And as the two opponents continued to probe each other like prizefighters searching for a weakness — Washington was reported by several British officers to have been observed personally raising a spyglass on a faraway hill — there were some on the commander in chief's staff who argued that Howe's northwest trajectory signaled not a move on Philadelphia at all, but a thrust toward the Continental caches of weapons and food stored in the state's interior. Washington publicly acknowledged the "Mystery" of Gen. Howe's plans, but privately entertained "little doubt" that the American capital city remained his ultimate target.

Finally, on September 8, Howe showed his hand when he ordered his troops north toward Philadelphia. Forty-eight hours later the two armies found themselves separated by mere miles on opposite sides of a wide and fast-flowing watercourse called Brandywine Creek.

Brandywine Creek, often mistaken for a river because of its width and depth, is formed by the confluence of two smaller rivulets with headwaters in Pennsylvania's western Chester County. On its journey to Delaware Bay it courses through a terrain of plunging ravines and rocky rises blanketed by thick spinneys of tulip poplars and towering black oak. Its current is strong enough to power gristmills, sawmills, and even the paper mill that pressed the sheets on which the Declaration of Independence was written. Washington recognized immediately that this topography formed the last natural line of defense on the road to Philadelphia, some 25 miles to the northeast. The British, having shorn themselves of all "tents, trunks, chests, boxes, other bedding and [extra] cloaths," were camped in the craggy hills that rose from the creek's western bank. The Americans, traveling similarly light, occupied an eight-mile belt on the opposite side of the water.

Of the half-dozen possible crossings along the Brandywine, the optimal one was Chadds Ford, a stretch of waist-deep water running about 150 feet from bank to bank situated on the "Great Post Road" that connected Baltimore to Philadelphia. Washington detached small units to guard the fording sites to the north and south with the intention of funneling the British toward Chadds Ford. He placed six or seven field pieces on the high ground overlooking the ford, and took as his headquarters the stone house of a miller just east of the crossing. He knew well what was at stake on the banks of the rushing Brandy-wine.

Washington was a reluctant public speaker, and days earlier he had used a General Order to inform his troops that they were about to embark upon what very well might be the most decisive battle of the war for independence. A defeat of the British here and now, he'd announced, "and they are utterly undone — the war is at an end. The eyes of all America, and of Europe are turned upon us [and] the most important moment is at hand . . . [where] glory awaits to crown the brave." To emphasize the importance of every soldier steeling himself for this momentous engagement, he had each commander muster his troops to announce that any men caught fleeing the battlefield "would be instantly shot down as a just punishment to themselves and for examples to others . . . to prevent the cowardly from making a sacrifice of the brave." Now, with their "arms cleaned and put in the best possible order . . . their bayonets fixed . . . and their flints screwed in fast," the Continentals were, in the words of the Rhode Island general Nathanael Greene, "in high spirits" and burning for a fight.

Of his senior officers, Washington was fondest of Greene, who at 33 was the youngest major general in the Continental Army until Lafayette was commissioned. Dubbed the "Fighting Quaker," Greene had quit the

Society of Friends as a teenager after being scolded by his parents for ignoring his Bible studies in favor of military histories and journals. His fondness for alehouses further alienated him from his family's religious community. Ignoring the reprimands of his father, a prosperous iron forge and sawmill owner, Greene helped found a militia in his hometown, East Greenwich, Rhode Island, where his reading habits expanded to include poetry, philosophy, and even the satire of Jonathan Swift.

Though Greene suffered from bouts of asthma and walked with a pronounced limp from a childhood sawmill accident, portraits from the era depict him as a strikingly handsome man, with burning blue eyes, a narrow straight nose, full lips, and a pair of broad shoulders that tapered to a V-shaped torso. Appropriately, in Catharine "Caty" Littlefield, he had married one of New England's most beautiful women. Despite his lack of formal education, in 1775 Greene was at Washington's urging commissioned a brigadier by the First Continental Congress by dint of what one historian calls his "dawn-to-dusk work habits." His personal bravery and his grasp of both strategy and tactics had impressed Washington during the siege of Boston — it was said that the Rhode Island militia's tent camp was the most disciplined and professional in the entire army — and the commander in chief had even recommended to Congress that should he himself fall in combat, Greene be appointed to take his place.

Washington would need all of Gen. Greene's martial qualities, for by the evening of September 10, he had wheeled his army to face the Brandywine, with the greatest concentration of troops massed under Greene near Chadds Ford. It was a disastrous mistake. On the other side of the creek, Gen. Howe's intelligence officers had recruited a clutch of Pennsylvania Tories with an intimate knowledge of the local terrain. Washington had apparently overlooked or chosen to ignore Howe's oft-stated preference for flanking maneuvers as opposed to costly frontal assaults. It was one of the qualities that bound his men to him.

The previous evening the civilian Loyalists had sketched for Howe a route that would take him farther north, where he could skirt the farthermost American pickets and cross the upper Brandywine's two shallow forks. With Howe and his chief commander Lord Gen. Charles Cornwallis embarking on a lightning march up and across the streams, the British would fall on Washington's right wing in a surprise attack. To complete the ruse, Howe left a rump force of some 6,000 Hessians on the west bank of the creek near Chadds Ford with instructions to their commander, Gen. Wilhelm von Knyphausen, to act as if the entire army were preparing for a bold rush across the water and into the teeth of the Continental line.

So it occurred that in the predawn hours of September 11, guided by the local Tories under the cover of a dense fog, Gen. Howe and Gen. Cornwallis led close to 9,000 Redcoats north while the Americans, girding for battle at Chadds Ford, took von Knyphausen's bait. Soon after sunrise the Hessians began cannonading the Americans; they also initiated a few minor skirmishes about the river as Washington rode the length of his line to the sound of cheering troops and, increasingly, the crack of muskets and the thunderous reports of artillery fire. Washington maintained that courage and cowardice alike flowed from the leadership of an army, and he practiced what he preached. At one point a British cannonball took the head off an American artilleryman standing but a few feet from him, and at another an enemy sharpshooter was said to have had the American commander in chief lined up in his sights just as Washington turned his back to him. The chivalric rifleman, Maj. Patrick Ferguson, refused to pull the trigger and shoot a man in the back.*

* Though the latter incident has been subsequently refuted, in some quarters the fact that Washington

As it was, the skirmishing at Chadds Ford was thick enough to lull Washington and his staff into overlooking the scattered intelligence reports arriving by couriers that indicated enemy movements to the north. There was no little irony in Howe's subterfuge. The French and Indian War had taught Washington the valuable lesson that the rugged and thickly overgrown terrain of the New World inhibited the conventional warfare preferred by the great European armies, with lines of troops arrayed opposite one another on open battlefields. Whenever possible, Washington instead intended to fight the British as the French had done, with speed and stealth — "Indian style," he called it. Such cunning had worked for him at Trenton and Princeton, yet now here was Howe employing a feint-and-flank maneuver perfectly consonant with the linear procedures of the great eighteenth-century armies.

Around noon, Washington was informed that one of his scouting parties had spotted what they took to be several companies of Redcoats on the American side of the river to the north. But a second communiqué contradicted this and suggested that the movement was a British feint as the main army massed

---

was known to hew so close to the front lines is telling.

51

for an attack across Chadds Ford. It was not until midafternoon that a rider arrived at Washington's temporary headquarters with definitive word that the greater part of Howe's army had indeed crossed the Brandywine's northern forks. His grand battle plan undone, the commander in chief spurred his horse north at a gallop to save what he could of both his army and his reputation. But here it was Howe's turn to blunder.

Had the British struck immediately at the Americans' exposed right flank, the Continental Army would have shattered like spun glass. But by now the fog had lifted, the afternoon had turned into a humid swelter, and the Redcoats, having quick-marched nearly 17 miles since before daybreak, lagged in forming their attack columns. This gave Washington enough time to reach his two reserve divisions and instruct their commanders to take up positions atop a hill that rose between the enemy advance and the bulk of the patriot force. For one of these generals, William Alexander — an American-born ironmaster whose lapsed inheritance of a Scottish earldom entitled him to the honorific Lord Stirling — the order must have seemed eerily familiar. A year earlier, during the catastrophic Battle of Long Island, Gen. Lord Stirling had been captured while leading the 1st Maryland Regiment in fighting a rear-guard action that allowed Washington's main body of troops to slip away intact. Now, at the head of a division of New Jerseyans after a prisoner exchange, he and the Scotsborn Gen. Adam Stephen, commanding two brigades of Virginians, were being asked to again sacrifice themselves for the good of the greater whole.

General Howe moved on this makeshift line around four o'clock. Stephen's Virginians and Lord Stirling's New Jersey infantry had dragged several small field pieces to the crest of the hill, and their canisters and grapeshot combined with Continental musket fire to rip holes in the ranks of the advancing British grenadiers. This effectively gave the northernmost Americans stationed on the Brandywine — two brigades of Maryland regulars under the command of Gen. John Sullivan — time to fall back from the creek and join the reserve divisions, although they encountered murderous fire as they attempted to create a joined line with Stephen's and Lord Stirling's men.

General Sullivan, a former New Hampshire congressman in overall command of this right wing of the American army, had also fought in the Battle of Long Island. After the British had similarly surprised Washington with a flanking maneuver then, his Continentals had so botched their fallback that the Hessians had openly mocked them as they bayonetted to death those who had thrown away their arms and surrendered in panic. Now, however, the majority of Sullivan's soldiers stood rock-steady as the British softened up their positions with a cannon bombardment.* Finally, the British fixed bayonets and charged the division holding Sullivan's left flank. Following the lead of their confused commander, the Frenchman Gen. Preudhomme de Borre, most of the American units panicked and broke as Lafayette, who had turned 20 five days earlier and had pleaded with Washington to be allowed to take part in his first action, attempted to regain some of France's honor. Spurring his horse, the marquis galloped up and down before the stampeding troops and, in his broken English, exhorted them to stand and fight.[†] On several occasions he jumped from his saddle to tackle soldiers running toward the rear. It was during one of these scrums that an aide noticed blood pouring from his left calf and helped him back onto his horse. Despite his boot filling with blood, Lafayette refused to leave the field as thousands of charging Redcoats swarmed Lord Stirling's remaining division and the fight degenerated into "muzzle to muzzle" and hand-to-hand combat.

* The troughs plowed up by the British cannonballs across Birmingham Hill can be seen to this day.
† De Borre was drummed out of the Continental Army following this debacle.

Before they could be completely surrounded the New Jerseyans and Virginians under Gen. Lord Stirling and Gen. Stephen managed to fall back through the glades of the steep and rocky terrain pocked with giant bluestone volcanic rock, using the boulders and the thick trunks of pignut hickory and blackgum tupelos as cover as they crouched to reload and return fire. Like their English and German counterparts, most of the colonists were armed with smoothbore muskets, often called firelocks or flintlocks after the flint-striking-steel charge ignition in the gunlock. A well-trained soldier might load and fire such a weapon three times in a minute. But a portion of the backwoodsmen, particularly the Virginians, carried long rifles. Although these took longer to load, they were more accurate. This afternoon they made deadly use of them, and so slowed the enemy advance that even the haughty Lord Cornwallis was moved to concede to Gen. Howe that "the damn rebels form well" as he watched the fight unfold from a rise overlooking the battlefield. It was small consolation.

By this time Washington had returned to his headquarters, from where he could clearly hear the artillery and musket reports of a major engagement taking place behind him. Before him across the Brandywine, meanwhile, he watched Gen. von Knyphausen's Hessians prepare to attack. It was likely at

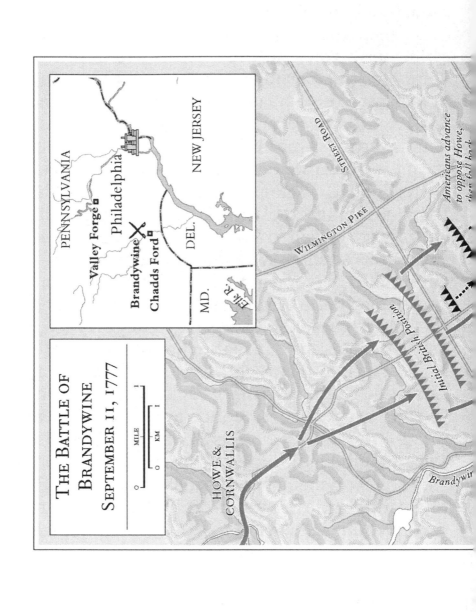

THE BATTLE OF
BRANDYWINE
SEPTEMBER 11, 1777

MILE

KM

PENNSYLVANIA

Valley Forge ◻

Philadelphia ◻

Brandywine

Chadds Ford ◻

DEL.

MD.

NEW JERSEY

Elk R.

HOWE &
CORNWALLIS

WILMINGTON PIKE

STREET ROAD

Initial British Position

*Americans advance
to oppose Howe,
then fall back*

Brandywine

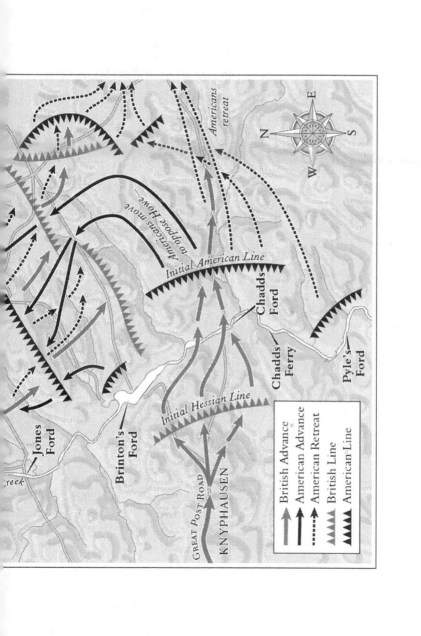

Americans retreat

Initial American Line

Americans move to oppose Howe

Chadds Ford

Chadds Ferry

Pyle's Ford

Initial Hessian Line

Jones Ford

Brinton's Ford

GREAT POST ROAD

KNYPHAUSEN

Creek

N E W S

British Advance
American Advance
American Retreat
British Line
American Line

this moment that he realized that he had lost the day.

Praying that Gen. Greene's regulars were as high spirited as he had boasted, Washington ordered Greene's two brigades of Virginians pulled from their original position on the lower Brandywine and rushed north. As Greene's division raced the nearly four miles up the east bank of the creek it actually had to break ranks to allow Gen. de Borre and his fleeing troops to pass through their battle line. After reforming on a battlefield that Greene described as raining "hot fire," his Virginians stood firm against the British attack for over an hour, the riflemen from the Old Dominion fighting like Vikings with iron and oak. Their efforts bought Washington enough time to begin pulling his remaining troops back up the road toward Philadelphia. Finally, as the sky purpled to the color of a mussel shell, Greene's troops, bone-weary and nearly out of ammunition, formed up and began to draw off in good order.

Back at Chadds Ford, Gen. von Knyphausen's Hessians along with several detachments of British foot soldiers had already routed a corps of American light infantry who had waded through the Brandywine to patrol its west bank. After hearing Cornwallis's cannons fire to the north, and sensing the depletion of the forces arrayed against him across the water, the German commander ordered a full assault. The air on the east bank of the creek was soon thick with flintlock smoke as tree branches cracked to the ground and cannonballs furrowed the forest floor. Outnumbered three to one, the 2,000 or so veteran Continentals remaining under the command of General Anthony Wayne held firm for several volleys before falling back. Great daubs of British and Hessian blood stained the creek red, but still the enemy came. Their advance was bolstered when a contingent of British Guards who had been lost in the forest fell in with von Knyphausen's troops.

Wayne, a 32-year-old Chester County native and Pennsylvania's only active general in the field, had no formal military training prior to the war. But Washington admired his zeal and innate quick thinking in the saddle. His faith proved prescient; Wayne's knowledge of the terrain and his savvy maneuvering during the running fight as his troops fell back pell-mell from height to height prevented von Knyphausen's combined force from completely encircling and devouring the Pennsylvanians. With the recently arrived Polish count Casimir Pulaski's 30 or so horsemen helping to blunt the British advance and screening the Continental retreat, the defeated Americans withdrew before halting at the town of Chester, Pennsylvania, some 14 miles to the east.

To Washington's astonishment, Gen. Howe declined to press his advantage that evening, deeming it out of the question to pursue the Continentals through the darkness without enough wagons to haul supplies, a decision he would be subsequently criticized for. While some exhausted Redcoats found shelter in nearby Tory farmhouses, most simply dropped and spread their blankets over the battlefield.

The British listed 587 casualties, including 93 dead. Although no official American casualty list survives, Gen. Howe reported to his colonial secretary with only slight exaggeration that his troops had killed some 300 Continentals, wounded another 600, and taken 400 prisoners.* The British had also captured 11 of the Americans' artillery field pieces. So many Americans lay bleeding out near the Brandywine's eastern bank and across the surrounding hills and fields that Gen. Howe would soon signal to Washington to send in Continental doctors under a flag

* The fact that three days later some 350 American prisoners of war were transferred from the field to a quickly established hospital near Wilmington, Delaware, suggests the validity of this latter figure. It would also indicate that only 50 or so Continentals had surrendered with either minor or no wounds.

of truce to minister to them. In the majority of cases this meant amputation without anesthetic.

The various Pennsylvania militias attached to the Continental Army had at times appeared bewildered by their first whiffs of gunpowder fired in anger. "Fighting is a new thing with these," Gen. Greene wrote to his wife, Caty, "and many seem to have a poor stomach for the business." This was evident by the some 315 names of militiamen later posted as deserters. Yet the greater part of the American regulars had acquitted themselves with martial professionalism during the fallback. Washington's officers, grasping for a silver lining, felt that the crumbling retreat they had overseen was actually a small victory of sorts, what one called a "mitigated defeat." That night, in a letter to John Hancock to inform Congress of the "misfortune of the day" — the first draft of which Washington found too dispiriting to send — the commander in chief managed to convey a touch of optimism. "I am happy to find the troops in good spirits," he wrote, "and I hope another time we shall compensate for the losses now sustained." Even in defeat, especially in defeat, Washington was aware of his duty to keep afloat his army's morale. And though it is tempting to view his communiqué to Hancock as a ploy to succeed in just that, his confident assurances were not all bluster or bravado.

Washington's private tendency was often to see the dark and pessimistic side in most of life's occurrences. But by the next morning as stragglers continued to trickle into the Continental camp, the consensus had been reached among American officers and enlisted men that the British had achieved their victory through a sort of quirk of fate — specifically, the enemy's reliance on sympathizers much more familiar with the terrain than the Continentals. Given the nature of Gen. Howe's surprise attack, this theory went, the Americans had in fact turned what could have been a deathblow into a mere bruising. As soldiers continued to wander into Chester from as far away as Wilmington, Delaware, there was already talk of regrouping for another assault.

Nevertheless, the stinging British victory at Brandywine Creek left more than enough grist for Washington's political enemies to mill. Why had he merely stalked Howe's army for weeks before choosing to fight? How could a foreign enemy have accrued such better knowledge of the landscape than an American force containing so many home-grown soldiers? How had a dust-raising force of over 8,000 Redcoats slipped past his reconnaissance units so effortlessly? It was also noted that at one point during their secret march the British had been forced to traverse a defile so narrow and deep that even their own officers feared their entire army could be pinned down by a handful of Continentals. Yet no Americans had been stationed to guard the pass. Most insidiously, the fiasco at Brandywine breathed new life into the vampirical criticism that had hounded Washington since his appointment as commander in chief — that he was a one-note general unable to adjust his field tactics on the fly and had surrounded himself with a staff of sycophants and toadies.

Washington was aware of the old whispers about him that would soon be recirculating from Richmond to Boston. He was also forthright enough to step in and protest when a faction of congressional delegates attempted to place the blame for Brandywine on Gen. Sullivan. At least he could take solace from knowing that the faith he had placed in the "freakishly brave" Lafayette had been repaid in such a public manner. For as his army prepared to move to a new camp just northwest of Philadelphia, more than a few hardened veterans continued to remark on the mettle and composure the Frenchman had displayed in the face of murderous ball and shell.

It was not until Lafayette had helped organize the orderly retreat from Brandywine Creek — forming his fellow soldiers into properly disciplined lines as they marched to

Chester — that he finally allowed the musket ball to be dug out of his calf. It had hit neither bone nor nerve. He was then carried to a medical barge bound for Philadelphia by, among others, the 18-year-old Virginia captain and future president James Monroe. Washington was standing on the riverbank when Lafayette's stretcher bearers arrived and advised the doctors on board the transport to treat the young Frenchman as if he were his own son. Given the American commander in chief's well-known impatience with the preponderance of European military "volunteers" washing up on American shores, this was a telling portent.

THREE:
THE FRENCH CONNECTION

Even his name swaggered: Marie-Joseph-Paul-Yves-Roch-Gilbert du Motier de La-fayette. He joked that he had been christened in honor of all the saints that could protect him in battle. He would need them.

Lafayette had yet to celebrate his second birthday when his father was cut down by British cannon fire at the Battle of Minden during the Seven Years' War. His mother died a decade later, leaving the 12-year-old marquis one of the wealthiest orphans in France. The boy was mentored by a bevy of aristocratic relatives on a rustic estate south of Paris in an area renowned for its redolent blue cheeses and a mythical man-eating wolf. He later wrote that his childhood was consumed by the same quest for military glory that had driven his forebears dating back to the Crusades. From an early age Lafayette exhibited a flair for horsemanship, and at 13 the ginger-haired youngster was commissioned an officer in King Louis XVI's household cavalry, the marvelously named *Mousquetaires Noirs,* or Black Musketeers. Three years later he married into the de Noailles family, a clan even more wealthy and powerful than his own. He was soon appointed a captain in his father-in-law's hereditary company of hard-riding dragoons.

Despite the social obligations of peerage, Lafayette shied from the decadent banquets and masked balls he and his 15-year-old child bride Adrienne de Noailles were expected to attend in Paris and Versailles. For such a skillful rider, he had a foal-like clumsiness that served to endear him to veteran soldiers but proved a major impediment at court. Once, while dancing with Marie-Antoinette, he demonstrated such left-footedness that the queen laughed in his face. Despite his frustration with the social obligations of his blue-blooded lineage, it was, ironically, a member of the English aristocracy who touched fire to the candle that would light Lafayette's journey to America.

Prince William Henry, Duke of Gloucester and Edinburgh, had fled to France from Britain in the wake of his older brother King George III's very public displeasure over his decision to marry the illegitimate granddaughter of the British statesman Robert Walpole. One night at a dinner party Lafayette listened rapt as the duke extolled the exploits of the "liberty-loving Americans" who had

66

just fired the first shots of the revolution at Lexington and Concord. The ambitious Lafayette, weary of what he called "the *longueur* of peace," had always harbored a personal contempt for the English who had killed his father. The duke's praise for the republicans across the Atlantic was all the push he needed. "From that hour," Lafayette wrote, "I could think of nothing but this enterprise."

He was not alone among adventuresome and ambitious Frenchmen.

The United States needed *la belle France* in their war, and the French knew it. So did the British. And though Great Britain and France were technically at peace with one another at the time of America's Declaration of Independence, the British were prepared to use their mighty Royal Navy to ensure that French provisions never reached the eastern seaboard of North America. However, despite the British mastery of the high seas, the Atlantic was a big ocean.

France was secretly colluding to supply the United States with everything from arms to uniforms to tents to blankets to shovels long before Silas Deane, a former Connecticut delegate to the Continental Congress, stepped off a clipper at the French port of Le Havre in July 1776 to help devise a way to smuggle those supplies. As the inestimable biographer of Lafayette, Sarah Vowell, has observed, "Jefferson's pretty phrases were incomplete without the punctuation of French gunpowder."

Deane was a rugged and handsome New Englander whose powdered wig obscured his ruddy complexion and thick shock of black hair. At 38, he had sailed to France posing as a merchant — not a stretch, considering that he had made a fortune in the West Indian sugar trade. In reality he had been authorized by the Continental Congress's Committee of Secret Correspondence to lever France's hostility toward England into support for the American uprising. The French were naturally bitter that the treaty that ended the Seven Years' War in 1763 had all but wiped out their holdings in the New World. Yet their defeat in that conflict had also depleted Louis XVI's national treasury.* The French king and his bankers knew that they could not af-

* In no small slice of irony, the successive British levies that sparked the American Revolution — the Stamp Act of 1765, the Townshend Revenue Act of 1767, the Tea Act of 1773, and the Coercive (or "Intolerable") Acts of 1774 — had been largely instituted to pay off British war debts from the same conflict. So perniciously meticulous were the accountants in the British Exchequer that one of the Intolerable Acts' demands was repayment for the 342 chests of tea tossed into Massachusetts Bay during the Boston Tea Party the previous December.

ford to trigger another overt war against the detested "Roast Beefs" across the Channel, particularly to prop up a rebellion that to this point had shown few signs of success. A needle in Great Britain's arse in the form of covert assistance to the Americans, however, was an appealing alternative to the rambunctious 22-year-old ruler who had assumed the throne three years earlier.

Aware of his king's predilections, France's foreign minister the Comte de Vergennes had already convinced Louis XVI to agree to secretly purchase military matériel to aid the Americans even before Deane arrived in Paris with cocked hat in hand. More than a decade before the Continental Congress's ratification of the Declaration of Independence, de Vergennes had predicted that the American colonies would eventually rise against the British. He had more recently warned that, should their rebellion prevail, the United States would undoubtedly turn a lusty eye toward French holdings in the Caribbean.

As a sort of insurance policy to forestall any such outcome as well as secure postwar amity with the Americans, the French king had allocated one million francs to fund de Vergennes's scheme. He even convinced his cousin on the Spanish throne to match the donation. De Vergennes used the money to set up a shell company in the name of a nonexistent Spaniard to mask the shipments. The clandestine affair rose to opera buffa heights when the French polymath and budding secret agent Pierre Beaumarchais, celebrated author of *The Barber of Seville* and *The Marriage of Figaro,* was placed in charge of the operation. That Beaumarchais — originally Pierre-Augustin Caron — had fabricated a family coat of arms to complement his fake last name made no difference to Deane, who hinted that future repayments for this extended line of credit would be made in favorable tobacco contracts.

By December 1776, as Washington was preparing his stunning Christmas-night Delaware crossing that resulted in the capture of Trenton, nearly 300,000 pounds of French gunpowder, thousands of firelocks and cannonballs, and scores of field artillery pieces and mortars had been secreted aboard French vessels allegedly carrying grain and wine to the French Caribbean. But there was a problem. The British spy network on the European continent, including a double agent whom Deane had hired as his private secretary, had the particulars of the plot in hand. When Great Britain threatened France with war should those ships weigh anchor, Louis XVI backed down. In a public humiliation, the foreign minister, de Vergennes, was forced to issue a proclamation ordering the immediate arrest of any sea captain delivering succor to the American rebels and any French army officer attempting to sail for America to volunteer his services. A small consolation prize for Deane and the revolutionaries was the three large merchant vessels that had already begun the transatlantic passage prior to the royal decree to stand down. They managed to dock at Portsmouth, New Hampshire, and offload crates of clothing, gunpowder, 58 cannons, 12,000 muskets and bayonets, and enough tents to house 10,000 men.

Lafayette viewed this as a start. He was soon to follow.

By the time news of the American victories at Trenton and Princeton reached France, Benjamin Franklin had arrived in Paris to oversee Deane's secret treaty negotiations with Versailles. When Deane introduced him to Lafayette, Franklin instantly recognized the value of the "young Nobleman of great family Connections & great Wealth." The American envoys happily accepted Lafayette's offer of service and supplied the teenage marquis with a letter of introduction to John Hancock. Within weeks, however, Louis XVI made it a crime for any Frenchman to aid the colonies. Lafayette was nonplussed. Despite his wife's first pregnancy, he had already purchased a 268-ton merchant ship in Bordeaux, renamed it *La Victoire,* and furtively stocked it with food and armaments. When his guardian and mentor the Comte de Broglie could not talk

Lafayette out of his wild and now illegal adventure, de Broglie did the next best thing by recruiting the Bavarian soldier of fortune Baron Johann de Kalb to accompany Lafayette on his journey. De Kalb, a hulking 55-year-old whom the British had previously expelled from North America on charges of spying for the French, was more than eager to resume his antagonism toward the Crown.

Perhaps feeling last-minute pangs of guilt over abandoning his pregnant wife for this "unique opportunity to distinguish myself, and to learn my profession," Lafayette abruptly confessed his plans to his father-in-law Jean-Louis-Paul-François de Noailles, the fifth duc d'Ayen. He had given his word to the Americans, he told the duc, "and you would not have respected me had I gone back on it." De Noailles was not happy with his son-in-law's decision, but he reluctantly agreed to keep it secret. Writing years later of "the secrecy with which this negotiation and my preparations were made," Lafayette set sail for the United States to join *les insurgents* in April 1777. The marquis spent most of the voyage studying the English language, blissfully unaware that Parisian salons and coffeehouses were atwitter with news of his audacity. By the time he arrived in Philadelphia in July, the king had privately forgiven him and Voltaire had even visited his wife, Adrienne, to bow in homage to her husband's *beau geste.* It was this deftness with older male authority figures that allowed Lafayette to rapidly assume a filial role in Washington's inner circle.

The two met when the 19-year-old, sporting a major general's sash, brashly introduced himself to Washington in Philadelphia's City Tavern on the last evening of July. Elegant and slim, with full lips, an upturned nose, and a prematurely receding hairline, Lafayette charmed Washington with his youthful brio for poetic pronouncements as well as his ability to segue from diffident self-abasement to fervent ambition in mid-sentence. Adding to his cachet was his physical stature. In an era when men's average height was five feet eight inches, the young Frenchman could directly meet the gaze of the Continental Army's commander in chief. Washington invited Lafayette to join him the following morning for a tour of the Continental defenses along the Delaware River.

The American general was certainly not blind to the diplomatic advantages of befriending a well-connected French nobleman. Yet Washington, whose own youth was rife with romantic paeans to justice and fair play, also saw something deeper in Lafayette's earnest devotion to American liberty. "The happiness of America is intimately connected to the happiness of all mankind," the marquis had written to his wife upon making landfall in the United States. Even if Washington expressed such sentiments less floridly, they were very similar to his own. There was, however, a limit to the commander in chief's forbearance.

Before intruding on Washington's supper, Lafayette had presented himself to John Hancock armed with his letter of introduction from Franklin and Deane. In the accreditation papers, which Lafayette had apparently not read, the American diplomats cautioned Congress that the young man was so well ensconced in the French aristocracy that any harm that came to him might negatively affect the delicate treaty negotiations Franklin was conducting. Congress, impressed with Lafayette's proposal to serve at his own expense, massaged this complication with a compromise. He would be commissioned a "volunteer" major general in the Continental Army — thus the sash upon his meeting with Washington — with the understanding that the appointment was expressly an honorary title. The delegates presumed that Washington would take Lafayette under his wing as an aide and keep him out of danger. This presented a problem: no one had informed the marquis of the arrangement.

Not long after their river tour, Washington was perplexed when Lafayette requested two aides-de-camp. He also informed both Hancock and his new commander in chief that, as he was new to the conflict, he was graciously willing to initially test his mettle on the general's staff before eventually being "entrusted with a division of the Army" due an officer of his rank. Washington was flabbergasted and complained to a fellow Virginian, the congressman Benjamin Harrison, "If Congress meant that this rank should be unaccompanied by Command, I wish it had been sufficiently explained to [Lafayette]. If on the other hand it was intended to vest him with all the powers of a Major Genl why have I been led into a contrary belief, & left in the dark with respect to my own conduct towards him?"

Washington was used to masking his true emotions when dealing with the civil authorities. His political calculations often took the guise of false modesty. Sometimes these feelings were even genuine, as when he tearfully confessed to his friend Patrick Henry his inner fears of disgrace and failure upon accepting the commission to lead the Continentals. More often than not, however, his shows of humility were convenient contrivances that bordered on the sarcastic. In this instance, in case his point to Harrison proved too subtle, he added, "I know no more of this than the Child unborn, & beg to be instructed."

Despite this confusion, Lafayette's infectious enthusiasm struck a chord in Washington's fragile psyche. Throughout his service during the French and Indian War the young Virginia planter had chafed at the second-class citizenship to which the Crown had relegated him and his fellow colonial officers. His requests for a royal commission in the king's regular army had been repeatedly rebuffed. And though he had risen to the rank of colonel in the militia, to his lasting resentment he too often found himself groveling for recognition from proper British officers of lower rank who treated him — as was their prerogative under the imperial system — as a provincial subaltern. It was a slight that rankled him still.

In Lafayette, however, he had discovered an officer from a lofty and professional European army who proffered not only respect but subservience of rank to the diffident former member of Virginia's middle gentry. Upon their initial inspection of the Continental Army, for instance, Washington's old insecurities surfaced when he apologized to Lafayette for the threadbare clothing and substandard armaments of his troops. Without hesitation the Frenchman replied that he had come to the United States to learn from the Americans, and not to teach. Washington never forgot the moment.

But Lafayette's self-effacement in no way hid his thirst for battlefield accolades — the Frenchman's very essence, observed one biographer, regularly required "the dignity of danger." Though Washington may have viewed Lafayette's passionate chivalry as a mirror reflection of his own youth, not all of his new American hosts were quite so taken. Thomas Jefferson and John Adams were both initially leery of yet another arrogant and interloping Frenchman's bountiful appetite for fame and flattery. Moreover, many of Lafayette's detractors, descended from good Puritan stock, found off-putting his Gallic habit of hugging people at the slightest provocation. Throughout his life, Washington had always shied away from any physical familiarity, instant or deliberate. His trust, respect, and friendship had to be earned. Even at that, a salute or a handshake would usually suffice. Yet there was something about Lafayette that penetrated the commander in chief's hard shell. The young man was at heart an idealist who, despite his thirst for glory, was a true believer in the American cause. In other words, he was a rarity.

On the whole, Washington had little use for the scores of French officers who swarmed to the United States to accrue personal glory fighting the hated British. Unlike Lafayette, whose English was by now at least rudimentary, many spoke none at all and were therefore useless in commanding American troops. Worse, from Washington's point of view, the language barrier left them unable even to help raise recruits. Moreover, their ubiquitous demands for stations well above their European ranks stole jobs from more worthy Americans and engendered a deep "disgust" in the Continental Army's officer corps. Although thankful for hardened warriors such as de Kalb, Washington repeatedly remonstrated with Franklin and Deane for burdening his command with the louche offspring of wealthy French aristocrats whose "every new arrival is only a source of embarrassment to congress and myself." He went so far as to warn Hancock of the "evil" this transatlantic pipeline was bringing upon the revolution.

At one point the army's redoubtable chief artillery officer, Gen. Henry Knox, offered his resignation when Congress attempted to supersede him with a French "general" endorsed by the increasingly harried Deane. The Frenchman's sole claim to expertise with cannon and shot was apparently a close affiliation with the ceremonial artillery displayed at Louis XVI's Versailles palace. Henry Knox was not a soldier Washington could afford to lose, nor were the generals Greene and Sullivan, who also threatened to resign if Knox was supplanted by the French interloper. Luckily for the commander in chief, the stalemate ultimately resolved itself when the foreign courtier imperiously spurred his horse toward a ferry departing the banks of the Schuylkill, missed the platform, and drowned in the river. The horse swam to safety.

But the *contretemps* was indicative of the larger problem. Franklin, more circumspect than Deane, had a better reading of the French character. In a nation besotted by both Enlightenment ideals and Rousseau's teleological paeans to nature, the urbane Franklin had taken to playing up the homespun nature of his fellow Americans by wearing a fur trapper's beaver cap on his visits to Versailles. But Franklin was also acutely aware of Washington's frustration at having to accept a modicum of vain and preening adventurers as the price to pay for future French comity. He only half facetiously observed that he had become reluctant to accept invitations to Parisian salons for fear of being engulfed in a sea of military supplicants in their pink collars and velvet lapels.

Conversely, one group of French volunteers whom Washington did hold in high esteem were the country's military engineers. Most of these officers had graduated from the prestigious Royal Engineering School at Mezières and were considered the finest in the world. Despite Washington's wariness about the efficiency of their *chevaux-de-frise* to hamper British naval advances, over the course of the Revolutionary War he relied upon them to erect fortifications, map terrain, and lay out trenches and encampments. Among these officers was the 34-year-old Louis Duportail, who arrived in America as a volunteer in early 1777 and by that July had risen to the position of chief engineer of the Continental Army. Duportail had an impressive reputation for reforming and revising the regulations of the French army's corps of engineers, and Washington's regard for his skills was such that he almost always deferred to the Frenchman's opinion. Although Lafayette lacked the combat experience of Duportail and was not an engineer by training, he proved "a fast study, showed courage under fire, and had an imaginative mind for military schemes." And as he had demonstrated at Brandywine, he also possessed a knack for inspiring soldiers while chasing the martial honors he so badly wanted.

Hence it was fair to wonder how Washington felt the news of Lafayette's injury during the fight on the Brandywine would be received in Versailles, as he stood on a bank of the Delaware and watched his wounded protégé sailing upriver on a medical barge. Little did he know that rumors would soon spread through Paris, and beyond, that Lafayette was dead.

FOUR:
BURNED FORGES

Three days after what came to be known as the Battle of Brandywine Creek, George Washington and his Continental Army were encamped near the settlement of Germantown, about six miles northwest of Philadelphia's old town center. The hamlet, since incorporated into the city proper, was at the time a patchwork of dense hardwood forest broken by natural meadows and cleared fields of wheat, flax, and corn set amid neat rows of peach and cherry orchards. The lush plantations, founded by Quaker and Mennonite families almost a century earlier, were irrigated by scores of rocky, spring-fed brooks splashing down to the Schuylkill — Dutch for "Hidden River" — from the surrounding hills. Seventy-two hours of rest and recuperation in such a pleasant landscape had given the American troops a new wind.

As the Continental companies and regiments licked their wounds and re-formed, there was a palpable ripple of excitement.

Washington's brigadiers realized that the number of dead and wounded was far lower than they had feared. Even most of the army's baggage, such as it was, remained secure, having been evacuated before the fight. The soldiers, particularly the officers, were in a combative mood; the yearning for retribution was amplified when news spread that the British, still camped along the Brandywine, were so desperate for medical assistance that they had begun forcibly conscripting Chester County's civilian doctors. Several bellicose junior officers vowed to be the first to dance a victory minuet in Philadelphia after they'd had another go at Gen. Howe's Redcoats. Their attitude was reflected by Alexander Hamilton, who informed the New York congressman Gouverneur Morris, "The militia seem pretty generally stirring, [and] our army is in high health and spirits." Nathanael Greene went even further, boasting to his wife that "the next action would ruin Mr. Howe totally. We are gathered about him like a mighty cloud charg'd with destruction."

As usual, Washington himself was more circumspect. He was gratified by the combination of courage and initiative his troops had exhibited while extricating themselves from the enemy's flanking maneuver along the Brandywine. But he also recognized the great part that fortune had played in the escape, particularly in the long time it took Howe's battalions to form a battle line after crossing the creek's upstream branches. Overall, he could take solace from the fact that his soldiers, so many of them green recruits, had come face-to-face with the world's foremost military machine and had not collapsed. This was something to build on. But that construction could begin only with an influx of troops. To that end, while his force girded for a rematch, he pressed Congress to supply him with more able bodies.

In Philadelphia, John Laurens's father, Henry, proved a sturdy ally. In his capacity as an influential member of Congress, Henry Laurens dispatched riders to the commanding officers of the New Jersey and Maryland militias requesting immediate reinforcements for the Continental Army. He had also taken in the wounded Lafayette and would soon spirit him to the town of Bethlehem, Pennsylvania, where a sect of German-American Moravians had set up a field hospital.* The Frenchman, unaware that rumors of his death would soon to be rocking the court at Versailles, spent his days writing blithe missives to his wife, Adrienne, extolling the sights, the

---

* The Moravians were as rigidly antiviolence as the Quakers and detested the war despite the fact that they cared for colonials wounded in it.

sounds, even the smells of battle. He also added the occasional aside recording his surgeons' astonishment at his body's rapid healing powers. It would be weeks until his letters reached Adrienne, informing her, and all of France, that he was alive.

It was not lost on Washington that he trod a political fault line with his increasingly strident requests for more troops. From its inception, the Continental Congress had been wary of establishing a standing army of professional soldiers. Only 14 months earlier it had declared its independence from a despotic king whose arbitrary and unaccountable law enforcement policies had been carried out by a collection of "forced men" and mercenaries — "Swarms of Officers to harass our People, and eat out their Substance," as the Declaration of Independence had it. The delegates feared that such a homegrown institution might one day become a similar instrument of tyranny. Instead they hoped to throw off the British yoke with citizen militias formed within the individual colonies and aided by several corps of federally funded if temporary "provincial regiments."

The British occupation of Boston had altered this romantic notion considerably. On June 14, 1775, two months after Continental militiamen had forced the Redcoats to retreat from Lexington and Concord, the congressional delegates voted to place the Massachusetts militia under its authority and ordered the establishment of 10 additional regular-army rifle companies from Pennsylvania, Maryland, and Virginia. The following day it voted unanimously to offer command of this nascent Continental Army to Washington. This made eminent political sense. Virginia was the union's wealthiest and most populous state, and the delegates determined that for the sake of political solidarity the common ruck should cohere around the laconic experimental tobacco farmer from Mount Vernon. Moreover, John Adams's quip that Washington was selected because he was always the tallest man in the room hints at the physical majesty conveyed by the new commander in chief. Still, not all were thrilled.

In appointing Washington, Congress had chosen a man more familiar with Indian forest-fighting tactics than with leading and directing large bodies of troops. He had never commanded any unit larger than a regiment, and had only recently begun rather frantically purchasing books to teach himself the intricacies of cavalry maneuvers, artillery deployment, and military engineering. This was not lost on several New England officers who felt that their efforts at Lexington and Concord had been slighted. Nor did Washington's inexperience pass unnoticed by two

British-born American generals, Horatio Gates and Charles Lee, soon to be selected by Congress to serve under the new commander in chief. Both men were highly decorated veterans of previous Crown campaigns; both had settled in the colonies and volunteered to fight for the cause of independence; both would harbor simmering resentments throughout the revolution at having to understudy what they considered a tomahawk-wielding bumpkin from the cow paths of Virginia.

At the same time that Congress stood up a national American army it also stipulated that the force's regulars would serve for just one year. Rather astonishingly, the delegates believed that the British would be driven from the former colonies within that period. By 1777, as reality set in, the subscription limit had been raised to three years, and eventually it would be extended "for the duration of the war." Regiments accepted volunteers as young as 16 years of age, 15 with parental consent. An artillery "man" from New Jersey named Jeremiah Levering, who enlisted at 12, is cited by historians as probably the youngest soldier to volunteer. Yet the civil authorities to whom the commander in chief deferred still preferred to wage their revolution with state militias that, as one experienced American officer noted, "may as well stay at home, for not one fourth of them are of any use [and] three fourths of them run off at the first fire." The respected French engineer Col. Duportail — soon to be charged with laying out and overseeing the construction at Valley Forge — was still more waspish in his appraisal. Even if an infusion of militiamen bloated Washington's force to twice its current size, he wrote, "we would not double our strength by a great deal, we would triple our trouble." Portraits of Duportail emphasize his symmetrical face graced by an aristocratic nose and hooded eyes that seem to sparkle ominously, as if expressing both amusement and threat. His views of the Continental Army captured both emotions.

In any case, Washington took personally these intra-army criticisms. At the same time, he understood and respected the unique responsibility Congress had granted him to lead a force of citizen-soldiers, with the emphasis on *citizen.* Sixteen years of service in Virginia's House of Burgesses had ingrained in him a reflexive esteem for the fundamental proposition of civilian control over the military. He recognized that this principle was no mere nicety, but essential to the democratic rule for which he was fighting. The signers of the Declaration of Independence understood that they were in the process of creating a new kind of government, one designed to prevent precisely the system of martial decision-making advocated by strategic thinkers as ancient as Thucydides. Though the Athenian general was cognizant of war's corrosive effect on a democracy, his observation that military conflicts are fought for either one or a combination of three reasons — fear, honor, and interest — certainly still held. But it was in the interest of Washington's military strategy that no matter how meddling the delegates, civilians should always set policy. He was merely tasked to execute it. If they preferred militiamen to full-time soldiers, so be it.

As duly appointed commander in chief, however, he needed no political permission to realign his regulars. In his desperate attempts to swell his regiments he immediately dispatched officers to scour the temporary military hospitals scattered about western Pennsylvania for able-bodied convalescents. He also sent riders into Philadelphia with warnings that any household, inn, or tavern lodging wayward American regulars would be subject to forfeiture. Simultaneously, he ordered a brigade of 1,000 Continentals from the Hudson River Highlands to immediately march south from Poughkeepsie, New York. These soldiers, under the command of Gen. Israel Putnam, were acting as a buffer between the British troops who had remained in New York City and Gen. Burgoyne's army storming down the Champlain Valley from Canada. Washington's order incensed Gen.

Putnam, who felt his defenses were already stretched too thin along the river. It was well understood by combatants on both sides that what was then called the "North River" was, in the words of Washington's biographer Douglas Southall Freeman, "the jugular of America, the severance of which meant death" to the revolution. Washington ignored Putnam's protests. He needed every musket-bearing man available for the return engagement with Gen. Howe.

Meanwhile, the high spirits among the troops at Germantown were far from being shared in Philadelphia. There, both the Continental Congress and the state legislators, taking a more realistic view of the events at Brandywine Creek, were already making preparations for the defense of the city in haste that bordered on panic. Militiamen were hurriedly formed into construction gangs to dig breastworks and haul cannons to the fords and ferry crossings along the Schuylkill River northwest of the city; the Liberty Bell was crated for passage to Allentown so it could not be melted down by the British for ammunition; and all of the city's printing presses save one for emergency proclamations were disassembled and carted into the state's interior.

Within days the presses were followed by the delegates from both houses who, sensing the futility of staving off a professional army with a collection of half-trained farmers and shopkeepers, voted to reconvene in the town of Lancaster some 80 miles to the west. While the state legislators remained in Lancaster, the national delegates of the Continental Congress were again soon on the move, relocating their operations to the small town of York another 30 miles distant. These signals were not lost on Philadelphia's Whigs, who were soon enough piling their own belongings onto wagons, carts, and carriages in anticipation of the arrival of an occupying force.

While civilians' anxieties were concentrated on the imminent arrival of Gen. Howe's army, Washington fretted equally over the Royal Navy vessels lurking somewhere about the mouth of the Delaware. Philadelphia is a city virtually surrounded by water, with the Schuylkill to the west and the Delaware to the east forming natural barriers before their confluence south of the city. If Adm. "Black Dick" Howe's fleet managed to break through the obstructions the Continentals had strung across the lower Delaware or, worse, to over-run the American riverbank forts, Washington suspected that instead of hosting dances for young American officers, the city's taverns and bawdy houses would soon reverberate with the lyrics of British and German drinking songs.

■ ■ ■ ■

Back on Brandywine Creek, Gen. Howe continued to be stalled by a shortage of wagons to carry supplies and remove his wounded. Washington took advantage of the enemy's standstill to withdraw across the Schuylkill and march back through Philadelphia to position his own force northwest of the city in eastern Chester County. There he would form a line of defense between the British and the capital. He also posted pickets on the roads that led to the Continental storehouses farther inland. While passing through Philadelphia his army was met by a decidedly muted reaction compared with that of a month earlier. This time green sprigs were in short supply, and many American officers noted the absence of fighting-age men among the thin, sullen crowds lining the lanes.

From here events played out rapidly. On the evening of September 14, Howe's scouts informed him that they had located the Continental Army in Chester County. In hopes of swiftly finishing what he had started on the Brandywine, Howe had his troops marching the next morning — by pure coincidence the same day that Washington, having followed his lifelong farmer's habit of rising at dawn, led his army out of its camp and recrossed the Schuylkill. The next afternoon advance parties from the two forces stumbled into each other quite by accident 26 miles west by northwest of Philadelphia. Neither of the commanders had planned on a major engagement quite so soon. As they frantically assembled their lines, providence intervened in the form of a ferocious northeaster, part of a tropical storm system that roiled the entire Mid-Atlantic region that day.

It began as a thick mist that hardened into a cold drizzle. Then the sky turned livid, awash with blinding neurons of white lightning as buckshot bursts of rain inundated the two armies. The downpour came in blinding sheets, so saturating each side's cartridges and powder horns that what was later dubbed the Battle of the Clouds was in reality not much more than a sidewise skirmish. Desultory shots were fired from the opposing lines before both sides fell back through the bulking gloom, a retreat not entirely to Washington's dissatisfaction. As the historian Ron Chernow notes in his masterly biography, "Despite his own hard-charging nature, Washington realized that, in view of the fragility of his army, it was sometimes better to miss a major opportunity than barge into a costly error."

With the inevitable fight postponed, Gen. Howe pushed southeast toward Philadelphia with his troops, the Hessians in particular, plundering and burning as they marched. The Continentals plodded across swollen streams and through calf-deep mud before again fording the Schuylkill and moving northwest toward the small German Lutheran enclave of Yellow Springs to obtain dry powder. Washington left behind Gen. Wayne and close to 2,000 of his best Pennsylvania regulars as a rear guard. Wayne's orders were to track the British troops' movements and harass their baggage train. Wayne was also told to expect reinforcements from the nearly 2,000 Maryland militiamen under the command of Gen. William Smallwood racing north in answer to Henry Laurens's appeal. The idea for one final and massive strike on the British before they reached Philadelphia was already forming in Washington's mind.

On September 18, two days after the aborted Battle of the Clouds, Gen. Howe paused to camp his force near the dozen or so fieldstone farmsteads and adjacent ironworks that constituted the hamlet of Valley Forge. Just over 20 miles northwest of Philadelphia in Tredyffrin Township, the small community occupied a strategic location at the confluence of Valley Creek and the Schuylkill River. The Americans used Valley Forge as a supply distribution center, and its warehouses were currently holding both foodstuffs and military arms — including some 3,000 bushels of wheat and 20,000 tomahawks. The British seized these stores after chasing off a small contingent of Continental dragoons led by Alexander Hamilton that had attempted to retrieve them. Then they fell on the civilian farms. It was the height of the harvest season, and scavenging parties systematically ravaged the area, confiscating crops and flour sacks by the wagonload and relieving the locals of almost all of their cows, pigs, and sheep — "flesh" or "hooves" in the contemporary vernacular. Howe had ordered his foragers to spare the stock and larders of any families known to be Loyalists. But in the swarm of war, hungry soldiers were not likely to be too thorough in their discrimination.

Before departing Valley Forge, the British burned its sawmill, blacksmith shop, waterwheels, cooperage, and workers' housing. Most strategically, they also destroyed the complete ironworks — finery, chafery, bloomery, and slitting mill — that lent the valley its name. This was more than the usual callous depravity of combat. There was a method to Howe's severity. He knew he was in patriot country. The historian Alan Taylor estimates that about 20 percent of all American colonists — 500,000 people — remained loyal to the Crown during the American Revolution, while some 40 percent favored rebellion. The remaining 40 percent constituted a fluctuating middle who based their allegiance on their own safety and, in Taylor's study, their "relationships with neighbors and kin." In and around Valley Forge, however, revolutionary sentiments ran stronger, with about three quarters of the population in sympathy with separation from England. General Howe also understood that Pennsylvania was the leading iron manufacturer for the Continental Army.

Though there were forges scattered up and down the east coast of North America, most were located near mines that yielded an inferior form of the metal called bog iron. The iron deposits up the Schuylkill Valley and into the larger Lehigh Valley, however, were of a purer grade, with the added advantage that they were also nearer to the surface. The rolling hills surrounding Valley Forge were thick with hardwood — great groves of oak, maple, ash, walnut, and sycamore, and particularly dense stands of chestnut. Burning these trees provided ample fuel for the forges. This, combined with the waterwheels powered by the Schuylkill, allowed the local ironmongers to fire-forge a superior brand of pig iron. From the works at Valley Forge the giant blocks of "pig" were shipped inland to smiths who, employing 80-pound trip-hammers, would fire them again while great bellows injected oxygen into the metal to produce wrought iron, a low-grade steel. From this process emerged all manner of end products beneficial to Washington's army, from wagon wheel hubs and nails to musket and cannon barrels. General Howe did not hesitate to disrupt this rebel manufacturing pipeline.

At the time the British were putting the torch to Valley Forge's ironworks, farther west at York the relocated Continental Congress was attempting to fulfill Washington's petition for more men and supplies. Washington was informed that in addition to the Marylanders, 2,000 Virginia militiamen had been rallied at Williamsburg awaiting his orders to march. He immediately sent for them. And after consulting with his fellow delegates, John Hancock went so far as to send the commander in chief copies of congressional resolutions granting him the authority to seize provisions from local populaces in exchange for promissory notes issued to farmers and merchants guaranteeing future repayment.

Although well meant, this proclamation was the seed of the civilian animus toward the Continental Army that would bloom into a withering rage over the coming winter at Valley Forge. The weather had yet to turn, and his army was already in dire need of supplies ranging from food to weapons to shoes to blankets. Still, Washington sensed "the melancholy truth" that Hancock's resolution could well "involve the ruin of the army, and perhaps the ruin of America" by turning the locals against him and his troops. In an eleventh-hour effort to forestall that outcome, Washington instead dispatched Alexander Hamilton to Philadelphia to procure what provisions he could, including blankets and, with over 1,000 of his men marching barefoot, at least 3,000 pairs of shoes he understood to be warehoused in the city. What Hamilton could not carry out he was to burn.

Yet even this option disturbed Washington. "I feel, and I lament," he wrote to Hamilton, "the absolute necessity of requiring the inhabitants to contribute to those wants which we have no other means of satisfying." In follow-up instructions to Hamilton the next day he was even more morose at the notion of Americans looting their countrymen. "The business you are upon I know is disagreable," he wrote, "& perhaps in the execution, you may meet with more obstacles than were at first apprehended & also with opposition; call in such a number of Militia as you may think necessary, observing however over the conduct of the whole, a strict discipline, to prevent evry species of rapine & disorder."

For now, however, as fresh soldiers and a bare minimum of provisions leached toward him from several directions — including enough ammunition procured from Philadelphia to issue 40 rounds to each soldier — a harrowed Washington faced other questions:

What exactly would be Howe's next move? With Philadelphia abandoned by Congress as well as by most of its Whigs, would the enemy still find symbolic glory in capturing the rebel capital? Or, given the British army's own fractured supply lines, would Howe instead veer west in an attempt to seize the Continental Army's inland storehouses, particularly its vast holdings at Reading and Carlisle? Washington had received somewhat vague congressional orders to protect Philadelphia. But was there really anything left to protect, particularly at the expense of his vital winter provisions? And where was the British fleet? If Gen. Howe could consolidate his army with his brother's warships and supply ships somewhere on the Delaware, Philadelphia would be lost in any case. Perhaps best to strike now, before that stood a chance of happening.

As Washington pondered these hypothetical questions, Anthony Wayne's rear guard was about to receive a rather more empirical answer.

Five:
Fix Bayonets

By September 20, British troops were still camped near Valley Forge as Gen. Howe, again mirroring Washington's instincts, contemplated a thrust west to meet the Continental Army. In the meantime, Gen. Wayne's Pennsylvania division had crept to within three miles of the enemy lines, perilously close to within long cannon shot and near enough to hear the British drummers beat reveille. Wayne had bivouacked his 2,000 or so regulars on the edge of a copse along a plateaued rise near a tavern perhaps regrettably named for the Corsican revolutionary Gen. Pasquale Paoli. Paoli, once popular in America for his attempts to drive the French colonizers from his island, was at present the latest celebrity-in-exile gracing London's salons. No one thought to change the name of the tavern. Wayne was still waiting for Gen. Smallwood's Maryland reinforcements and what he hoped would be orders from Washington to attack. He assumed, wrongly, that the presence of his own troops had been undetected by the British.

Journals and diaries kept by soldiers from both sides describe an ominous cloud cover rolling over the area late that Saturday afternoon, and by nightfall completely obscuring the full moon and stars. Wayne was aware of his precarious position; his original plan was to move out under cover of darkness. But with Gen. Smallwood and his militiamen inexplicably delayed and the scent of another heavy rain in the air, he instead instructed his men to fashion a series of what the Continentals called "weather booths" — primitive lean-tos constructed of tree branches, thick cornstalks, and trimmed saplings that would keep dry both the soldiers and the little powder they were carrying. As his troops went to work on their improvised huts Wayne and a small group of aides rode off to reconnoiter their perimeter.

This was familiar and, for the most part, friendly territory for the young general. Wayne — the grandson of Anglo-Irish immigrants who had been the recipients of an extensive royal land grant in what was to become Chester County — had been born only a few miles away. Prior to the revolution he had established himself as a successful farmer, state politician, and surveyor — he'd once laid out plans for a settlement on land in Nova Scotia owned by Benjamin Franklin and a consortium of merchants — and when war broke out he'd raised a regiment of Pennsylvania militiamen. Although he had no formal military training, what one historian calls his "zeal and spunk" soon led to his appointment as a colonel in the Continental Army.

Wayne and his Pennsylvanians had subsequently distinguished themselves during the failed invasion of Canada, where Wayne was wounded during the Battle of Three Rivers. Wayne's natural athleticism belied his vicar's visage, and his boundless energy and fighting skills — what harder-eyed observers might describe as his reckless abandon — had caught Washington's eye. Upon his recovery he was promoted to brigadier general in early 1777. Wayne's mettle and knowledge of the territory had rewarded Washington's judgment at Brandywine Creek, and if the American commander in chief trusted anyone to cover the local terrain while playing cat and mouse with a British force that outnumbered him seven to one, it was the lord of Waynesboro Manor.

Yet neither American took into account the possibility that the same Tories who had guided Howe across the upper branches of the Brandywine would inform the British of Wayne's location. While Wayne was off on his scouting mission, Gen. Howe was quietly assembling some 2,000 elite British and Scottish raiders to fall on the Pennsylvanians. This light infantry, under the command of Gen. Charles Grey, was well versed in the swift, stealthy movements of ranger tactics. Before departing camp, Grey ordered most of his soldiers to remove the flints from their .75-caliber "kings arms" — the ubiquitous musket soon to be known around the world as the deadly "Brown Bess." It was fitting that Grey, a small, thin officer with a face as pinched as a hatchet, so resembled a metal instrument of destruction; the night attack he had been chosen to lead was to be purely a bayonet assault.

The British bayonets were triangular in shape, ensuring that even if the 18-inch blade did not puncture a vital organ, at least one facet of the weapon would always be slicing near a heart, a kidney, a liver. Moreover, the tips of the bayonets were not sharpened but blunt, cast to tear at an opponent's flesh like a shark's tooth instead of inflicting a surgical cut that could be easily sutured. It was a perfectly deadly tactic for a dark, rainy night. As Grey's second in command, Capt. John André, confided to his journal: "It was represented to the men that firing discovered us to the Enemy, hid them from us, killed our friends and produced a confusion favorable to the escape of the Rebels and perhaps productive of disgrace to ourselves. On the other hand, by not firing we knew the foe to

102

be wherever fire appeared and a [bayonet] charge ensured his destruction; that amongst the enemy those in the rear would direct their fire against whoever fired in front, and they would destroy each other."

Although Wayne had dashed off a communiqué to Washington the previous morning assuring his commander that Howe "knows nothing of my Situation — as I have taken every precaution to Prevent any intelligence getting to him," there are indications that he had been warned by at least one local patriot that the enemy was aware of his camp. When he returned to his headquarters tent around 10 that night he took the precaution of increasing his picket posts from four to six, with each squad consisting of roughly 20 sentries. These included a mounted picket called a vidette.

With Smallwood yet to appear, Wayne was loath to break camp and complicate their rendezvous. Washington had indicated to Wayne that once his and Smallwood's troops were combined, they would make up one half of the pincer movement buffeting Howe's rear. The commander in chief's much larger force, already on the move from Yellow Springs, would form the other half. So certain was Wayne of Smallwood's imminent arrival that he instructed his company commanders to be prepared to move at the first sight of the Marylander's forward scouts. As the Pennsylvanians waited, the British force under Grey was already on the march beneath the starless sky.

Guided through the murk by an American deserter and a local blacksmith coerced into cooperation, Grey took no chance of tipping his prey and flanked out skirmishers to sweep up and detain every man, woman, and child in his path. Sometime before midnight a company of these advance guards was spotted by two of the American videttes, who fired on it before galloping back to camp with the alert. Wayne immediately ordered his entire division turned out to arms. He was too late. Moments later the Americans heard a volley of flintlock fire perhaps three quarters of a mile to the north. Then silence. They had no idea that one of their picket posts had been overrun by a bayonet charge. Wayne next issued orders to evacuate the camp, beginning with the two dozen wagons hauling his four field pieces, spare ammunition, and commissary and quartermaster supplies.

As the division filed into columns, the Continentals heard more gunfire to their northeast. It was a second, closer American picket getting off final musket shots before being cut to pieces. Moments later, on the cry of "Dash, Light Infantry!" the first battalion of 500 enemy troops poured into Wayne's right flank. The Americans were overwhelmed. The campfires still burning beside the weather booths served as homing beacons for the wave of Redcoats who cut and slashed their way into the middle of the American camp, their blades flashing in the firelight. At such close range, musketeers had little chance against bayonets, particularly at night. Those who did manage to use their weapons in the mounting chaos proved Capt. André prescient. Panicked Americans pulled their triggers at any firelock flash they saw. The British had still not fired a shot.

Meanwhile, Wayne's retreat across a fenced-in meadow stalled when one of the forward wagons hauling a field piece broke down and blocked the adjacent road. This was a perfect example of what the preeminent Prussian military theorist Carl von Clausewitz referred to as "friction" — the unexpected and seemingly innocuous battlefield occurrence that sets off a string of unintended effects resulting in disaster. With the remainder of the wagon train now stalled, the rush of American foot soldiers attempting to shove past the obstruction between fences created a bottleneck for slaughter. A second wave of 350 British infantrymen, accompanied by a dozen or so of the Queen's Own Light Dragoons atop snorting warhorses, saw to it. To shouts of "No Quarter" the enemy surrounded the jumbled body of Continentals and ran at them in flights of bayonet rushes. Any American who managed to escape the mayhem was run down by the mounted dragoons, who wielded their three-foot broadswords like scythes. Wayne and his company commanders were attempting to wheel the writhing mass of bleeding humanity into a semblance of a defensive line when another 300 British soldiers emerged from the woods behind them and charged.

The early evening's light rain had grown thicker, and the battlefield, if it can be called such, was by now a soupy brew of mud, blood, and gore. The broken wagon was pushed off the road, and the Americans who made it out of camp now streamed west with the rush of a river current. The wounded were carried by comrades as best they could be, while the able-bodied left behind were beyond putting up any organized resistance. Hand-to-hand fighting was their only recourse. Eyewitnesses later testified that Continentals attempting to surrender were surrounded by as many as a dozen British infantrymen who took turns running them through with steel blades. A subsequent compilation of wounds to the dead would confirm this. For Gen. Grey, all that was left was to administer the *coup de grâce.* This was accomplished by what one chronicler of the fight called "the largest and most terrifying menace of the night."

Grey had held in reserve two companies of the Royal Highlands Regiment, the ferocious

Black Watch, for just this occasion. Now, at his signal, the nearly 600 Scotsmen in their short red jackets and tassled blue bonnets were released in a double-ranked battle line. They had adopted canvas "trews," or trousers, in place of their traditional kilts. Savage Gaelic battle cries filled the air as the Scots swept across the killing field in a solid front without breaking ranks. They put to the bayonet any wounded or stragglers they encountered and began systematically burning the weather booths, often with frightened Americans still hiding inside. As Capt. André laconically observed, "We stabbed great numbers."

While Gen. Wayne attempted to form yet another rear guard not far from where the artillery wagon had broken down, Gen. Smallwood and his 2,000 or so Maryland troops were finally approaching Paoli along the muddy, rutted roads leading east. Smallwood digested the reports of the fighting from the first retreating Pennsylvanians he met and decided to fall back about a mile to higher ground and form a defensive line behind which Wayne's forces could regroup. He had done much the same 13 months earlier during the Battle of Long Island. Despite that engagement's disastrous outcome, his rearguard action at Brooklyn Heights was credited with saving hundreds of American lives. Smallwood had barely issued the order to form up when his left flank was raked by a volley from a company of British light infantry chasing Wayne's stragglers. Earlier, back at Howe's camp, this particular group of infantrymen had been exempted from the order to remove their flints after their commander promised to hold himself personally responsible for any of his men who fired their weapons. Now they had expressly disobeyed the order not to fire.

This made little matter to many of Smallwood's militiamen, who promptly fulfilled the French colonel Duportail's grim forecast by flinging away their weapons, turning tail, and running like foxes before the hounds. Those who did not flee fired madly at anything that moved. General Smallwood himself narrowly escaped this friendly fire when a dragoon riding beside him was blown off his horse and killed by an American musket ball. Nearly half of the Maryland men vanished into the Pennsylvania countryside that night, never to be heard from again, before Smallwood's officers finally regrouped the remainder to form a defensive line. There they waited for Wayne and the roiling cluster of his surviving regulars while bracing for the British and Scottish in pursuit.

Yet by this time the blare of trumpets had recalled the enemy troops back to the smoking, reeking scene of what can only be called a massacre. The overwhelming success of the operation stunned even the most presumptuous British officers. Of the 272 men reported missing from Wayne's division, nearly 60 lay dead on and around the battlefield. Despite the unofficial "No Quarter" strategy, the British did manage to take some 71 American prisoners, more than half of them seriously wounded. They had also captured nine of the Continental supply wagons piled with food and baggage. Their own losses came to three dead, eight wounded, and two horses killed. By dawn they had returned to Howe's camp near Valley Forge to ringing huzzahs.

Washington had the ignominy of learning the results of the Battle of Paoli from the enemy himself. The next morning, before Wayne's riders reached the commander in chief's new camp across the Schuylkill, a British messenger forded the river offering a flag of truce to Continental burial details. General Howe, as he had at Brandywine, also allowed passage to surgeons to treat the most severely injured prisoners who had been deposited at local homes, inns, and taverns in British-controlled territory. The doctors were appalled at having to dress the multiple stab wounds, often a dozen or more per soldier. Many of the wounded would not see October.

Even by the standards of eighteenth-century combat, the unprofessionalism shown by the British who killed and maimed surrendering

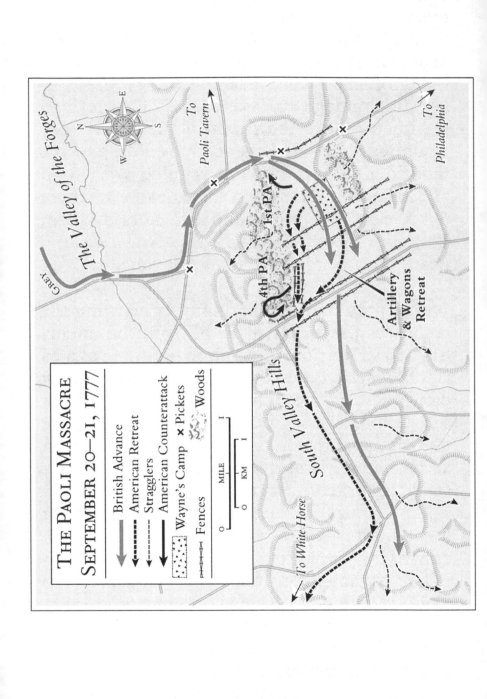

THE PAOLI MASSACRE
SEPTEMBER 20—21, 1777

British Advance
American Retreat
Stragglers
American Counterattack

× Pickets
Wayne's Camp
Woods
Fences

MILE
KM

The Valley of the Forges

GREY

To Paoli Tavern

To Philadelphia

4th PA 1st PA

Artillery & Wagons Retreat

South Valley Hills

To White Horse

Continentals that night was scandalous and would blight the careers of the officers who led them, Gen. Grey in particular, who that night acquired the nickname "No Flint Grey." It would even affix a taint of dishonor to Howe himself. The general's defenders argued that a "No Quarter" order had never been given. Their proof — the 71 American prisoners in Crown hands. The same defenders conveniently elided the fact that nearly every American prisoner had been the victim of multiple bayonet wounds. For his part, Howe saw no point in adhering to the informal yet generally recognized European "laws of war" that prohibited the killing of wounded or unarmed soldiers. The American colonists — a mere "herd of fugitives," according to Capt. André — were in rebellion, and thus traitors to the Crown not entitled to the presumptions of such established custom.

The Continentals naturally viewed the events in a different light. To their sensibility, the acts of butchery by the enemy that night, against unarmed men, could be expected of hired mercenaries, particularly the Germans contracted by George III to fight in North America. But the viciousness with which the English and Scottish had treated their erstwhile American "cousins" revealed a loathing for the rebels that seethed just below the surface throughout the revolution. It would not soon be forgotten, and "Remember

Paoli" was to become an American battle cry long before the Alamo or the battleship USS *Maine.*

When an official American inquiry was convened to explore the roots of the "Paoli Massacre," some were inclined to charge Gen. Wayne with gross misconduct. Instead, the court of inquiry found him guilty of only tactical errors centered on his failure to decamp earlier. He was nonetheless outraged at even this minor rebuke, and as was becoming more common among the fragile egos of the Continental Army's officer corps, he demanded a full court-martial to clear his name. A panel of 13 officers thereafter ruled that he had indeed acted with honor on the fateful night.

Howe and his army broke camp at dawn the morning after the fight. The British general, having ascertained that Washington's defensive position was too strong to breach, instead headed for Philadelphia. Across the Schuylkill in the American bivouac, a Pennsylvania officer who had escaped the Paoli killing fields summed up the experience in a rather stunning understatement. Describing the engagement in a letter to his wife, he wrote, "Fortune has not been sublime to our Division."

Perhaps deeming that euphemism insufficient, he felt compelled to add, "The carnage was very great."

Six:
A Perfect Scribe

The day after the Battle of Paoli, Gen. Howe directed several of his regiments northwest in a strong feint toward the Continentals' Reading storehouses. It was only a ruse, but it worked. By the time he recalled his troops, Washington had responded by withdrawing north, away from Philadelphia, and forming a defensive line between the British and the Pennsylvania interior. The city's fate was sealed.

Moving at a leisurely pace, Howe's army of some 14,000 took nearly a week to reach Philadelphia. As it lumbered through the suburbs of Norristown and then Germantown clad in a rainbow of uniforms — dragoons in crimson coats faced with dark blue lapels; grenadiers in brick red with their multicolored facings reflecting their parent regiments; artillerymen in dark blue, their buttonholes laced yellow; Hessian Jägers sporting their customary forest green, their omnipresent waxed mustaches cultivated to such a density as to qualify as topiary — onlookers (and spies) noted its surly disposition. In contrast to the sprightly Continentals who had marched into Philadelphia just over a month earlier, the British appeared anything but happy to be here, an ocean away from home, chasing an elusive enemy who refused to stand and fight like proper European adversaries.

Finally, at noon on a crisp Friday, September 26, with Gen. Lord Cornwallis in the van of the parade marching down Second Street and up Vine Street, Howe claimed his prize unopposed by a single musket shot. Cornwallis's triumphal entry into the city proper was accompanied by row upon row of lace-coated fifers and drummers playing "God Save Great George Our King." Each of Howe's soldiers had tied a sprig of green to his hat or his horse's tail. It is not recorded if the crowd of mostly women and children — the majority of the town's men were gone — recognized the mocking allusion.

Three thousand troops under the command of Cornwallis were billeted in the city proper. The remainder, under Howe, were encamped six miles away at Germantown. Soon, Howe would move into the city, settling himself and his staff in a 110-year-old, three-and-a-half-story brick mansion on the corner of Sixth and Market Streets that had once been the home of William Penn's grandson.* But, for now, he remained on the periphery to ensure that his greater force formed up properly as a bulwark between Philadelphia and Washington's army. He had arranged, however, for one further derisive gesture beyond his troops' green sprigs. While the lower floor of Independence Hall was converted into a barracks for a small company of grenadiers, Howe ordered the upper floor of the statehouse where the Declaration of Independence had been signed converted into a holding pen for some 70 American officers, predominantly Virginians and Pennsylvanians, captured at Brandywine and Paoli.

Only months earlier Washington would have considered the capture of the capital of the United States a fatal blow to the revolution. Now, just as the bend of the river compels the pilot's course, the fall of Philadelphia proved more academic than calamitous, particularly with the Continental Congress safe in York and, thanks to Alexander Hamilton, most of the city's storehouses either emptied or destroyed.

A week before the first clomp of British horses echoed across the cobblestones of Market Street, the redoubtable Hamilton had

* Masters-Penn House, known today as President's House, was later home to both President George Washington and President John Adams.

led a small party of dragoons to the city's outskirts. They were in the process of burning a brace of flour mills along the Schuylkill when a company of British cavalry, drawn to the flames, ambushed them in the dark. One American was killed, another wounded, and Hamilton's horse was shot out from under him. While the rest of his mounted company fled, Hamilton and four other Continentals managed to secure a tiny, flat-bottomed skiff and row to the middle of the river as Redcoats swarmed the bankside and "emptied their carbines and pistols at the distance of ten or twelve paces." When their boat was caught in the eddies in the middle of the river, Hamilton and his compatriots dived in and swam to safety. From the opposite riverbank he dashed off a message to John Hancock warning that the British were closer to the city than anyone imagined.

The irascible corset maker turned pamphleteer Thomas Paine, whose *Common Sense* had electrified the movement for American independence a year earlier by demythicizing the aura of a benevolent King George, recalled the panic that ensued. Even at midnight, Paine wrote, Philadelphia's moonlit streets resembled market day at high noon as disbanding militia companies rushed about wildly and hundreds if not thousands of citizens hitched teams to overloaded wagons and carts to flee west.

Washington, meanwhile, was distraught when the horsemen under Hamilton's charge reached camp and reported their leader dead. But just as the commander in chief was digesting this hard communication, who should appear at the entrance to his tent on a borrowed horse but the sodden and disheveled dead man himself. It was the best news of a bad time.

Hamilton, then all of 22, had come to Washington's attention a year earlier during the Battle of Harlem Heights, one of the few bright spots of the New York campaign. The commander in chief had been impressed by the precocious artillery officer's proficiency at constructing defensive earthworks, and had invited Hamilton to his headquarters. As the two conversed, Washington was further taken with the young man's military acumen. It is likely Hamilton did not bring up an incident from weeks earlier, when during the Battle of Long Island his cannoneers, some of them drunk, had been decimated by British warships sailing up the Hudson. Since the abandonment of New York, Hamilton's reputation had only risen. During the engagement at Trenton the pinpoint accuracy of his field pieces had sent the Hessians into a panic. The following day at Princeton, when a company of some 200 British soldiers took refuge in the school's main hall, lore has it that one of Hamilton's cannonballs blasted through the head of a portrait of King George II, compelling their surrender.

Two months later, in March 1777, Washington had brought the short, slim "Little Lion" onto his staff as his principal aide. This was no small promotion. When Congress had tabbed Washington to lead the army two years earlier, it had also authorized a military secretary and three aides-de-camp to assist him. To Washington the two positions were interchangeable, as both job descriptions consisted of composing letters and orders, delivering messages on and off the battlefield, leading scouting missions, interrogating prisoners of war, and helping to run the various spy rings that sprang up during the revolution.

The commander in chief well knew the sacrifices these men made — most who accepted the positions would have preferred more prestigious posts as line officers. In a letter to John Hancock decrying the pittance that Congress set aside for his staff's salaries, Washington provided a stark insight into the character of the men with whom he surrounded himself. "Aid de Camps are person's in whom entire Confidence must be placed," he wrote. "It requires Men of abilities to execute the duties with propriety and dispatch where there is such a multiplicity of business as must attend the Commander in chief of such an army as our's; and perswaded I am that nothing but the zeal of those Gentlemen who live with me and act in this capacity for the great American Cause and personal attachment to me, has induced them to undergo the trouble and confinement they have experienced since they have become Members of my Family."

Given the mortification Washington had felt at being betrayed by the man Hamilton was replacing, Joseph Reed, it was something of a wonder that the commander in chief retained such high opinions of his aides. The charming and loquacious Reed, a prominent Philadelphia attorney, was Washington's original secretary and aide-de-camp. Reed attended Princeton before studying law at London's Middle Temple, and his academic credentials probably overimpressed the Virginia planter, ever self-conscious about his own lack of higher education. As the biographer Joseph Ellis notes, "Instead of going to college, Washington went to war," and his innate solitariness, manifested by his reluctance to place his complete trust in anyone except his wife, Martha, was legendary. Yet he grew to view Reed not only as a confidant, but as a friend. Which made it all the more devastating when, after the retreat from New York, Washington discovered that Reed was conspiring to have Congress throw him over and vault Gen. Charles Lee into the supreme command of the Continental Army.

General Lee had since been captured by the British while undertaking a foolhardy escapade involving a tavern girl. And Washington, though seething inwardly, had granted Reed a temporary furlough to tend to his law practice. In the four months since the incident, Washington had been overburdened by bureaucratic clerical duties, and Hamilton seemed the correct fit to step in. In the interim between Reed's dismissal and Hamilton's hiring, Washington's vast network of correspondents had become accustomed to receiving communiqués in the commander in chief's distinctive and imposing handwriting, marked by frequent if erratic use of capital letters. Washington considered effective communication a key to his management style, and to his mind this included an emphasis on presentation. If anything, Hamilton's beautiful penmanship, written in a consistent, elegant slope imbued with a series of decorative loops, outdid his new commander's. How he had acquired his many talents was a strange story.

Alexander Hamilton was born a bastard on the Caribbean island of Nevis. His mother, Rachel, died from a tropical fever when he was nine, leaving him to look after his younger brother James. With the help of a Scottish Presbyterian minister named Hugh

Knox, he found employment in the custom-house in the bustling port of Saint Croix and appeared destined for an anonymous life as a mid-level clerk, or "quill driver." Then lightning struck — literally and metaphorically — when a descriptive letter he wrote at the age of 14 to his departed father in the wake of a ravaging hurricane was reprinted in a local newspaper.* This caught the attention of a company of local merchants who, taken with the boy's natural industriousness and intelligence, set up a fund to pay for his formal education.

Denied entrance to any Church of England school because of his illegitimacy, he sailed to America in 1772 to enroll at the Elizabethtown Academy in New Jersey. Like Lafayette, Hamilton displayed a penchant for attracting the attention of influential older men, not least of them the future governor of New Jersey, William Livingston, with whom he found lodging. Livingston was already a proponent of independence from Great Britain, and his young charge carried this revolutionary notion along with his ever-present bag of books to New York when he enrolled at King's College, now Columbia

* In the letter, Hamilton described "the prodigious glare of almost perpetual lightning, the crash of the falling houses, and the ear-piercing shrieks of the distressed."

121

University.

Hamilton was still a student at King's College when he published a series of pamphlets and gave a string of speeches advocating American independence. But he had also matured into a man of decency and integrity, and he was credited with saving the life of the college's president, Myles Cooper, when Cooper was attacked by a mob for his Loyalist leanings. When the revolution broke over the 13 colonies, Hamilton and a few of his classmates formed a militia company, dubbing themselves the Corsicans. Later, perhaps feeling betrayed by Gen. Paoli's conversion from resistance fighter to London dandy, they renamed their unit the Hearts of Oak. By now Capt. Hamilton's sack of books was heavily weighted toward military tactics and history. As he employed his autodidactic learnings to real-world effect in battles from Harlem Heights to White Plains to the Raritan River to Trenton, his fearlessness and composure under fire were evident enough to prompt Gen. Lord Stirling and Gen. Alexander McDougall, a Scottish-born former privateer now serving under Washington, to invite him onto their staffs. He turned down both, stating his preference to remain a field officer. It is worth noting that he accepted Washington's similar offer only when it was proffered in conjunction with a promotion to lieutenant colonel.

By the time the British marched into Philadelphia, Hamilton was so deeply immersed in his position as Washington's chief secretary and aide-de-camp that, as the bibliographer Chernow notes, he was "the surrogate who was not only a good scribe but could intuit the responses [Washington] himself would write." No further proof of this is needed than the hundreds of letters to Congress, governors, and senior officers that Hamilton composed in his exquisite penmanship in Washington's name. He wrote, as the popular Broadway musical based on his life put it, as if he was running out of time. During his tenure on Washington's staff — he would not officially resume field duty until July 1781 — Hamilton formed with Lafayette and John Laurens a triad of bright and eager young men who filled a void in the childless general's military family. It is rather astounding that, by the fall of 1777, three men barely out of their teens had become some of the most essential figures of the American Revolution.

Like the prickly John Adams, who viewed the enemy's occupation of Philadelphia as a "gloomy, dark, melancholy, and dispiriting" occasion, Hamilton was crestfallen at the capture of America's capital city to the point where he wondered if this meant the beginning of the end of the revolution. Yet not every American patriot saw the event as quite so dispiriting. The great propagandist Paine, for instance, now serving as secretary to the Foreign Committee of Congress, noted that the quest for independence was not a fight for "a field of a few acres of ground, but a cause we are defending." And half a world away in France, when 71-year-old Benjamin Franklin was breathlessly informed that Gen. Howe had captured Philadelphia, he waved off his courier's conspicuous anguish.

"No," he quipped, "Philadelphia has captured Howe." For all of Franklin's quick wit, there was usually a kernel of truth at the heart of his pithy aperçus.

By late September the first frost of the season had already whitened the rolling green hills of southeastern Pennsylvania. Short of a pitched battle to retake Philadelphia, Washington understood that his best chance to stymie Gen. Howe was to keep the British fleet literally at bay. If the Americans could prevent Adm. Howe from sailing his supply ships up the Delaware River, his brother would soon enough be hard pressed to feed his army. This meant relying on the Continentals' riverside forts, and to that end Washington detached a regiment of close to 1,000 men to reinforce the stockades on the lower Delaware. He felt able to spare these troops upon receiving word that the brigade he had summoned from Poughkeepsie was now but a day's march away. Yet when he discovered that this unit consisted of only some 900 men and officers, he sent word to Gen. Putnam to hurry another 1,600 troops south to Pennsylvania.

Upon receiving this order Putnam was again astonished and angry — why not just invite the British to stroll up from New York City and seize the entire Hudson Highlands? Such were the perils of the era's communication lines that Putnam and the other American generals stationed in the north were under the impression that Washington commanded an army of some 40,000 men — enough, one commented, to make the British in Philadelphia "but a breakfast" for the Continentals.

In fact, not counting the 2,000 soldiers marching from Virginia and the combined detachments from Putnam's command, at the moment Washington could field only around 5,000 fighting men, with but 2,000 of them considered battle-hardened regulars. A salient fact about the Revolutionary War is that out of a population of three million, the 13 colonies never managed to raise an army of more than 50,000 men at any one time, including state militias. Even that figure is misleading, as it counts the rolls of soldiers who technically enlisted but may or may not have served for any length of time. In truth, the entire Continental Army never numbered more than around 20,000, and Washington never had more than 12,000 or so troops under his direct command.

For all of Putnam's obstreperousness, Washington had a soft spot for the gnarled 59-year-old. With his crop of thick curls turned badger-gray to match the great puffy pouches underlining his eyes, "Old Put," as his soldiers called him, wore the face of a melancholy sheepdog. He had been a popular and inspiring leader of men since his Indian-fighting days with Rogers' Rangers, and it was only half-jokingly remarked that he was totally unfit for any venue except the battle-field. As a civilian Putnam had tried his hand at farming and sheepherding — he was rumored to have crawled into a wolf's den to kill the last she-wolf in the state of Con-necticut — but soldiering was his true call-ing. It was Putnam who at Bunker Hill had growled the command to hold fire "until you see the whites of their eyes," and as a senti-mental sop to the old warhorse, Washington sent instructions allowing him to consolidate his farther-flung American outposts spread about the Hudson Highlands. But even this peace offering received Putnam's derision, with one of his officers fuming at the "Paper Men" of Washington's army and mocking the "boasted Courage of the Southern Heroes." After Brandywine and Paoli, the patriots of the north country had no idea of how much worse it would get for the paper men in Pennsylvania.

On September 28, Washington summoned a war council to solicit opinions about whether to "make a general and vigorous attack upon the enemy, or to await further reinforcements." Early in his military career, while fighting in the French and Indian War, Washington had discovered that he made his best decisions after listening to a spectrum of suggestions from his subordinates. He found that weighing the judgments of others reliably led him to the correct course of action — a course he invariably stuck to once he had decided upon it. On this occasion the vote to defer an assault on Philadelphia until more troops arrived was nearly unanimous — a consensus that, historians suggest, Washington was in agreement with and knew was coming. It was often noted that Washington exerted more influence on events by concealing rather than advertising his preferences. "He possessed the gift of silence," as John Adams noted years later. Within 48 hours the Virginia troops had reached York to the delight of the Continental Congress, whose members watched them step smartly through the town. Washington was decidedly less enthusiastic when he discovered their conspicuous dearth of firelocks.

Still, as September wound down Washington was again cautiously stalking the British, moving his army to within 16 miles of Germantown. Congress, particularly the Pennsylvania delegation, was pressing him to attack. But he was not certain he had sufficient firepower to stand and fight the bulk of the British regulars stationed at Germantown, much less the total British force. Surprising the enemy would be his only recourse. But when and where? As it happened, events in the north went far toward settling the decision for him. For when word reached Congress that Gen. Gates was successfully blocking the British path to Albany, the pressure on Washington to mount an offensive only grew. As the Valley Forge historian Wayne Bodle writes, "The news [from the north] had its intended effect as a morale booster, and seemed to call for a corresponding triumph in the southern theater."

Once again, Gen. Howe solved his counterpart's problem. As Washington suspected, by occupying Philadelphia, Howe had created an internal crisis. On the march to the city his troops had provisioned themselves by living off the countryside, particularly the farmsteads around Valley Forge. Now, however, his quartermasters reported their food and gunpowder supplies dwindling. It was imperative for Howe to break the stranglehold the Americans had on the Delaware River and allow his brother's supply ships to pass.

About four miles below the city, on either side of a narrow section of the Delaware, Continental regulars manned two forts that constituted a strategic choke point. In addition to the redoubts, a small flotilla of American ships — facetiously dubbed "George Washington's Navy" and consisting of a motley collection of merchantmen turned privateers and several floating artillery batteries — patrolled the waters near the outposts. These were abetted by smaller craft crewed by local Pennsylvanians.

Taken together, the forts and the ships constituted a formidable defense, and Gen. Howe was neither prepared nor inclined to meet it head-on. A few miles below the two riverside outposts, however, rose a much more vulnerable, half-completed earthen fortification at Billingsport, where the Delaware's main channel swung hard against the New Jersey embankment. This outpost could conceivably form a threat to his brother's supply ships offloading provisions farther downriver to be conveyed overland to Philadelphia. This would be the British general's first target. He had no idea that his decision to assault the dilapidated stockade at Billingsport would inadvertently lead to a pitched battle 27 miles away, at Germantown.

SEVEN:
A BLOODY DAY

It was the opportunity for which Washington had been waiting. On September 29 his scouts reported two regiments of British soldiers departing Germantown and marching south. Washington correctly surmised their intention to seize the fortification at Billingsport. He had already ordered the stockade there abandoned and burned and its six cannons spiked. Which is how the enemy found it when they arrived 48 hours later. In the meantime, Washington led his army to within 15 miles of Germantown and convened another war council. It was one of the rare occasions when he was not content to act as a neutral sounding board for his generals. "The term of mercy having expired," he wrote in his General Orders for October 3, "our dearest rights, our dearest friends, and our own lives, honor, glory and even shame, urge us to fight."

General Howe, he added, "Has left us no choice but Conquest or Death." It was time to strike the enemy, hard, before winter set in. By dusk on the evening of October 3 the entire Continental Army had broken into four columns. These marched all night in preparation for a daybreak attack.

The two center columns, led by the generals Sullivan and Greene, were made up of regulars, now numbering close to 8,000 men. Three thousand militiamen under the command of Gen. Smallwood and Pennsylvania's Gen. John Armstrong were apportioned to either wing. Nothing was to be carried that could not fit into a haversack greased for rain, and each soldier was issued a sheet of white paper to affix to his hat in order to distinguish him from the enemy. Their objective: to encircle and converge in waves on the British at Germantown, driving them south toward Philadelphia before Cornwallis could lead reinforcements up from the city. Given the timing, tactics, and terrain, it was an intricate if well-conceived battle plan. It failed miserably.

It was Washington's bad luck that by sunrise on Saturday, October 4, the gorges and defiles that dominated the landscape in and around Germantown were obscured by a strange and unsettling fog so thick that his men could barely make out compatriots advancing a few yards away. Initially the two columns of regulars moved on parallel tracks through the misty shroud, with one of Sullivan's divisions under Gen. Wayne's command so surprising the British pickets as to make matchwood of their defenses. While the bulk of the enemy force fell back helter-skelter for nearly two miles, trilling cries of revenge for Paoli filled the air as the Continentals advanced into the village of Germantown itself. Wayne's officers attempted, without much success, to prevent the furious Pennsylvanian troops from bayoneting wounded Redcoats left behind by comrades fleeing in wild disorder. This early stage of the battle proved both the highlight and the lowlight of the American effort. Though it appeared for a brief moment as if the rout would continue to Philadelphia — Washington watched from horseback as his regulars poured past abandoned enemy tents and discarded cannons — the militiamen on either flank inexplicably failed to push forward to engage and engulf.

The offensive took an even more pernicious turn when the two inner columns, hindered by the fog, were unable to form up as planned to create a solid front. Greene's plank had to this point made good headway, but now one of his divisions commanded by the Virginian Gen. Adam Stephen stumbled in behind Wayne's men and began firing at any movement before it.* The identifying pieces of

---

* It did not help matters that Gen. Stephen was vis-

white paper proved ineffectual and the most forward Continentals were caught in a cross fire of musket balls, quick throbs of light in the soupy murk, at first a light patter, then a downpour. Some came from the direction of the retreating Redcoats, others from the upper stories of the town's plethora of stone houses occupied by the enemy. And now more came from the mystery force to their rear. Many of Wayne's troops turned and fired on Stephen's soldiers. Though Gen. Armstrong's Pennsylvania militia had tepidly engaged the Hessian Jägers on the British left flank, there was no sign of Smallwood and his men as the battlefield was transformed into a chiaroscuro of dripping mist and sulfurous gun smoke punctuated by the ripping-silk sounds of metal shot.

The confusion accelerated when British sappers began to torch Germantown's fields of hay and buckwheat. Plumes of black

---

ibly drunk for the duration of the fight. He was later court-martialed, found guilty of "Drunkenness, or drinking so much, as to act frequently in a manner, unworthy [of] the character of an officer," relieved of command, and cashiered from the service. (Washington's "General Orders, 25 October 1777," in *The Papers of George Washington*, Revolutionary War Series, Vol. 11, ed. Chase and Lengel, pp. 604–6.)

smoke further obscured the terrain until the bewildered American regulars finally collapsed onto themselves, Leonardo da Vinci's lost *Battle of Anghiari* come to life. Officers raced up and down what they could only guess were the front lines, urging staggering units forward. Washington himself whirled like a top on his white charger, shouting commands to advance and striking retreating soldiers with the flat of his sword. When this failed he ordered a remuda of dray horses arrayed across the green meadows and pale amber fields abutting the main Germantown road to block any Americans falling back. Fleeing Continentals ran around the animals or crawled beneath their flanks.

By now, nearly three hours into the engagement, Cornwallis's reinforcements were streaking up from Philadelphia and pouring into the fight. Howe, at his headquarters perhaps a half mile behind the British main line of defense southeast of the village square, initially thought that he was responding to — and that his soldiers were running from — a raiding probe. It never crossed his mind that Washington's rebels would dare attempt another pitched battle so soon after Brandywine and Paoli. It was later reported that in order to prevent one of his "stupefied" battalions from breaking and running, Howe had castigated them with cries of "For shame, Light Infantry. Form! Form! It is only a scouting party." Yet with American grapeshot rattling the trunks and branches of the chestnut trees about him, an incredulous Howe soon realized that he was indeed facing an all-out assault. His admiration for the enemy's temerity was matched only by his organizational skills. He and Cornwallis regrouped and rallied their troops as the Continental momentum ground to a dazed halt amid the miserable shouts and murmurs of bleeding men. Within moments, as the Redcoats and Hessians counterattacked, the American trickle to the rear became a torrent.

For the third time in less than a month George Washington's troops were in retreat. To Gen. Armstrong, they had seemingly "fled from victory." Many blamed the miserable showing on the militiamen, including Gen. Armstrong's. Armstrong himself later equated what he called "the infamous falling off" of his own troops with what "may with great justice be called desertion." His words were echoed by scores of exhausted Continental regulars who finally came to a halt some 20 miles north of the battlefield.

As at Brandywine, American officers who had been in the thick of the fight appeared to recognize how close they had come to Howe's annihilation, and spoiled for another clash. Washington's old friend and fellow Virginian Gen. George Weedon bemoaned the loss of the "Trophies that lay at our feet." His Virginians, he wrote, "had no Objections to another tryal which must take place soon." And Tench Tilghman, one of the commander in chief's longest-serving aides, wrote to his father that only the "excessive fogginess" had saved Howe's forces from defeat. One American surgeon wrote to his father that the men from whose bodies he had extracted musket balls were in such good spirits and so anxious for retribution that they were determined "to see it out this fall." A New York company commander even boasted "that we are far superior in point of swiftness [and] in high spirits. Every action gives our troops fresh vigor and a greater opinion of their own strength." Even Washington's chief intelligence officer Lt. Col. Benjamin Talmadge — a circumspect spymaster rarely given to metaphor — lamented that he had watched a unit of Connecticut regulars chase the British from "post to post" before being forced to withdraw.

General Lord Stirling was even more emphatic, if perhaps fanciful, in his assessment. Like the best Continental generals from Washington on down — and in stark contrast to most of their European counterparts — Lord Stirling was not content to view the bloody fighting from afar. He had been in the thick of it, and writing as if the complex arrangement for the four American columns to converge had actually succeeded, he noted,

"This affair will convince the World that we Can out General our enemy, and that we know how to Retreat in good Order and defy them to follow us." Like the others, Lord Stirling appeared to thirst for another crack at the British. "The Enemy will find that after every Battle our Army will increase and theirs diminish," he wrote. "This is fighting at such a disadvantage that they must soon be Convinced that they can never Support the war in America."

Perhaps it was only natural for the optimistic officers to gild what was, under any circumstances, a distressing setback. The final tally would be 150 Continentals killed, some 520 wounded, and 400 captured, against 70 British dead, 450 wounded, and 15 Redcoats and one small terrier in American custody.* Nevertheless, when the reports of victory in defeat reached York, congressional enthusiasm was difficult to temper. Delegates called for Washington to maintain a relentless offensive posture that would drive the British not only from Philadelphia but, within the

---

* When Washington was informed that the dog's collar indicated that it belonged to Gen. Howe, he had the animal bathed, combed, and returned to Howe with a note penned by Hamilton that read, "General Washington's compliments to Gen. Howe. He does himself the pleasure to return him a dog, which accidentally fell into his hands."

month, from the nation's shores. Once again there was talk of patriotic Christmas pageants and balls in the city's inns and taverns.

On the other hand, Washington's bruised and bleeding rank and file tended to leave less writing for posterity. It is doubtful that they were as giddy as their superiors and the distant politicians over the prospect of a rematch. But in the aftermath of what Washington described to his brother John as "a bloody day," the commander in chief's impression of the engagement can be fairly summarized in several communiqués. To John Hancock he described the events as "rather unfortunate" although far from "injurious." He later sent an addendum observing, "The tumult, disorder, & even despair, which seems to have taken place in the British Army were scarcely to be paralleled." And in a letter to Thomas McKean, president of the Delaware House of Assembly, he dismissed any notion of his own troops faltering and, instead, encouraged all patriots to "rejoice that we have given a severe blow to our Enemies."

True to his written sentiments, within days the Continental Army was indeed slowly inching back toward Philadelphia. Even as squads of soldiers were assigned to moccasin-sewing duty to cover the hundreds of Continental bare feet and deserters were hanged in the camp's parade ground, expectations ran high that the order to attack would come at any moment. Not even news of the British Gen. Clinton's expedition from New York City to capture two American forts on the Hudson Highlands could dampen the aspirations of Washington's troops. The same could not be said for Israel Putnam, who had predicted as much when the commander in chief had weakened his northern forces. Putnam could only sputter oaths over the fact that days before the British had taken his redoubts, Washington had assured him that if Clinton were to make a military move at all, the foray would almost certainly be through New Jersey "to form a junction with General Howe."

Then, on October 14, breathless riders from upstate New York arrived at the commander in chief's headquarters with details of the first of several running series of clashes between Gen. Gates's northern army and Gen. Burgoyne's Redcoats that would come to be known as the Battle of Saratoga.

Four months earlier, on June 20, "Gentleman Johnny" Burgoyne had departed Quebec with the appropriate pomp at the head of a force of just over 8,000 men. His army included nearly 4,000 hardened British regulars and 3,000 blue-coated German Brunswickers belting out their Lutheran hymns. Within a week the outnumbered

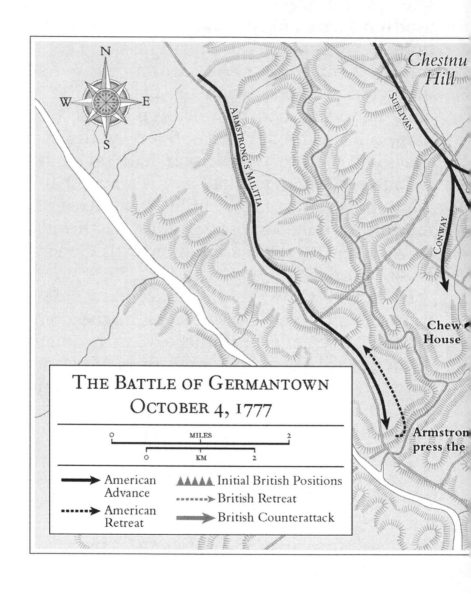

THE BATTLE OF GERMANTOWN
OCTOBER 4, 1777

MILES
0   2
KM
0   2

→ American Advance   ▲▲▲▲▲ Initial British Positions
------> American Retreat   ------> British Retreat
                                    → British Counterattack

Chestnu
Hill

ARMSTRONG'S MILITIA

SULLIVAN

CONWAY

Chew
House

Armstron
press the

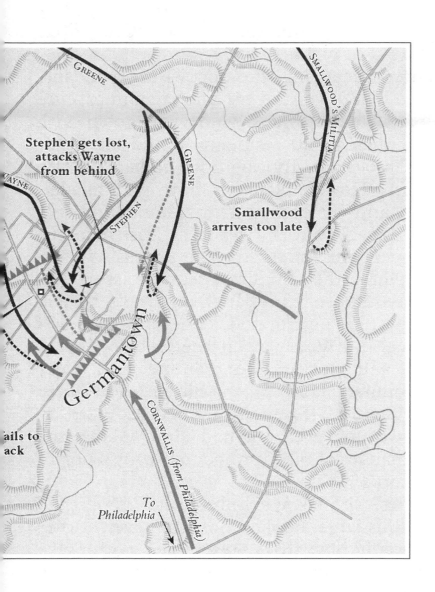

GREENE

SMALLWOOD'S MILITIA

Stephen gets lost, attacks Wayne from behind

WAYNE

GREENE

STEPHEN

Smallwood arrives too late

Germantown

ails to ack

CORNWALLIS (from Philadelphia)

To Philadelphia

patriots defending Fort Ticonderoga at the narrows near the south end of Lake Champlain would hear that chorus echoing from the heights overlooking their redoubt. They had no choice but to abandon "Old Ti" in the dead of night.

After occupying the fort, Burgoyne surmised that the rest of his campaign to capture Albany, at the time a wilderness town with fewer than 4,000 residents, would fall naturally into place. By this time he had learned of Gen. Howe's plans to move on Philadelphia, and he counted on Gen. Clinton's troops in New York City to at least theoretically keep the Americans guessing as to when and where they might expect an assault on their southern flank. In Burgoyne's typical bombast, he proclaimed, "The messengers of Justice and Wrath await the [rebels] in the field, and Devastation, Famine, and every concomitant Horror . . . will bar the Way to their Return." It remains unrecorded whether the warning ever reached Gen. Gates, the commander of the Continental Army's northern corps.

Gates, with his matronly spectacles perched upon his large, hooked nose and ever clad in a slovenly blue frock, resembled nothing so much as a blowsy midwife from a Gainsborough painting sprung to life. Yet his countenance disguised the 49-year-old's lust for power and position. Gates, who was the illegitimate son of a Kentish chambermaid impregnated by the duke for whom she worked, possessed a nimble and martial mind. After obtaining a military commission at the age of 17, he had risen to the rank of major during the French and Indian War before purchasing a plantation in the Shenandoah Valley and settling in America. A relentless ingratiator and wily political operative, one year earlier he had opted out of Washington's Christmas-night crossing of the Delaware by feigning illness and had galloped off to Philadelphia to attempt to persuade Congress to install him as commander of the Continental Army's Northern Military Department.* That the department was at the moment being ably run by Washington's friend Gen. Philip Schuyler was beside the point. Schuyler, a wealthy New Yorker intensely disliked by the New England contingent to the Continental Congress, nevertheless had a circle of influential friends whom Washington counted on for political influence and backing. As two historians of the

* The Continental Army's Northern Military Department covered northern New York and the New England states; the Southern Military Department consisted of Virginia, the Carolinas, and Georgia; the Middle Military Department's purview included Maryland, Delaware, Pennsylvania, New Jersey, and parts of southern New York.

American Revolution have observed, "Although there were clear limits to [Gates's] not inconsiderable military talents, there were none to his ambition."

As the general pleaded his case before Congress, at least one delegate was repulsed by Gates's "vanity, folly, and rudeness." "His manner was ungracious and totally void of all dignity, his delivery incoherent," wrote the New York representative William Duer to his friend Gen. Schuyler. Yet, in the end, his undermining of Schuyler succeeded. Now, nine months later, the "unhappy figure" whom the representative Duer had described as stabbing his fellow American officer in the back was charged with preventing Burgoyne's force from gaining control of the Hudson River and severing New England from the rest of the United States.

The initial engagement between the two northern armies, centered on an abandoned farmhouse set deep in the Adirondack woods, took place on September 19 when a wing of Gates's 6,000-man force under the command of Gen. Benedict Arnold ambushed a column of Burgoyne's Redcoats. By advancing on the British, Arnold had exasperated the more defensively inclined Gates, who had bivouacked his main body behind the barricades he had ordered thrown up some 25 miles north of Albany. But Arnold's instinctive tempestuousness prevailed, and the enemy suffered more than 600 casualties, including the deaths of a bevy of British and German officers. Much of the damage was done by a provisional regiment of picked riflemen led by Washington's old Virginia acquaintance Col. Daniel Morgan.

If Morgan were nature, he would have been sleet. He was well over six feet tall and broad of shoulder, with a frontiersman's ruddy face, and in his 49 years he had acquired a reputation as a gambler and tavern brawler of backwoods renown. He had honed his fighting skills breaking trail with his cousin Daniel Boone, and was known to communicate with his troops by turkey gobbles. Two years earlier he and his unit had been surrounded and captured during the disastrous attack on Quebec. True to his obstreperous nature, Morgan refused to present his sword to a British commander and instead handed it to a French-Canadian priest. He spent 14 months in British custody before returning in a prisoner exchange, albeit only after refusing a general's commission to fight for the Crown. Morgan's guerrilla tactics were infamous among the British, who considered his penchant for targeting officers a shocking breach of honor and etiquette. Yet they were effective, as evidenced by the next clash in which he and his riflemen were involved.

In the two weeks since Gen. Arnold's triumph in what was already being called the

Battle of Freeman's Farm, the Continentals and Crown troops had dug in and engaged in daily skirmishes that produced no clear outcome. In a last-ditch effort to fulfill his promise to capture Albany, Burgoyne attempted to outflank Gates's defensive works. His target was the high ground on the Continentals' left wing: a thickly wooded plateau known as Bemis Heights, by this time of the season a portrait of scarlet and gold. Once again Morgan, and later Arnold, stymied his maneuvering — although it is a wonder that Arnold was present at all.

Gates had relieved Arnold of command and replaced him with Morgan after the fight at Freeman's Farm, ostensibly for disobeying orders. In reality the general was wary of Arnold, who made no secret of his continued friendship with Gen. Schuyler, the man whom Gates had replaced. Their relationship further deteriorated when Gates failed to mention Arnold in his official dispatch to Washington detailing the engagement near the farmhouse. Arnold had few equals in seeking public approbation, and he was not a man to brush the many chips off his shoulders. When he found out about the slight he burst into Gates's tent and erupted with a string of profane oaths. Gates yelled back, and Arnold stomped away. Arnold had been in Washington's favor since his daring maneuvers had broken the siege of Fort Schuyler in the Mohawk Valley two months earlier, and now only the interference of several friendly officers restrained him from forsaking the northern campaign and riding off for Pennsylvania to complain directly to the commander in chief.

Like a modern-day Achilles, Arnold was sulking in a corner of Gates's headquarters tent on the afternoon of October 7 when the officers' afternoon mess of charred oxen heart was interrupted by the sound of gunfire some two miles away. Arnold begged Gates, twice, to be allowed to investigate. After his second appeal, Gates granted him leave on one condition — that he not personally participate in the action. When Arnold arrived at the scene on a borrowed Spanish mustang, a British force of some 1,500 troops had already been caught in a murderous cross fire. Earlier that morning during their stealth march to Bemis Heights the Redcoats had stumbled across an abandoned wheat field. Their commanding officer, the Scottish General Simon Fraser, had paused and granted his men permission to forage. As they scythed the wheat stalks they were spotted by an American picket who reported the enemy's presence to Morgan. Morgan immediately led his brigade on a circuitous route through the thick wood that surrounded the wheat field and fell in behind the enemy column on its left flank. The New Hampshire General

Enoch Poor, commanding a mixed regiment of New Hampshiremen and New Yorkers, had bought Morgan time by engaging the British right flank and center.

As Gen. Fraser formed up his soldiers to fend off Poor's ambush, Morgan's cohort burst from the forest and poured rifle fire into the stunned British flank. The Redcoats were falling back in disorder as Arnold galloped onto the battlefield and spotted Gen. Fraser atop his huge Highland gray struggling to develop a second defensive line. An instant later, at Morgan's command, one of his Virginia sharpshooters blew Fraser from his saddle. All was now chaos. Arnold took advantage.

Drawing two brigades about him, he led a charge into the center of the disintegrating British front, splitting the enemy's defenses and opening a wide corridor through which Gen. Poor's troops poured. Next Arnold raced across the length of the enemy's purview to lead an attack on its right flank. "He behaved, as I then thought, more like a madman than a cool and discreet officer," noted a Connecticut trooper who fell in behind him. At this point one of Gates's aides caught up to Arnold with orders that he return to headquarters. He ignored the man and, spotting a unit of Brunswickers defending a hastily constructed redoubt not 500 yards from the Freeman farmstead, swept up Morgan and his riflemen, pointed his sword, and galloped into the teeth of enemy fire. A study in frenzy, he made it as far as the little fort's sally port before his luck ran out. As Morgan and the others were overrunning the fortification, Arnold was being carried off the field with a ball in his right leg. It was the same leg he had broken two years earlier during the luckless attempt to make Canada the fourteenth state. The wound would pain him for the rest of his life.

By nightfall nearly half of Burgoyne's would-be flanking corps were dead, wounded, or missing, including Gen. Fraser. American casualties totaled about 150. Only darkness and fatigue prevented the Continentals from finishing off the expeditionary force, and the Americans managed to seize some 330 tents, eight brass cannons, assorted lesser field pieces, and multiple "kettles boiling with corn." Over the next several days Burgoyne slowly withdrew his starving army north through the rain and cold, their wounded left behind, their dead unburied. Gates's regiments harassed their every step. The constant echo of cannon blasts and flintlock reports through the mountains of upstate New York must have seemed to "Gentleman Johnny" Burgoyne the death rattle of his once grand designs to spread "Devastation, Famine, and every concomitant Horror."

By mid-October what was left of the British army had taken refuge in the hills outside the hamlet of Saratoga. Their safety was but temporary. The British were surrounded as, farther north, a force of New Hampshire militia had blocked the road to Fishkill, Burgoyne's last potential escape route, while a separate regiment of Massachusetts militiamen were raiding Fort Ticonderoga's surrounding outworks. With his force in tatters, Burgoyne's last, best hope was a rescue by Gen. Clinton. To that end he sent a string of messengers south pleading for help. All were captured by the Americans, including one who was caught swallowing a hollow silver ball that contained the written communiqué. It was recovered when a Continental surgeon administered to the man a strong emetic.

When Burgoyne finally learned that Clinton had led his troops back to New York City after capturing the American forts on the Hudson, he realized that his last, best hope for survival had evaporated. On the morning of October 15 he dispatched his adjutant general to Gates's headquarters with the terms of his surrender. Gates's aides and officers were astounded when the American commander, contrary to the usual practice of generals at the head of victorious armies, accepted them without demanding counterterms. Historians have since speculated that Gates, unaware that Gen. Clinton had marched his troops back south, was still leery of his last-minute arrival and wanted Burgoyne's troops disarmed as quickly as possible.

Three days later, 5,000 Crown troops and German mercenaries tromped into a cleared meadow and, unit by unit, laid down their arms. The procession included over 300 officers, seven generals among them. Particularly galling was the company of American fifers leading a loud serenade of "Yankee Doodle." The words to the centuries-old tune had originally been composed by British soldiers to mock the Continental troops as homosexual rubes. But by this point in the war the song had been adopted by the colonists as a paean to their industriousness and grit. Looking on, Daniel Morgan, Enoch Poor, and the others who had been responsible for the British capitulation were merely satisfied at having furthered the cause of the revolution. Benedict Arnold, on the other hand, still simmered. Gates had again failed to mention him in his after-action dispatches. The hard feelings of Saratoga were the roots of his descent into treason.

Following the humiliating surrender ceremony, Gen. Burgoyne was escorted on horseback to the head of Gen. Gates's camp. There he wordlessly presented his sword to the American commander. Whether Burgoyne was aware that his counterpart had never left his barricaded headquarters nor issued a

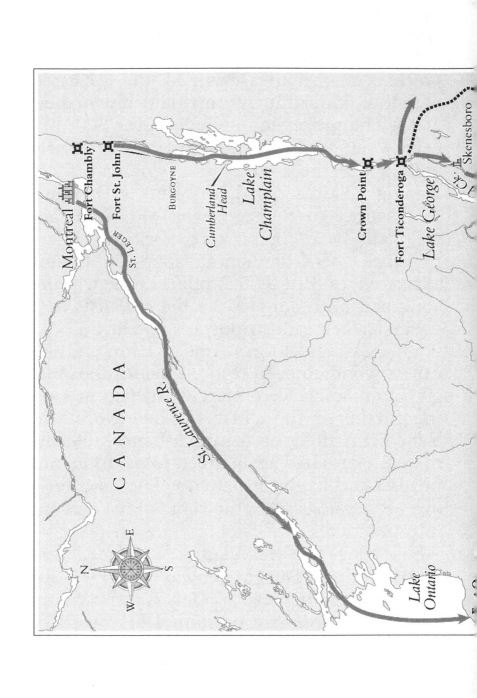

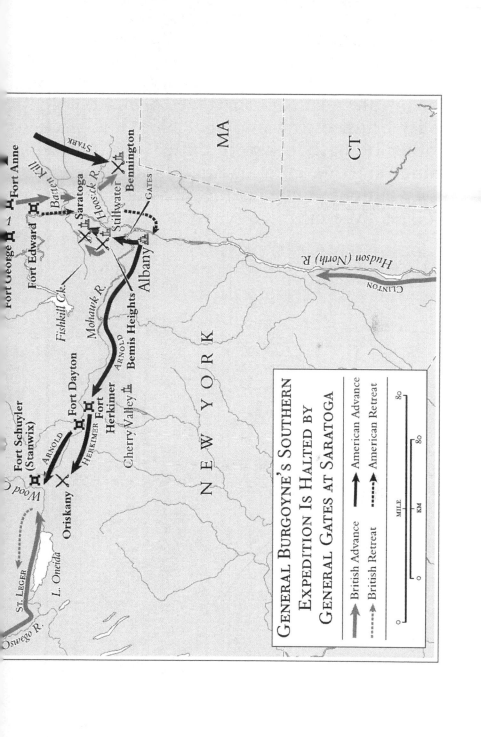

GENERAL BURGOYNE'S SOUTHERN
EXPEDITION IS HALTED BY
GENERAL GATES AT SARATOGA

British Advance ➤ American Advance

British Retreat ➤ American Retreat

MILE

KM

80   80

NEW YORK

MA

CT

Hudson (North) R.

CLINTON

Albany

Bemis Heights

ARNOLD

Mohawk R.

Fort George

Fort Anne

Fort Edward

Fishkill Ck.

Saratoga

Batten Kill

Hoosick R.

STARK

Bennington

GATES

Stillwater

Fort Dayton

Fort Herkimer

HERKIMER

Cherry Valley

Fort Schuyler
(Stanwix)

ARNOLD

Oriskany

ST. LEGER

L. Oneida

Wood Cr.

Oswego R.

combat command during the fortnight of fighting remains unrecorded. Burgoyne was, as usual, impeccable in uniform, his service coat dyed a rich royal scarlet with expensive cochineal and the lush velvet of his falling collar brushed to a midnight blue. His black leather riding boots were buffed to a mirror shine, and his gold epaulets and polished silver buttons glinted in the mid-autumn sun.

Gates wore his plain blue frock.

EIGHT:
THE IDEALIST

As Washington certainly recognized, the astounding news from the north constituted a doubled-edged sword. General Burgoyne's surrender, combined with the fall of the American forts on the Hudson Highlands, only increased the pressure on the commander in chief to force another assault on Philadelphia. For Washington's congressional critics, Gen. Gates's triumph was precisely the measuring stick to hold up against the defeats at Brandywine, at Paoli, and at Germantown — no matter how orderly and professional the retreats. Nor was it lost on the delegates that the enemy's capture of the two Highland forts was the likely result of Washington's thinning of Israel Putnam's ranks. If the commander in chief had to detach men from Putnam's command, why was he not using them against Howe? From as far away as Saint Croix, Hamilton's old mentor Hugh Knox wrote to his former charge of the "Immortal Gates; another bright Star in the Constellation of American Heroes." Knox added that he and his fellow republicans "tremble in Suspence . . . Expecting to hear that Gen. Washington has done Something like the same by Gen. Howe!" Even a faction of Washington's own officer corps agitated for an attack.

The brigadier general Jedediah Huntington, for instance, was a renowned tactician who had led one of Putnam's detached Connecticut brigades south from Peekskill. Once integrated into Washington's main force he adjudged only two options appropriate in the wake of Saratoga — a forceful winter siege of Philadelphia, the British-held capital city, or an immediate assault on it "to fight them in their stronghold." Huntington and others made clear that they preferred the latter. Less than a month after the defeat at Germantown, Gen. Greene, who was strongly loyal to Washington, eagerly wished "to get to fisticuffing of it with Mr. Howe" as soon as possible. For his part, Washington nourished no such delusions.

Despite publicly urging his own soldiers to match the feats of the heroes of Saratoga — "What shame then and dishonour will attend us, if we suffer ourselves in every instance to be outdone?" he asked in one General Order — Washington knew that springing another surprise on the now vigilant Howe was impossible. Moreover, his campaigns in the

Ohio wilderness a decade earlier had left him with a better understanding than most of how long it took an army to retrench and refit after an engagement such as at Germantown. It was sage leadership to grant his foot soldiers time to recover both their strength and their morale. He and his strategists also had to prepare for the possibility, however slim, that the British might follow up with a counterassault of their own. As it happened, Washington could not know that Gen. Howe, having withdrawn his troops into Philadelphia proper after the Germantown fight, wanted to avoid another large engagement.

Unlike George III and his combative advisers, Gen. Howe was a sphinx without a riddle, more interested in suppressing the rebellion by driving the Americans into submission rather than despair. Howe's older brother Richard was even more conscientious, the admiral having before the war exhibited decidedly pro-American leanings, particularly in his view that the colonists were being unfairly taxed by Parliament. Their eldest brother, George Howe, had died fighting alongside Americans in the French and Indian War, and they admired the grit of the Americans. Both brothers also feared that an utter military victory, while feasible, would in the long run continue to bleed England by necessitating a semipermanent occupation force in North America. They had reluctantly answered the call to lead British forces against the rebels on the condition that they also be authorized to negotiate a peace settlement — with the terms, naturally, dictated by Whitehall.

But Gen. Howe also understood that Britain could not benefit from the profitable trade with its vast web of colonies without asserting martial authority over them. If in his personal philosophy he preferred maneuver to battle — not only to conserve Britain's manpower, but to demonstrate its army's military superiority — that was not an option either the king or his prime minister Lord North condoned. Howe was not a soldier to buck orders. Now, however, he had been stung twice. The first blow was the Crown's refusal to provide him with the manpower he felt he needed to tamp down the rebellion. The second was the growing public criticism in and outside of Whitehall that his failure to send Gen. Clinton to Burgoyne's rescue had precipitated the British defeat at Saratoga. In the face of this dual burden, he wrote to George Germain requesting "his Majesty's permission to resign the command [and] to be relieved from this very painful service."

Several of Gen. Howe's officers gingerly proposed abandoning Pennsylvania and consolidating forces with Clinton in New York. At this Howe dug in his heels and condoned a petulant frenzy of citywide burnings and lootings "so brutal and cruel" that the revolutionary diarist Christopher Marshall found it "tiresome tracing them with a pen." Marshall, a former Philadelphia chemist and pharmacist now enlisted in the Continental Army, received regular, smuggled letters from his son chronicling the "many instances of wanton cruelty in his neighborhood, among which is the burning of the house where Col. Reed did live, the house where Thompson kept tavern, with everything in it, [and] all the hay at Col. Bull's [including] fifteen hundred bushels of wheat with other grain [and] his powder mill and iron works." It is safe to say that it was not a happy time to be a revolutionary in Philadelphia.

General Howe, meanwhile, had finally absorbed Washington's propensity for sudden, unforeseen strikes. As a result he positioned his army behind a line of trenches and redoubts his engineers constructed north of the city. The defensive front stretched for two and a half miles from the Schuylkill to the Delaware and was pocked with 12-pound artillery pieces strategically placed among howitzers and lighter cannons. Within days it would be further bolstered by the arrival of reinforcements Howe had requested from Gen. Clinton in New York. To the Continentals it might as well have been the walls of Asgard. Washington's chief artillery officer Gen. Henry Knox noted "the improbability

& impracticability of surprising 10,000 veteran troops in a well fortified city." Washington valued not only Knox's guns, but his opinion. When Gen. Knox cast doubt on the success of a potential operation, the commander in chief took notice.

Henry Knox weighed in at north of 300 pounds; the only thing missing from his ample paunch was barrel staves. Yet his Father Christmas–like countenance belied one of the most ingenious military minds of the revolution. The Boston-born Knox was the grandson of Northern Irish immigrants whose father had deserted the family when young Henry was 12. Forced to drop out of the Boston Latin school and seek employment to help support his mother and three younger siblings, he was hired by a local bookseller who, taken with the boy's warm and gregarious personality, assumed the role of surrogate father. Knox was allowed free rein among the shelves before and after store hours, which he used to immerse himself in volumes of military history, engineering, and advanced mathematics. He also mixed easily with the British soldiers who frequented the shop. When not picking their brains about strategy and tactics, he found the time to teach himself French. By his mid-teens Knox had acquired an extraordinary reputation in his neighborhood near Boston Harbor as a self-educated polymath as well as a fearsome street fighter.

Knox opened his own bookstore in Boston at the age of 21 just as his republican inclinations were hardening into deed. A year earlier he had been a witness to the quelled riots that became known as the Boston Massacre, and stepped forward to testify in court against several British soldiers who had fired indiscriminately into the crowd. His breaking point arrived in 1774 with Parliament's passage of the Coercive Acts, the punitive retributions for the Boston Tea Party known in the colonies as the Intolerable Acts. These called in part for the closing of Boston Harbor to international trade. As Knox's livelihood depended upon book shipments from London, the laws effectively put him out of business. The loss to literate Bostonians, however, was a boon to the American cause. With time on his hands, Knox devoted himself to drilling with a local patriot militia called the Boston Grenadiers. More important, he put his idle hours to use broadening his self-education into the mechanics and maintenance of heavy ordnance.

Knox and his Boston Grenadiers had fought well at Breed's Hill — known to posterity as the Battle of Bunker Hill — and by the time Washington arrived in Boston to take command of the new Continental Army the opposing forces had more or less settled into a stalemate. The British occupied Boston proper, including its harbor, which allowed their troops and Loyalists to survive on provisions shipped from Canada. The Continentals controlled the higher ground surrounding the city but lacked the firepower to implement a proper siege. One day as Washington was inspecting the breastworks Knox had helped to engineer on the heights of Charlestown, the former bookseller introduced himself to his new commander. He then volunteered to journey the over 200 miles to Fort Ticonderoga and return with the cache of artillery recently captured by Ethan Allen and Benedict Arnold. The harsh New England winter notwithstanding, a skeptical Washington signed off on the harebrained scheme.

That November, Knox and his brother set off for Lake Champlain. Two months later they reappeared with 43 cannons, 14 mortars, and a brace of howitzers they had hauled up and over the snowy Berkshires on sleds pulled by oxen. Washington was astounded. So were the British who, staring up at the guns, abandoned the city on Saint Patrick's Day 1776. Washington had retained a soft spot for the portly cannoneer ever since. He also had to take seriously Knox's doubts about dealing the British in Philadelphia a decisive blow before the snows set in. As it happened, the commander in chief had a more immediate foe to confront.

In a stinging coda to the setback at German-town, Washington's antagonists both in and outside the military had begun to exhume old whispers about what they viewed as his central deficiency: an inability to make and enforce command decisions on the battlefield. Benjamin Rush, a Philadelphia physician and influential former congressman who had volunteered as a surgeon during the Pennsylvania campaign, was perhaps the most public voice attributing the defeats at Brandywine and Germantown to this shortcoming. Rush, a signer of the Declaration of Independence who once counted Washington as an ally, was a zealous republican reformer who now blamed the commander in chief — wrongly, as it was — for the scrofulous state of the Continental military hospitals and medical stations. In a bitter letter to John Adams at the Continental Congress in York, Rush charged that Washington had been "out-generald and twice beaten" by Howe, and went on to suggest a solution. "I have heard several officers who have served under General Gates compare his army to a well-regulated family," Rush told Adams. "The same gentlemen have compared Gen'l Washington's imitation of an army to an unformed mob."

That Rush had written specifically to Adams, or that Adams had appeared to welcome and agree with the doctor, was no surprise. Adams had long viewed Washington's growing popularity with both the American citizenry and the military's rank and file as posing a threat to the young republic. Upon receiving news of Burgoyne's surrender, Adams had written to his wife, Abigail, of his satisfaction that it was Gen. Gates who had earned the victory and not a certain general too close to being considered "a deity or savior." Further, with the impending retirement of John Hancock due to ill health, Adams had become the center of a new generation of delegates whose loyalty to the commander in chief was more abstract than personal. Rush and Adams were in fact in the middle of the stirrings to replace Washington with either Gen. Gates or Gen. Charles Lee, the two British-born generals fighting for the Continentals — notwithstanding the fact that Lee was currently a British prisoner of war.

To no one's surprise, the imperious Lee had also weighed in with his own scalding contempt for Washington's performance at Germantown. When informed of the British victory, he told his jailers that his putative commander in chief "was not fit to command a sergeant's guard." Lee was a blister of a man unencumbered by charisma who preferred the company of his hunting hounds to human beings. Human beings who came into contact with him felt similarly. Yet he was also a decorated veteran of the Seven Years' War and considered one of the Continental Army's soundest military strategists. Lee's bloated ego notwithstanding, his critique was shared by more than a few delegates. Adams's fellow Massachusetts congressman James Lovell predicted that Washington would lose more men "marching and countermarching over hills and thro rivers than in *battles*." And even Lafayette, though he would never entertain the thought of replacing Washington, could not help extolling Gates's "glorious" virtues. "I find myself very happy to have had the pleasure of your acquaintance before your going to take command of the northern army," he wrote to the general from his convalescent's bed in Bethlehem.

By mid-October Henry Laurens was alarmed enough at the anti-Washington sentiments in York to confide to his son John, "The general opinion is that the difficulty arises from the want of discipline in the American army." John Laurens of course passed this on to his commander in chief. Though Washington seemed to take the criticism with equanimity in the presence of his aides, he complained to an old friend from the Virginia House of Burgesses about "the jealousy which Congress unhappily entertain." More overtly — and quite out of character — in one of his last letters to the outgoing president of the Continental Congress, John Hancock, Washington expressed his "most anxious impatience" over the fact that he had yet to receive an official report from Gen. Gates regarding Gen. Burgoyne's surrender. That the ambitious Gates had ignored the chain of command and reported the details of his victory directly to Congress was another cutting display too obvious to overlook. Washington had publicly congratulated Gates on his "signal success," calling his mastery of Burgoyne "an event that does the highest honor to the American Arms." In private, however, he bristled over his subordinate's impertinence. In a letter to his friend Richard Henry Lee, a delegate from Virginia, he admitted feeling "most bitterly of Genl Gates' neglect in not giving me the earliest authentic advice of it." And in his one public hint of churlishness over Gates's severance of military protocol, he sarcastically inquired of Hancock, "If Congress have had authentic advices about [Burgoyne's surrender], I wish to be favor'd with them."

In hindsight, there were many reasons put forward for the failure at Germantown — the risk that Washington's baroque battle plan would not cohere; the confusing fog and smoke; the friendly fire that panicked Wayne's advancing troops; the auspicious arrival of

Cornwallis's reinforcements. In his invaluable wartime diary, the Connecticut private Joseph Plumb Martin even postulated that the retreating British were emboldened to turn, stand, and ultimately counterattack when the fog carried the voices of the most forward Continentals desperately crying for more ammunition. Washington's political enemies, however, focused on one incident that reflected a particularly unfavorable light on him.

About midway through the fight, the gathering American thrust was stopped short when one of the forward columns under the command of Gen. Sullivan was enfolded in a hail of musket fire emanating from a three-story stone residence on its flank. The estate — belonging to Pennsylvania's Chief Justice Benjamin Chew, currently under house arrest in New Jersey on suspicion of being a Crown sympathizer — had been commandeered by over 100 British foot soldiers who had barricaded themselves inside. Washington had convened an impromptu horseback conference with several of his officers and aides to decide whether to lay immediate siege to the Chew House or keep moving forward and take the hornet's nest later. All but one favored leaving the house surrounded by a company of soldiers and pushing on. The lone dissenter was Henry Knox, whose cannons were already trained on it. Washington sided with Gen. Knox. The artilleryman's judgment and expertise had, after all, served him well on the Charlestown heights overlooking Boston. This time Knox was wrong.

For over an hour Knox's three- and six-pounders failed to make a dent in the structure's sturdy schist facade. British marksmen stationed at the upper windows also repelled three separate assaults by American regiments, leaving nearly 80 dead Continentals lying splayed across the handsomely manicured lawn. A few charging soldiers managed to reach the blasted-out ground-floor windows only to be dispatched by British bayonets. Finally, too late, Washington ordered the stronghold cordoned off and his troops moved forward. The decision to delay the American push, Washington's detractors charged, had turned the momentum of the battle by giving Howe the time he needed to re-form his lines. In the end, however, Thomas Paine, riding with Gen. Greene as an observer, probably said it best: "I can never . . . and I believe no man can inform truly, the cause of that day's miscarriage."

Paine's notion has the whiff of the true nature of the confused fight, though this did not stop the campaign of innuendo against the commander in chief. First his strategy at Brandywine had been questioned. Now his tactics at Germantown were under scrutiny. Washington was by nature reserved and aloof, and he had cultivated a knack for distancing himself from others that well served his leadership. That said, he was also hypersensitive to criticism, and only a general of steely self-possession and fortitude could have bucked such a tide of insinuation without countering with an assault on Philadelphia to relieve the political pressure. Yet buck it he did. Moreover, if there was a silver lining to the unfortunate events surrounding the fight at the Chew House, it came in the form of the valor displayed by John Laurens during the failed siege.

Laurens had been riding with Gen. Sullivan when in the opening moments of battle a British ball tore through the fleshy part of his right shoulder. Ignoring the wound, he pressed on through the fog until Sullivan halted his troops outside the Chew House. One of Sullivan's French aides, watching Knox's cannonballs bounce off the estate's thick walls, hatched a plan to burn the British out and tabbed Laurens as his second. The two streaked across the killing field to gather straw from a nearby stable. Their arms filled with the combustible hay, they crept beneath one of the house's ground-floor windows. When the Frenchman ripped open what was left of the shutters, a Redcoat fired. He missed, but Laurens drew his sword and made for the window. He had nearly reached it when he was spun to the ground by another ball, this one lodging in his side. The two escaped without further injury — unless one counts the anxiety that overcame Laurens's father. When Henry Laurens learned of his son's wounds, he dashed off a letter pleading with John to appreciate the difference between genuine courage and reckless temerity.

Washington had quite the opposite reaction. Two days after the battle he summoned John Laurens to his headquarters and, acceding to the young man's long-standing request, appointed him an official member of his staff. Though Laurens had served as a voluntary aide-de-camp to the commander in chief since August, he was now formally inducted into the small, elite circle of admirers granted access to the innermost thoughts of the patriarch of the American Revolution. Aside from Hamilton, at the time these included the 31-year-old Virginian Richard Kidder Meade, a superb horseman who, like Hamilton, was often charged with secret military and diplomatic missions; Tench Tilghman, a 33-year-old Philadelphian whose primary responsibility was handling the voluminous correspondence that passed into and out of the commander in chief's headquarters; and the "Old Secretary" Robert Hanson Harrison, a Maryland lawyer who, though only 32, had served as Washington's attorney since before the war.

It was electrifying company, and John Laurens, as devoted to the commander in chief as his new associates were, felt as if he had been born for the position.

In his voluminous letters, John Laurens's free-flowing prose attempted to affect a worldview of Machiavellian clarity. In truth, his romantic vision of combat and the thirst for honor and glory presaged the Byronic action-hero's appearance on the world stage by half a century. The plumage of young Laurens's detailed and entertaining accounts of battles waged, conspiracies uncovered, and strategies concocted constitute one long ode to the American Revolution. Though his recollections are little known to the general public today, historians are grateful to have them.

Ten months earlier, in January 1777, Laurens was newly married and pursuing his legal education at London's Middle Temple when he abruptly informed his pregnant wife that he was quitting law school and returning to America to fight for the revolution. Naturally, his decision to "to offer his services to his Country" did not sit well with his in-laws, members of the English gentry. More surprising was the reaction of his father, Henry, the South Carolina delegate who would succeed John Hancock as president of the Continental Congress. Henry Laurens had accumulated enough of a fortune to send his three sons, of whom John was the eldest, to study in Europe. Although Henry was a successful merchant and rice planter, much of his wealth was derived from his half ownership in the largest slave-trading house in North America. Henry made it clear that he preferred John to establish a law practice and perhaps follow him into politics rather than risk the great social leveler of the battlefield, "whose bullets and cannonballs proved indiscriminating, felling gentleman officers and common soldiers alike." But the father knew better than to try too hard to dissuade his headstrong son.

Henry Laurens had already won the career battle with John by steering him away from his early interests in science and medicine and convincing him to take up law. His influence, however, had proved temporary, and John had conspicuously failed to seek his father's blessing when he married Martha Manning, who would give birth to their daughter while John was voyaging to America. Moreover, John's ambivalence toward the institution of slavery was not merely a philosophical tenet he had picked up while studying in Europe. It was his opinion that Americans could not fight for their own freedom while owning slaves, and as a practical matter he would act on his beliefs two years later by petitioning the Continental Congress to authorize his recruitment of a brigade of

3,000 slaves who in exchange for fighting for the United States would be freed after the Continentals' victory.*

As it was, by the time John Laurens strode into Washington's Philadelphia headquarters in July 1777, he and his father had crafted a tentative peace. His circuitous return to America had taken him from London to Paris, where he met three times with Benjamin Franklin to offer his services. From Paris he journeyed to Charleston, South Carolina, by way of Bordeaux and the French West Indies. In an accident of history, Laurens presented himself to Washington in the same week that an even younger adventurer, the Marquis de Lafayette, had arrived in America's capital city. As with the voluble Frenchman, Washington immediately took to the budding lawyer with the rings of sleeplessness around his low-lidded eyes. Apart from the obvious political advantage of mentoring the son of one of the most powerful members of Congress, the commander in chief was particularly impressed with Laurens's proficiency in French, Latin, and Greek, as well as his familiarity with classical literature, mechanics, and — a field close to Washington's heart — surveying.

* Congress acceded to the request, but in the end the South Carolina Provincial Congress rejected the proposal before John Laurens could effect it.

Yet what stirred Washington most about John Laurens was his intense devotion to the ideal of the United States — his *amor patria,* as the commander in chief would describe it in a letter to the historian Rev. William Gordon. Unlike Lafayette's, however, Laurens's application for official duty on Washington's personal staff was initially rejected. Washington preferred that he serve as a volunteer aide, albeit one, he promised, eventually destined to "become a Member of my Family." Now, several months later, as Henry Laurens fretted over his son's safety, John had proved himself a fearless fighter, first at Brandywine — where Lafayette himself made note of his grace under fire — and later at Germantown, most notably with his actions at the Chew House. To some who witnessed Laurens's perhaps foolhardy valor that October morning it appeared as if he had crossed the line between the coddled son of a gentrified planter and a hard-shelled warfighter. As his biographer Gregory D. Massey observes, "In constructing his new identity as a gentleman officer, John threw himself wholeheartedly into the struggle for liberty. So long as the British army remained a threat to America, he would remain an officer, renouncing his family in order to fulfill what he conceived to be his public duty."

Laurens and Alexander Hamilton rapidly became best friends despite their disparate backgrounds and, perhaps more pertinent, despite the latter's natural veneer of reserve. Their shared antipathy toward slavery proved a building block. Hamilton never forgot the slave auction houses of his youth on Saint Croix, an island whose population was 90 percent of African descent. That this was but a way station for the human chattel en route to withering labor in the cane fields and sugar mills sparked in Hamilton an intense desire to get away. "I would willingly risk my life, tho' not my character, to exalt my station," he wrote to a friend at the age of 12. He foresaw only one route: "I wish there was a war."

Moreover, as Hamilton helped nurse Laurens back to health the two discovered their mutual admiration for the stern code of honor observed by the heroes of ancient Greece and Rome. Idealists in thought, word, and deed, they shared a vision of the future United States as modeled on archaic Greece's Amphictionic League, and at one point Hamilton copied and presented to Laurens a passage from Plutarch's *Lives* regarding the bonds formed by Spartan soldiers. "Every lad had a lover or friend who took care of his education," Plutarch quotes the Spartan military reformer Lycurgus as explaining, "and shared in the praise or blame of his virtues and vices." To modern ears the overtones of homoeroticism are inescapable, and though some historians have claimed with tenuous evidence that Laurens was a closeted homosexual whose marriage and child were a necessary cloak, an alternative interpretation through the lens of the era is more probable. Although alien to today's military culture, for officers like Laurens and Hamilton the notion of applying the romantic imagery of the classical age to their unique status, separate as it was from both civilians and the rank and file, was quite flattering. For such peers in Washington's army, thirsting for fame and glory while fighting for a cause larger than any individual, the battlefield bonds of friendship did indeed encompass a sense of *love*.

However it stood, not long after the Battle of Germantown, Laurens was again preparing to share with Hamilton in either the praise or the blame for the Continental Army's victories or defeats. As he saw it, with Washington's troops recovering their spirit and Fort Mifflin and Fort Mercer constituting a virtual Scylla and Charybdis on the banks of the Delaware, he was certain the British would soon be feeling the pressure from an American grip. As he wrote to his father, "If . . . we do our duty, Genl Howe will find himself in a situation which will require the utmost exertions of military talents to bring him off with honor." In a postscript he added another provision to Howe's downfall: "If our forts hold out."

Nine:
An Eerie Foreboding

As autumn progressed, Washington, beset by military and political travails, was also facing an existential threat to his army as acute as any British cannon or congressional critic. From his new command center in Whitemarsh, Pennsylvania, a limestone-laden tract 13 miles northwest of Philadelphia first purchased by William Penn nearly 100 years earlier, he took stock. The day after the retreat from Germantown, his Commissary Department reported that three days' worth of provisions had been lost during the confused fallback. This was only the beginning of the Continental Army's supply woes. On paper, the rations promised to an enlisted man appeared hearty enough. Every recruit was theoretically entitled to a daily pound of bread, three pints of dried vegetables, a pint of milk, a quart of spruce beer or cider, and a pound of either beef, pork, or salted fish, with one soldier observing that salt was "as valuable as gold." The reality of the situation was something else. Men could not eat theories.

The rapid depletion of the congressional treasury had combined with inept management of the army's supply chain to make shipments of food, clothing, blankets, and ammunition sputtering at best. Salted meat and beef on the hoof were nearly nonexistent in camp, flour was in short supply, and the all-important stores of liquor were also diminishing. By this point in the war the typical Continental soldier considered beer as much of a necessity as bread, and Washington himself had long been a healthy consumer of English porter.* When informed that his soldiers were selling their clothing in order to purchase beer and whiskey from local brewers and distillers, he issued a General Order forbidding the sale of liquor by private vendors in and around the encampment. Should these "tippling house" purveyors persist, he warned that their alcohol would be seized and they would be lashed. But no executive decree could magically fill the

* Following the signing of the Declaration of Independence he had forsworn British comestibles in favor of home-brewed — "I use no porter or cheese in my family, but such as is made in America," he wrote to Lafayette — but now even those staples were scarcely arriving. (Hucklebridge, *The United States of Beer,* p. 108.)

army's larders. Soon the officers in charge of the commissaries were hard pressed to provide victuals on a day-to-day basis, much less enough to sustain an all-out engagement against a dug-in enemy. If an army marches on its stomach, Washington's troops were nearer to crawling, and the commander in chief was reduced to pleading with his quartermaster general, Thomas Mifflin, to rectify the situation as quickly as possible.

Mifflin was an odd case. The son of a prominent Philadelphia merchant of the Quaker faith, he was a spirited orator and had once been described by John Adams as "the heart and soul of the rebellion." Mifflin had graduated from the city's eponymous college, now the University of Pennsylvania, and been elected to the First Continental Congress alongside Benjamin Franklin before resigning and — breaking with his family's religious antiwar dictates — enlisting in the Continental Army.

With his deep, wide-set eyes, sculptured cheekbones, and classic Roman nose, Mifflin cut a striking figure in his hand-tailored uniform. Washington had met him two years earlier while traveling to Boston to assume command of the army, and he was impressed enough to select the then 31-year-old as an aide-de-camp to complement Joseph Reed. He also promoted Mifflin to the rank of brigadier general. But Washington never lost his Virginia planter's instincts, and was always more interested in the stalk lurking beneath the showiest bract. The vain, urbane Mifflin may have looked as if he'd been robed in a vestry, but Washington was more intrigued by the young radical's ardor for the revolution. Yet, again, he had acted in error. For all his lofty ideals, Mifflin proved an inadequate soldier.

Their relationship had begun to fray the previous summer during the catastrophic Battle of Long Island. By relieving Washington's rear guard too soon, Mifflin had nearly botched the Continental Army's predawn evacuation from Brooklyn to Manhattan across the East River. In a rare instance of public censure, Washington exploded at Mifflin, "Good God! I am afraid you have ruined us." Though the escape was eventually effected, Mifflin's skin was as thin as his commander's, and he never forgot nor forgave the shaming. Even after Mifflin's actions at Trenton and Princeton had earned him a promotion to the quartermaster general's post, he carried a grudge against the man who had recommended him for the position. The final straw for Mifflin was Washington's failure to prevent his hometown, Philadelphia, from falling into British hands. For Washington's part, sketchy rumors had begun to reach him that Mifflin was enriching himself and the civilian cronies he had hired to staff the Quartermaster Department's supply depots. The two now circled each other warily.

Whatever the commander in chief's differences with Mifflin, more important was the near collapse of the Continental Army's already tenuous supply chain. On October 14, after surveying the clothing needs of his troops, Washington penned a beseeching letter to John Hancock. "It gives me pain to repeat so often the wants of the Army," he began, "and nothing would induce me to it, but the most urgent necessity. Every mode hitherto adopted for supplying them has proved inadequate, notwithstanding my best endeavours to make the most of the means, which have been in my power. The inclosed return will shew how great our deficiency in the most essential Articles."

The return Washington "inclosed" reported a shortage of 3,084 coats; 4,051 waistcoats; 6,148 breeches; 8,033 stockings; 3,236 pairs of shoes; 6,330 shirts; 137 hunting shirts; 4,552 blankets; 2,399 hats; 356 overalls; and 1,140 knapsacks. More distressingly, these figures did not include shortfalls from nine regiments whose commanders had yet to report in. Washington neglected to mention to Hancock that he and his aides had been sharing their meals on one tin plate for weeks.

Toward the end of his supplication he added a coda that, in hindsight, reads like a rough draft of the more alarming communiqués he would soon be issuing from Valley Forge. "It is impossible that any Army so unprovided can long subsist," he wrote, "or act with that vigor, which is requisite to ensure success." In a dark harbinger of the events that would later alienate much of southeastern Pennsylvania's civilian populace, he then commanded his foraging parties to seize arms, clothing, blankets, and food from any homesteads whose owners had either abetted Crown forces or refused to swear allegiance to the new republic. And in a move that surely dismayed his hungry troops, he ordered the dismantling of all gristmills at local farms lest they provide succor to the British.

Yet even as the weather turned there remained in Congress a rather large bloc of delegates who audibly questioned why a commander in chief as allegedly brilliant as Washington lost so many battles. It was this faction that continued to urge Washington to make a final attempt to drive the enemy from Philadelphia. From a strategic point of view, however, Washington now had more pressing concerns. For after British engineers completed their great defensive barrier across the north end of the city, Gen. Howe again turned his gaze south toward the American forts blockading the Delaware River.

■ ■ ■ ■

Contrary to both the popular contemporary and the historical conception, the vast majority of the British occupiers of Philadelphia that autumn were not in fact whiling away their days frequenting taverns and bawdy houses nor attending dances and theater productions by night. Crown officers, dwelling comfortably in private homes, did take advantage of the few delights the city offered. Yet the majority of Howe's army — now swollen to nearly 15,000 with the reinforcements from New York — as well as the 2,000 or so women and children camp followers were for the most part stacked like tinned fish in hastily constructed barracks, warehouses, and the outposted wooden guard huts along the Schuylkill River defenses. The British brain trust understood that with the Delaware blocked and daily American patrols prowling the outskirts of town to confiscate provisions from local farmers heading into the city, the troops would be near to starving by midwinter. Prices of staples such as clothing, salt, and candle wax had already soared, and, as at the Continental camp at Whitemarsh, some foodstuffs such as beef had disappeared altogether. Firewood was so scarce that several of the town's wooden structures had already been earmarked for demolition to provide heat when the cold set in. Howe was desperate to open the river to his brother's supply ships, and the first Continental outpost to feel the British probe was Fort Mercer.

Fort Mercer had been laid out and constructed on the high ground of Red Bank, New Jersey, by the Polish engineer Tadeusz Kosciuszko, and was defended by 600 men and 14 artillery pieces. Across the river, just below the point where the Schuylkill poured into the Delaware, rose Fort Mifflin — a stone-and-wood fortification originally built by the British atop a marshy hump of cripple meadow known locally as Mud Island. Fort Mifflin was garrisoned by 200 regulars operating 10 cannons. Together, the two forts were capable of directing a nearly impenetrable wall of artillery fire at any ship that dared sail beneath their parapets. Yet either fort was useless without the other, as enemy vessels could merely skirt the opposite shoreline. Howe's first target was the stronger of the two.

A few weeks earlier the British had attempted to bomb the Americans out of Fort Mercer with a desultory land-based artillery barrage that came to nothing. This time Gen. Howe took a different tack. Under cover of darkness on the night of October 21 he ordered a unit of over 2,000 Hessians under the command of Colonel Carl von Donop ferried across the Delaware to Camden, New Jersey. Von Donop's orders were to march south to Red Bank and attack Fort Mercer from the rear. Prior to this assault, six British men-of-war from Adm. Howe's fleet would sail upriver and soften the fort's defenders with a cannonade. Von Donop's troops had been thrashed by the Continentals at Trenton, and he was eager to avenge what he considered a humiliation. As he vowed to his men, "Either the fort shall be called Fort Donop, or I shall have fallen."

At dawn the next day von Donop divided his regiments into two columns while the British warships lobbed shells into Fort Mercer. At a signal, the cannon fire ceased and the Hessian colonel ordered his Jägers forward. Von Donop personally led the southern spur of his force, which was encompassed in a murderous hail of musket and cannon fire before it even reached the fort's nine-foot parapets. His northern prong fared little better. Though some men did manage to scale the ramparts of an abandoned section of the redoubt, once over the walls they were met by an abatis — a tangled mass of felled trees whose interlaced branches had been sharpened into deadly spears facing outward. As the Hessians clawed through this barricade they became easy targets for American marksmen firing down from the main wall of the fortification. Soon enough they joined von

Donop's wing in retreat. The colonel himself was wounded in the thigh during the assault and temporarily abandoned on the battlefield. Within two days he had bled out and died in the shadow of the fort he had vowed to rename after himself.

The following morning a squadron of British ships returned to bombard Fort Mifflin. They were immediately swarmed by the swifter and more maneuverable American gunboats. Two of the enemy vessels — the ship of the line HMS *Augusta* with 64 cannons and the 18-gun sloop HMS *Merlin* — ran aground on shoals while attempting to thread the naval attacks and the embedded *chevaux-de-frise*. British sailors burned the listing *Merlin* to prevent it from falling into American hands. The *Augusta*'s crew ultimately managed to extract their ship from the shallows, but not before Continental artillery had raked it from stem to stern with ball and grape. The *Augusta* sailed back downriver aflame, and exploded the next day.

When news of the successful defense reached Washington's headquarters in a cramped farmhouse at Whitemarsh, he and his staff were ecstatic. American spies in Philadelphia reported that the Hessians had lost nearly 350 men killed, including von Donop, with another 20 either captured or missing. The American casualties totaled 14 dead and 27 wounded. Washington immediately detached a brigade of regulars as a further bulwark against future pressure on both forts and dispatched a smaller force to cut off the wagon trains that the British had begun running by night between the fleet and Philadelphia. Finally, in a move designed to choke off any relief for what remained of the beleaguered Hessians still retreating through New Jersey, he petitioned the state's governor, William Livingston, to have his militia lay ambushes for Redcoats marching to their rescue. He also ordered his light cavalry south to harass the enemy lines surrounding the city. The horsemen often galloped to within two miles of the city center, inflicting severe if scattered damage on enemy pickets. They even managed to capture a number of British soldiers from scavenging parties sent forth to plunder food in the countryside.

These latter successes proved ephemeral, however, as they burdened the Continental commissaries with even more mouths to feed until the prisoners could be transferred to a holding camp in Morristown, New Jersey. One perhaps unintended consequence of these small units' operations was that they actually alleviated some of the pressure on the kitchens at Whitemarsh by allowing the participating troops to effectively provision themselves in the field on an ad hoc basis. And when the British foraging parties became larger and better armed, so too did the

American guerrilla units lying in wait for them along the roads and trails of Chester County.

On October 30, still simmering over having received no official word from Gen. Gates about his reported triumph at Saratoga, Washington dispatched Alexander Hamilton to upstate New York with instructions to collect two of Gates's three brigades to further shore up the Delaware River forts. The communiqué from the commander in chief that Hamilton carried began with another perfunctory congratulatory note on Gates's success at Saratoga. Then Washington slipped in the blade. "At the same time," he wrote, "I cannot but regret, that a matter of such magnitude and so interesting to our General Operations, should have reached me by [secondhand] report only." Had Gates's triumph so gone to his head, he wondered, that the general had neglected to send "a line under your signature, stating the simple fact"?

Riding hard, Hamilton covered the 300 miles to Albany in five days. Gates, irritated by the tone of Washington's letter, also took umbrage at having to deal on an equal footing with a representative he considered no more than a callow youth — an irritation that Washington may very well have intended. Gates initially attempted to stonewall Hamilton, insisting that he could spare not a man.

He was, he said, still wary of Gen. Clinton's attempting another foray north from New York City. At this, Hamilton slyly wrote to Washington, he "was sorry to find [Gates's] feelings did not correspond with yours for drawing off the number of troops you directed." After several cantankerous meetings during which an obviously frustrated Hamilton took pains to at least fake the proper deference, he finally inquired if it was Gates's position that he should return to Pennsylvania and report to the commander in chief that the general refused to obey his orders. At this Gates reluctantly agreed to part with one brigade. It included Gen. Poor's New Hampshire regiment and Dan Morgan's Virginia sharpshooters.

By early November it had become increasingly evident to both sides that the Pennsylvania campaign had devolved into a battle of nerve and attrition. The stalemate was exacerbated by the unusually heavy rains that flooded the roads that fall. The few Continental supply trains that could be mustered were unable to pass over the washed-out arteries, and Washington's commissary officers were driven to further despair. Concurrently, some 20 miles to the southeast, Gen. Howe's despondence over von Donop's miserable performance at the Battle of Red Bank was palpable. Entrenched in his command center in the elegant Masters-Penn House, the Brit-

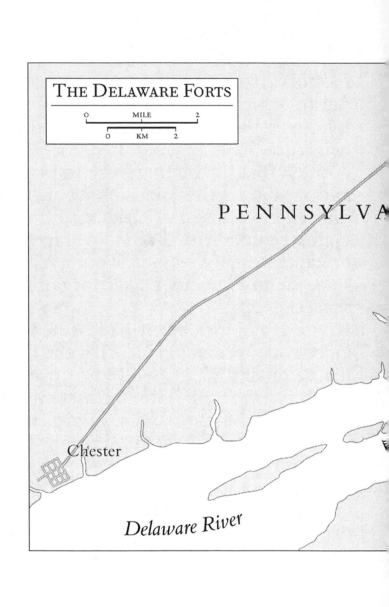

THE DELAWARE FORTS

O   MILE   2

O   KM   2

PENNSYLVA

Chester

Delaware River

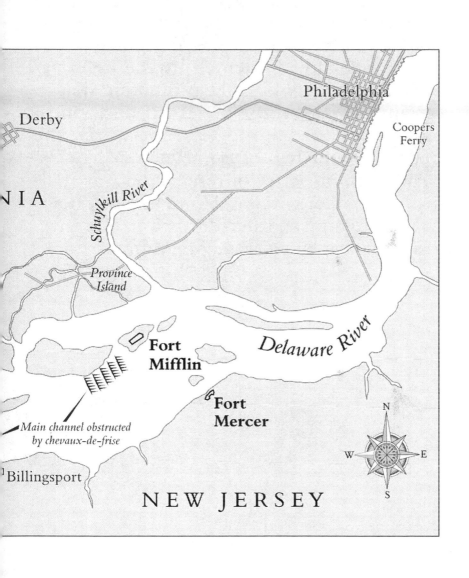

ish commander recognized that if the Continentals could continue to hold their river forts until the Delaware froze over — conceivably in mere weeks — he would have little choice but to abandon the city. His reputation as commander in chief of Crown forces in America already dented by the defeat at Saratoga, he could not help intuiting that in certain parliamentary circles his decision to move on Philadelphia was not worth the trade-off of the loss of Burgoyne's army.

Although his letter of resignation was dulling his taste for combat, Howe had no choice but to attempt another downriver offensive. This time his target was Fort Mifflin.

TEN:
BLOOD ON THE DELAWARE

For all his frustration with the course of the war, Gen. Howe was not a fool. He had now twice absorbed the lessons of attempting to dislodge the Americans from their riverside forts with a primarily overland assault. If the redoubts were to fall, it would have to be from a combined attack by land and water. So, in cooperation with his brother, he organized a plan to engage the defenders of Fort Mifflin with three times as much firepower as he had brought to bear the previous month against the larger and better-defended Fort Mercer. Less than two miles to the rear of Fort Mifflin on the Pennsylvania side of the Delaware, a spit of land called Province Island protruded from the river's shallows. For years it had been used as a sanctuary by local Indians harassed by a vigilante group of Scots-Irish known as the Paxton Boys. In the first week of November, the British general ordered the island's Indian population cleared as his cannoneers hauled their artillery onto the foreland that jutted out nearest the Delaware River.

In the interim since von Donop's strike at Fort Mercer, the garrison at Fort Mifflin had ballooned to some 400 Americans, including the young diarist Joseph Plumb Martin. At daybreak on November 10 they awoke to a fusillade that would be the largest extended bombardment of the Revolutionary War. Over the next four days British artillery from Province Island rained continuous fire on the rickety outpost — balls launched directly at its wooden barracks and walls; mortar and howitzer shells lobbed over its parapets; grapeshot rattling its bastions at the merest glimpse of a cocked hat or musket barrel. The fort's 10 cannons proved ineffectual in response, "a Burlesque upon the art of Fortification," wrote one Continental regular. When the Continentals' lone 32-pounder ran out of ammunition, the fort's commander offered a gill of rum, about four ounces, to any soldier who dared enter the parade ground to recover British cannonballs to be fired back at the enemy. Each night, under the tireless direction of the French engineer Maj. François de Fleury, the defenders attempted to repair the damage and shore up their crumbling walls. By the next afternoon the enemy's artillery would have reduced their efforts to rubble.

For the moment the Americans found

redemption only in the weather. A series of intense squalls had blown in from the north, roiling the currents on the river and preventing Adm. Howe's ships from reaching their target. On the night of November 14, however, the veil of clouds lifted to reveal a black canopy bristling with pinpoints of starlight. The *coup de grâce* was delivered the next morning, when the river tides carried eight British gunboats armed with 228 more cannons upriver. Keeping out of range of the artillery at Fort Mercer, the vessels encircled the little fort on Mud Island and fired at will. The waterborne show of force was no match for what even Washington referred to snidely as the "Gondolas and Guard Boats" of the Continental Navy. During one hour over 1,000 cannonballs reportedly fell within Fort Mifflin's walls.

With his gift for limpid, simple prose, the diarist Joseph Plumb Martin sketched a grisly portrait from the perspective of boots — or, in his case, bare feet — on the ground. "I have seen the enemy's shells fall upon it and sink so low that their report could not be heard when they burst, and I could only feel a tremulous motion of the earth at the time," he wrote. "At other times, when they burst near the surface of the ground, they would throw the mud fifty feet in the air." Martin witnessed comrades "split like fish to be broiled" while he himself "endured hardships, sufficient to kill half a dozen horses." He was six days shy of his seventeenth birthday.

As the battle progressed, the converted British East Indiaman *Empress of Russia* managed to ride the current into the narrow channel that separated the fort from the mainland. British marines, clambering to the ship's crow's nest, heaved scores of hand grenades down on the Continentals firing from the parapets. That night, with ammunition running low and over half of the redoubt's exhausted and starving men either killed or wounded, Fort Mifflin's commanding officer, Colonel Christopher Greene — a third cousin of Nathanael Greene — ordered its evacuation. Just prior to midnight, with the oars of their longboats muffled with sheepskins, the Americans slipped their dead into the Delaware's currents and rowed across the river to Fort Mercer. A small unit was left behind to spike the cannons and set the outpost ablaze before its members, too, crossed. The escapees included Joseph Plumb Martin. The following morning the British took possession of the charred and splintered remnants of the little citadel.

General Howe — buoyed by casualty reports of only 13 British dead and 24 wounded during the siege — immediately ordered Gen. Cornwallis to lead 3,000 men to storm Fort Mercer. Washington briefly considered reinforcing the New Jersey outpost, but a team of generals he sent to assess that contingency advised against it. On November 20, five days after the fall of Fort Mifflin, Col. Greene ordered Fort Mercer's walls abandoned. Cornwallis's detachment moved in the following morning. To his delight, Cornwallis also found himself in possession of 400 head of cattle, which he ordered driven to Philadelphia as a gift to Howe's hungry troops.

With the Delaware River now open to Adm. Richard Howe's large transport vessels, any hope of starving the British out of Philadelphia slipped away like a smuggler's schooner. Washington, under pressure from Congress to react, could do no more than dispatch an undersized division of roughly 2,000 men under Nathanael Greene to southern New Jersey with discretionary instructions to engage Cornwallis whenever a suitable opportunity presented itself. Riding with Greene was the peripatetic Marquis de Lafayette.

Lafayette had spent his short convalescence dashing off *billets-doux* to Adrienne, updating his powerful father-in-law on the vigilance and righteousness of the American cause, and pestering Washington for a command of his own. Finally, having received no reply from his patron, in early October he had quit his hospital bed, wrapped his game leg in a blanket, bidden his Moravian hosts *adieu,* and ridden off to Whitemarsh. There he slept on the floor in the commander in chief's hovel of a headquarters, shared the general staff's one tin plate, and continued his lobbying. This persistence eventually broke down Washington's inchoate reservations, and in one of his first letters to the new president of Congress, Henry Laurens, Washington wrote of his "delicate situation with respect to the Marquis Le Fayette."* Washington advised the senior Laurens that a refusal to grant the Frenchman's request "will not only induce him to return [to France] in disgust — but may involve some unfavorable consequences." Moreover, in the wake of Lafayette's heroism at Brandywine, he was now inclined "to gratify him his wishes."

"The Marquis," Washington added with what may be imagined as a sigh of resignation, "is determined to be in the way of danger." While awaiting Laurens's directions, Washington attached Lafayette to Gen.

---

* John Hancock, in failing health, resigned from the post he had held since May 1775 on October 31, 1777. The following day the delegates voted near-unanimously to elect Henry Laurens to the post. The only dissenting vote was cast by Laurens himself, a chivalrous action meant to show his uninterest in placing personal promotions over his civic duty.

Greene's expeditionary force in a sort of trial run.

By late November, Greene had stalked Cornwallis's force to the town of Gloucester in southwest New Jersey. There he put 400 riflemen under the command of Lafayette and tasked him with probing the enemy lines. On the afternoon of November 25, Lafayette, still hobbling on his wounded leg, crept to within yards of the Redcoat camp to conduct a troop count. As he was making his return circumference he came upon a stand-alone picket of some 400 Hessians. Fulfilling Washington's forecast — and perhaps his worst fears — the Frenchman gathered his infantry and attacked. The Americans routed the Hessians, killing or wounding close to 40 and chasing the rest for a good half mile before the combination of British reinforcements and darkness ended the engagement.

General Greene's reconstruction of the action for Washington was evenhanded in its praise for the marquis. More impressive, Lafayette's own précis of his "little success" stressed the heroics of the American troops while downplaying his own role as "not very considerable." If nothing else, Lafayette had learned to say what his commander in chief wanted to hear. Immediately after receiving both communiqués, Washington relayed to Congress his own summation of the encounter, again suggesting that Lafayette be given a greater role in the army. This time Congress agreed, and on December 1, Lafayette was placed in charge of the division of Virginians formerly led by the disgraced Gen. Stephen. In the meantime any hopes Washington had of Greene's luring Cornwallis into a fight evaporated when Cornwallis and his troops were recalled to Philadelphia. If Gen. Howe was going to force a major engagement, he was going to do it on his own terms.

On December 4, American scouts reported that the entire British army with Howe at its head was marching from Philadelphia toward Whitemarsh. Sensing a final opportunity for a conclusive confrontation before winter set in, Washington roused his troops and, in John Laurens's words, "paraded our men so as to make them acquainted with the ground and its advantages." The following morning when the British hove into view the Continentals were already positioned in the fortified hills overlooking a deep swale in front of the camp. The Redcoats were then greeted with a series of feints designed to draw them closer to the defile, including a fusillade into their right flank from Dan Morgan's rifle corps. General Howe, proving either too savvy or too indifferent, refused to take the bait. "We wished nothing more than to have them engage us," recorded the prolific Joseph Plumb Martin, who had arrived at Whitemarsh the previous day: "For we were sure of giving them a drubbing, being in excellent fighting trim, as we were starved and as cross and illnatured as curs." His sarcasm is understandable.

Instead, for the next 48 hours the British probed the American battle lines for weaknesses, finding none. Howe then withdrew his army in such haste that Continental soldiers raced to scavenge the abandoned blankets and cooking kettles, some of the latter with fires still burning beneath them. Howe's imminent return to England — and the prospect of explaining another defeat on the heels of the humiliation at Saratoga — probably influenced his decision to seek the succor of Philadelphia. And in that instant the expectation of another large-scale engagement that had buoyed what Washington called his "soldiery" since Germantown became as meager as their paydays and daily rations. What the commander in chief and his staff of confidants considered a moral victory at Whitemarsh left a sour taste in the mouths of many others, not least in the halls of Congress.

Again the *sotto voce* grumbling circulated, this time not quite so *sotto.* Would not someone like Horatio Gates or Benedict Arnold have carried the fight to the enemy from those limestone hills? "Two battles he has lost for us by two such Blunders as might have disgraced a Soldier of three months standing," sniped the New Jersey delegate Jonathan Dickinson Sergeant to his fellow congressman James Lovell of Massachusetts. Now that the opportunity had passed, all that remained was the prospect of a cold and hungry season of waiting. As Jedediah Huntington wrote to his father in Connecticut, "What probability is there of recruiting our Army? Money will not do it for it has almost intirely lost its Value. How is it possible to clothe our men? They have worn out their Blankets & other Clothing and I see no prospect of renewing them." Or, as the historian Wayne Bodle observed, "In the camp of the American Army, the winter of discontent had begun early."

With the farmsteads and mills surrounding Whitemarsh bled dry by the two voracious armies, there was nothing left for Washington but to find another area to stake winter camp. So it was that in the waning autumn weeks of 1777, mounted messengers pocked the sodden roads between Whitemarsh, York, and Lancaster — the seat of Pennsylvania's state legislature — as Washington, the Continental Congress, and the local politicians debated various options. Some of Washington's aides pressed for a chain of winter cantonments meandering from Reading to Lancaster, the better to protect what little Continental stores remained. Others argued that fragmenting the army in such a manner would lead to a flood of desertions. Still other general officers — including Greene, Lafayette, and Wayne — put forth the proposition of marching the troops to winter quarters as far south as Wilmington, Delaware. The irascible Count Pulaski, echoing the sentiments of a healthy swath of junior officers and the more bellicose members of Congress, called for an immediate attack on Philadelphia. General Lord Stirling's was the lone voice suggesting that the army consider wintering over in the "Great Valley of Trydruffin," or Valley Forge, some 13 miles to the west. A circumspect Washington was more wary than usual of voicing his opinion on the subject. For ultimately any decision would entail a delicate balancing act.

On the one hand was the covey of congressional delegates, abetted by some of his own lieutenants, majors, and colonels, who still wanted to take the fight to the enemy. On the other was the political reality of the state government, which expected the Continental Army to remain near enough to Philadelphia to prevent, as one representative put it, "the ravages and insults of the enemy" across its suburbs. That both these strategies broke against Washington's own intuition and military experience was the conundrum. To this point the entire Pennsylvania campaign had been an exercise in experimentation after the decisive victories at Trenton and Princeton that closed out the previous year. To Washington's critics it had been a failed experiment incurring a cascade of defeats. In reality it had consisted of little more than several inconclusive, though violent, tactical clashes punctuated by extended periods of strategic regrouping. There was, however, a larger picture to consider.

By early December the news of Burgoyne's surrender had reached Versailles. King Louis XVI and his ministers were so overjoyed that it inspired a *démarche,* with the king himself notifying Benjamin Franklin that now was a propitious time for the Americans to officially resubmit their bid for French aid. More surprisingly, France's military minds appeared to be just as impressed by reports of Washington's attack on Howe at Germantown as they were by Gates's victory. The irony was palpable — while at home Washington endured harsh criticism for his army's failure, across the Atlantic his stab at Germantown, coming so soon after the defeat at Brandywine, was viewed as a dazzling display of audacity. Despite the mixed outcomes, the news that an American army still in its infancy and consisting of citizen-soldiers had defeated the British on one front and thrown a major scare into them on another nearly 300 miles away was taken as a sign of an ascendant United States. As the French foreign minister wrote to Franklin and Deane,

"This, promises everything."

Washington could well imagine how the news of Saratoga would play in Paris, though he would not learn for months how strongly the Germantown engagement influenced the French. He was, however, certain of one thing — his bedraggled and bedeviled troops were in no condition to conduct a major offensive against Philadelphia. He had personally journeyed to the city's edge to view the British defenses, and John Laurens, who accompanied the observation party, described them in a letter to his father as "redoubts of a very respectable profit, faced with plank, formidably fraised, and the intervals between them with an abbatis unusually strong." The French engineer Col. Duportail delicately advised Washington that even a Continental Army doubled in strength would break on the enemy's ramparts. Young Laurens was equally direct, telling his father that any attack on the city would constitute "madness."

Convinced that his American forces were far too weak to storm Philadelphia, Washington settled on the next best strategy. As he wrote to his old friend Patrick Henry in Virginia, "Next to being strong, it is best to be thought so by the enemy." Another defeat, the commander in chief knew, would expose his army's fragility not only to the British, but also to potential allies across the Atlantic. His troops needed the winter to restore their vigor and morale. Ideally this rehabilitation site would be somewhere inland, far from harm's way. Yet to suggest such a path would be anathema to the federal and state civil authorities. There had to be another way to make his point. In a brazen act of political jujitsu, he decided to turn the criticisms of his leadership skills to his advantage.

Three days after confiding his fears to Patrick Henry, Washington penned a letter that confronted his doubters head-on. "I am informed that it is matter of amazement, and that reflections have been thrown out against this Army, for not being more active and enterprizing than, in the opinion of some, they ought to have been," he wrote to the president of Congress, Henry Laurens. He then went on to detail "the best way to account for" these defamations — specifically the scandalous dearth of arms, ammunition, shoes, clothing, blankets, and wages that his soldiers had been promised. Even if these commodities were to somehow miraculously appear, he continued, Gen. Howe's forces still massively outnumbered his own army. To drive home the point, Lafayette addressed his own letter to Henry Laurens, describing "the quite nacked fellow [soldiers]" warming themselves at his campfire, and proclaimed, "How happy I would be if our army was drest in a comfortable manner."

The dual complaint prompted a congressional fact-finding committee to journey to Whitemarsh where — as Washington had presumed — the delegates were shocked by the camp's ragged condition. A third of the Continentals remained without blankets, shoes, and socks, and the congressmen were shamed into unbuckling their own footwear to hand over to freezing soldiers. They also vowed to press their fellow congressmen for an untangling of the army's supply line upon their return to York. In their official report, however, they could not resist tossing a dart at the commander in chief. The promised reforms, the committee noted, could be accomplished only with a commensurate upturn in the army's lax discipline. None of this, of course, answered the question regarding a site for a winter camp.

Washington's official papers during this period are noticeably sparse and betray little of his personal feelings over this tumultuous debate. Moreover, unfortunately for historians, fearing the capture of a personal journal, he had discontinued his diary entries early in the revolution. This leaves to posterity's conjecture many of his intimate thoughts on events through eight years of war. Happily, in many instances the writings of acolytes such as Laurens, Hamilton, and Lafayette provide guideposts to his innermost reflections. In this instance, one can assume that John Laurens's views mirrored those of the general he cherished when, in a letter to his father, Henry, in early December, he itemized the reasoning behind the Continental Army's requirement of "exemption from fatigue in order to compensate for their want of clothing." The men needed safe, warm quarters, he wrote, in order to discourage desertion, encourage enlistment, and fine-tune the force's discipline and training. Yet he also recognized the realities of abandoning the local populace to the mercies of the Crown. Without naming a specific location, he then suggested a compromise that "leaves us within distance for taking considerable advantage of the Enemy and covering a valuable and extensive country."

There were manifold facts to parse in selecting the site. It had to be secure enough to fend off a British attack in force while central enough to afford the citizens throughout the countryside around Philadelphia protection against lesser enemy excursions. It had to lie between the army depots and hospitals at Lancaster, Reading, and York yet still be close enough to the capital city should some as yet unfathomable opportunity for a winter assault present itself. Fresh water would need to be available, as would enough wood to build barracks cabins and keep fires burning. It was a military and political conundrum that Washington was still mulling when, at the urging of Lord Stirling, Gen.

Wayne — born in Chester County and thoroughly familiar with the area — came around with the answer.

Wayne joined Lord Stirling in suggesting "hutting" atop the undulating, triangular plateau overlooking the Valley of the Forges. Washington immediately recognized that the site met both civil and military prescriptions. Some 23 miles northwest of Philadelphia, it was close enough for American horsemen and outlying pickets to react to any British "ravages" or "insults." Yet at a day's march from the city, it was also far enough from the enemy stronghold to make it virtually immune to surprise attack. In the event of a major British assault, its natural contours — it was bounded by steep falloffs on two sides and the Schuylkill on the third — would provide excellent defensive terrain. It was blessed with an abundant supply of fresh water from both the river and copious creeks and wells. Finally, the thick carpet of virgin hardwood forests on the western rises anchored by the 426-foot Mount Joy and, behind it, the slightly higher Mount Misery, would prove integral for the sustainment of a winter camp's two vital B's — burning and building.

Perhaps more important, the site lay on the western rim of the fall campaign's sundry battlegrounds. The farms, orchards, and mills to the southeast had been virtually picked clean by both armies. But to this point western Chester County had been the scene of relatively little pillaging. While the Schuylkill remained ice-free it would provide a thoroughfare into the Pennsylvania interior for both communications and supplies. And once the river froze, Valley Forge's road network, though susceptible to washouts, afforded at least two sturdy cobblestoned avenues, both laid down in the 1740s and generally passable for Conestoga wagons delivering provisions from points farther west. Moreover, in a worst-case scenario, the large artery formed by the confluence of the two roads could be used as an escape route that ran some 60 miles west all the way to hilly Lancaster, perfect terrain from which to conduct guerrilla operations.

Unlike Washington's current encampment at Whitemarsh, Valley Forge was not wilderness. It was farm country, and it would require all the expertise the French engineer Duportail and his subordinates could muster to construct adequate field fortifications. But, overall, it was as stable an anchor from which to run the far-flung business of war as the commander in chief could expect to find. It would do as the bloodied and desperate Continental Army's home for the next six months.

■ ■ ■ ■

PART II

■ ■ ■ ■

I am Sick — discontented — and out of humour. Poor food — hard lodging — cold Weather — fatigue — nasty cloaths — nasty cookery — Vomit half my time — smoak'd out of my senses — the Devil's in't — I can't Endure it — why are we sent here to starve and Freeze — Here all Confusion — smoke and cold — hunger and filthyness. A pox on my bad luck.

— ALBIGENCE WALDO,
CONTINENTAL ARMY SURGEON,
DECEMBER 14, 1777

George Washington reviews troops at Valley Forge.

Eleven:
The Relics of an Army

The Continental Army broke camp at White-marsh on December 11 and crossed a raft bridge spanning the Schuylkill the next night. In an odd counterpoint to the maxim that history is written by the victors, even the most meticulous scholars and researchers have never been able to establish exactly how many soldiers George Washington led from Whitemarsh in late 1777. The consensus puts the total at somewhere between 11,000 and 14,000. As it was, all of these troops and most of their officers had no idea as to their destination.

After a brief skirmish with a startled British foraging party led by Gen. Cornwallis, the battered column of Continentals spent the next week following the cobblestoned road west, descending deeper into the dank and rugged defile that the original Welsh settlers, the most numerous in any of the 13 colonies, called the Gulph — "valley" or "glen" in their home language. By day sheets of cold rain blew sideways beneath vivid bursts of cloud-shrouded lightning and turned the road into a trail of mud. Come sunset the downpours froze into a wet, heavy snow that virtually interred the men, Brueghel's peasants bathed in a Rembrandt's gloom. During preparations for the battle that did not occur at Whitemarsh, most of the army's tents had been sent north for safekeeping. Now, canvas strips sliced from the remaining few became the raw material to fashion makeshift shirts, shoes, and stockings. "A cavalcade of wild beasts" was how Joseph Plumb Martin described himself and his compatriots, their personal Via Dolorosa traced across the landscape by the trails of blood left by the thousands of barefoot men. At one point he and his company managed to run down a scrawny cow that was immediately killed and skinned, its untanned hide fashioned into crude moccasins.

But the march was most miserable for the long roster of sick and wounded. Because of a shortage of wagons — fewer than 40 were on hand for the entire army — most of the injured were either carried on improvised stretchers or supported by strong shoulders. Influenza, typhus, typhoid, dysentery, and scurvy were only just beginning their winter sweep through the ranks, and the dreariness of the landscape was aptly described by the Connecticut surgeon Albigence Waldo as "a place where nothing appears pleasing to the Sicken'd Eye & Nauseating Stomach." Despite his prolific journal entries, not much is known of the 27-year-old Waldo's personal life other than that, as he wrote, he had left behind "a good and loving wife" and his "pretty children" in Putnam, Connecticut. Waldo was attached to the 1st Connecticut Infantry Regiment, the unit Gen. Huntington had led south from Peekskill three months earlier, and his diary entries provide an invaluable snapshot of Continental Army operations through the fall and winter of 1777 and 1778. Waldo was a sturdy campaigner and an ardent revolutionary, but by December even the indefatigable surgeon wrote like a man slowly perishing. Waldo stretched the horizons of his vision to recall and lament the mouthwatering "fine stock of provisions, hens, turkeys, pigs, ducks, wine and cider" available aboard the packet he had served on, plying the Hudson River. He could not help ruing the "wiffling wind of fortune" that bore upon it the "disappointments, anxieties, and misfortunes" bracing the American force. Perhaps it was because someone had stolen his shoes.

Whatever the case, as Waldo and his fellow soldiers slogged forward he was far from alone in considering the army's dire circumstances. As scant rations had been issued since the breaking of camp at Whitemarsh, anyone lucky enough to have snatched a turnip or an ear of winter corn from the fields along the route devoured it raw. At night, gazing about over the thousands of campfires that blackened their faces and stung their eyes, the wraithlike soldiers could not have helped concluding that they resembled nothing so much as what one future historian would deem "the relics of an army."

As the mass movement neared Valley Forge on December 18, a messenger from York arrived with news that Congress had declared this a national day of "Thanksgiving and Praise" in honor of the victory at Saratoga. With the Continental Army having lurched a mere six miles in six hours, Washington halted the march outside a country inn named in honor of the king of Prussia. It had stopped snowing, and the night felt as if it were holding its breath as chaplains conducted services before the regiments and brigades. Following the devotions, while his soldiers gathered damp twigs to light feeble fires, Washington and his senior officers lumbered into the tavern, where a painting of the dashing and victorious Frederick the Great seemed to mock them.

Washington recognized that the announcement of a day of thanks was a shot across his bow from the faction of delegates cozying up to Gen. Gates. Nevertheless he ordered his commissary officers to drain their kegs, slaughter their last drift of hogs, and literally scrape the bottoms of their flour barrels to provide some of the troops a meager celebratory feast of beer, ham, and bread. Others, like Joseph Plumb Martin, made do with half a gill of rice and a tablespoon of vinegar to ward off scurvy. Such a feast, he wrote, was complemented by "a leg of nothing and no turnips." Since mid-October the commander in chief had been a supplicant before both Congress and Pennsylvania's state authorities in a determined attempt to keep his army supplied. Now, two months later, the consequences of the delegates' failure to heed his warnings were manifest in the bobtail force that limped toward Valley Forge like a line of tattered scarecrows.

As the days dragged on, Washington periodically reined his horse to the side of the road to linger and bear witness as his ghost of an army straggled past. First the officers on horseback leading their stumbling and footsore regiments, then the juddering baggage wagons, and finally the 400 or so "camp women" with their untold children bringing up the rear. These were primal moments. As the commander in chief beheld so many of his soldiers "without Cloathes to cover their nakedness — without blankets to lay on — without Shoes," it must have crossed his mind that the preponderance of his hungry and half-clad men were present in great part out of personal loyalty to him. Nor could the irony have been lost on him that his days as the leader of this army might well be numbered, through either political perfidy or, as seemed more likely at the moment, the complete dissolution of his vagabond force. By the same token, one cannot help wondering if any of the young troopers he now gazed down upon, their listless eyes sunk deep into gaunt faces, reminded him of the defiant youth who over two decades earlier had undertaken his own hazardous missions into the wilderness on behalf of an empire that was now his sworn enemy.

In many ways the parallels are striking. Just as Washington's first command in the Revolutionary War had driven the British from Boston, to worldwide acclaim and astonishment, so his initial military foray in the French and Indian War had resulted in a measure of international fame. It had occurred in 1753, when the 21-year-old Virginian was dispatched into the vast hinterlands west of the Blue Ridge Mountains. Washington had volunteered to carry a letter from Virginia's royal governor addressed to the commander of the French troops currently occupying and fortifying territory in the wild Ohio Country. The communiqué informed the French that they were trespassing on ground claimed by "His Britannic Majesty" and were to depart forthwith. Though the French, in effect and politely, laughed off the English king's pretensions and sent Washington on his way, he had served as the vehicle for the firing of the first, symbolic shot of the French and Indian War.

Upon Washington's return to Richmond, his journal from the expedition was published by a local newspaper. Its tales — of settlers murdered and scalped by marauding Indians, of Alleghany mountain passes traversed through waist-deep snow, of fording icy rivers that froze the legs off pack horses — caused an immediate sensation in the colonies. When the narrative was reprinted by newspapers and magazines from London to Edinburgh, the adventures of the young fourth-generation colonial planter were suddenly the talk of Great Britain's salons and coffeehouses. More important, the travelogue shone light on a trait Washington would cultivate for the rest of his military and political career — "that of a man of action," as his biographer Joseph Ellis writes, "determined to tell us what he did, but equally determined not to tell us what he thought about it."

Yet just as Washington's success in Boston in 1776 was followed by catastrophe in New York and — after a brief respite at Trenton and Princeton — by bitter disappointments and recriminations in the aftermath of Brandywine, Paoli, and Germantown, so too did the trajectory of his early military career take a sharp downward turn. In the years following his successful foray into the Ohio Country, Washington, by now an officer in the Virginia militia, was twice more involved with excursions to dislodge the French from the British-claimed territory. Each ended in a fiasco. He led the first mission, which resulted not only in the rout of his rum-soaked militiamen, but also in charges that he had allowed the small band of Indian allies who accompanied him to kill a French nobleman on a diplomatic mission. During the latter expedition he was attached to a much larger army of British regulars charged with capturing Fort Duquesne, a sturdy redoubt the French had constructed at the confluence of the Alleghany, Monongahela, and Ohio Rivers where Pittsburgh, Pennsylvania, now rises. The bulk of the Crown forces, unaccustomed to the forest-fighting techniques adopted by the French from their Indian allies, were wiped out with brutal efficiency. Nearly every officer around Washington was killed; he escaped with bullet holes in his hat and in his coat. Thereafter he told friends that he felt as if "Providence was saving him for something larger."

Washington could take small solace from the plaudits he received for rallying the few survivors into an orderly retreat. He was now considered an assassin in France, and in

Virginia his luster was badly tarnished. As a Richmond newspaper editorial coolly observed, although Washington may have acquired "a high Reputation for Military Skill, Integrity, and Valor; Success has not always attended his Undertakings." For the rest of his life he could never erase from his memory the wails of the wounded or the images of the dead scalped by the enemy's own Indian accomplices. Nor would he ever forget the wily guerrilla tactics that had vanquished the British force. If he could not bring his compatriots back to life, he could ensure that any soldiers serving under his future command would be well versed in bush-fighting techniques.

Back home at Mount Vernon, Washington began to apply these lessons. At just 23 he was charged with raising a colonial regiment from the primarily Anglo-Saxon and Celtic immigrants pouring into Virginia. The company he recruited and trained, the historian Ellis notes, "combined the spit-and-polish discipline of British regulars with the tactical agility and proficiency of Indian warriors." Although by this point the major campaigns of the French and Indian War had gravitated farther north, Washington's Virginia Blues — named after the indigo uniforms that he had personally designed — honed their expertise patrolling the homestead-dotted Shenandoah Valley west of the Blue Ridge that was subject to frequent French-directed Indian attacks.

Each of the Virginia rangers, as he called his enlisted men, was issued a detailed battle plan that Washington had written himself. Based on his earlier experiences, it addressed a variety of contingencies. If his men were ambushed in an open forest clearing, for instance, instead of forming up in a European-style defensive square, they were to rush the woods and flank their attackers. He dictated that the area around any potential stockade site was to be cleared of brush and trees to just beyond the 70 yards of a musket's range — rectifying an oversight that had helped to doom his first military foray against the French. If troops should happen upon the aftermath of an Indian massacre, they were to harvest the corn crop before moving on. And despite his lifelong love of dogs, he ordered that before a surprise attack was mounted, all dogs roaming the camp were to be killed lest their barks and growls alert the enemy. He was also a harsh disciplinarian to officers and rangers alike. Any man found drunk on duty faced lashes, sometimes numbering in the hundreds. Captured deserters were summarily hanged. Washington was a compassionate man, but the exigencies of war prevailed.

His Virginia Blues eventually played an integral role in the final defeat of the French at Fort Duquesne in 1758. During that campaign, which was led by the renowned British military administrator Gen. John Forbes, Washington took advantage of his proximity by copying Forbes's orders into notebooks that he would keep for future reference. By the war's end his regiment of Provincials was regarded as the most effective colonial fighting force in America. Now, almost two decades later, as Washington watched the threadbare Continentals shamble toward Valley Forge, sometimes pausing to boil their shoes in an attempt to make them digestible, a simple question arose: Would he be granted the same time and leeway to restore and retrain these soldiers as he had done with his Virginia corps? Or would that long-ago newspaper editorialist prove prescient; would military success "not always attend his Undertakings"? In truth, given the horror still facing the raw, unkempt men and boys passing before him, his prospects looked as improbable as a human being's having the strength to fling a silver dollar across the wide Potomac.*

Added to this burden was his recognition that *he* was now the physical embodiment of

* The legend of a young Washington displaying such prodigious strength probably arose from his ability as a boy to clear Virginia's 300-foot-wide Rappahannock River with a rock as he and his friends waited by a ferry stop.

the American Revolution, the man and the cause having fused into a single entity. Three weeks earlier Henry Knox had advised Washington, "The people of America look up to you as their father, and into your hands they entrust their all." The Jeffersons and Adamses, the Hancocks and Franklins and Paines may have set in motion a rebellion based on ideals not contemplated since classical Athens. But no one in York or Lancaster, no one in Boston or Albany or Charleston, could lead the political movement those philosophers of freedom had birthed. Pericles may have moved men's minds, but Leonidas made them get up and march. In practice and in deed, the Spartan mantle of breaking the bonds of stratified British colonialism fell to Washington, and Washington alone.

In his youth he had been granted a glimpse of the immensity of a continent whose eastern rim was now consumed by revolution. His decisions and actions in the weeks and months to come would determine the fate of those thousands of miles rolling westward that would constitute the future United States of America. Given the gravitas of such a task, it is no wonder that a sense of desperation hung no less heavy over the Gulph Road that December than the storm clouds saturating his army.

TWELVE:
CHAOS IN THE EAST

December 19 dawned dank and windy beneath a dove-gray sky. As the army trudged forward through the pale sunlight, the scent of rain was in the air. It was into the afternoon's gathering mist that Washington cantered down into the declivity that would form Valley Forge's outer defensive ring and up onto the triangular plateau. He was accompanied by his aides, his personal guard, and the contingent of French military engineers. When they topped the rise's western slope, he and the others were disappointed, but not surprised, to find no sign of the supply wagons promised by the Pennsylvania state government. The Frenchmen, long accustomed to what they considered the Continental Army's slipshod procurement process, had other things to fret over. They were already mentally sketching the layout for the thousands of log huts to be erected as well as the sites for the redoubts needed to defend the winter cantonment.

One month earlier, at Washington's urging, Congress had officially sanctioned the creation of a rudimentary Army Corps of Engineers, which over the next two centuries was destined to serve the country through an invasion of Mexico, a civil war, countless Indian subjugations, and multiple overseas conflicts. The delegates had selected Louis Duportail to lead this new cadre, over objections from representatives who had met and dealt with the imperious Frenchman. They had also promoted him to the rank of brigadier general. As the wind picked up and a light rain began to fall, Washington's first executive decision at Valley Forge was to order Duportail and his assistants to join several of his general officers in traversing the campsite to survey and map the rolling meadows. As Duportail's English was limited, the bilingual Richard Kidder Meade was assigned as a translator and liaison.

Washington next summoned the commanders of the regiments he planned to detach to patrol the roads leading into Philadelphia. Several hundred Pennyslvania militiamen under Gen. John Armstrong were sent back east across the Schuylkill with instructions to split into small, mobile units and turn back any local tradesmen attempting to haul goods into the city. They were also charged with interdicting the enemy's lines of communication between New Jersey and New York and, when possible, harassing British foraging parties. Simultaneously, a smaller command of Pennsylvania militiamen supplemented by Dan Morgan's rifle corps were fanned south to serve as forward pickets. Finally, Gen. Smallwood and a division of regulars were dispatched to Wilmington, Delaware. Smallwood's orders, like Armstrong's, were threefold — to shore up the town's defenses against a surprise attack, to assist the navy in distressing Adm. Howe's ships along the lower reaches of the Delaware, and to serve as a bulwark against a British raid on the Continental food magazines some 20 miles inland near what is now Elkton, Maryland.

For months Washington had pushed back against the idea of confiscating provisions from civilians loyal to the revolution. When Henry Laurens succeeded John Hancock and broached just such an idea, the commander in chief foresaw the negative ramifications. Such a step would undercut the very ideals for which the Americans were fighting. The immortal preamble to the Declaration of Independence often diverts attention from the guts of the document — that is, the 27 specific accusations leveled against the tyranny of George III. One of these accused the British monarch of sending "Swarms of Officers to harass our People, and eat out their Substance," and another of affecting "to render the Military independent and superior to the Civil Power." The representatives of the 13 colonies who formed the Second Continental Congress did not take these intrusions lightly, and neither did Washington. For Washington to declare himself "superior to the Civil Power" and turn on the local citizenry to "eat out their Substance" was a hypocrisy that could very well doom the revolution.

From a military perspective, there were also practical considerations. Washington recognized that the arrogation of civilian goods would serve, in effect, to open up another front against his beleaguered force. As he wrote to Henry Laurens, "The mode of seizing and forcing supplies from the Inhabitants, I fear, would prove very inadequate to the demands while it would certainly imbitter the minds of the People, and excite perhaps a hurtful jealousy against the Army." Since the sending of that letter, however, the army's supply stem had wilted to the point of near-complete dysfunction. Much of this could be laid at the feet of the sad lot of civilian teamsters hired to deliver provisions to the camp from the inland warehouses. To lighten their loads over rough roads, for instance, they had washed the brine from salted meat, allowing it to spoil; and salt herring "arrived in such condition that the fish had disintegrated into a sort of paste." To further ease their journey, flour was removed from barrels and poured into the bed of supply wagons to mix with all manner of muck and grime. As for beef on the hoof, what little the Continentals managed to obtain was often unrecognizable.

Rhode Island's Gen. James Varnum, fresh from the defense of Fort Mercer, noted that his men had gone four days, including their first two at Valley Forge, without bread or meat. When they finally procured beef, he added, "it is of such a vile Quality, as to render it a poor Succedanium for Food." Joseph Plumb Martin, now an 18-year-old veteran, reported that after two days with no food his unit was supplied with "a beef creature" so skinny that it was "quite transparent. I thought at the time what an excellent lantern it would make." As a compromise against growing calls to allow his army to seize any and all foodstuff from civilians wherever it was found, Washington granted leave to the detached militiamen to commandeer any trade goods they discovered being taken to Philadelphia. He added that all wagons and carriages captured during these encounters were to be driven back to Valley Forge, carrying whatever extra food was not needed by the patrolling troops themselves.

This pruning of his main force served to reduce the number of mouths to feed at Valley Forge, as many of Gen. Armstrong's Pennsylvanians had local roots, and the commander in chief expected them to be capable of living off the land. Although Gen. Howe may have considered the area a bulwark of rebellion when he destroyed its iron forges, the Quakers populating the surrounding countryside constituted a potential fifth column. Washington hoped that sending the militiamen out into their own neighborhoods would dampen temptations for the populace to trade with the British or, worse, share information. The establishment of even this tentative, porous land blockade around Philadelphia was, however, a military trade-off, for by disseminating his troops as such, Washington had also loosened his grip on his control of them. He would have to rely on a communications system consisting of daily, and sometimes hourly, riders delivering and receiving messages and orders to and from the many spokes of his far-flung wheel.

Meanwhile, as well-worn campaign tents and temporary brush booths sprouted like mushrooms across the Valley Forge plateau, work crews began emptying the firewood sheds dotting the rolling fields — although, on Washington's orders, the sheds themselves were left standing. The snake-rail fencing erected by local farmers was dismantled, and the teams of woodcutters climbing into the thick stands of timber west of the site reminded Thomas Paine of "a family of beavers" invading the flanks of Mount Misery and Mount Joy. Horses and oxen were in such short supply that the men were reduced to yoking themselves to jerry-rigged carts to haul the bounty back from the forests. The commander in chief's General Orders specified that tree trunks were to be hewn into sections of "sixteen to eighteen feet" for cabin construction, while all larger branches were stockpiled to construct the abatis that would ring the camp's fortifications. Whatever remained was added to the firewood store. By the time the first of these creaking barrows laden with wood had begun to return, the French surveyors had laid out the sites for the cabins and the defensive redoubts.

Washington ordered all of his regimental commanders to divide their units into 12-man squads, junior officers included, to erect their own living quarters. The cabins were "pitted," that is, their floors were dug several feet below the frost line, with the rough specifications for each hut set at 16 feet deep by 12 feet wide by six feet high. A dozen straw-covered bunks were to extend from the walls. The soldiers' work gangs stacked the log walls; trimmed cedar, pine, and chestnut planking for roof shingles; and left but a single opening for a door. The gaps between the ill-jointed logs were chinked with mud and clay to keep out the rain and snow. Though wood for flooring was so scarce that it was distributed only for officers' huts, and glass for windows was out of the question, some of the teams installed crude fieldstone chimneys in their cabins. But since Washington had offered a 12-dollar reward to the squad in each regiment that completed its cabin first, most rose without fireplaces.* By the time the nearly 2,000 huts were completed — an optimistic number that would never come close to housing its capacity of 24,000 soldiers — the five-square-mile plateau that rose from the Valley of the Forges nonetheless constituted the fifth most populated "city" in the United States.

Duportail and his staff laid the cantonment's rough thoroughfares along the flanks of the plateau, with the fronts of the cabins facing each other in parallel lines. The effort expended to assemble these simple structures was evidenced by a Connecticut surgeon's mate who wrote to his father that he and his fellow soldiers had raised their entire structure with but "one Poor ax & no other Tool." Though some of his general officers had made arrangements to rent rooms in nearby farmhouses, Washington, as a show of solidarity with his troops, vowed to live in his linen "sleeping marquee" erected next to his headquarters tent until the log cabins were completed. He had barely settled in the

* The first winners of the bonus had their cabin erected by the evening of the second day in camp.

232

shadow of a ridgeline in the far northwest of the campsite before he was faced with another, quite unexpected problem.

During the slog from Whitemarsh hundreds of summer soldiers, many of whose enlistments were set to expire on December 31, had simply walked away from their commands. Over the ensuing days these semi-desertions became so intolerable that Washington and his staff were deluged with reports of roving gangs of half-uniformed Continentals wandering the countryside looting the farmsteads of friend and foe alike. The state of affairs was exacerbated when word began to circulate among the detached Pennsylvania militiamen that their homes and families were being accosted. The idea of patriots with guns leaving their posts to confront other patriots with guns was a burlesque almost too dark to contemplate. In an effort to halt the exodus, Washington took the extreme step of issuing garrison orders — that is, no man was allowed to set foot outside the cantonment without a written *laizzez-passer* from his brigade commander. Riders were dispatched to inform local civilians, including Quakers, that anyone whose fields, livestock, or corn-cribs had been plundered could apply for restitution at the Valley Forge commissary. As this was invariably empty, most petitioners had to settle for certificates of seizure: notes vouchsafing future repayment for stolen goods.

The garrisoning of the encampment, however, could not prevent those same civilians from taking advantage of the chaotic conditions in the war-torn countryside. One Loyalist gang in particular had long been a burr beneath Washington's saddle. The Doan Gang, as it was known, consisted of five hulking brothers and a cousin reared in the loamy farmland of nearby Bucks County. They turned to outlawry when the brothers' father, Joseph Doan, a devout Quaker who refused to cut ties with England, was jailed for failure to pay taxes to Pennsylvania's new Whig government and his homestead was seized. The Doan Gang specialized in horse theft and also took a particular satisfaction in robbing Whig tax collectors. Predictably, the Doans offered their services to the British as spies. It was their leader, the eldest brother Moses Doan, who 16 months earlier had informed Gen. Howe of the unprotected Jamaica Pass that allowed Crown troops to surprise the Continental Army at the Battle of Long Island.

Since then the gang had roamed the Middle Atlantic states and even as far west as the fringes of the Ohio Country, with Bucks County serving as its nominal base. When the British took Philadelphia, the Doans embarked on a virtual reign of terror with the complicit backing of Gen. Howe. They ransacked patriot homesteads, rustled cattle, and helped escaped British and Hessian prisoners make their way back to the city through American lines. Over the winter of 1777–1778 the Doans were said to be responsible for stealing more than 200 horses in and around Bucks County alone, and in turn selling them to the Redcoats. Although many of the Quakers residing in the county came to regard the brothers as modern-day Robin Hoods, the area's patriots considered them demons incarnate.

Even as the Doans ran wild, a more insidious threat to Washington's authority arose. Bands of young men calling themselves Continental Volunteers began appearing on the roadways surrounding Philadelphia, setting up tolls, and refusing to let pass anyone who would not, or could not, pay. More organized than the common deserters, these men were primarily civilian opportunists taking advantage of the area's anarchy to waylay unwary travelers. More than a few, however, were undoubtedly soldiers from the same units who had deliberately separated from their commands on the march from Whitemarsh. Washington had already threatened 100 lashes for any Continental seized outside camp without a pass. Now he ordered platoons of light cavalry into the countryside not only to track the Doans, but to apprehend and return the American stragglers. As a further precaution he issued General Orders forbidding any man inside the encampment to carry a weapon or ride a horse. His regimental officers were instructed to double their daily roll calls, and any soldier caught discharging a firearm in camp was to receive 20 lashes "on the spot."*

Even the strongest threats of punishment, however, could not feed and clothe troops, a horrified Lafayette noted, "whose feet and legs turn black with frostbite." Warnings that his starving soldiers were close to open revolt arrived at Washington's headquarters almost daily. A colonel from New York's brigade wrote to his governor, George Clinton, that all but 18 men in his regiment were unfit for duty, with the rest "wholly destitute of clothing [and] perishing in the field." And Gen. Varnum concluded his letter describing the inedible beef with a caution that among some regiments there was talk of taking to the countryside en masse on plunder raids. "The Men must be Supplied," he wrote to Washington, "or they cannot be commanded." Yet again it was the omnipresent surgeon Waldo's

---

* These punishments were administered with a whip that ended in several knotted cords that tore into the skin. In order to survive the ordeal, men receiving the lash resorted to biting their lead bullets, the origin of the phrase.

vivid prose that captured the dichotomy. "Were soldiers to have plenty of Food and Rum," he wrote, "I believe they would storm Tophet." Instead he was left to wander the camp listening to chants of "No Meat! No Coat! No Bread! No Soldier!"

The outcries were not limited to the native-born. The French engineers grumbled — "as of course the French will do," noted Benjamin Franklin — as they went about their business of standing up a professional military camp for an amateur army, and less than a week after arriving at Valley Forge, Lafayette's Bavarian companion Gen. de Kalb complained to a Parisian patron, "The idea of wintering in this desert can only have been put into the head of the commanding general by an interested speculator or a disaffected man." Calling Washington "the bravest and truest of men," de Kalb nonetheless regretted that the commander in chief had not held hard to his first instinct to select a campsite deeper in the Pennsylvania countryside awash with game, fresh fish, and friendly farmers. Blaming the American politicians' interference for the soldiers' current plight, he concluded his letter with the distinctly Teutonic lament that "congress . . . has the foible of interfering with matters which it neither understands nor can understand."

Lafayette was sympathetic about his Bavarian mentor's disappointment, if more sensitive to its cause. Writing years later, he observed that in this time and place, "The American situation was never more critical. Its paper money, which had no solid foundation and was not supplemented by any specie, was counterfeited by the enemy and discredited by the partisans. The Americans were afraid to establish taxes and had still less power to collect them. Since the people had revolted against English taxes, they were astonished to have to pay even more now, and the government lacked the power to force them to pay." These were problems seemingly without answers — at least without any answers that the marquis could provide. Luckily for him, he was at least distracted from the camp's misery by news that his wife, Adrienne, had given birth to a second healthy daughter.

Meanwhile, across the Schuylkill the situation was equally dreary. General Armstrong was already complaining that he had far too few militiamen to maintain order across a vast territory that stretched all the way to New Jersey. He also reported that skirmishing with the larger and better-armed British foraging parties was out of the question. Local farmers and traders were hiding in barns and root cellars, watching the roads for his foot patrols to pass before sneaking into Philadelphia. He was also chagrined upon discovering that Continental regulars had been sent to fortify Wilmington, and he began lobbying for a similar number of men to be detached to his purview. Washington was sympathetic but resolute. He informed Armstrong that he could spare no more than a few more companies of Continental light horse.

It was clear to the commander in chief that even if the contents of every farmer's wagon and cart hauling goods into Philadelphia could have been magically diverted to Valley Forge, it would have made but the merest dent in his supply shortage. And despite granting the militia commanders in the hinterlands the power not only to seize provisions but to inflict corporal punishment on the purveyors, he recognized that not every civilian trafficking goods into Philadelphia was a Loyalist to the bone. Some were surely motivated by greed. But most were simply capitalists who had no faith in the debased American currency, much less the certificates of seizure. The British, after all, paid for provisions in hard specie. No, if Congress and the states expected him to carry out this war, it would ultimately fall on those civil authorities to feed and clothe the American army.

These tensions were reaching a crescendo when, with Christmas approaching, word reached the American camp that the British were again stirring.

THIRTEEN:
TRENTON REDUX?

General Howe did not need the Doan Gang or any other Loyalists to know that Washington and his army were wintering a mere 23 miles northwest of Philadelphia. Following the brief skirmish near Whitemarsh, Gen. Cornwallis's scouts had shadowed the Continentals all the way to Valley Forge. Howe, however, was less likely to have understood the American army's nearly crippled condition. As it was, the British were facing their own supply travails. Despite Gen. Armstrong's complaints, his Pennsylvania militiamen on the east side of the Schuylkill had done a fair job of slowing local produce that was being slipped into Philadelphia. Howe's quartermaster reported that his storehouses were stocked with enough to feed the army for only about the next 100 or so days. More ominously, ice was beginning to form on the Delaware, meaning that the 15,000 British troops cooped up in Philadelphia would soon be cut off from Adm. Howe's supply ships.

With Washington distracted by the construction of his cantonment, Gen. Howe seized the opportunity to mount a large foraging expedition.

Beginning on December 20, American intelligence officers began delivering daily communiqués to Washington's headquarters regarding British maneuvers — construction crews digging entrenchments leading out of Philadelphia, engineers hastily throwing up a pontoon bridge over the Schuylkill west of town, hundreds of horses blanketed and saddled on the city common. These were followed by a report that 1,000 Redcoats had crossed the Delaware into New Jersey to sweep away patriot resistance in order to establish a temporary farmers' market. Nearly simultaneously, close to 100 wagons accompanied by a small contingent of Hessians forded the Schuylkill and ventured some five miles southwest of the city, where they loaded the carts with hay from fields near what was then called Derby, now the borough of Darby, Pennsylvania. In one baleful missive, the commander of an American scout team shadowing this caravan bemoaned the fact that he did not have enough men to ambush such an easy target. Washington convened his aides and generals to discuss the enemy movements. Something was afoot. But what?

The Americans received their answer two days later, on the morning of December 22, when 8,000 Crown troops led by Gen. Howe himself crossed the Schuylkill over the temporary bridge. The enemy, marching in a slender column that stretched for four miles, was again moving in the direction of Derby. When the empty wagons in the van of the train reached the Derby farmsteads, the rear of the detail fanned into protective wings flanking the scythe-wielding threshers. This time the British were not only gathering hay, but sweeping up the cattle that grazed in the surrounding marshes. Whether such a large force would strike north for Valley Forge after the foraging expedition Washington could only guess. In any case, with the enemy but 20 miles south of his encampment, he had to somehow respond. This proved problematic.

In addition to the burgeoning rolls of American sick and wounded, nearly 3,000 soldiers at Valley Forge had been declared unfit for duty because they were missing shoes, clothing, weapons, or some combination thereof. It was against this shortfall that Washington issued his General Orders for December 22: his brigade commanders were instructed to choose from each of their units eight officers and 50 infantrymen in fighting trim "fit for annoying the enemy in light parties." Each of these hit-and-run units, perhaps one tenth of Washington's total force, was to be issued several days' worth of rations and 40 rounds of ammunition before marching south. Confusion ensued.

Most of these skirmishing companies snaking out of Valley Forge had tentative orders to report to Gen. Lord Stirling, who days earlier had ridden from Valley Forge to combine the Pennsylvania militia pickets and Dan Morgan's riflemen into a unified force under his command. But the officers in charge of these disparate units now being sent to join Lord Stirling were also given ambiguous instructions to engage any British they encountered en route to their rendezvous. The result was an obvious rupture in the chain of command. Several of the companies simply headed off on their own, while many of the Continentals who managed to link up with Lord Stirling arrived at his camp with no sense of their mission and, despite Washington's instructions, no rations whatsoever.

Upon first impression, neither Lord Stirling nor Col. Morgan was optimistic as to the new arrivals' usefulness or purpose. Morgan in particular viewed their lack of provisions as merely adding a greater burden to the field force, and predicted that if any of these companies did manage to engage the British, two Americans would be captured for every enemy soldier cut down. Unsure of what to do, Lord Stirling pointed most of these new men toward Derby and in essence instructed their commanders to do their best to fall on any light cavalry patrols venturing forth from

Howe's main foraging party. As the bulk of the men in the Crown column had been ordered to hold their line in order to protect the hay gatherers, the American general assumed there was little chance of a major encounter.

Dan Morgan considered this a saving grace. But he and Lord Stirling, by now accustomed to working with the undisciplined militiamen, had underestimated the seasoned regulars who had arrived as reinforcements. Dispatches soon began reaching the two officers describing American skirmishers giving as good as they got, swarming enemy horsemen and chasing them hither and yon while inflicting heavy casualties and taking prisoners. Initially surprised by these reports, the two commanders began to reconsider their strategy. Morgan sent out riders with orders for the American companies to consolidate under his banner. The next morning he and Lord Stirling marched the entire force to the nearby village of Radnor, where they incorporated another regiment of Pennsylvania militiamen into their command. Still, the Americans remained too few to face the British in a head-on engagement. But perhaps, Lord Stirling felt, his orders to harass the enemy could now be accomplished with more vigor.

In Derby, Gen. Howe also faced a decision. His scouts and spy network had followed

Lord Stirling's movements, and he was aware that his force outnumbered the Continentals at Radnor. But, as at Whitemarsh, he was not tempted to engage. In what was becoming a pattern, he kept his troops close to his threshers and cattle drivers until it became clear to Washington that the British had no intention of moving on Valley Forge. Howe's inaction opened another opportunity. With so many Crown troops tied up gathering provisions, large swaths of the countryside to the north of Philadelphia had been left unattended. Lord Stirling sent riders to Valley Forge with instructions to return with as many wagons as possible. He then dispatched his own foraging parties. In exchange for Continental certificates of seizure, these men gathered a fair amount of cattle and sheep as well as several carts of clothing, blankets, and even baskets of dried persimmons.

Clothes, meat, and fruit — Washington was delighted. Only that morning he had informed Henry Laurens that his commissaries contained "not a single hoof of any kind to slaughter and not more than 25 barls of flour." Despite the unexpected bounty, he continued to remain wary of Howe's intentions, and dashed off a note to Lord Stirling reminding him that his paramount assignment was to continue to track the British movements. It was sage advice, for Howe, even as his force denuded the fields around

Derby, ordered a regiment on an all-night quick march to within seven miles of Radnor. It was only a feint, but it was timed perfectly. When farmers in the area were spooked by the sounds of a vicious thunderstorm they mistook for cannon fire, they panicked. Rumors rapidly spread that Crown forces were marching on their farmsteads. Within hours the farmers sent a procession of over-stuffed wagons streaming toward Philadelphia on the justification that it was better to receive seven shillings for a pound of butter or 16 shillings for a bushel of potatoes than to allow the Crown forces to descend on their larders like locusts.

The thin line of Pennsylvania militiamen who had not joined Gen. Lord Stirling had little hope of stemming this tide. And even after Washington's intelligence officers reported that the British stab toward Radnor was merely a ruse to inspire exactly the hysteria that ensued, it was too late to halt the civilian stampede. Oddly enough, the anxious farmers' parade of provisions heading toward the city produced an unexpected boon for the Continentals. With so much traffic on the roads, Armstrong's men were able to confiscate substantial amounts of goods that would have typically slipped by them.

As reports detailing these events trickled into Valley Forge, Washington absorbed each new development with an equanimity that his aides considered conspicuous even for their unflappable commander in chief. What they did not know was that from the moment he had discerned that the enemy intended no assault on his encampment, the seeds for another grand offensive were germinating in his mind.

It is difficult to overestimate the impact the previous year's Christmas raid on Trenton had on the psyche and morale of the Continental Army and its commander in chief. Certainly what Washington termed the "victorious defeats" across the intervening 12 months — at Brandywine, at Germantown, at Fort Mifflin and Fort Mercer — could not dull the luster of that marvelous memory. Nor was it lost on Washington that the most glorious celebration of the anniversary would be to stage a replication. As his long-time aide Tench Tilghman wrote to Lord Stirling, "I wish we could put [the British] in mind . . . of what happened this time twelvemonth." Given the insouciance with which Howe's troops were ransacking Philadelphia's inner suburban belt, the idea that another surprise attack was beginning to cohere in Washington's mind is far from remarkable.

Washington intended to begin the engagement with a ruse of his own. On Christmas Eve, Lord Stirling's and Dan Morgan's combined forces, already in the area, would fall on the left flank of the British column at Derby as if they were the point movement of a major assault. Washington assumed that Gen. Howe would naturally attempt to quick-time the bulk of his force back to Philadelphia while leaving several detachments, most likely his light horse, to screen his retreat as well as cover the Schuylkill's northern fords. Then, while the 6,000 Crown troops who remained in Philadelphia under the command of the Hessian general von Knyphausen rushed to cover Howe's fallback, a Continental shock corps of some 4,000 men advancing in two columns — between 50 and 60 men and eight officers drawn from each regiment — would dash to capture the British ramparts north of the city. Once these battlements were taken, the right column of Americans would rush south along the Schuylkill to seize the four ferry crossings and destroy any temporary bridges, stranding Howe's rump army on the west bank of the river and cutting him off from von Knyphausen.

The left wing of the shock corps, meanwhile, would penetrate Philadelphia proper, free the American prisoners of war, and demand von Knyphausen's surrender "under promise of good Quarter in case of compliance, and no Quarter if opposition is given." As Continental artillerymen turned the captured British cannons on any of His Majesty's ships berthed in the harbor, Gen.

Armstrong's Pennsylvania militiamen would recross the Schuylkill to the west, join Gen. Smallwood's regulars rushing up from Wilmington, and reinforce Lord Stirling's attack. Howe and his troops, their backs to the Schuylkill, would be left with no choice but to surrender or be swept into the river.

Even if Washington viewed the battle plan as "a work which depends more upon secrecy and dispatch than Numbers," it nonetheless flew in the face of a hard-and-fast military dictate of the era — that is, an attacking force should always be at least double the size of the defenders. Moreover, the daunting metrics only complicated the scheme. A victorious outcome, after all, hung not only on Washington's correct reading of Howe's tactical thinking, but upon several and various moving parts all working in conjunction — a set of tumblers clicking into place and locking the Continental Army into a commitment that might well end the war, or destroy the revolution. Washington did not need to be reminded that his strategy at Germantown had relied upon similar intricacies of balance and symmetry. Such was the agenda's mutability that the commander in chief eschewed his customary habit of convening a war council. Instead he decided to put out feelers to a small coterie of confidants via one of his most trusted advisers, Gen. Sullivan, who was presently overseeing the construction of a bridge to span the Schuylkill on the northern outskirts of the Valley Forge encampment.

When Sullivan arrived at Washington's headquarters tent the commander in chief laid out his proposed operation, which included Sullivan commanding the right wing of the shock corps. He then asked Sullivan to circulate through camp and gather feedback from a select few of his fellow general officers. In the meantime, Washington also shared his thoughts with Gen. Lord Stirling. Since Lord Stirling would be the sacrificial lamb in the attack, Washington felt he was owed an explanation. Finally, he conferred with Gen. Knox, whose artillery would be the key to the assault on the city's northern bastions; Washington had to be certain that his guns were fit to take the field. Knox told him that the cannons could indeed be prepared for immediate transport. But he expressed his doubts that the troops were in similar readiness.

Within hours Sullivan returned with correspondingly tepid reactions. Several of the generals cautioned that only if the British were to move on Valley Forge would such a major battle be worth the risk. Others preferred bypassing Philadelphia altogether and instead concentrating an all-out assault on Howe's right flank, not only to sever the Redcoats' escape route across the Schuylkill, but also to block any reinforcements pouring out of the city. General Greene's thoughts were perhaps the most frank. He well knew the near-messianic fervor with which Washington sought to drive the British from Philadelphia, no matter how well hidden behind a facade of executive sobriety. But he reminded Washington that only a month earlier, while chasing Cornwallis across New Jersey, he had counseled the commander in chief about the danger of "consulting our wishes rather than our reason."

If anything, Sullivan's synopsis of the numerous opinions was personally heartening to Washington, although professionally dismaying. Washington's general officers were willing to follow him onto any field of battle, even to Derby, with ragged, hungry, and outgunned troops, to attack a strong British contingent. But few could muster much enthusiasm for the action. Even Lord Stirling, as prickly as a Highlands thistle, was skeptical if willing.

In the end, Washington heeded their advice and decided to stand down. It was indeed, as his biographer Chernow put it, "sometimes better to miss a major opportunity than barge into a costly error." Yet the dearth of documentation regarding this Christmas Eve attack makes it difficult to discern just how serious the commander in chief was about the proposal. Some historians argue that Washington, his naturally aggressive temperament at odds with his adopted Fabian strategy, viewed the Continental Army as in such dire straits that he was willing to risk its survival on long odds rather than see the force disintegrate from a lack of food and supplies. Others, more conspiracy-minded, suggest that he viewed an attack on Philadelphia as an ultimate make-or-break political moment. The enemy's presence in America's capital city was an affront to his own personal honor and reputation, and an assault would result in either a stunning victory or a catastrophic defeat that would shock the Continental Congress into finally recognizing his army's acute distress. Still others, such as the usually sobersided historian Wayne Bodle, wonder if the "sugar-plum reveries" of Washington's battle plan were an outgrowth of nostalgia for the glories of Trenton enhanced by "a holiday induced overindulgence in hemp or Madeira at Headquarters." For the record, there is no indication that marijuana had filtered into the winter cantonment.

As the aborted project disappeared into the churn of history, a heavy snow began to blanket Valley Forge. It would continue for three days, the worst blizzard of the season thus far. It was during this Christmas whiteout that Washington transferred his headquarters to a small fieldstone cottage hard by the confluence of the Schuylkill and Valley

Creek.* Known as the Isaac Potts House, or Potts House, the dwelling belonged to the eponymous Quaker whose family's gristmill and ironworks had been destroyed by the British two months earlier. Potts had rented the two-story structure to his late brother's wife, to whom Washington paid 100 pounds in Pennsylvania currency for her inconvenience while she left to live with her brother-in-law. The structure consisted of two ground-floor rooms, three upstairs bedrooms, a detached kitchen, and a rough basement and attic. While his personal guard began construction of their own cabins close by, Washington, his staff, and their servants moved in. On any given day, 18 to 25 people were squeezed into the cramped, musty quarters that for the next six months would serve as the de facto capital of the United States.

Meanwhile, on the afternoon of December 25 the troops of the Continental Army filed from their half-built huts and tattered tents like weakened animals emerging from their burrows. Many with their feet wrapped in rags, they hunched past barefoot sentries

* Though Washington's pledge to live in his tent until all huts were completed was sincere, he soon discovered that operating from a crowded "marquee" was not the most efficient way for a commander in chief to conduct operations.

standing on their hats to receive a Christmas dinner of burned mutton and watery grog. The scrappy holiday meal was courtesy of a small flock of sheep Gen. Lord Stirling's foragers had delivered to camp. It had been the standard practice of the commander in chief to order a gill of rum distributed to each soldier on special occasions. On this holiday Washington's commissary officers used the last of it to mix the grog.

Washington spent the evening picking over a small meal of mutton, veal, potatoes, and cabbage with several officers and aides, including John Laurens and Lafayette. The latter, "adapted to privation and fatigue," remarked in his memoirs on the "simple, frugal, and austere" repast. There was no Madeira, much less hemp.

That night a Continental soldier from Connecticut's 7th Regiment known to posterity only as Jethro was found dead in his tent. His skin was as cold as the dirt floor on which he lay, and a crude autopsy attributed his death to a combination of malnutrition and exposure. This was the initial fatality recorded on the rolls at Valley Forge. It would be but the first of many such shrieks from Casca's bird of night to echo through the winter encampment. That Jethro was one of the hundreds of freed black men at Valley Forge who had enlisted to fight for the cause of American liberty injects an even more tragic note.

FOURTEEN:
STARVE, DISSOLVE, OR DISPERSE

Three days earlier, toward the end of the morning when Washington dispatched skirmishers from Valley Forge to harass Gen. Howe's foragers, the commander in chief had received a letter from Henry Laurens. The president of the Continental Congress informed him that Congress retained serious reservations regarding the advisability of the Continental Army establishing a winter cantonment. The delegates were still in fact debating whether the troops should remain in the field across the coming months for one last "vigorous effort" at dislodging the British from Philadelphia. Washington was astounded and angry. He considered the matter of a winter camp at Valley Forge settled. And after conferring with his generals about a surprise Christmas assault on Philadelphia, he by now nourished no delusions that the emaciated condition of his soldiery would allow for the large offensive the delegates were suggesting.

As it happened, before receiving Laurens's

letter, Washington had been composing his own dispatch to Congress. In it he again called attention to the dismal conditions under which his troops were being asked to survive. He seemed to sense that the British expedition just kicked off to his south afforded him leverage over the recalcitrant civil authorities who, in his view, had failed so miserably in supporting and sustaining his troops. Ever since the victories at Trenton and Princeton, Washington felt as if he were fighting on two fronts — a straightforward military exercise opposing Crown forces and a bureaucratic rearguard action against his own civilian government. Now, if Howe did decide to attack Valley Forge — in the early morning hours of December 22 this was still very much a possibility from Washington's perspective — his starving and half-clothed force was in grave peril.

After reading Henry Laurens's missive, Washington added a resoundingly testy postscript to his own communiqué, expressing his "infinite pain and concern." He prefaced this with a sincere statement that he was in no way exaggerating the crisis at Valley Forge. He then wrote, "Unless more Vigorous exertions and better regulations take place in that [supply] line, and immediately, this Army must dissolve. I have done all in my power by remonstrating, by writing to, by ordering the Commissaries on this Head . . . but without any good effect, or obtaining more than scanty relief." He added that he took personal responsibility for the decision, now firmly made, to stake winter camp at Valley Forge. Finally, as in his earlier letter to Congress regarding Lafayette's status, he turned to sarcasm to answer the statesmen's primary questions about his defensive plans for the Middle Atlantic area.

"It would give me infinite pleasure to afford protection to every individual Spot of Ground in the whole of the United States," he wrote. "Nothing is more my wish. But this is not possible with our present force." Then, as if to twist the rhetorical knife, he referred specifically to congressional queries regarding the defense of New Jersey. He was, he wrote, "most sensible to her sufferings" if, alas, completely powerless to ease them. By the next morning Washington was still chafing as he dictated an even more contentious letter to Henry Laurens and Congress, doubling down on the threat of the army's dissolution. This missive was destined to become one of the most famous communiqués in American history. It is worth quoting at length.

Washington opened this second dispatch with a blunt formulation: the ad hoc system in place for supplying his troops was simply not working. Now, more than ever, the British movement into Derby afforded "fresh and more powerful reasons" to effect an "immediate capital change" in the system of feeding and clothing his army. When he learned that Howe had taken the field with 8,000 men, he continued, "I order'd the Troops to be in rediness [for an attack] but behold! to my great mortification, I was not only informed, but convinced, that the Men were unable to stir on Acct. of Provision. All I could do under these circumstances was, to send out a few light Parties to watch and harrass the Enemy." His troops, he repeated, were immobilized because of a lack of supplies for which the United States' civilian authorities bore complete responsibility.

More personally, he argued that by not fulfilling its promises to adequately feed and clothe his soldiers, Congress had tarnished his good name and reputation. No man, he wrote, "ever had his measure more impeded than I have, by every department in the Army. Finding that the inactivity of the Army, whether for want of provisions, Cloaths, or other essentials, is charged to my Acct., not only by the common vulgar, but by Those in power, it is time to speak plain in exculpation of myself."

His biting scorn was remarkable; he rarely displayed such withering derision in public. Then he went further, specifically addressing the members of Pennsylvania's state legislature who, he charged, expected him to defend their rights and property without themselves making the requisite sacrifices. "I can assure those Gentlemen that it is a much easier and a less distressing thing to draw remonstrances in a comfortable room by a good fire side, than to occupy a cold bleak hill, and sleep under frost and Snow with no Cloaths, or Blankets." He even resorted to stark exaggeration, transforming what had been warnings from his regimental commanders about grumbling among the troops into the specter of a "dangerous mutiny." One such uprising, he wrote, had occurred just the previous evening, and had been put down only with the "spirited exertion" of himself and his officers.

With an oratorical flourish Washington had succeeded in composing a symphony of destitution in which his hungry and barefoot patriots were reduced to insubordination by the feckless actions of comfortable civilians in the rear.

As the dispatch continued, Washington's ire cooled. He again listed his suggested changes, paramount among them a comprehensive reorganization of the military supply system. Perhaps no single piece of business was more crucial to the commander in chief's plans than the appointment of a competent quartermaster general. The post was the financial fulcrum from which nearly every department of the Continental Army was supported, including the procurement and delivery of provisions and the collection of forage. The idea of contemplating future campaigns without such a powerful lever was unthinkable.

General Mifflin, citing illness, had resigned from his post as quartermaster general six weeks earlier. Most assumed he left in a fit of pique over not being assigned a frontline command. His subsequent congressional election to the Board of War was viewed as a way of mollifying him. Given the circumstances, Mifflin's former position was in truth a thankless job, and to fill the vacated spot Washington stressed his need for an officer with battlefield service who would be granted the authority to take a sword to the department's congealed bureaucracy. That man would in turn have to be buttressed by a civil authority with the power to fulfill his needs. No longer could Congress and the Pennsylvania state officials be allowed to slough off responsibility onto each other for supply-line failures. Then, as if sensing he had the politicians precisely tuned, Washington played his final, searing chord.

He wrote that he was now convinced "beyond a doubt" that unless Congress quickly complied with his requests, "unless some great and capital change suddenly takes place in that [supply] line, this Army must inevitably be reduced to one or other of these things. Starve, dissolve, or disperse, in order to obtain subsistence in the best manner they can."

Starve, dissolve, or disperse. It was the gauntlet thrown. At worst it hinted at the elimination and possibly even the surrender of the Continental Army and thus the end of the war against the British across the middle states. At best it evoked visions of armed and desperate men roaming the Pennsylvania countryside singly and in feral packs, scavenging by any means or manner for food and clothing. It was not difficult for the statesmen to imagine these troops eventually overrunning and tearing into the American storehouses in Reading and Easton, in Lancaster and York. It was precisely the image Washington meant to convey.

George Washington's "starve, dissolve, or disperse" letter left America's civilian authorities with little choice. They could accede to the commander in chief's demands that they immediately reconstruct his army's supply chain under the supervision of a competent military officer. Or they could allow the revolution to teeter on the brink. It was a stark option. But was it all a masterful bluff?

Regarding the issue of starvation, it was true that there were technically no cattle in camp at the time of Washington's writing on December 23. His commissary officers also reported fewer than 30 barrels of flour on hand, a situation which accounted for the handpicked skirmishers detached to Gen. Lord Stirling the previous day with little or no rations. Yet by that same morning Washington had already received word from Radnor, just 10 miles away, that foraged provisions including mutton and beef were on the way to Valley Forge. In addition, dispatch riders from Gen. Armstrong east of the Schuylkill had reported that Armstrong's militiamen had taken advantage of the British absence to round up another 200 head of cattle that were at present being driven to the winter camp.

In truth, there had been no "dangerous mutiny" the previous evening, merely the muttering and bickering of weary soldiers. Washington's subordinates were certainly voicing genuine concern in their reports of the troops' low morale. Yet he recognized that such grumbling was inherent to battlefield camps since time immemorial. As for the prospect of Gen. Howe's 8,000-man force marching on Valley Forge, it was likely that by the time Washington sent his mail rider galloping off to York with his second dispatch of December 23, his forward scouts and pickets had informed him that the British movement appeared to constitute no more than a very large forage thrust. Once more the reluctance of Gen. Howe to engage the Continentals in any meaningful way had proved one of the Americans' few advantages.

But the strongest indication that Washington's fiery words were designed to further his political agenda was the fact that at the same time he was writing to Henry Laurens he was also consulting with his generals about attacking Philadelphia. How could an all-out assault on the enemy stronghold possibly square with the bone-weary pittance of an army he had just described to Congress? Of course, Washington recognized that with no politician present on the cold and dreary front lines, there was no civil authority to refute his critical depiction. In the end, as was his wont, the master strategist had left the delegates a way to save face. In his "starve, dissolve, or disperse" letter, he also suggested to Congress that a face-to-face meeting with a committee of delegates might resolve their disputes. As there was no way he could leave his troops and journey to York, the committee would have to come to Valley Forge.

As the commander in chief awaited Congress's reply, some 20 miles to the south his tired, hungry scouts could only watch through the gathering snow as Howe's expedition marched back across the Schuylkill's pontoon bridge and reentered Philadelphia. The British carried with them over 200 tons of horse fodder and carts piled high with plundered furniture, and drove before them several hundred head of cattle and sheep earmarked for Crown commissaries. More dispiriting was the sight of the 40 or so American prisoners hobbling along in the herd's wake, their weakened condition enough to make John Laurens "weep tears of blood." The fact that the British teamsters had baled and packed the hay before it was completely dry, rendering most of it useless, provided small solace.

Nonetheless, with an otherwise well-provisioned enemy presumably settled into the city for the winter, Washington recalled Gen. Lord Stirling and his troops to Valley Forge. Any large military encounters had to be tabled for the moment. Not so his political battles. They were only just beginning.

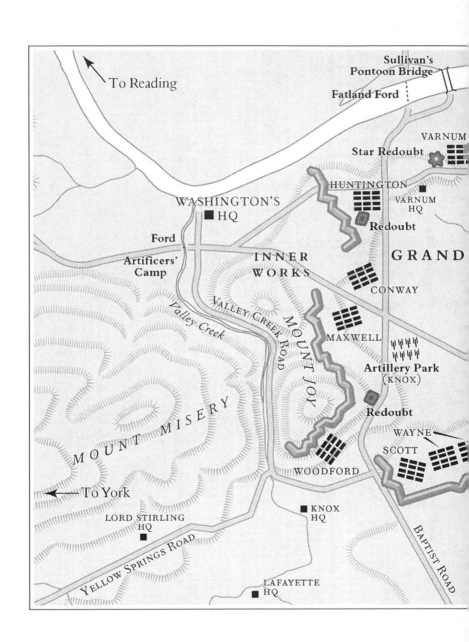

To Reading

Sullivan's
Pontoon Bridge

Fatland Ford

VARNUM

Star Redoubt

HUNTINGTON

VARNUM
HQ

WASHINGTON'S
HQ

Redoubt

GRAND

Ford

Artificers'
Camp

INNER
WORKS

CONWAY

Valley Creek

VALLEY CREEK ROAD

MAXWELL

Artillery Park
(KNOX)

MOUNT JOY

Redoubt

MOUNT MISERY

WAYNE

SCOTT

WOODFORD

To York

KNOX
HQ

LORD STIRLING
HQ

BAPTIST ROAD

YELLOW SPRINGS ROAD

LAFAYETTE
HQ

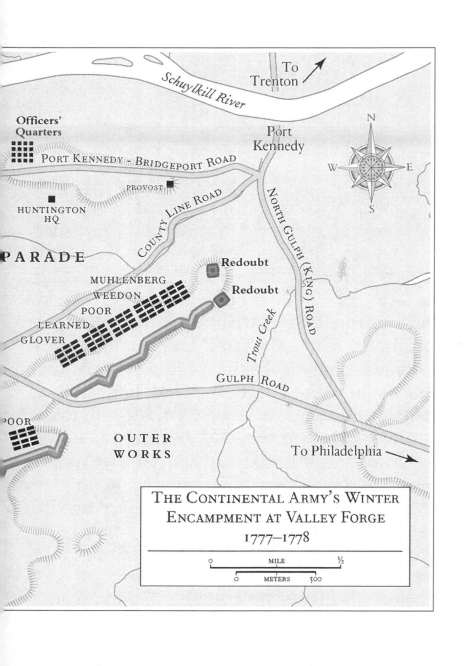

THE CONTINENTAL ARMY'S WINTER
ENCAMPMENT AT VALLEY FORGE
1777–1778

FIFTEEN:
THE BEST ANSWER
TO CALUMNY

By this point in the war the commander in chief was no stranger to bureaucratic fisticuffs, and he seemed to take an odd pleasure in what his Irish troopers would call a nasty hooley. A year earlier, for instance, following the string of Continental defeats in New York, Washington had instructed his second in command Gen. Charles Lee to lead two brigades from Peekskill, New York, to join him in his flight across New Jersey. Lee hesitated. Lee may have been, in Washington's words, "fickle and violent," but he was nothing if not shrewd. Lee had sensed that Washington's reputation was crumbling in the aftermath of the British victories across the state from Long Island to Manhattan to Westchester County. His plan was to become the default replacement when the civil authorities finally recognized the Virginia planter's inadequacies. In 1775, the First Continental Congress had been hesitant to hand a foreign-born officer such as Lee or Horatio

Gates complete command of its military. But after the failed New York campaign, Lee wagered that the country's desperate straits would alter that approach. He had never been burdened by either humility or introspection.

At 46, Lee was a gifted linguist who spoke six languages and consumed the classics in the original Greek and Latin. Though short and lamppost lean — a bantam figure with a restless demeanor and a discursive speaking style that lent him the aura of a davening rabbi — Lee's ravenous ego compensated for his physical deficiencies. As a young lieutenant stationed in North America during the French and Indian War with Gen. Braddock — a body of infantry that included fellow junior officers George Washington and Horatio Gates — he had entered into a "marriage" with the daughter of a Seneca war chief, a rather bizarre arrangement for a man whose racist screeds against the Irish were legendary. His bewildered new father-in-law, playing on Lee's choleric nature, bestowed on him the Iroquoian name "Boiling Water," and Lee himself admitted that he suffered from "a distemper of mind." However, he also had a windfall inheritance from his late father, allowing his "distemper" to not hinder his rise through the British army's ranks. Severely wounded at the Battle of Fort Ticonderoga in 1758 — he directed such a steady stream of invective at the attending physician that the doctor later tried to kill him — he secured his military reputation four years later in Portugal, routing a far superior Spanish force during a daring night raid.

Following the Peace of Paris in 1763, Lee's regiment was disbanded and, sidelined with a major's half pay, he resigned his commission. He was rescued from a life of roaming London's gambling halls by King Stanislaw II of Poland, who employed him as an aide-de-camp and promoted him to the ceremonial rank of major general. He later saw action as a British observer attached to the Russian army during the czar's war against the Turks and, sensing greater opportunities in the American colonies, in 1773 he purchased an estate near the home of his old friend Gates in what is now West Virginia. Two years later, with the outbreak of revolution, he volunteered his services to the First Continental Congress.

Lee raged at being passed over for the post of commander in chief. His indignity was assuaged only by his certainty that the delegates would eventually see the error of opting for an upstart provincial over a seasoned professional soldier. In the meantime, his scorn for Washington did not prevent him from grudgingly accepting the position of Washington's second in command. Though Lee's overweening self-regard, turbulent personality, and bouts of paranoia led some in Washington's circle to consider him mad, his military expertise were never questioned. Even the debilitating attacks of gout that sometimes forced him to be carried into battle on a litter were viewed as a badge of martial discipline.

Washington had always considered himself an adept reader of men. Why he remained blind for so long to Lee's dangerous ambition remains something of a mystery. He welcomed Lee as a war counselor and even renamed Fort Constitution on the New Jersey side of the Hudson in Lee's honor after dispatching him from Boston to oversee the construction of New York City's defensive works. Perhaps it was Lee's cosmopolitanism that clouded an insecure commander in chief's judgment. If so, Washington was not alone. Congress soon tapped Lee to take command of the Southern Military Department where, in June 1776, he was lauded for the breathtaking victory over a British fleet at the Battle of Sullivan's Island in Charleston Harbor.* His adventures in the south earned him a recall to New York as well as accolades

---

* Most historians have since concluded that despite loudly taking credit for the fight, Lee had little impact on the Continental victory, and even less to do with the subsequent triumphant defense of Fort Moultrie, located on Sullivan's Island, when the British counterattacked.

in and outside the army — including a $30,000 bonus from an adoring Continental Congress whose delegates Lee privately likened to a herd of cattle. When Washington's fortunes ebbed following his failure to defend New York City, there were factions among the Continental Army's officer corps who viewed Lee's ascension to the top post as the last best hope for the military's survival.

Late in 1776, as Washington fought his rear-guard action across 100 miles of New Jersey's cold, muddy plains and hills, he grew increasingly impatient over Lee's whereabouts. He had no idea that the general was purposely stalling as he conspired with members of Congress and several likeminded officers to wrest command from Washington. It was during this retreat that Washington had been betrayed by his original military secretary Joseph Reed. Reed had slipped a private note into the mail satchel that carried Lee's orders to move south from Peekskill. In it he accused Washington of "fatal indecision" during the New York campaign, and proposed that Lee approach Congress with a strategy to re-form the Continental Army with Lee at its head. Incredibly and quite imprudently, Lee not only gave an affirmative response, but shared with Reed his plan to disobey his marching orders.

That November, Reed was on a field assignment when Lee's communiqué reached

Washington's headquarters in New Brunswick, New Jersey. The anxious commander, seeing that it was from Lee, opened the letter and discovered Reed's and Lee's perfidy. Reed offered to resign when confronted with the proof, but Washington demurred. Their relationship, however, was never the same. For Lee's part, Washington did not let on that he had seen the correspondence; he merely reiterated his order that Lee lead his 3,000 troops into New Jersey, ford the Delaware north of Trenton, and unite with him in Pennsylvania. When Lee finally crossed the Hudson he informed Washington, in a startling act of insubordination, that he believed his force would be more effective harrying the enemy's flanks and rear. Privately, he wanted nothing to do with what he saw as Washington's inevitable defeat.

By mid-December, Lee was still dallying close to the British lines in northern New Jersey when he visited a local inn. There remains some question as to whether the establishment also constituted, in the era's euphemism, a romp through Cupid's grove. A commander's venturing to a brothel so near enemy territory was unsound policy, if not hubristic lunacy. Sure enough, that night a local Tory informed a patrol of British dragoons of Lee's whereabouts. Early on December 13, 1776, 70 horsemen led by Col. Banastre Tarleton, notorious for his brutality toward the rebels, surrounded the tavern. They easily routed Lee's small guard and captured the general in his slippers and nightshirt. A Hessian trumpeter sounded a mocking *trombatensto* to mark the occasion. Lee was also taken with a letter addressed to Gen. Gates in which he maligned Washington's military judgment as "damnably deficient." The irony was lost on the British, and Lee spent the next 16 months under loose and luxe guard importuning the man he had tried to supplant to send him his horses, his hunting shirt and rifle, and his beloved hounds.

The British, who viewed Lee much as he saw himself, were ecstatic over his capture. Tarleton and his company were feted by a regimental band concert and toasted with copious rounds of spirits, some of which they apparently used to inebriate Lee's horse. Conversely — as the historian John Buchanan notes — when the news of Lee's capture spread through the Continental Army, "consternation swept the rebel ranks." The exception was Washington. Upon receiving the "melancholy intelligence" two days later, he wrote a terse note to John Hancock "sincerely regret[ting] Genl Lee's unhappy fate." Though his compassion was no doubt sincere, one senses that he was also relieved at no longer having to parry with his barmy and scheming number two.

It was during the Continental Army's plodding march through New Jersey in late 1776 that Thomas Paine, accompanying the troops, published another pamphlet, entitled *The Crisis*. In *Common Sense*, Paine's incessant hectoring of George III as "The Royal Brute of Great Britain" shattered the king's image as a benign monarch manipulated by Parliament into burdening the colonists with onerous taxes. *Common Sense* had been a key factor in turning American public opinion against the Crown.* In *The Crisis* — whose 13 chapters were dedicated to the 13 colonies — Paine composed a paean to the Continental soldier's fortitude under duress. The tract contained Paine's most famous lines: "These are the times that try men's souls. The summer soldier and the sunshine patriot will, in this crisis, shrink from the service of their country; but he that stands by it now deserves the love and thanks of man and woman."

Washington befriended Paine along the trek, and by the time he led his 3,000 or so shivering troops across an ice-strewn bend in the Delaware into Pennsylvania's Bucks County, he had ordered copies of *The Crisis* distributed to company commanders to be

* Such was Paine's mastery of propaganda that he had in fact managed to transform an amiable and befuddled old "farmer king" most comfortable ambling through his fields into an ogre of tyranny.

read aloud to the soldiers huddled about their campfires. Days later, his force now swollen to some 5,000 troops with the addition of Pennsylvania and Delaware militiamen, the Continental Army recrossed the Delaware and captured Trenton. As it would turn out, Washington's laconic handling of the Charles Lee affair provided the template with which he would address future political struggles.

The paucity of food and clothing was not the only burden that Washington bore as he braced for the hard winter of 1778. By New Year's Day, with the raising of the log huts soon to be completed and no major military engagements on the horizon — combat in the world's northern climes was at that time generally an eight-month-a-year proposition — there was only so much work to conjure to keep his men busy. As a result, a dispiriting boredom began to pervade the entire parenthesis-shaped line buffering Philadelphia from Trenton in the north to Wilmington in the south. This was particularly true in the thick center of the crescent at Valley Forge.

Washington tried his utmost to assign tasks to his troops. Scouts regularly patrolled the roads leading to Philadelphia to interdict smugglers and gather intelligence on enemy movements. Select senior officers were instructed to begin the planning for next spring's campaign. And the work of compiling the reports the commander in chief intended to present to the congressional delegation soon to arrive from York proceeded apace. But as the lack of purposefulness hung more heavily over the camp, Valley Forge twitched with feuds and frictions great and small — a reminder, Washington's biographer Joseph Ellis notes, "of an earlier era's conviction that character was not just who you were but also what others thought you were."

From his days captaining the Virginia Blues, Washington was accustomed to attending to the minutiae of military matters. He now found himself adjudicating squabbles between junior officers protesting the promotions of their peers, company commanders disputing each other's jurisdictions, and a long line of officers demanding courts-martial to answer vague rumors of their battlefield cowardice or negligence. Scores of officers resigned their commissions, and hundreds more threatened to do so. Although technically against army regulations, duels over real and perceived slights were fought so often that John Adams complained to his wife that Washington's soldiery had devolved into "quarreling . . . Cats and Dogs worry[ing] one another like Mastiffs . . . Scrambling for Rank and Pay." The discord was not limited to the lower rungs of the officer corps.

In one case, Washington was forced to rule on what he considered an unseemly grab for the spoils taken from the British brig HMS *Symmetry,* which in late December had run aground near Wilmington and been captured by Gen. Smallwood. Smallwood's detachment claimed a proprietary interest in the shirts, shoes, bolts of cloth, and kegs of rum discovered in the vessel's hold. Several general officers at Valley Forge challenged this, claiming that their own superior rank entitled them to a share of the bounty. Washington ultimately ordered the goods transferred to the winter cantonment while burdening Smallwood's command with housing and feeding the 80-odd British prisoners, including several officers' wives. This opened what would become a long-standing gash in the relationship between the two men.* In another instance, Washington was petitioned by a group of regimental commanders objecting to the lack of beer, cider, or rum in their daily rations. He had to remind them that their troops faced the same, if not worse, privations. It is not recorded whether Washington watched with a ravening eye when he later ordered the captured kegs of spirits tapped. Each noncommissioned officer and enlisted man was issued a gill of the hard

---

* Smallwood's attempt at a reconciliation with his commander in chief was dashed when Washington coolly rebuffed his truce offering of a matched pistol set taken from the brig.

liquor while the officers received none.

These shallow if virulent intramural annoyances boiled over in late December when word reached Valley Forge that Congress had bypassed its own commander in chief's universal military authority and named Thomas Conway, an Irish-born former colonel in the French army, to the heretofore nonexistent post of inspector general. Gifted with a silver tongue and, per his portraits, a visage resembling a clenched fist, Conway had arrived in America six months earlier bearing a brigadier's commission from Silas Deane. At 42, Conway had fought with competence at Brandywine, but was accused of abandoning his brigade at Germantown as it broke against the enemy's left flank. He had also made no secret of his contempt for America's provincial army officers nor, as an avowed fortune hunter, of his desire to ride the tailwind of America's revolution into a more lucrative posting upon his return to the French army.

Conway haunted the halls of Congress during his serial visits to York in the aftermath of Germantown and insinuated himself into the delegates' graces via, among various patrons, the Board of War's Gen. Mifflin. It helped that the awestruck statesmen, desperate for any positive military tidings, were susceptible to what John Laurens labeled Conway's "preposterous panegyricks of himself." Alexander Hamilton, less florid, settled for "the vain boasting of foreign pretenders." In addition to being a braggart, Conway was also a whiner. When he learned that a fellow French brigadier had been promoted to major general, he threatened to resign and return home unless offered the same rank. In response, Gen. Mifflin advocated the creation of the post of inspector general, which carried with it the promotion Conway desired. As news of the foreigner's elevation spread through the winter cantonment, Washington's squabbling collection of more experienced and longer-serving brigadiers revolted.

John Laurens was one of the first to sense the dissident stirrings. "The promotion of Gen. Conway has given almost universal disgust," he informed his father: "His military knowledge and experience may fit him for the office of inspector general, but the right of seniority violated, without any remarkable services done to justify it, has given a deep wound to the line of brigadiers." By this time the young Laurens had become an unofficial back channel from which Henry Laurens could take the pulse of the army, and he cautioned his father to expect further tumult. It was a warning borne out when Nathanael Greene wrote to Congress protesting Conway's advancement and nine other brigadiers — including Henry Knox, Enoch Poor, and

Jedediah Huntington — signed a petition complaining of the irregular nature of an appointment that Hamilton described as "most whimsical favoritism." The entire misadventure was indicative of the broken connection between America's civil authorities and its military.

On the whole, the Continental Army's officer corps was a self-doubting class, their temperamental insecurities heightened in relation to rank. Unlike their European counterparts — whose birthrights, wealth, and even coats of arms often trumped merit — America lacked a stratum of nobility. As a result, American military officers valued their honor above all else, often including property, wives, and family. The concepts of reputation, prestige, and rank were virtually inseparable, with rank being the "only honourable badge of distinction" separating them from mere commoners. In Conway, these men now found themselves subordinate to a condescending soldier of fortune whose ascension had overstepped the bounds of military protocol. As John Laurens added in his letter to his father, Conway's promotion had united the officers in camp in a "universal anger" that had "convulsed the army."

Washington's attachment to the principle of military subordination to civil authority was strong. He nonetheless recognized a snub when he saw one. He had allowed his nine generals to submit their letter of indignation through his office, demonstrating at least a tacit approval of its contents. Though he filed no formal protest of his own — and even went so far as to falsely assure Conway that his appointment "has not given the least uneasiness to any Officer" — he shared his true feelings about the usurpation of his power in a letter to the Virginia congressman Richard Henry Lee. "If there is any truth in a report which has been handed to me, that Congress hath appointed . . . Brigadier Conway a Major General in this Army, it will be as unfortunate a measure as ever was adopted. General Conway's merit, then, as an Officer, and his importance to this Army, exists more in his own imagination, than in reality."

Washington also made it known to Conway and Gen. Gates that he was aware of a letter to the latter in which Conway impugned the commander in chief and his senior staff as "a weak General and bad Counsellors." The snide remark about Washington's inner circle is what undoubtedly set Hamilton off on a tirade like Laurens's. He wrote to his friend George Clinton, the governor of New York, decrying Conway's "impudent importunity," calling him "a monster," "vermin bred in the entrails of this chimera dire," and, finally, "a villainous calumniator and incendiary." Compared with Hamilton's diatribe, Washington's assessment of Conway as a "bad scribe" seems almost quaint.

Much as with his deft handling of Gen. Lee, Washington found a pretext for simply refusing to recognize Conway's appointment when the new inspector general arrived at Valley Forge on December 29. He could not officially acknowledge Conway's authority, he said, until the Board of War notified him of it in writing. That such a communiqué was, for reasons lost to history, never forthcoming did not prevent Conway from attempting to exercise the prerogatives of his new office. On New Year's Eve he had delivered to the Potts House a letter demanding that a detachment of mid-level officers, sergeants, and corporals be culled from each regiment and placed under his command. These troops were to be drilled in maneuvers that they would then use to instruct the rest of the army. Conway boasted that he had personally witnessed successful European armies train in this manner. Washington refused to even respond, and instead referred Conway's letter to Congress, again citing the official silence from the Board of War regarding the general's authority.

Conway spent the next week stewing over the cool reception he had received at Valley Forge. He finally penned another letter to Washington, accusing him of acting like an "absolute King." As if addressing an unschooled bumpkin, he wrote that if Washington's thin skin had been bruised over the disparaging remarks in his correspondence with Gen. Gates, well, that too followed the sophisticated Old World manner of European officers freely critiquing their superiors. He ended the dispatch with an ultimatum. "I do not wish to Give you or any officer in the army the Least uneasiness," he wrote. "Since you will not accept of my services, since you can not bear the sight of me in your camp, I am very ready to goe Where ever Congress thinks proper and even to france. And I solemnly Declare that far from resenting the undeserv'd rebuke I met with from you, I shall Do everything in my power to serve this cause. These are the true sentiments with Which I remain sir your Excellency's Most obedt humble servant."

For several days Conway's challenge hung in the air like a mote of dust. Washington, checking his temper, sensed a trap and refused to be drawn into a political dispute with a man whose patronage was so powerfully proved. Finally, he effortlessly deflected the bluff by informing Conway, "It remains with Congress alone to accept your resignation." He surely took sly pleasure in adding that should the delegates indeed acquiesce in their new inspector general's fit of pique, "you will have my hopes for a favourable passage and a happy meeting with your Family

& Friends." As Washington expected, Congress refused to accept Conway's resignation.

Washington may have held his tongue at Conway's impudence, but the Irishman's patronizing words were more than his longtime aide Tench Tilghman could swallow. Tilghman surely spoke for Washington's inner circle when he wrote to Pennsylvania's Gen. John Cadwalader that Conway "has come down full of his own importance and wrote the General a letter for which he deserved to be kicked." Intimating a duel, John Laurens noted that had Conway condescended so to any officer other than the commander in chief of the Continental Army, the insult would have been "revenged in a private way."* Yet even as Conway continued to bombard Gen. Mifflin and congressional delegates with complaints about Washington's icy reception, Washington did not engage. As he would explain to the governor of New Jersey, William Livingston, "To persevere in one's duty, and be silent, is the best answer to calumny."

* As it happened, seven months later, on July 4, Cadwalader would severely wound Conway in a duel. After his bullet passed through Conway's mouth and neck, Cadwalader is said to have stood over the bleeding Irishman and remarked, "I have stopped that damned rascal's lying, anyway." (Chernow, *Alexander Hamilton,* p. 322.)

Shunned by nearly every officer at Valley Forge, Conway found himself operating in a sort of limbo and took to quartering himself and his staff some 20 miles north of the camp in the village of Pottsgrove. Washington, meanwhile, saw a more sinister hand than the bumptious Conway's driving the imbroglio. His suspicion fell on the generals Gates and Mifflin. The entire affair might have struck him as a plot device from Goldoni's slapstick *A Servant of Two Masters,* a version of which he had surely attended back in Virginia.

It had long chafed foreign-born officers such as Gates, Lee, and Conway that Washington's leadership style kept faith with a meritocracy that favored young, competent homegrown generals with little formal military education over so-called professional soldiers. That the likes of Nathanael Greene, Henry Knox, and Anthony Wayne had ascended to key positions in the Continental Army was seen as an insult to the established hierarchy. Foisting an auditor like Thomas Conway upon the commander in chief was one of the few means Gates had of putting Washington in his place. But Conway's promotion and appointment were only one front in a multifaceted assault.

Earlier that fall Congress had approved a long-debated plan to professionalize the

Board of War to more closely resemble Britain's War Office. No longer would rotating congressional delegates make up the committee; it would now consist of three permanent members and a clerical staff tasked with acting as sole intermediaries between Congress, state authorities, and the army. The board's original purview — compiling officer rolls; securing prisoners of war; and monitoring the movements of troops, arms, and equipment — was also expanded to include the supervision of recruiting operations and the oversight of arms production and procurement. General Mifflin, Adjutant Gen. Timothy Pickering of Massachusetts, and Washington's fellow Virginian and military secretary Robert Hanson Harrison were initially elected to constitute the board's directorship. But Harrison wished to remain at Washington's side in the field and declined the post. His seat was awarded to the former commissary general, Connecticut's Joseph Trumbull. At this Gen. Mifflin persuaded Congress to expand the board to five permanent members and recommended the appointments of the board's former secretary Richard Peters and Gen. Gates to fill the new slots. Congress agreed and, again at Mifflin's suggestion, Gates was named the board's president.

If Mifflin did not hide his disdain for Washington, Gates was more subtle. The

"Hero of Saratoga" had already shown himself to be a wily political operative, and as president of the new Board of War he was unlikely to remain satisfied with an offstage role filing regimental rosters or tending to prisoners. Behind the scenes he wisely juxtaposed his victory in the north against Washington's stalled Pennsylvania campaign, so much so that, to most observers, Gates seemed, like Gen. Lee before him, to have set his sights on Washington's job. For now, however, the board's most urgent task was provisioning Valley Forge, and to that end its ukases flew fast and furious toward Lancaster, seat of the Pennsylvania state assembly ostensibly tasked with supplying the winter camp. The Board of War's directives, though couched as suggestions, were intended to demonstrate to the state representatives that the national government would no longer abide their foot-dragging.

Congress also authorized the board's principals to journey to the winter encampment on an official inspection tour. This mission fell apart almost immediately, fractured by personal politics worthy of the Byzantine court. After seeming to acquiesce in the congressional mandate, Gen. Gates announced suddenly that he and his fellow members were entirely too busy with reorganizing the board's affairs to venture so far from York. Though the excuse fooled few, no delegates objected. It was left to soldiers like Connecticut's truculent Gen. Huntington to speak plain. "I fancy they don't like us well enough to come," he bluntly informed his friend Joseph Trumbull.

Yet Huntington and officers of a similar mind had missed the forest for the trees. It was Gates's offhand mention of the board's reorganizational efforts that should have raised eyebrows. In fact, Gates and his fellow board members were in the process of securing from Congress unprecedented concessions, including the power to establish a network of supply depots throughout Pennsylvania and western New Jersey independent of Washington's control. These would be manned by purchasing agents and transportation superintendents appointed by the board, in effect overriding the army's established commissary department. Although the term would not enter the American vernacular for another 150 years, these were the first steps of a classic power play Gates and his cohort planned to spring against Washington.*

Not everyone in Washington's orbit was as obtuse about the board's intentions as Gen. Huntington. It took the Marquis de Lafayette

---

* The first appearance of *power play,* in 1921, related to an American football formation. A decade later it had gravitated to hockey, and in 1941 the term was applied to politics.

less than a week after Gen. Conway's arrival at Valley Forge to deduce the true intent of his presence. The young Frenchman wrote to Washington that before departing his home country he'd "believed that all good Americans were united together." Now, however, he professed himself shocked at the Board of War's duplicity, and in a separate note to Henry Laurens he warned the president of Congress to keep a watchful eye on Gates. The general's successes in the north country, Lafayette noted, "have turned all the heads and raised his party to the highest degree. Some have been audacious, ungrateful, and foolish enough as to hope it would reflect on General Washington's reputation and honor — men indeed to be pitied as well as despised." Thus the new year opened with more and increasingly varied reports of "dirty arts and low intrigues" making their way to Washington's headquarters.

Few of these "intrigues" came by official post or mail coach. Instead most arrived at Valley Forge by hint and rumor, like daylight emanating from a sun so beclouded that neither particle nor wave carried it directly. One old friend alerted Washington that Gates's allies had convinced influential congressional delegates, particularly the New Englanders, that it was only the commander in chief's terminal mismanagement that had allowed the British to take Philadelphia.

Another reported whispers in York that the Continental Army actually outnumbered Gen. Howe's troops by a factor of three or four, yet for some reason Washington refused to engage. Patrick Henry forwarded an anonymous letter he'd received in Virginia that scorned Washington's leadership and posited, "We have wisdom, virtue and strength *enough* to save us if they could be called into action. The northern army has shown us what Americans are capable of doing with a GENERAL at their head. The spirit of the southern army is in no ways inferior to the spirit of the northern. A Gates, a Lee, or a Conway would in a few weeks render them an irresistible body of men." Henry and Washington both recognized the author's handwriting as that of the general's old ally turned antagonist Dr. Rush.

This is where the personal embodiment of the world's first laboratory of democracy stood in the thirtieth month of the American Revolution — blamed for losing both New York and Philadelphia; his troops resembling an army of beggars; his supply lines a laughable calamity; and his authority nibbled and nipped at from all sides by jealous and power-hungry subordinates. All this might have been enough to induce a commander of lesser character to throw up his hands and return home to his wife and family. Washington, needless to say, was not that commander.

SIXTEEN:
INTEGRATION

While Gen. Gates attempted to leverage his victory at Saratoga to attain a new role leading the Continental Army, some 4,000 miles away Benjamin Franklin was also working to exploit Gen. Burgoyne's surrender. His aim was to use the British defeat to ramp up the enmity between France and England. This argument began and ended with the simple and quite obvious assertion that Britain's loss of its North American colonies would be France's fiscal, political, and psychological gain.

Franklin, sailing with his two grandsons aboard the American merchant brig turned warship *Reprisal,* had arrived in the French port city of Nantes in late November 1776. The bespectacled 71-year-old polymath's celebrity had preceded him; he was hailed by the French as the world's most famous American and feted at every stop on his journey to Paris. He took rooms on the Right Bank of the Seine in the Hôtel de Valentois some three miles outside the city proper in the fashionable suburb of Passy, now a part of the 16th arrondissement. From there, sporting a decidedly frumpy brown suit and fur cap, the son of a simple Boston soap maker cut a swath through the world's fashion capital, making near-daily calls on government officials and financiers as well as influential aristocrats and intellectuals, all anxious to learn more about the United States' noble experiment of representative democracy and its chances of survival. In his little spare time, Franklin sought out fellow scientists eager to discuss both his experiments and his philosophical pursuits. A notorious flirt, he also made the acquaintance of several of the French court's prominent *coquettes.*

Despite the adulation — which included several medallions struck in his image — Franklin found that convincing France to officially throw in its lot with the American Revolution was difficult. Though the shocking victories at Trenton and Princeton had mitigated some of the stain of Washington's loss of New York, Franklin was increasingly hard pressed to explain away the likes of Brandywine, Paoli, and Germantown. He was not aware that the French, particularly their foreign minister de Vergennes, secretly admired the pluck Washington and his army had demonstrated by even attempting to engage the British at Germantown so soon after the defeat at Brandywine.

That newfound esteem soared when, on the morning of Thursday, December 4, news of Saratoga reached Paris. Within days de Vergennes informed Franklin that the result at Saratoga had convinced Louis XVI to recognize the United States with a treaty of trade and alliance, but there remained one obstacle. A 16-year-old mutual defense pact between France and Spain stipulated that the Spanish monarch Charles III would need to participate in any Franco-American federation. When French attempts to rally Spain failed — Charles III and his ministers rightly viewed the American Revolution as threatening their own holdings in the New World's southern hemisphere and did not want to risk British retribution unnecessarily — Franklin resorted to subterfuge.

He knew well that Paris was awash in French and British spies. The Crown's agents assigned to pry into his secrets would rummage through his trash, break into his writing parlor, reserve tables near his in his favorite *boulangerie,* and even copy his laundry lists.* Each Tuesday, detailed reports of what they had gleaned were indexed in invisible ink, rolled into a bottle, and depos-

* One of these operatives, it was later revealed, was the American diplomatic delegation's own chief secretary.

ited in a hidden hollow at the southern boundary of the Tuileries gardens. Later that night the British ambassador's secretary would retrieve the notes and forward them to London by the next packet ship. If the ambassador had instructions for the agents, he would leave them beneath the flowing roots of a nearby boxwood tree. One night, frustrated by the pace of the talks with Spain, Franklin purposely allowed it to slip to an associate that France was tilting toward accepting the United States as a sovereign nation. Learning of this, George III rushed an envoy named Paul Wentworth across the Channel to meet with Franklin and his colleagues. Had Franklin's transatlantic passage been intercepted by a British frigate a year earlier, Wentworth would have happily watched the American traitor hanged. Now he was assigned to parley.

Wentworth's first target was Silas Deane, a fellow Freemason whom the British considered much less strident than Franklin. Wentworth and Deane met for 11 hours, during which the king's agent proposed a reconciliation plan that would in essence repeal all offensive parliamentary acts passed since 1763 as well as allow the Americans to maintain their Continental Congress. As a further inducement, he also promised that in exchange for helping to bring about the cessation of hostilities, Deane and Franklin would be awarded knighthoods and generous pensions. Franklin himself subsequently arranged an ostentatiously public dinner with the British emissary, certain that the news of their rendezvous would reach Versailles before coffee and dessert. During the encounter Wentworth repeated his offers, which Franklin had no intention of accepting. But he continued to stall his suitor long enough to unnerve the French king. As he had assumed, within days Louis XVI ordered the Comte de Vergennes to hurriedly hammer out a treaty with the United States, with or without Spain.*

Washington at Valley Forge naturally knew nothing of these foreign machinations. And when his dream of a Christmas assault on Philadelphia faded, he finally resigned himself to a protracted war. Given its present course, he reasoned that the conflict would be likely to take years to conclude, with or without French assistance. Until that time, the preservation of the Continental Army would be his primary concern. As the flurry of construction banged on about him and the desks and tables at the Potts House groaned under rising stacks of paperwork, he surely wrestled with the idea that the army whose disintegra-

* One year later Spain did join the entente, albeit without making any commitment to American independence.

tion he was charged with preventing resembled no other on earth.

When Washington took command of the "Troops of the United Provinces of North America" in 1775, one of his first General Orders was to proclaim "that all Distinction of Colonies should be laid aside; so that one and the same spirit may animate the whole." Save for the officer corps, the Continental Army of two years earlier bore little resemblance to the legion that had tromped into the winter encampment hard by the Schuylkill. The early stages of the revolution had produced a soldiery of largely middle-class New Englanders of Anglo-Saxon extraction. But as the abbreviated enlistments of these yeoman farmers and shopkeepers expired, the Continental Congress had enacted new recruitment terms. The troops who had since stepped forward to fight for three years, or in some cases "for the duration of the war," emerged from a distinctly lower rung of colonial society — a disparate contingent of indentured servants; younger sons faced with primogeniture; a wave of recent immigrants dominated by impoverished Irish, Scots, and Germans; and even free blacks.

For the most part these young men and teenagers were uneducated, wildly undisciplined, shockingly under-armed, and strikingly unkempt.* The last particularly nettled the commander in chief. From his days organizing the Virginia Blues, Washington had taken great pride in the appearance of his troops. He had even ensured that his personal guard, then and now, were tall, broad-shouldered, and well-groomed troops whose martial carriage set them apart. But the motley collection of soldiers now under his command routinely defied their superiors' orders regarding the length of their hair and regularly decorated their uniforms, such as these were, with whatever bits of animal fur, ribbons, and feathers struck their fancy. Further, even in the best of times, throwing together a mix of southern sharecroppers, cosmopolitan seaport dwellers from the middle states, and flinty New Englanders would have resulted in a complex disharmony. As living conditions at Valley Forge deteriorated, these animosities began to take on a distinctly regional tenor.

The first 400 huts erected, for instance, were located just past the defensive redoubt facing Philadelphia at the camp's southeast

* According to the American Revolution specialist Arthur S. Lefkowitz, a mere 830 American college degrees, predominantly from Harvard, Yale, and the College of New Jersey at Princeton, were awarded between the years 1769 and 1775. (Lefkowitz, *George Washington's Indispensable Men*, p. 8.)

corner. They housed troops from Virginia, Massachusetts, New Hampshire, New York, and Pennsylvania. The Virginians, naive about the rigors of northern winters, complained that their New England counterparts had purposely failed to show them how to construct these "outer line" cabins for maximum warmth. Similarly, urban units invariably contained more artisans than their rural counterparts, and the skilled carpenters scoffed that the frontiersmen's quarters were barely a step above lean-tos. As the revolutionary historian John Milsop observed, "The New Englanders resented the southerners, while the southerners resented the New Yorkers."

Milsop's remark was understated. The Maryland papists were never fully accepted — even those who proclaimed themselves merely "Catholic around the edges." And no one seemed to like the Pennsylvanians. Joseph Plumb Martin, noting that the New England contingents contained not a few soldiers of puritan leanings who were more conversant with Savonarola than with Paine, observed in his journal that his fellow Nutmeg Staters considered even the "Fighting Quakers" little more than "savages." But among certain ranks, particularly in southern regiments, the greatest enmity was reserved for the free blacks.

By 1775, blacks made up some 20 percent

of the colonial population; close to half a million men, women, and children. Ninety-nine percent of them were enslaved. Washington had wavered over accepting the nation's few free blacks into the army's ranks from the onset of the revolution. Although considered a compassionate slaveholder by the standards of the era, he was nonetheless a Virginia planter who upon his appointment as commander in chief continued to *own* 135 human beings. He was of course aware of the loyalty and grit shown by black volunteers who had fought for the colonies in and around Boston. And by now most patriots were familiar with the story of Crispus Attucks, the fugitive slave considered the first casualty of the revolution when he was killed during the Boston Massacre. On a more personal level, Washington respected the opinions of his personal manservant William "Billy" Lee and appreciated the hardships Lee had shared with him since he had taken the field. (Lee was one of the few slaves granted the dignity of a surname.) Yet the idea of arming black men weighed heavily on a class of gentry whose subconscious was so invested in the fear of slave uprisings that they included this concern in the Declaration of Independence.★ It was not until a Loyalist

★ The Declaration's twenty-seventh and final accusation against George III included the charge,

politician outmaneuvered Washington on the subject that he reluctantly acknowledged the need for black soldiers.

In the wake of the British evacuation of Boston, the royal governor of Virginia, Lord Dunmore, incorporated what he called an Ethiopian Regiment into his state's Loyalist forces. The unit was composed of slaves promised their freedom in exchange for deserting insurrectionist masters and fighting for the Crown. Slaves at the time outnumbered the white population in Virginia, and when Patrick Henry informed Washington that his manpower was being stretched to its limits pursuing these fugitives, the reaction was swift. Washington wrote to John Hancock that Lord Dunmore's policy might not only swell the British ranks with escaped slaves, but also encourage free blacks to turn coat. These freemen, he had decided, should be granted the right to fight for the cause, albeit awarded smaller enlistment bonuses. Congress acquiesced, and over the course of the revolution some 5,000 black men enlisted in the Continental Army and, to a lesser extent, in various state militias. This was the first and only time an American fighting force was integrated until the Korean War. These

"He has excited domestic insurrections amongst us," a clear reference to slave revolts.

enlistees included the more than 750 black soldiers who had marched from Whitemarsh to Valley Forge.

Concerning his attitude toward slavery, historians have generally viewed Washington through a complex lens: that is, as a man who held slaves but also expressed reservations about the institution of slavery throughout his public career. Although he left ambiguous writings on the subject — including a 1778 letter to his cousin and estate manager Lund Washington prohibiting Lund from selling Mount Vernon's slaves against their will — it is safe to assume that he shared the attitude of his fellow Virginian Thomas Jefferson. "Nothing is more certainly written in the book of fate that these people are to be free," Jefferson wrote in his autobiography. "Nor is it less certain that the two races, equally free, cannot live in the same government. Nature, habit, opinion had drawn indelible lines of distinction between them."* It thus came as something of a surprise when John Laurens — a man from an even more aggressive and pernicious slave state — broke with those prevailing instincts.

In the early days of 1778, the younger Laurens — whose family fortune was built on the backs of captured Africans passing

* That first sentence is inscribed on the Jefferson Memorial. Tellingly, the following sentences are not.

through his father's auction houses — began to agitate to raise his own regiment of freed black soldiers. He was probably influenced by Rhode Island's Gen. Varnum, who convinced his state's legislature to stand up a battalion of freed chattel upon the condition that their masters were fairly compensated.* An excited Laurens wrote to his father with an overture "to augment the Continental Forces from an untried Source." In lieu of any future personal family inheritance, he went on, "I would solicit you to cede me a number of your able bodied men Slaves . . . those who are unjustly deprived of the Rights of Mankind [to] reinforce the Defenders of Liberty." In an earlier letter, Laurens had emphasized to his father that he had "long deplored the wretched state of these men," and insisted that his "black scheme" was far from "a chimera" of a young and foolish mind.

Laurens's arguments were heavily influenced by the writings of John Locke, perhaps the Enlightenment's greatest liberal thinker. Laurens had fallen under the seventeenth-century philosopher's spell while studying his writings in Geneva, and Locke's doctrines attacking taxation without representation had

* So estimable in drill and maneuver was Rhode Island's all-black battalion of 130 men that Massachusetts and Connecticut soon followed suit.

originally drawn him to the patriot cause. Similarly, Locke's contention that all men were born equal regardless of skin tone struck the young man like a blast from Gabriel's trumpet. Unusually progressive for a son of South Carolina, Laurens reasoned that African Americans' alleged intellectual deficiencies and lack of social refinement resulted only from decades if not generations of enslavement. He believed that given the educational opportunities afforded to whites, black men — he never spoke of women of color — would naturally reveal their potential as full contributors to American society. Yet for all his noble intentions, Laurens remained a creature of his era. Reading his words today, no matter how virtuous their design, still makes one's gorge rise.

He contended, for instance, that the violence of the south's peculiar institution had prepared the slaves for the hard life of infantrymen. "Habits of subordinations, patience under fatigues, sufferings and privations of every kind, are soldierly qualifications, which these men possess in an eminent degree," he wrote. "Those who fall in battle will not lose much. Those who survive will obtain their reward." Laurens even proposed a uniform design for the regiment, a white coat with red facing "to form a good Contrast with the complexion of the soldier." Whether the warmly dressed Laurens recognized the speciousness of arguing for the universal "Rights of Mankind" while retaining at Valley Forge his own half-clothed manservant, a slave named Shrewsberry, remains unrecorded.

What posterity does reveal is Henry Laurens's surprising reaction to his son's entreaties. Henry replied that he was not personally averse to John's proposition. He merely considered it improbable. After immersing himself in the cause of American independence he had gradually changed his views on the institution and become a proponent, if a tepid one, of emancipation. Of his own slaves, he wrote to John, "I am devising means for manumitting many of them & for cutting of the entail of Slavery." This was far from the prevalent view among his peers, and Henry Laurens knew it. "Great powers oppose me," he added, specifically citing "the avarice of my Countrymen." The elder Laurens ultimately decided that bucking those great powers was a fool's errand. As he informed his son, "I will do as much as I can in my time & leave the rest to a better man." He then suggested that if it was more troops John needed, he travel home to South Carolina and use the powerful Laurens name to raise a regiment of white men who would eagerly flock to his banner.

John Laurens, however, had by now become such an intrinsic member of Washington's staff that the idea of taking even temporary leave from Valley Forge was out of the question. It is debatable, in any case, whether Washington would have given him permission. He had only reluctantly acceded to allowing free blacks to enlist, his hand forced by Lord Dunmore. A regiment of former slaves could well have been a bridge too far. Moreover, by this point even the indefatigable commander in chief had become too reliant on the diligence of his young kitchen cabinet as they oversaw a plethora of administrative duties.

Washington was no longer the foxhunting Virginia squire who had ridden off to war 30 months earlier. He was now the porcelain crucible of the nascent United States, and he recognized in the southern passion of Laurens, in the erudite insouciance of Hamilton, and even in the Gallic *je ne sais quoi* of Lafayette the molten material with which the new nation would be sculpted. Perhaps even more than he needed his favorite generals, he needed these surrogate sons now. For amid the flurry of construction activity at Valley Forge as the calendar rolled into 1778, he sensed that the solidarity of his officer corps was steadily disintegrating.

Most of the Continental Army's enlisted men were accustomed to hard labor in adverse conditions. They were farmers and blacksmiths, carpenters and miners, fishermen and stonecutters whose sunburned faces and callused hands attested to their ability to withstand the rigors of nature. The majority of Washington's officers, on the other hand, were sons of America's aristocracy, patricians whose vision of war tended toward heroic cavalry charges followed by giddy minuets in Philadelphia taverns. Their illusions were obliterated by the reality of shoeing one's own horses or boiling one's own lye and lard to make soap. Moreover, hanging over Valley Forge like Banquo's resentful ghost was the specter of a provisionless winter. The conditions made for a grousing gentry.

The Christmas forage sweeps conducted by Lord Stirling and Gen. Armstrong had provided a short-term reprieve from the gnawing hunger afflicting the troops. But Washington well understood that the link between adequate supplies and good morale that sustained an army was close to shattering. A telling example was the experience of Gen. Armstrong himself after he and his militiamen had secured their prize of close to 200 cattle. They had driven the herd all Christmas Day and night, forded the Schuylkill, and arrived at Valley Forge some 24 hours later. Once the beef was delivered to the commissary, the proud Pennsylvanian general, formerly a prosperous civil engineer and surveyor, was reduced to abjectly approaching his commander in chief to beg that he be allowed to cull six of the cows in order to feed his own hungry and exhausted soldiers.

Even the troops whose short-term enlistments were about to expire presented Washington with a double-edged sword. Though their departure would mean fewer mouths in camp, by contract and the rules of basic morality they were also due enough provisions to last them through the duration of their homeward trek. John Laurens aside, South Carolina and Georgia — busy with fending off threats from the Royal Navy at Charleston and Savannah — were the only two states not represented at Valley Forge. This meant supplying comestibles for journeys into the upper reaches of New Hampshire or deep into North Carolina's piney woods. Given these and too many similar circumstances, Washington worked at the edges as best he could to maintain his army's equilibrium. One solution was to detach more units, as he had done several weeks earlier with Armstrong's Pennsylvania militia. This would serve the dual purpose of lessening the strain on his kitchens while fulfilling his commitment to Congress to protect the territory surrounding Philadelphia. With hay and oats particularly precious commodities, his gaze fell first on the four companies of General Casimir Pulaski's light horse dragoons.

The 32-year-old Pulaski had arrived in the United States the previous July an abject pauper, having been driven into exile when the czar's armies crushed the Polish-Lithuanian resistance to Russian hegemony over the Baltic states. Born to a noble family and having been a soldier since his teens, Pulaski was by the age of 21 already a renowned horseman who had raised a Polish cavalry unit, or *choragiew,* that for close to a decade had struck fear into the far larger armies of his country's Russian, Austrian, and Prussian oppressors. The failure of the quixotic Polish rebellion was the American Revolution's gain, and by September Congress had acceded to Washington's request to grant Pulaski command of the Continental Army's horse service. In a letter to John Hancock recommending the commission, Washington showed his softer side for this budding Sobieski "who has sacrificed his fortune engaged in the liberty and independence of his country." His compassion paid immediate dividends when Pulaski rallied the disorganized American light horse in the latter stages of the Battle of Brandywine Creek.

In the interim between Brandywine and the Battle of Germantown, Pulaski set about writing the Continental Army's first cavalry manual and transforming the force's few hundred mounted scouts and mail carriers into a formidable fighting unit. With his dashing black mustache and swarthy good looks set off by his favorite white sable uniform collar, Pulaski was instantly recognizable galloping at the head of the Continental dragoons. Yet even the greatest horseman is only as good as his steed. And in an effort to spare his horseflesh from Valley Forge's deprivations, Washington dispatched Pulaski and his men to a winter garrison at Trenton. Pulaski was given instructions to provide for the city's security and, perhaps more important, to rest and nourish his emaciated animals as best he could in order to have them battle ready by spring. A smaller mounted detachment with similar orders was carved from Pulaski's charge and sent to reinforce the Continental regulars holding Wilmington, Delaware. There the failure of the Maryland and Delaware militias to turn out in force had left the American remuda decimated, so that mail riders had been reduced to mounting mares heavy with foal.

With Pulaski's horsemen departed, Washington took a moment to turn his eye toward the distant future. He pressed the camp's quartermasters to work with his staff in drawing up plans for provisioning the next spring's offensives, and dispatched junior officers whose troops had been decommissioned to scour the southern states for deserters while fanning others north to secure arms and supplies from New England. He then requested that his remaining regimental commanders compile lists of the specific deprivations from which their units suffered, as well as recommendations to remedy the deficiencies. His aides were instructed to collect and collate these files in order to present them to the congressional delegation that Washington was gambling would agree to journey to Valley Forge.

How confident the commander in chief was in Congress's reaction to his entreaties for a personal consultation, and how much of this was a show of bravado to stay the morale of his officer corps, is difficult to determine. In either case, so eager were his subordinates to vent their frustrations that the Potts House was soon awash in thousands of pages of exhaustive memorandums. In the meanwhile, Washington allowed a full week to pass after sending his "starve, dissolve, or disperse" letter. He had made his case and said his piece. In the interim, his silence spoke for itself. This proved yet another shrewd political tactic. For 80 miles to the west, his deliberate reticence was having its desired effect.

SEVENTEEN:
FIRECAKES AND COLD WATER

Throughout 1777, Washington's plaints to the Continental Congress, while urgent, had reflected the same quiet constancy with which he commanded his army. The delegates, however, could not help reading his dispatch of December 23 as full-blown fulmination. Henry Laurens in particular, prodded by his son, recognized that the commander in chief had crossed a metaphorical line.

Since succeeding the sickly John Hancock as the president of Congress, the elder Laurens had thrown himself into the job with the same zealous enterprise and industriousness that had carried his Huguenot forebears from France to the shores of the New World. And as his power became concentrated, so did his revolutionary fervor. Once a member of the moderate class who as late as 1775 had counseled caution about breaking away from England, he was now as insurrectionary as any fire-eating Bostonian. Though bedridden by a nearly crippling attack of gout, upon receiving Washington's stark warning he roused himself to coax his fellow congressmen into supporting what he called the general's "proper and sensible" case. He also argued that now that the question of the Continental Army's winter encampment had been settled in the field, the logistics of a supply pipeline could and should be more easy.

Laurens was a persuasive and powerful personage. Within days of his lobbying campaign, Thomas Wharton, the president of Pennsylvania's supreme executive council in Lancaster — a position analogous to governor* — was besieged by communiqués from delegates in York calling the army's situation "distressed beyond description." One of Wharton's fellow Pennsylvanians, Daniel Roberdeau of the Continental Congress, warned him that unless "flour and fat Cattle" were quickly gathered and shipped to Valley Forge, "the army will be reduced to the necessity of abandoning their post." Roberdeau sagely neglected to mention Washington's belittling of the state politicians, safely ensconced "in a comfortable room by a good fire side" while his troops slept under canopies of frost and snow.

After the usual haggling over the formation of a task force dedicated to streamlining the

* As we will for convenience refer to him.

313

military's supply chain — three separate panels were established; each would rapidly dissolve amid regional acrimony and finger-pointing — the delegates finally enlisted the Board of War as a sort of cudgel to work in conjunction with the civil authorities.* One of the board's first edicts was to direct the state legislators at Lancaster to immediately begin procuring the goods Washington required or face the official withdrawal of the Continental Army from the Philadelphia area. It was one thing for Wharton and his assembly to receive veiled threats from the military commander in the field. It was quite another to officially hear this from the body appointed by the Continental Congress to oversee the war effort. The board also warned Wharton that if his commissary officers could not rise to the challenge via bureaucratic channels already in place, their task should

---

* The third congressional commission included the Massachusetts congressman Elbridge Gerry. Though little remembered today, the future vice president contributed mightily to the modern lexicon of politics. In 1812, as governor of the Bay State, Gerry signed off on a scheme to redraw the boundaries of its electoral districts to the benefit of his Republican Party. One of these new state senate districts resembled nothing so much as the outline of a salamander, and thus was the word *gerrymander* introduced into the political vocabulary.

be accomplished even if it meant "giving umbrage" to the civilian population. This was a pointed reminder that forcible seizures of provisions would not be ruled out.

Governor Wharton rightly considered both ultimatums a form of blackmail. He also recognized that he was left with little choice if the citizens of his state wanted troops to protect them. He therefore informed Congress that it would take at least several weeks to get a new procurement process and its delivery system up and running. There was food and clothing to be collected, wagons to be located, drivers to be hired. The question arose — would there be an army left to provision by the time this was all accomplished?

Congress next drafted a letter to all Continental officers at Valley Forge requesting that they temporarily forgo the extra rations to which their rank entitled them in order to conserve the limited amount of food already on hand. In exchange for this forbearance, each officer would be issued cash payments commensurate with his sacrifice. The delegates also passed legislation to award every noncommissioned officer and enlisted man an immediate bonus of one month's pay. Given the depleted national treasury, the fact that Congress was powerless to levy personal taxes, and the loosely confederated states' intrinsic antipathy to nearly all forms of taxation, no one in York seriously expected this bill to be enacted. But, for now, it was hoped that the mere *idea* of an infusion of scrip into Valley Forge might dampen any mutinous inclinations. The delegates then took up Washington's petition for a personal audience. As they palavered, a messenger from Valley Forge arrived on New Year's Day.*

This time the tone of Washington's dispatch was disconcertingly conciliatory. He reported on the capture of the British brig by Gen. Smallwood's Wilmington forces as well as unconfirmed rumors of another British vessel run aground and taken by New Jersey militiamen. Regarding the quartermaster general's post vacated by Thomas Mifflin, he casually suggested that he had received warm reports about a Scottish-born colonel named Udney Hay, currently serving as the deputy quartermaster at Fort Ticonderoga. "I thought it my

* January 1, 1778, was only the twenty-seventh occasion in the 45-year-old Washington's lifetime that the new year officially began on January 1. Prior to 1752, New Year's Day had been celebrated in England and in its colonies on March 25. This was the date the Catholic Church had pegged to coincide with the Solemnity of the Annunciation, when the Angel Gabriel appeared to the Virgin Mary to inform her that she would give birth to Jesus Christ, the son of God. The stubborn British had stuck with that date long after most of Catholic Europe had returned to the Julian calendar.

duty to endeavor to find out a Gentleman who I could venture to recommend," he wrote in a matter-of-fact tone. "Either from my own particular knowledge or from that of others."* In a similarly modulated voice he very nearly apologized for not having the time to apply the same due diligence to researching officers capable of filling the empty position of adjutant general. The delegates were befuddled by this insouciance. What did it indicate?

Congress aimed to find out. Within 10 days it had convened yet another fact-finding commission whose three members — Francis Dana of Massachusetts, John Reed of Pennsylvania, and Nathaniel Folsom of New Hampshire — were to accompany the members of the Board of War to Valley Forge under the vague aegis of adopting "such other measures as they shall judge necessary for introducing economy and promoting discipline and good morals in the army." When Gates, Mifflin, and their compatriots again declined to travel, two more committee members were added — Virginia's John Harvie and Gouverneur Morris of New York.

Judging from their copious letters, none of these delegates appeared quite certain as to

* In the end, Gen. Gates, who knew Hay and was aware of Hay's admiration for Washington, persuaded Congress to demur.

317

the point of their mission. Were they to be investigators? Advisers? An amalgamation of the two? How far did their executive powers extend? How wary should they be of injecting politics into the minutiae of day-to-day military comportment? None of these questions had an immediate answer. Common sense dictated that it would have been folly for the civil authorities to issue recommendations for any sort of military reorganization prior to an on-site inspection of the camp. Yet historians can be pardoned for wondering exactly what these committeemen hoped to accomplish with their enigmatic intent of "reducing battalions," "reforming regiments," and even restructuring the allocation of army chaplains.

More confusingly, the delegates preparing to journey to Valley Forge were tethered to a political body in exile that at times put forward diametrically opposite opinions regarding their assignment. The New Jersey delegate John Witherspoon perceived the army's "chief obstacle to success" as the bickering and "insubordination" among its officers. Yet Henry Laurens praised those same officers for their "humble Representation" and "valuable meritoriousness." Either way one viewed the impasse, the much-needed reformation and reconstruction of the Continental Army were off to a confounding start.

Meanwhile, the ensuing fortnight at Valley Forge was a harbinger of the harsh conditions to follow. Anthony Wayne, the blunt general from Chester, complained to his governor, Thomas Wharton, that a third of the army were without "Shoes, Stocking, or Shirts." He received no response. Yet though the supplies pledged by the state of Pennsylvania had yet to appear, by mid-January the junior officers whom Washington had dispatched to New England were trickling back with a modicum of food, clothing, and all-important blankets. Connecticut's contribution to the haul even roused the irascible Gen. Jedediah Huntington to write a congratulatory note to his father, a fellow Connecticut general and an active member of the Sons of Liberty — although the younger Huntington could not help appending his usual dose of gloom. "We live from Hand to Mouth," he lamented, "and are like to do so, for all anything I see." Huntington may have been a morose soul, but he was an acute observer. If anything, his prophecy did not do justice to the calamities that had befallen the camp.

By mid-January the frenetic early pace of cabin construction had ebbed — most of the eventual 2,000 or so huts had been raised — and an arctic front had settled over Valley Forge. With it the malaise that had incited the mood of the officers began to spread into a more serious disquiet among the enlisted men. By this point there was even less make-work for Washington and his officers to assign. The construction of the bridge spanning the Schuylkill, under Gen. Sullivan's management, had been halted, owing to both a lack of proper tools and a spreading silent protest against the camp's living conditions that took the form of intermittent work stoppages. What other building tasks still remained were consigned to small work gangs under the direction of French engineers expanding the nearly three miles of slit trenches and excavating the five ravelin-like dirt-and-log redoubts placed at strategic points along the plateau. Even for these men, the freezing temperatures made the work slow, dangerous, and cheerless.

The consequence was a raft of desertions, which multiplied daily up and down the line from Trenton to Wilmington. A year earlier, before the victories at Trenton and Princeton, a lack of both rations and pay had combined with the generally foul conditions to prompt as many as a quarter of Washington's troops to slip away. Now the number of men simply vanishing from Valley Forge reached such proportions that Washington was forced to issue a series of General Orders requiring his regimental commanders to convene multiple daily roll calls — the best way to ensure that men abandoning the army could not get too far.

Many of the Continental runaways set out for Philadelphia in hopes of securing food and clothing as prisoners of war. This was in and of itself almost incredible, considering the tales told by American escapees who had made their way back to Valley Forge. These men related shudder-inducing stories of trapping and roasting the rats infesting their cells, pulling up grass in the prison yard in order to eat the roots, and even plucking and swallowing the lice on their bodies. Some captives held on decrepit troopships set fire to the vessels to end their collective misery. And a few, driven mad by the dearth of food, had gnawed their own fingers to the knuckle.*

As for clothes, those who agreed to fight for the Crown were indeed issued uniforms at first. But so many deserted back to the Continental side once they received shoes, stockings, pants, and shirts that Gen. Howe had taken to distributing the clothing only on board British ships. The Americans were then impressed to serve in theaters ranging from the Caribbean to the East Indies. Continental officers who deserted were also treated to a rude awakening. Considered by the enemy as

* Nearly 12,000 American prisoners of war perished in captivity during the revolution, more than in all its battles combined.

men of bad character — in contrast to the sheeplike rabble who composed the rank and file — most had been thrown, as ballast, into the filthy holds of ships returning to England. They were now languishing in British dungeons.

Despite the terrible tales, still the soldiers left. The absentees were not limited to the rank and file going over to the enemy. Upon his return to Valley Forge from Radnor, Lord Stirling found that one of his key brigade commanders, having been denied leave, had simply packed up his kit and disappeared with all of his unit's scant supply of salt. Washington found this type of delinquency among his officer corps particularly nettlesome, and nearly each of his daily General Orders throughout January addressed the issue. "Notwithstanding the orders repeatedly given for calling the absent officers to camp," began a typical example, "the Commander in Chief is informed, that many are still scattered about the Country, misspending their time, to the prejudice of the service, and injury of those officers who remain and attend their duty in Camp — He therefore directs, that the Brigadiers and officers commanding brigades forthwith make a strict enquiry, concerning all the officers absent from their brigades; and such as are absent without leave from proper authority, or having had such leave remain unnecessarily absent, are to be immediately notified to return to camp without delay on pain of being suspended or cashiered."

For those who persevered, stacked like cordwood in their rustic huts, life remained wretched. Much of the firewood was still so green that when the stove-lengths did manage to catch flame the cabins were inundated with black, choking smoke that left the camp in a permanent twilight. And though slit latrines known as "vaults" had been dug haphazardly about the living quarters, exhausted and hungry men were unlikely to be meticulous about their sanitary habits. Filth rapidly accumulated in and around the cabins, and disease spread unabated. Adding to the dread miasma, when a workhorse died — as close to 500 such horses would before the winter was over — it was quickly butchered for its meat while the carcass was left to rot where it lay.

In the absence of horse meat, the troops subsisted for the most part on a crude mixture of flour and water they dubbed fire-cakes. Either these were baked in kettles or, more commonly, the moist globs were simply lumped onto a rock placed in the center of a campfire. Since there was no yeast or other leavening available, the resultant biscuit-like concoctions were dense; they were also tasteless, and inevitably enveloped in a layer of black ash. In the absence of beef, pork, and mutton, the dead weevils and maggots that had found their way into the flour barrels and thence into the firecakes were often a soldier's only source of protein. On the rare occasions when meat was procured, the large amount of salt needed to preserve even the flesh of dead horses produced something that had to be soaked repeatedly in order to become remotely edible. Moreover, since animal fat is less prone to spoilage than muscle, most of the "meat" dispensed tasted more like chunks of salty lard.

The ubiquitous Albigence Waldo describes weeping to the heartrending strains of a lonely violin being played in a nearby tent as he forced down yet another serving of firecakes and cold water. Once, when a scrawny cow became available, he reported himself and his unit feasting on "a bowl of beef soup — full of burnt leaves and dirt."

One suspects that Waldo, with his eye for graphic detail, would have made a fine photographer had the camera been invented but a few decades earlier. History is left instead with his plaintive journal entries. "There comes a Soldier, his bare feet are seen thro' his worn out Shoes," begins one. "His legs nearly naked from the tatter'd remains of an only pair of stockings, his Breeches not sufficient to cover his nakedness, his Shirt hanging in Strings, his hair dischevell'd, his face meagre; his whole appearance pictures a person forsaken and discouraged. He comes, and cries with an air of wretchedness & despair, I am Sick, my feet lame, my legs are sore, my body cover'd with this tormenting itch — my Cloaths are worn out, my Constitution is broken, my former Activity is exhausted by fatigue, hunger and &Cold. I fail fast I shall soon be no more!"

Concludes the account: "I don't know of any thing that vexes a man's Soul more than hot smoke continually blowing into his Eyes, & when he attempts to avoid it, it is met by a cold piercing Wind."

The tormenting itch Waldo describes refers to smallpox, the scourge of armies from Hannibal to Cortés. Washington himself was by now immune to the disease, having contracted and survived a mild case at the age of 19 when he accompanied his tubercular brother Lawrence to Barbados.* Though the experience had left him with barely visible pocks on his body and face, he knew well how smallpox could not only devastate a standing army, but frighten away prospective recruits. At one point, Enoch Poor informed

* This was the only occasion in Washington's entire life when he left what became the United States. Two other American presidents, Andrew Jackson and Abraham Lincoln, were also survivors of the disease.

325

New Hampshire's governor that close to half his brigade was down with the pox. And such was the fear of contagion that the pickets and guards posted about the camp's perimeter were instructed to examine anyone entering for telltale signs of the "dimpled death." As the virus can be transmitted by air, this precaution was for the most part in vain. Nonetheless, at the first sign of smallpox or any other communicable disease, ailing soldiers were evacuated and carried off in open carts through pelting rain, sleet, and snow to the area's crude, filthy hospitals. If they survived the journey, they were deposited on the doorsteps of what the contrarian doctor Benjamin Rush aptly labeled "the sinks of human life in the army."

Even these soiled sinks were soon overflowing. The Continental Army had barely settled into Valley Forge before all existing medical centers on either side of the Schuylkill and as far away as New Jersey were overwhelmed. This, despite vociferous local protests, necessitated the seizure of village meetinghouses, churches, barns, schoolhouses, and even some private residences in the predominantly religious communities to the west and south of the winter camp. The exact number of these unofficial infirmaries has never been recorded, although it surely ran into the scores if not the hundreds. In any case, they were not so much hospitals as abattoirs.

Ostensibly supplied with sugar, milk, barley, mutton broth, and perhaps even a meager measure of medicinal port or Madeira, in reality they provided at best a warm bath and a scanty ration of rice while nurses, usually camp followers paid two dollars a month, watched and waited for the patients to die, as some 1,700 men did in these facilities over the winter of 1777–1778. The few who did recover often reported back to duty wrapped in blankets or even naked, as the doxies had stolen their clothes. Washington attempted to tighten security by stationing a field officer in each facility to act as a ward master. This did not have much effect on the pilfering; nor did the commander in chief's numerous personal visits to raise the spirits of the ailing and dying men.

By mid-January, Washington had seen enough. Horrified and exasperated by the filthy, overcrowded conditions of the general hospitals — it was not unusual for 20 patients to be packed into a room meant for a half dozen — he ordered the brigade commanders at Valley Forge to construct a series of what he termed "flying hospitals" to tend the less seriously ill. These structures, generally 15 feet by 25 feet, were erected at a distance of no less than 100 yards from each brigade's headquarters, and were essentially a larger version of the hut lodgings — with two exceptions. No sod or dirt was to be used as chink, as Washington believed such chinking caused unhealthful dampness; and there were to be windows on two walls for aesthetic purposes. But no porthole view, no matter how glorious, could offset the eighteenth century's primitive medical mores.

In both the more established infirmaries and the flying hospitals, patients with contagious diseases mixed with soldiers recovering from minor wounds or illnesses. This gave rise to a new term, "hospital fever," referring to a condition that would kill as surely as the frequent outbreaks of dysentery, typhus, and typhoid known collectively as camp fever. Medical science of the era had no idea of the relation between body lice and typhus, and infected blankets and straw used by the recently deceased were issued to new patients. Surgeons' tools were rarely washed, much less sterilized, before amputations with no anesthetic were performed, and postsurgical infections spread like the ubiquitous vermin that carried them. Moreover, as the early signs of typhus and smallpox bore a striking resemblance to one another, doctors often treated men for the wrong disease. This, however, mattered little when one constant of the medical centers was taken into consideration — there was never enough medicine available. Regimental physicians made do almost exclusively with the conventional practices of blistering, bleeding, and administering a mixture of the extremely toxic tartar emetic with a drug known as "jalap," a purgative extract from the tuberous roots of plants in the morning glory family. It is not recorded how many died from the treatments meant to heal them.

As a result, so frightening was the idea of being consigned to one of these slaughterhouses that not a few soldiers instead opted to conceal their fevers and die in their huts. In what may seem a minor clerical inconvenience but was in fact a bureaucratic nightmare for a commander in chief bent on shaping an army for its next campaign, many of the men who died — either in a hospital or in a hut — were carried on the active-duty rolls for months afterward. There was but little army doctors could do to successfully treat the majority of pestilences swirling in and around Valley Forge that winter. Yet one of the few medical triumphs they could claim resulted from the controversial steps Washington took to eradicate the dread smallpox.

A year earlier, as the army overwintered in Morristown, Washington had experimented on small units with an inoculation technique known as "variolation." The procedure had been practiced for millennia in China, but was new — and therefore mysterious and frightening — to western minds. It consisted of deliberately exposing healthy soldiers who had never contracted the virus to small doses of infected smallpox scabs or pus, churned into a powder and rubbed into superficial cuts on the skin. The patients would develop pustules and other symptoms similar to those of naturally occurring smallpox — fever, nausea, fatigue, muscle aches. But after a few weeks these manifestations would subside and be followed by recovery and immunity. While at the time the death toll from smallpox outbreaks hovered at around 16 percent of those who contracted it up and down America's eastern seaboard, less than one percent of the soldiers at Morristown who underwent variolation died. At Valley Forge, Washington went even further, insisting that the entire army undergo the inoculations. The purposeful infections began in January and were done in secret, lest the British be alerted that at any given moment whole brigades might be incapacitated. According to some reports, after 4,000 or so troops had been treated by mid-March, deaths from smallpox dropped to a seventeenth of what they had been. This was but the smallest of comforts.

So vile were the deteriorating conditions at the winter camp that even the flintiest officers were prone to sympathy. In the same letter in which he detailed the smallpox outbreak, Gen. Poor also asked his governor how he could possibly inflict punishment on any soldier arrested for desertion, "when they plead in their justification that on your part the Contract is broken? That you promised to engage them and supply them with such things that were requisite to make them comfortable here, and the situation of their families tolerable at home, this they say they had an undoubted right to expect."

The 41-year-old Poor was no tender shoot. Tall and handsome enough to have sat for the Polish-Lithuanian military engineer and amateur portraitist Tadeusz Kosciuszko, prior to his heroism at Saratoga he had survived the disorganized retreat from Quebec following the invasion of 1775. And before throwing his lot in with the Continentals he had fought for the British in some of the most brutal battles of the French and Indian War. General Poor knew suffering. Yet despite his hard bark, Valley Forge was nudging even him close to a breaking point. It is doubtful he imagined that the conditions could get worse.

EIGHTEEN:
CIVIL WAR

Given the ravages of winter quarters, it might have been easy for many soldiers to forget that there was still a war on. Washington could not. Though the weather restricted both antagonists' movements in New England, upstate New York, and even New York City, he was constantly apprised of Continental defensive designs from Savannah to Richmond. He considered Charleston, South Carolina, especially its key harbor, particularly vulnerable to a siege. His daily conversations with the Palmetto State's John Laurens may have heightened his awareness of that front, and messengers from Valley Forge riding south with warnings and instructions were a common sight.

Closer to home, he continued to dispatch daily patrols to police the roads leading into and out of Philadelphia. Their primary purpose, as always, was to enforce the ban on commerce with the enemy and to gather intelligence, particularly concerning any British excursions out into the counties neighboring the city. Washington encouraged his field commanders to harass these British patrols whenever feasible, and his campaign of bedevilment even included an attempt to disrupt the enemy's supply deliveries by floating mines down the Delaware to blast the provision ships in Philadelphia's harbor.

The idea was the brainchild of the inventor David Bushnell, a thin, stern-faced Connecticut Yankee with a knack for gadgetry. Bushnell was the oldest of five children in a farming family; after his parents died, he sold his share of the homestead to his brother and enrolled at Yale University at the relatively mature age of 31. There he studied the natural sciences, which led to his successful detonation of several waterproof kegs packed with gunpowder beneath the surface of the Connecticut River. With the help of two New Haven clock makers, and his own precision, Bushnell managed to concoct a crude timing device attached to a musket's gunlock to explode his "torpedoes," as he named them. Four years later the gun smoke had barely cleared from the fields of Lexington and Concord when he offered his unique services to the Continental Army.

Benjamin Franklin, another famous tinkerer, was the first to advise Washington of Bushnell's peculiar talents. The commander in chief immediately sensed the potential of these underwater time bombs as a weapon against the mighty Royal Navy. But the question hung — how to deliver them with accuracy? Bushnell's answer: the world's first documented use of a submarine in warfare. With his experiments, Bushnell was following in the tradition of a group of visionaries and scalawags who had attempted to pioneer the science of underwater machinery.

The Dutch-born Cornelis Drebbel is often credited with creating the world's first submarine. In 1605, Drebbel journeyed to London, where he persuaded King James I to underwrite the construction of a submersible boat propelled by oars fitted into leather joints to make the rowlocks watertight. Drebbel claimed to have conducted a maiden voyage beneath the Thames — but there were in fact no first-person accounts other than his own. Still, even if the Drebbel submarine "was simply an elaborate hoax perpetrated on a guileless king by an ambitious mountebank," it helped spark genuine innovation by a series of inventors. The most prominent of these was Edmond Halley, the British royal astronomer for whom the comet is named. A century after Cornelis Drebbel's invisible feat, Halley attached a string of lead weights to a primitive diving bell, procured a volunteer, and sank the contraption into a lake. When its operator detached the weights after a few minutes, the trapped oxygen floated it back to the surface with its occupant un-harmed. Now, decades later, it was left to the American David Bushnell to design a craft that could both travel underwater and sustain its driver for more than a few moments of breathing time.

Bushnell constructed the frame of his one-man submersible by joining two tortoise-shell-shaped oaken slabs in an upright posi-tion. A windowed conning tower large enough for a man's head was affixed to the top of the craft between two snorkels that automatically closed upon submersion. The watertight gaskets were then slathered with tar before the entire contraption was bound with wrought iron staves. Bushnell once again turned to his clock makers for assistance with the ship's mechanics. They helped him devise a valve-controlled bay that could fill with or flush seawater in order to control the ship's depth, a form of ballast still employed today. Two screw propellers — one to maintain propulsion and one projecting upward to as-sist in ascents — were operated by foot ped-als and hand cranks.

Because its tiny compartment held so little air, the vessel Bushnell dubbed the *Turtle* could remain submerged for only a few minutes. This perforce limited its use to night operations. The ingenious Bushnell solved the problem of operating the machinery in the murky depths by coating his instrument panel and compass needles with bioluminescent fox fire, a species of fungus found in decaying wood that glows in the dark. With more ballast attached to its hull to keep the vessel upright, the *Turtle* — which actually more resembled a walnut — was deemed fit for operation in the fall of 1776. Its first target was none other than Adm. Howe's 64-gun flagship of the line HMS *Eagle*, at the time engaged in the blockade of New York Harbor.

The *Turtle* was transported overland to the Hudson River and fitted with a torpedo two and a half feet long packing 150 pounds of gunpowder. Late at night on September 6, Continental whaleboats towed the contraption along the surface in New York Harbor to just outside the range of the *Eagle*'s cannons. During trials on the Connecticut River and in Long Island Sound, the *Turtle*'s volunteer pilot, Sgt. Ezra Lee of Connecticut's 10th Infantry Regiment, had been trained to submerge the vessel when he approached an enemy ship. He would then bore a hole in its hull with a large screw controlled by the hand cranks, guide the torpedo into the opening, and set the explosive's timer. Like so many of the Continentals' best-laid military plans, the *Turtle*'s initial mission fell apart almost immediately. Bushnell and his fellow planners had failed to take into account the Hudson River's strong currents.

After Sgt. Lee was cut loose from the whaleboats that night it took him over three hours of furious pedaling to reach the *Eagle*, by which time the sun was already peeking over the eastern horizon. In addition, the Americans were unaware that copper plating had only recently been laid over the *Eagle*'s hull to protect against shipworms. Whether the *Turtle*'s screw failed to penetrate this metal sheathing or was thwarted by the thick iron plate attached to the *Eagle*'s rudder hinge is immaterial. Lee, running out of air, exhausted, and possibly suffering from carbon dioxide poisoning, abandoned the scene. As he made for the New Jersey riverbank in broad daylight he was spotted by enemy sentries on Governors Island, who launched an oared guard boat in pursuit of the floating globe. Lee managed to frighten them off by detonating his torpedo. But with the element of surprise eliminated, the *Turtle*'s future effectiveness was compromised. Although the British maintained that no such thing as a submarine had attacked them, they subsequently intensified their lookout for any bizarre little boats toting what they referred to as exploding "infernals."

Within the month Bushnell tried again. Sailing this time with the tide, Sgt. Lee pedaled the *Turtle* toward a British frigate anchored off Manhattan. But he was spotted by the ship's night watch and forced to retreat under a salvo of flintlock fire. A few days later the *Turtle*'s tender vessel, with the submarine on it, was sunk by enemy cannon fire off New Jersey's Fort Lee. The *Turtle* may have been gone; Bushnell's tenacity remained. In early January 1778 he journeyed to Valley Forge and approached Washington with a plan to prepare a fresh batch of torpedoes and float them down the Delaware toward Philadelphia's harbor. There would be no need for timing devices, as the triggers on the bombs were set to detonate on contact with the hull of a ship. The city's moorings were then so crowded with enemy vessels that Bushnell and Washington hoped the torpedoes might ignite a wharf fire which would engulf Adm. Howe's entire fleet.

The sun had only just risen on January 5 when two boys walking along the Delaware's riverbank north of Philadelphia spotted one of the first powder-packed kegs approaching on the ebb tide. Thinking the flotsam might contain something valuable, they secured a small boat to investigate. When they gaffed the object, the "infernal" blew them and their craft to pieces. The explosion alerted lookouts who had been posted near the harbor to warn of floating ice chunks. Within moments panicked British sailors manning berthed warships unleashed a broadside of cannon fire at the remaining torpedoes while half-dressed soldiers rushed to the riverbank to pour shot into the water. The barrage lasted for hours, long after it had destroyed the floating bombs before they could do any physical damage. The psychological bruise to the British, however, was captured smartly by the New Jersey congressman and author Francis Hopkinson, whose subsequent 15-stanza poem, "The Battle of the Kegs," lampooned the enemy's hysterical reaction to what they thought was an amphibious invasion. Hopkinson's mocking parody, with specific references to Gen. Howe leaping from the bed of his mistress to don his battle attire, was published in newspapers from Massachusetts to Georgia, and became a staple recited around Valley Forge campfires.

Bushnell went on to develop other types of waterborne mines that could be delivered without his submarine, and Continental forces successfully deployed several of his prototypes along the Delaware and in New London Harbor. Years later Washington hailed his pet inventor as "a man of Great Mechanical Powers, fertile of invention and master in execution." Yet he also admitted that Bushnell "labored for some time ineffectually, and though the advocates for his scheme continued sanguine, he never did succeed." That the commander in chief of the Continental Army deigned to embrace David Bushnell's eccentric enterprises reflected Washington's desperation as well as his tendency to try anything that might addle the enemy's superior force. As for Bushnell, though he was often referred to as the "father of submarine warfare," his name — once as celebrated as Fulton's and Whitney's — has since faded into the mists of time.

The floating time bomb having come to naught but embarrassment to the British, by mid-January 1778 Washington had returned his attention to his increasingly bifurcated land operations. Since arriving at Valley Forge he had in effect split his winter command, using the Schuylkill as the dividing line. To the east of the river, the vast tract that stretched nearly 50 miles to New Jersey remained the nominal responsibility of the Pennsylvania militia, now under the temporary leadership of 23-year-old Gen. John Lacey. Lacey had been appointed after Gen. Armstrong, citing ill health, withdrew on temporary leave to his home in Carlisle, Pennsylvania. Like his predecessor, Lacey never came close to commanding the 1,000 troops the state had promised. His ranks were further thinned when scores of Pennsylvania men of fighting age subject to the compulsory militia laws simply refused to report for duty. So undermanned were Lacey's regiments that American spies in Philadelphia reported the city's markets suddenly awash with goods trundled in by the "country folk" predominantly from Montgomery County and Bucks County north of the city. One alarmed informant reported that there were enough flour sacks pouring into the city to keep 10,000 Redcoats in bread each day. The Continental blockade was further hamstrung by armed Tories banding together to escort caravans of overstuffed supply wagons and herds of cattle into the city, literally daring Lacey's militiamen to stop them.

In response, a clearly exasperated Washington turned to desperate measures. He wrote to one militia commander, "With respect to your future treatment of the Tories, the most effectual way of putting a stop to their traitorous practices, will be shooting some of the more notorious offenders wherever they can be found in flagrante delicto." He also toyed briefly with the idea of depopulating the problematic Montgomery and Bucks counties by forcing their inhabitants to pack up and move a minimum of 15 miles farther north from Philadelphia. Inevitably recognizing the impracticability of such a scheme, he instead dispatched a company of Continental regulars across the Schuylkill to anchor Gen. Lacey's right wing, and ordered Casimir Pulaski's already overburdened and undernourished cavalry to recross the Delaware from New Jersey whenever they could to buttress the Pennsylvanians' left flank.

Pulaski's light dragoons had encountered a

chilly reception in Trenton, whose pastures and infrastructure were still recovering from the ravages of both the Hessians' occupation and the previous Christmas's fighting. The fact that Pulaski's unit arrived with a reputation as horse thieves did not ease tensions. Only weeks earlier Washington had been forced to reprimand Pulaski for his liberal interpretation of his instructions to confiscate horses from Loyalists only. Moreover, New Jersey's capital city, consisting of barely 600 structures, was already garrisoning several hundred American sailors who had participated in the defense of Fort Mercer and Fort Mifflin. Its sullen citizenry was loath to welcome more mouths, human or equine, to feed and shelter. For his part, the Polish count repeatedly complained to Washington that the Navy's "galley men" had so stretched the township's limits that he had difficulty finding beds for his troops, much less stalls for his animals. As the days passed, Pulaski's increasingly shrill communiqués arrived at the Potts House as regularly as the Angelus — which is to say as often as petitions from Trenton's civil magistrates imploring the commander in chief to find another winter billet for either the sailors or the cavalrymen, if not both.

Washington trod delicately around the two squabbling factions. As much as he relied on a healthy and rested cavalry corps for his spring campaign, he could ill afford to alienate the New Jerseyans. After he abandoned his plans for a Christmas attack on Philadelphia, his strategy was more focused on the long view of the war. Accordingly, he suspected that when fighting resumed it would center on New York rather than Philadelphia. This meant that key battles were likely to take place throughout New Jersey. To that end Washington had cultivated a cordial relationship with the state's governor William Livingston, who was also the commander of the New Jersey militia — precisely the musket men whom he expected to play a prominent role in future engagements. Now, Livingston had taken up the cause of Trenton's grumbling town fathers. Placating Pulaski was not worth the risk of compromising the goodwill he had built up with Livingston. Pulaski was in essence left to his own foraging devices as long as he hatched no more "plundering schemes."

Pulaski, finding the area too fallow to support his dragoons, ultimately split his four companies between the New Jersey towns of Flemington and Pennington to Trenton's northwest. The count himself, when not attempting to fulfill his orders to patrol Bucks County, remained in Trenton with a small coterie of horsemen whose mounts were quartered in hay fields miles from town. These arrangements inevitably rendered the concept of quick strikes against Pennsylvania's Tory smugglers rather negligible.

Meanwhile, the mutual distrust that arose between Lacey's state militiamen and the army regulars sent to reinforce them took on the trappings of a cold war within the hot war. If the New Jersey irregulars in and around Trenton grudgingly accepted the presence of the American sailors and Pulaski's horsemen, the Pennsylvanians flaunted their outright hostility toward the Continentals. They accused the regulars of taking bribes to allow supply wagons to pass into Philadelphia, and of the more heinous crime of confiscating supplies from patriotic farmers and selling them to city-bound Loyalists. Regular-army officers answered these accusations by painting the militiamen as too frightened to stop and fight the gun-toting civilians, particularly the Doan Gang.

Struggling to maintain some shred of equanimity, Washington reacted as best he could to the charges and countercharges, sending a fact-finding mission across the river to report back on the situation. But a string of outraged General Orders evidenced his frustration — "It is with inexpressible grief and indignation that the General has received information of the cruel outrages and robberies lately committed by soldiers, on the other side of the Schuylkill: Were we in an enemy's country such practices would be unwarrantable; but committed against our friends are in the highest degree base, cruel and injurious to the cause in which we are engaged," read one.

In the end, his investigators found some merit in both arguments. A few Continentals suspected of selling travel passes were reprimanded and transferred back to Valley Forge. At the same time, Washington urged Gen. Lacey to step up his efforts against the armed supply caravans. But for the most part, the commander in chief's hands were tied, and any joint embargo effort on the part of these two groups was a pipe dream. Even if he could have afforded to buttress the patrols east of the Schuylkill with more of his regulars — which, given his finite resources, he could not — it had long been decided in York and Lancaster that the territory in question was under the nominal military purview of the state of Pennsylvania. Picking another fight with the state's civil authorities was pointless, particularly since a congressional delegation was soon due in camp. The agreement to bottle up the British in Philadelphia had been a joint pact between the army and Pennsylvania's statesmen, after all, and if they were overly worried in Lancaster about the ample amount of provisions reaching Gen. Howe's troops, it was their responsibility to strengthen their own force to halt it.

By late January the enmity between the

militia and the regulars had so calcified that the American efforts on that side of the river were more sieve than blockade. As more marketers flooded the roads into the city, the price of food in Philadelphia actually began to fall. Allowing the bad blood to persist between the state militiamen and his regulars — and allowing the British to get fat off the intramural rift — was about the best of Washington's several terrible options. Until, that is, he could make his case to the delegation from York. At least the situation on the west bank of the Schuylkill was more manageable.

Washington considered the area just below and to the west of Valley Forge the most vulnerable to a British probe, and thus the more dangerous defensive assignment. In addition to the trenches and redoubts excavated beyond the 400 "outer line" cabins facing Philadelphia, another mile-long slit trench pocked with rifle pits had been dug as a fallback position on the western edge of the camp near the base of the double-humped Mount Joy. This trough roughly followed the contours of the base of the mountain, atop which the Continentals had erected a 38-foot observation tower with sweeping views down the Schuylkill Valley. The tower was staffed day and night by lookouts supplied with spyglasses and signal flags. In addition, there were some 800 to 1,000 pickets constantly patrolling the territory to the southeast between Valley Forge and Philadelphia.

Given the wretchedness of camp life, it was considered something of a plum detail to be detached for anything that smacked of real soldiering. To that end the task of proscribing smugglers west of the Schuylkill as well as guarding against any British raids fell primarily to Dan Morgan and his rifle corps, the Continental Army's most effective guerrilla fighters. Morgan's men were bolstered by a small corps of mounted dragoons under the command of his fellow Virginian, 21-year old Captain Henry Lee III. The dashing Lee, nicknamed "Light Horse Harry," was a scion of one of Virginia's first families and considered one of the finest horsemen in the state. He had graduated from the College of New Jersey four years earlier with a degree in Latin and the intent of pursuing a legal career. The war changed that, and upon volunteering his services he was commissioned a captain.

The Lees had known the Washingtons since Mount Vernon, and Capt. Lee had in fact declined the commander in chief's invitation to join his staff as an aide-de-camp. He was flattered by the offer, he wrote, and thanked Washington for the opportunity, "certainly the first recommendation I can bear to posterity."* But he remained, as he put it, "wedded to my sword," and preferred to continue in the field. His gracious decline of the post was in keeping with his outsize reputation for professional and personal concern for his riders.

Chester County had a population of some 30,000 at the time, with Quakers making up a sizable portion, and the county's lower reaches were known to be dominated by an increasingly Tory-inclined populace. In addition to maintaining security and disrupting trade with the enemy, Lee's assignment on the western periphery of Valley Forge was also to broaden the army's network of spies and informants. It was hazardous duty. Any Whigs thought to have contact with the Continentals, or even a favorable impression of their cause, faced harassment and, in some cases, British-condoned kidnapping. Moreover, Gen. Howe had offered a bounty of 40 to 60 "hard dollars" for every captured American officer, and the risk of encounter-

* Little did Lee know that "the first recommendation I can bear to posterity" would in fact be to father a son he named Robert Edward, who married the daughter of George Washington's adopted step-grandson George Washington Parke Custis and, on April 9, 1865, surrendered his sword to Ulysses S. Grant in the town of Appomattox Court House.

ing Loyalist informers made it too chancy for Lee's limited detachments to linger in any one vicinity for more than 24 hours.

Despite the risk, not only did Capt. Lee become Washington's unofficial geographer in the area — scouting the countryside and recommending the most favorable junctions to place pickets and erect guard posts — but he and his 25 or so horsemen interacted with the local population perhaps more than any other American troopers. As the historian Wayne Bodle observes, Lee's "rapport with the common soldiers seemed to extend to the class of common citizens from which they were drawn." This sympathy led Lee to keep meticulous payment records for farmers under his jurisdiction who supplied him with food and shelter as well as offer them protection from both British and Continental foraging parties.

As it happened, the mutual bonds of trust Lee cultivated with these local patriots led to one of the most exciting sidebars of the war. On the night of January 19, one of Lee's constituents allowed him and his small escort of seven riders to bunk in his farmhouse. The Americans were awakened at daybreak by the sound of Redcoats attempting to batter down the farmer's oaken front door. Lee, rushing to a window, counted a sizable British patrol consisting of some 130 mounted dragoons surrounding the property. Only later would he discover that the company was commanded by the despised Banastre Tarleton. The farmhouse had more windows than Lee had men, but he positioned his Virginians so expertly that the British were soon retreating under what Lee drolly described as a "very warm" cascade of musket balls. Tarleton then threatened to burn Lee and his men out. This was met with jeers, hoots, and taunts reminding the British colonel that the structure was made of stone.

In an attempt to salvage his advantage, if not his dignity, Tarleton finally ordered his troops to seize the Americans' horses. But as the Redcoats approached the adjacent stable they were intercepted by Lee and his reckless squad, who rushed from the farmstead with their carbines blazing. The enemy turned tail and fled down the road toward Philadelphia. Lee and his men saddled quickly and, joined by a small company of Morgan's foot soldiers drawn to the sound of the gunfire, gave chase. The British riders rapidly outdistanced the Continentals afoot. With three of his horsemen bleeding from minor wounds, Lee opted for discretion over valor and called off the pursuit. A minor engagement soon forgotten. Or so he thought.

From a military perspective, the tactical significance of Lee's skirmish was close to nil. Two of the British dragoons had been killed, with Lee counting another four, including Tarleton, wounded. But the spreading tales of the outnumbered company's derring-do sent a vicarious shiver through the Valley Forge campsite. John Laurens was naturally agog, lauding the audacity "of the officers and men who had the honor of forcing such an incomparable superiority of numbers to a shameful retreat." And a 19-year-old New Jersey captain named William Gifford, writing to his best friend in the state's militia, encapsulated the mythology born that morning by describing how Lee's "superior bravery . . . and vigilance baffled the [British] designs . . . Obligat[ing] them to disgracefully retreat after Repeated & fruitless attempts." Washington personally congratulated Lee on his gallantry, and included in his General Orders for January 20 "his warmest thanks to Captn Lee & Officers & men . . . which by their superior Bravery . . . baffled the Enemy's designs."

Within days Lee's exploits at the farmhouse had become the stuff of legend, a fable masked by reality. One of the reasons Lee found himself bushwhacked with such an underwhelming force was that no American commander at Valley Forge, regardless of the value of his assignment, could muster much in the way of manpower or, in Lee's case, horsepower. As noted, two days before Christmas, Washington had reported to Congress that between one quarter and one third of his force — nearly 3,000 troopers — did not possess the clothing to render them fit for duty. Now, a month later, that number had risen by another 1,000. It was only natural for men living amid such misery to direct their anger toward local and state legislators who had sent them off to war and now seemingly abandoned them.

General Poor, for instance, having apparently given up on receiving redress from his governor, wrote to the New Hampshire state assembly about being barely able to tolerate the shame of having to inspect his troops each morning while listening to their "lamentable tales of distresses" that were beyond his power to alleviate. His starving and half-naked soldiers, Poor wrote, were solely dependent "on the cold hand of meek-eyed charity alone." As with the implied menace in Washington's "disperse" letter, Poor intimated that unless the situation was rapidly remedied, he did not know how much longer he could hold his troops in the field. Similarly, a lieutenant colonel with Massachusetts's 12th Regiment described to his state's executive council the appalling sight of assembling his company each morning in the snow and slushy mud. Some 90 of his soldiers, he wrote, "have not a Shoee to their foot and near as many who have no feet to their Stockings."

At least the young New Jersey officer so

aroused by Light Horse Harry Lee's gallantry was willing to give the civil authorities back home the benefit of the doubt. In the same letter to his friend, Capt. Gifford wrote that he could not believe his state representatives were venal; they were merely ignorant of the hardship facing him and fellow New Jersey-ans. "If they had any idea," he wrote, "they certainly wou'd do more for us." After fighting through the fall campaigns, Gifford and his companions had expected to be assigned a winter bivouac closer to home. They were, after all, less than 50 miles from the New Jersey border. Instead, they found themselves "very bare for clothes" atop a snow-swept plateau in southeast Pennsylvania, forced to shelter in what he called dilapidated Indian "wigwams."

Gifford's charity toward his state's civil authorities was the exception. The 26-year-old Massachusetts lieutenant colonel John Brooks spoke for most when he concluded that if in fact the "bare footed, bare leg'd, bare breech'd" condition of his troops was merely a lack of foresight, "then the Lord pity us." But, invoking the principle *res ipsa loquitur,* he added that if their plight was brought about "thro' negligence or Design, is there not some chosen curse reserv'd for those who are the cause of so much Misery?"*

The groundswell of grievances from the enlisted ranks did not go unnoticed by the officers they held responsible for their plight. Food purchasing agents rarely set foot within the confines of the Valley Forge encampment after a commissary officer was killed by a mob of hungry soldiers. And representatives from the clothier general's department attached to the army so feared physical retribution that they staked winter quarters some five miles northwest of the camp. The Continental Army's paymaster in York, aware of his unwelcome presence at the cantonment, quite simply wrote to Washington that there was no sense in his visiting until Congress somehow managed to raise enough money to actually pay the soldiers.

Washington was left to cope with this myriad of colliding catastrophes while still concentrating on his overarching strategy of keeping his army a disciplined, confident, and competent force. Yet there was one hurdle he was never able to clear. For if there was a common and overriding enemy aside from the British, aside from the Tories, and aside

* Brooks would later practice what he preached when, as commander of his state's militia in 1787, he made sure that his soldiers were well-clothed, well-armed, and well-fed when he ordered them into the field to put down Shays' Rebellion.

from the bickering lawmakers upon whom the American troops longed to loose their wrath, it was the members of the numerous pacifist religious sects who populated much of southeastern Pennsylvania. Many a Continental soldier went to his grave hating the Quakers.

NINETEEN:
AN AMERICAN ARMY

When William Penn founded his eponymous Commonwealth in 1682, he and his followers preached open-mindedness toward the various Mennonites, Dunkers, Amish, Moravians, and smaller if similar religious communities that settled in Pennsylvania and, to a lesser extent, Delaware and southern New Jersey. To the Continental soldiers, these somewhat diverse groups were lumped together under the rubric of the largest faith among them, Penn's own Society of Friends, or Quakers — the latter name referred to the physical trembling before God that they advocated and sometimes performed at their religious meetings. In late 1777, nearly a century after Penn's grand experiment in tolerance, it was the progeny of these early settlers who quite conspicuously refused to take up arms in defense of the American Revolution. This proved contentious at Valley Forge, particularly to the Virginians and Carolinians, who already cast a wary eye at the members of the Society for their antislavery sentiments.

The resentment was understandable. For five months Washington's troops had crisscrossed the farmlands and villages of Quaker country fighting and dying for a cause they felt represented all Americans. These men had watched friends and compatriots fall while the inimical "Dutchmen from this Sanctified Quaking State" remained neutral at best and antagonistic at worst. More than one bitter patriot echoed the sentiments of the Massachusetts officer John Brooks — the dyspeptic lieutenant colonel who had called down curses on his own state government — when he wondered, regarding the outcome at Saratoga, whether his fellow New Englanders exhibited the same nonviolent tendencies toward Gen. Burgoyne's army "which the cringing, nonresisting ass-like Fools of [this] State have shown towards Howe." Perhaps more chillingly, in an age when religion remained a fundamental theme of life *and* death, there were few premonitions more frightening to the righteous than the possibility, as Rhode Island's Gen. James Varnum put it, "of dying in a heathenish land, depriv'd of a Christian burial."

As most Quakers were at the time forbidden to earn academic degrees, they had come to dominate eastern Pennsylvania's manufacturing and commerce economies. The hostile interactions between Continental troops wintering over at Valley Forge and what they dubbed the local "Thees and Thous" were exacerbated by rumors — sometimes verified; often not — that Quakers were integral to the Tory smuggling trade. The outlaw Doan Gang had Quaker ties, and it was undeniable that Quaker farmers and merchants, like many non-Quakers, preferred British specie to the devalued Continental scrip. Moreover, as several of the 13 colonies maintained separate currencies, exchange rates jounced wildly from region to region and in some places there was an 800 percent inflation rate. Though the federal government printed and issued its own money, this was not backed by gold supplies. For that reason, and because of a concerted British counterfeiting effort that flooded the colonies with forged dollars, American paper money was virtually worthless by this point in the war.*

Given Valley Forge's location, this proved a bitter paradox. For Washington's army *should* have had much greater access than the British to the agricultural resources of the ter-

---

* In late 1776 the First Continental Congress voted to hold a convoluted national lottery to raise money that, in essence, resembled nothing so much as a Ponzi scheme. After various iterations, the first drawing was finally offered to the public in May 1778. It proved an utter failure.

ritories surrounding Philadelphia. The bountiful fields of Bucks County and Montgomery County in particular had in 1777 produced crop yields that were among the highest of the decade. And it was clear to all noncombatants that the British seldom played favorites among the settled towns and villages through which they tramped and looted. The Hessians in particular had earned a reputation for leaving devastation in their wake, and the nonviolent religious communities were just as likely to have had their "wives ravished [and] houses Plunder'd and burn'd" as any patriot hamlet. The Potts family's mills and forges were testament to that. Yet not only did the Continentals lack money; their severe dearth of wagons made useless any provisions they might secure on credit.

At their Yearly Meeting in 1777, all Quakers were threatened with disownment by the faith not only if they took up arms, but also if they traded with soldiers or worked as teamsters, smiths, or foragers for either army. Further, relations between the desperate Continental troops and the local civilians who did arrive at Valley Forge on market day held little hope for improvement when, for instance, the flagging American scrip pushed the price of a pound of butter to one dollar, a small bread pie sold for double that, and the cost of a pair of shoes was nearly equal to a soldier's monthly pay, which by this point was a very theoretical $25.*

Two days after the battle of Germantown, Quakers in Philadelphia had sent deputations to both Howe and Washington testifying to "the ungodliness of war and their equal love to all men." To the American commander in chief in particular they pleaded their case as nothing more than conscientious bystanders to the carnage surrounding them. This was a hard sell to the average Continental soldier. Even the more enlightened felt that if the Quakers' religious principles prevented them from lifting a firearm in anger, they at least had an obligation to support the cause by selling provisions at fair and humane prices. Some Pennsylvania officeholders who knew the sects best went even further, theorizing that if only the right feelers were put out, the Quakers might be persuaded to act as secret couriers and even spies in exchange for official exemption from military service. To make this case they pointed not only to the "Fighting Quaker" Gen. Greene but also to the man in charge of the Valley Forge commissary, 37-year-old Col. Clement Biddle.

Prior to the war, Biddle had worked in his father's burgeoning shipping business.

* Or around $600 in 2018 dollars, though it hardly mattered. The New England troops dispatched to Pennsylvania from Peekskill in September, for instance, had not been paid since leaving New York.

Though members of the Society of Friends, the Biddles were not prominent in Philadelphia's Quaker circles. When he was in his twenties Biddle discovered that he did not share his parents' and his brother Owen's pacifist views, particularly when it came to the outrages committed against the peaceful Conestoga Indians by the Paxton Boys. Biddle set about recruiting a volunteer militia of like-minded coreligionists to protect the Conestoga, who had taken refuge on Province Island. Ten years later, with the Declaration of Independence, Biddle and what had become known as his "Quaker Blues" threw their lot in with the Continental Army, and fought honorably and ably at Trenton, Brandywine, and Germantown.

The theory had it that if Biddle could convince his fellow Friends to take up arms in defense of godless Indians, what could prevent him or someone like him from recruiting eyes and ears in Philadelphia willing to pass on the latest military gossip? But a series of anti-Quaker events between Biddle's formation of his militia in the 1760s and the Continental Army's encampment at Valley Forge had opened a gulf too wide to bridge. Not the least of these events was a 1775 decree by the Pennsylvania state assembly making "defensive military service" compulsory in the state militia.

The law, which imposed a heavy tax on any

man who refused to serve, was directed toward Quakers like Joseph Doan. He and others who refused to pay the levy had their property seized and sold at auction. In defiance of the legislation, Quakers attending Philadelphia's Yearly Meeting in 1776 were advised to "unite against every design of independence." This earned them a public censure from Pennsylvania's Committee for Public Safety, which in turn sparked a series of anti-Tory riots in Philadelphia aimed at Quaker establishments. While most Society members fled to the countryside, a few held out, and even as Washington and his army paraded through the city in August 1777 the Continental Congress ordered 18 of the city's most prominent Friends banished to western Virginia under suspicion of "aiding and abetting the cause of the enemy."

Washington himself had a unique manner of dealing with Quaker intransigence. At the beginning of the Pennsylvania campaign he had issued standing orders that all millstones be removed from gristmills standing in the enemy's path. Once the British had passed through the area in question, the stones were returned to the mill owners — except if the millers happened to be Friends. This practice eventually led Gen. Howe to file an official complaint against the Continentals for "inflicting untold hardship" upon the territory's civilian population. Washington was not moved. Yet whatever his private feelings about the Society's pacifism, throughout the war and particularly later in life he publicly professed an admiration for the Quakers' "conscientious scruples of religious belief." After his defeat at Brandywine Creek, he had even dined and spent the night at the commodious home of one of Chester County's most illustrious Friends, the London-born trader James Vaux. He was unaware that, the evening before, Vaux had extended the same courtesy to Gen. Howe.

Washington's attitude toward the Quakers was undoubtedly influenced by Alexander Hamilton, who was drawn to their passionate antipathy to slavery. Hamilton also admired the pro-independence Philadelphian scholar, writer, orator, and lawyer John Dickinson. Though a semi-lapsed Friend, Dickinson retained strong Quaker leanings throughout his life — he said often that his real difference with the Society was that he thought it every man's duty to fight in a just war — and his famous polemic against parliamentary taxation, *Letters from a Farmer in Pennsylvania,* aligned precisely not only with Hamilton's republican bent, but with his Quaker-like belief that the essential right to happiness was bestowed by the Almighty, not by any king or general.

That the thoughts of a barely 23-year-old aide-de-camp — "that bastard brat of a Scottish peddler," per John Adams — could so sway Washington's mind-set offers insight into how close he had become not only to Hamilton, but to the group of young men with whom he shared such close living quarters at the Potts House. In his 1910 biography of his paternal grandfather, Allan McClane Hamilton observed that there was something about the "gay trio" of Hamilton, John Laurens, and Lafayette "rather suggestive of the three famous heroes of Dumas." Laurens, with his odes to either "glorious death or the triumph of the cause," and the swashbuckling Lafayette with his unquenchable thirst for military glory may have indeed aroused the commander in chief's natural martial impulses. But it was Hamilton in the role of Athos who best channeled Washington's analytical approach to both war and politics. Nothing illustrated this better than the "bastard brat's" input into the searing policy doctrine that Washington had prepared for the congressional delegates who in late January 1778 departed York for Valley Forge.

January 24 dawned warm and gray over the winter cantonment, with misty showers and jagged skeins of fog scudding down from the western hills. The cold front had broken, and the hoarfrost that had spangled the branches of the great chestnut trees was slowly dissipating, giving the impression of glass figurines melting into shapelessness. The unsettling warmth had also released a miasma that lay over the camp like an illness: the black smoke from cooking fires mixed with the effluvia of decomposing animals and overripe latrines leaching into the muddy soil. It was into this cloak of bone-aching damp and noxious haze that the five members of the congressional delegation arrived that afternoon.* One could not blame them for wondering what fresh hell they had ridden into.

The delegates were met by Washington personally at what was to be their quarters, Moore Hall, a grandly gabled Georgian pile hard by the west bank of the Schuylkill. The stone house had been rented by several American officers, including Gen. Greene and Col. Biddle, while the elderly Moores, an aristocratic and outspoken Tory family, had been relegated to a few rooms on an upper floor. After depositing their traveling gear at Moore Hall, the congressmen spent the next several days inspecting the soldiers' winter lodgings and consulting informally with commanders from their home states.

On the morning of January 29, Washington,

* The delegation now consisted of Francis Dana of Massachusetts, Gouverneur Morris of New York, Joseph Reed of Pennyslvania, Nathaniel Folsom of New Hampshire, and Virginia's John Harvie.

John Laurens, and Hamilton rode the two and a half miles from the Potts House to Moore Hall to convene the first session of what would come to be known informally as the Camp Committee. If the men who had journeyed from York were apprehensive about the opacity of their mission statement other than, as the delegation's chairman Francis Dana put it, "to rap a demi-god over the knuckles," the commander in chief was not. He and his staff had spent the previous weeks paring the thousands of pages of memoranda submitted by his officers into a 38-page handwritten report that one admiring historian described as "a carefully polished political tract."

Composed in the baroque vernacular of the era — "I have in the following sheets briefly delivered my sentiments upon such of them as seemed to me most essential; so far, as observation has suggested, and leisure permitted" — the 13,000-word manifesto was written in Hamilton's elegant cursive and entitled *A Representation to the Committee of Congress.* That Hamilton, recovering from pneumonia, had returned from upstate New York only a week earlier yet had still managed to compile a document burnished by his protean intellect was as astonishing as the content of its pages. For *A Representation to the Committee of Congress* was not only a blueprint for reforming the entire Continental Army, but an aggressive rebuttal of the implicit and explicit criticisms of Washington's leadership from military and civil authorities. Not the least of these was a 45-point critique of the commander in chief that had appeared on the steps of the congressional hall in York only two days earlier.

The savagery of the unsigned tract, entitled *The Thoughts of a Freeman,* was bracing. Fashioned in the form of a legal indictment, it referred to Washington, his aides, and his leading generals as the hellspawn demon "Baal & his worshipers" and accused the commander in chief alternately of cowardice and incompetence in allowing the enemy to capture Philadelphia.* It implied that the officers who had ordered the abandonment of Fort Mercer were treasonous; it warned the delegates that the state militias were the only force that stood between the republic and Washington's using the Continental Army to turn the United States into a dictatorship; it mocked the congressional delegates loyal to Washington for their "great weakness in the head"; and it concluded by charging the American people with "Idolatry by mak-

---

* This "Baal," the "King of Hell" in seventeenth-century occult writings, is usually spelled Bael and is a separate entity from the god of fertility worshipped by the ancient Canaanites.

ing a man their god" at the expense of offending "the true God of heaven and earth."

The Thoughts of a Freeman had been discovered on the steps of the county courthouse where Congress met and was turned over to Henry Laurens with its seal unbroken. Laurens read the anonymous screed and, without sharing its contents with any of the 13 congressmen in attendance at York, forwarded a copy to Washington. In an attached note he suggested that "the hearth was the proper depository for such Records." But it wasn't burned; Washington wrote back urging Laurens to submit the denunciation to Congress so he could defend himself against any accuser courageous enough to publicly step forward. None did, although "the malignant faction" aligned against him continued, as Washington put it, "to take ungenerous advantage of me."

Now, if the five delegates who constituted the Camp Committee expected to confront the general described as disaffected and indecisive by his enemies in and outside Congress, they were surely taken aback by the visionary breadth and depth of *A Representation to the Committee of Congress.* One section suggested restructuring the regimental, cavalry, artillery, and engineering units. Another included concrete recommendations for inducing all officers and enlisted men to commit fully to the war effort for the duration of hostilities. In the furtherance of this end, another long passage addressed standing up a regimented military hospital system between the Potomac and the Hudson with clear and uniform guidelines for treatment of the sick and wounded. But it was the army's bloated and barely functioning procurement practices and supply stem that ranked highest on Washington's list of grievances.

Traditionally, both the Commissary Department and the Quartermaster Department were headed by military officers. Yet the majority of employees working under the department heads, even those attached to army units, were civilians. As a result, ineptitude, shortsightedness, theft, and corruption were rampant, particularly in the form of fraudulent purchasing orders. In his report to the delegates, Washington was blunt, categorizing the Commissary Department as "defective" and "deplorable." He singled out the Maryland militia's Lt. Col. William Buchanan — the "present Gentleman" in charge of the Commissary Department — as the cause of the "utmost difficulty we are [having] to keep the army together" and went on to warn the politicians that unless "a considerable alteration takes place, I see no prospect of adequate supplies for the succeeding [spring] campaign."

Washington's policy statement emphasized that no longer could the bloated commissary bureaucracy continue the practice of provisioning and paying the troops on a "hand to mouth" basis. The document also hinted strongly that if the United States' civil authorities expected their fighting men to take the offensive come spring and thereafter, a smooth and reliable delivery system for supply and payment must be instituted, with the army's Quartermaster and Paymaster Departments staffed no longer by civilian employees but by military officers who had earned the positions by dint of their actions on the front lines. In an example of its wide-ranging purview, the report suggested that a deal be struck with the French court to purchase uniforms on credit, with each state embedding within its fighting brigades a clothier and quartermaster's assistant of some rank with the power and ability to distribute the uniforms as well as rectify losses and wants ranging from food to shoes to kettles to blankets to "spirituous liquors" and "vinegar vegetables and soap."

In a passage pertaining to the retention of troops, *A Representation to the Committee of Congress* prescribed a pension system whereby every officer who pledged to serve until the revolution prevailed would be awarded half pay for the rest of his life, with his widow and children equally compensated in the event of his death. In this manner Washington was advancing the reasonable premise that the offer of postwar compensation would reduce if not eliminate the pervasive disgruntlement of an officer corps riven by "apathy, inattention, and neglect of duty" resulting in large part, he felt, from financial insecurity. Conversely, the threat of dismissal and the loss of a promised pension would provide senior officers with a greater measure of discipline over their junior charges. One detects the hand of the eminently practical Hamilton in the argument that public virtue and civic duty "may for only but a time actuate men" to risk their lives for an ideal. But at the end of the day, the argument concluded, it was fair compensation that kept them on the line. This was merely human nature, and to think otherwise would necessitate "chang[ing] the constitution of man."

Perhaps with the militia-centric *Thoughts of a Freeman* lingering in his mind, Washington acknowledged that creating a semipermanent officer class would clash with the infant government's aversion to any semblance of a standing army, and even more with Congress's "well-intended frugality." However, he hinted that if their cause was to triumph, the legislators could not have it both ways. A great percentage of his most efficient and experienced officers at Valley Forge were in fact waiting to see if the new pension plan would be initiated "to reanimate their languishing zeal." If it was not, he predicted a slew of immediate resignations.*

If retirement at half pay was the carrot dangled before the army's officer corps, the stick for the enlisted men took the form of a national military draft. Voluntary enlistments in the regular army, Washington contended, could no longer make up for the decimation of its rolls due to deaths, injuries, illnesses, and "dayly desertions." He calculated that most if not all patriots willing to commit themselves to arms had already done so. If experience had taught him anything, he wrote, it was that forcing whatever men were left into uniform for the duration of the conflict, particularly members of the pacifist religious sects, "would not augment our general strength, in any proportion to what we require." He thus offered what he felt was the admittedly "disagreeable . . . but unavoidable" alternative of implementing a draft from within each state's militia. The colonies already required a year of militia service from every white male between the ages of 16 and 60, exempting the clergy and college students and in some cases proscribing free blacks and Catholics.† Washington's conscription plan

* In fact, 576 officers are believed to have left the army during the Valley Forge encampment.
† One of Gen. Horatio Gates's first proclamations upon his appointment to head the Board of War was directed to regular-army recruiters in Massachu-

would obligate militia draftees to serve one year in the Continental Army. When this 12-month commitment expired, he suggested that a reenlistment bonus of $25 be offered. If that bounty failed to keep the army fully staffed — as he suspected — the state-by-state draft would be conducted annually for as long as the fighting lasted.

Washington recognized that restocking the ranks of the regular army in such a manner was far from optimal. It was, however, "perhaps the best our circumstances will allow." Moreover, if the pension plan was adopted, at least there would also be in place a stable of veteran officers to train and shape the rotating draft classes. He even left the draftees an out by suggesting that should any men's "disposition and private affairs make them irreconcilably averse to giving their public services," they would be excused if they were able to "procure a substitute in [their] stead."

As Hamilton and John Laurens stood off to the side of Moore Hall's great room taking in their imposing commander in chief's oration, it surely must have dawned on them that they were witnessing history writ large. Washington — as always, the tallest man in the room —

setts. In it he forbade them to enlist "any deserter . . . nor any stroller, Negro, nor any under eighteen years of age."

was declaring his own colonial army obsolete, ineffective, and doomed to failure. And though neither aide left personal reminiscences about the meeting, it is easy to imagine the excitable Laurens barely able to contain himself during the scene he was witnessing, and to envision the more cerebral Hamilton calmly fixing his gaze on one delegate after another as the powerful message he had composed struck home.

A Representation to the Committee of Congress ticked off the commander in chief's exigencies like Homer cataloging the Achaean ships. His overtures to the national legislature ranged from the sweeping — a complete expansion and the reorganization of the cavalry service by adding some two dozen horsemen to each of the army's four mounted regiments — to a comprehensive facilitation of the minutiae of military command. He argued that the current limit of 100 lashes for recidivist deserters be raised, and pressed for an overhaul of a promotional system that rewarded political connections over valor in the field. He detailed intricate plans for streamlining a be-draggled battalion system stretched so thin by losses that regiments varied in size from larger than brigades to, in one case, a single unit consisting of three dozen men commanded by a corporal. He delineated the ranks of general officers who were to be put in charge of brigades, battalions, and divisional battle lines. And he suggested the institution of one of the first forms of military police — a mounted "Provost Marshalcy," he called it, to watch over the good order of the army, in camp, in quarters, or on the march and "to silence all quarrels, tumults, and riots, detect and hinder every species of marauding — prevent straggling and other unsoldierlike licenses among the troops — to apprehend spies, or persons, whose not being able to give a good account of themselves may render them suspicious — to establish and inforce good regulations among the suttlers, seeing that the articles they offer for sale are good in quality and at reasonable prices."

Addressing the matter of black troops, Washington warned against the induction of slaves, as they were too likely "to desert to the enemy to obtain their freedom" while taking Continental Army wagons and supplies with them. He did, however, implore Congress to consider hiring African American "freemen" from Maryland, Virginia, and North Carolina to replace the expensive and arrogant civilian teamsters currently hauling the army's provisions. And in order to counterbalance the enemy's use of "savages" against his troops, he asked "would it not be well to employ several hundred indians" as scouts and stealth skirmishers in the ensuing American campaigns. To that end he volunteered his friend Dan Morgan, who, he said, could be counted on to round up a party of Cherokee from Virginia, adding that he also knew a local clergyman whose influence among some more northerly tribes would be sufficient to fill in the remainder. He even invited Congress to consider differentiating each state's soldiers by subtle changes to the colors of their uniform as well as the cut of their collars and cuffs in order to improve morale.

If there was a single theme that permeated *A Representation to the Committee of Congress,* it was Washington's emphasis on the subtle perils of continuing to wage war, particularly a Fabian war, with nonprofessional soldiers. Discipline and subordination, he argued, had not yet had time to completely infiltrate the psyches of "a young army, like ours." At heart these men maintained a civilian's frame of mind, particularly acute to any slight that carried a whiff of injustice. These patriotic soldiers, Washington said, would fight, and fight well, but they must receive food, clothing, pay, and arms equal to their sacrifice.

The commander in chief had opened his position paper with due deference to the political body shaping the young nation. In its first paragraph he offered his hope that the delegates would see fit to consider his proposals as mere suggestions "conducive to remedying the Evils and inconveniences we are now subject to and putting the Army upon a more respectable footing." The underlying tenor, however, was more Hamiltonian in its substance — firm and obvious. The Continental Army that existed at its inception 30 months earlier could not be sealed in a bell jar. It was Washington's intention to create a modern *American* army from its fragments. He reminded the committeemen that they had been appointed by Congress "in concert with me" to reorganize his forces, while reiterating "the numerous defects in our present military establishment." The same accommodating opening paragraph climaxed with an insistent ultimatum — "Something must be done."

Throughout his analysis Washington had somewhat tempered the dire predictions enumerated in his "starve, dissolve, or disperse" proclamation. But his report also made clear to the delegates that the recommendations therein meant the difference between an army prepared to confront and defeat the British and "a feeble, languid, and ineffectual" force easily defeated come spring. In his conclusion Washington drove home the point that painting such a "disagreeable picture is a just representation of evils equally melancholy and important; and unless effectual remedies be applied without loss of time, the most alarming and ruinous consequences are to be apprehended."

A Representation to the Committee of Congress was a masterly amalgamation of distillation and presentation. The pension plan, for instance, had begun as a germ of an idea submitted by Gen. Greene, much as the expansion of the cavalry corps had been originally presented by Gen. Pulaski. Even the consolidation of the regiments had been suggested by the officers of the nine North Carolina battalions whose commands had been so thinned by attrition that they barely resembled robust fighting forces.

Given the broad contours of their mandate, the manifesto was, in all, quite something for the five delegates to digest. The commander in chief's singular tenacity was the trait that had set him above his peers on the battlefield. Now this same persistence was on display in the political arena. As the hours passed that evening, a significant fact became clear — Washington the soldier-statesman had captured the hearts and minds of the visiting delegates. They began work on his proposals immediately.

This portrait of tranquility of the falls of the Schuylkill River, five miles from Philadelphia, belies the fact that the area was to endure repeated conflicts between the British and American armies before and during the Valley Forge encampment.

Though King George III ruled Great Britain and its territories for six decades, he is essentially remembered as the monarch who lost the war for American independence.

Charles Willson Peale's iconic portrait of Marie Joseph Paul Yves Roche Gilbert du Motier, Marquis de Lafayette, who at 20 was a fearless major general in the Continental Army and who joked that he had been christened in honor of every saint who could protect him in battle.

Dubbed "that bastard son of a Scottish peddler" by John Adams, the 22-year-old Lieutenant Colonel Alexander Hamilton chafed for a battlefield command during the winter of 1777–78, but he was too indispensable as General George Washington's chief aide-de-camp.

John Laurens of South Carolina, son of the president of the Continental Congress and an idealistic aide to Washington, formed with Hamilton and Lafayette a troika of young men as completely devoted to the American cause for independence as they were to its commander in chief.

General "Mad Anthony" Wayne, a native Pennsylvanian and one of Washington's most trusted home-grown commanders, led his troops in every major engagement of the Pennsylvania campaign, including the ill-fated Paoli Massacre.

Reviled in London for their failure to put down the American rebellion, the British brothers General William Howe and Admiral Richard Howe are lampooned in this political cartoon as conspiring with the Devil to enrich themselves by prolonging the war.

Though many of the American troops lacked the skills and training of their British counterparts, for much of the Battle of Brandywine Creek on September 11, 1777, they repelled one British attack after another before being forced to withdraw.

"Treat him as you would my own son," Washington instructed the army surgeon who tended to Lafayette after he was wounded during the Battle of Brandywine Creek.

The British-born American General Charles Lee spent the winter of 1777–78 as a prisoner of war, only to be exchanged in time to lead the Continental Army to the brink of disaster at the Battle of Monmouth Court House.

Henry Laurens, president of the Continental Congress during the Valley Forge encampment, became a staunch ally of Washington's, aided by the fierce loyalty his son John had for the commander in chief.

The American General William Alexander—known as Lord Stirling because of his ancestral claims to Scottish nobility—was one of Washington's most courageous and loyal officers.

Nearly 200 sleeping Americans were bayonetted to death on the night of September 20, 1777, in what came to be known as the Paoli Massacre.

Still recovering from wounds suffered during his heroic actions at the Battle of Saratoga, General Benedict Arnold was placed in charge of Philadelphia after the British evacuated the city in June 1778.

The Virginia frontiersman Colonel Daniel Morgan led a rifle regiment of sharpshooters whose backwoods guerilla tactics struck fear into their British opponents.

Serving as second in command to both General William Howe and, later, General Henry Clinton, Lord Charles Cornwallis led the reinforcements who helped turn the tide at the Battle of Germantown.

Though Col. John Laurens was lauded for his bravery during the attack on the "Chew House" during the Battle of Germantown, the action proved a major and costly mistake.

Brigadier General Louis Duportail, who traveled from France to join the American cause, was the chief designer of the Valley Forge defenses; he and his team were appointed as the original U.S. Army Corps of Engineers.

WASHINGTON'S MARQUE

Before appropriating the Potts House at Valley Forge for his headquarters, Washington directed the Revolutionary War from this campaign tent. With the Continental Congress in exile and disarray, the canvas pavilion served as the de facto capital of the United States.

Contrary to popular belief, the winter of 1777–78 was not the coldest one of the Revolutionary War. The conditions, however, may have been the most harsh, exacerbated as they were by the near-complete dearth of food and clothing.

Many scholars contend that this scene of Washington praying in the snow at Valley Forge in February 1778 never actually occurred, yet it does represent the genuine anguish the commander in chief felt over the suffering of his troops.

Considered Washington's favorite general and chosen personally by the commander in chief to succeed him should Washington fall on the battlefield, Rhode Island's Nathanael Greene reluctantly volunteered to take on the additional duties of quartermaster general in order to scour the countryside for provisions to feed the starving troops.

Charles Gravier, the Comte de Vergennes, served as King Louis XVI's foreign minister and worked closely with Benjamin Franklin in negotiating the Franco-American alliance that brought France into the war on the side of the Americans.

This depiction of Benjamin Franklin being received at the court of Louis XVI reflects not only the French veneration of him for his scientific achievements, but his lifelong appeal to the fairer sex. Both qualities helped him, Silas Deane, and Arthur Lee negotiate an alliance with France.

Thomas Paine compared the Continental troops to an "army of beavers" in their zeal to construct the simple log huts that would provide some semblance of suffocating shelter during the Valley Forge encampment.

This house, owned by the Potts family of Valley Forge, served as the cramped headquarters and living quarters for Gen. Washington and his sprawling staff during that fateful winter.

During the British occupation of Philadelphia over the winter of 1777–78, the intelligence officer Captain John André romanced the beautiful American socialite Peggy Shippen, the future wife of Benedict Arnold.

A contemporary portrait of Peggy Shippen, daughter of a wealthy Philadelphia loyalist, drawn by Capt. André. Her marriage to Benedict Arnold would lead to his treason against the American cause.

The American general Horatio Gates, fresh from his astounding victory at the Battle of Saratoga, proceeded to scheme with a small circle of fellow officers—including General Thomas Conway and certain members of Congress—to replace Washington as commander in chief, in what came to be known as the "Conway Cabal."

Washington had little use for most of the foreign soldiers of fortune who flocked to America's shores seeking battlefield glory. The exceptions, from his immediate left, were Johann de Kalb, Baron von Steuben, Casimir Pulaski, Tadeusz Kosciuszko, and the Marquis de Lafayette, soldiers who fought—and in the case of de Kalb and Pulaski, died—for the cause of American independence.

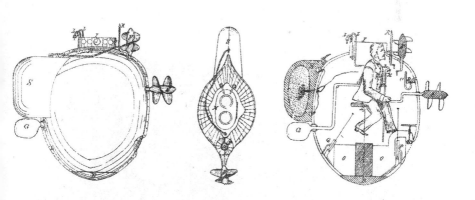

The American Revolution witnessed the first military use of a submarine, a one-man craft dubbed the *Turtle* by its American inventor, David Bushnell. While arming the submersible vehicle, Bushnell coined the term "torpedo."

With the ever-loyal Marquis de Lafayette at his side, Gen. Washington visits the troops soon after a January 1778 snowstorm.

During the Valley Forge encampment Gen. Washington sent out hundreds of letters, many of them written by Alexander Hamilton, to officers, lawmakers, family, and others, providing details on the conduct of the war. Over the winter of 1777–78, Washington essentially was the personification of the government of the United States.

The arrival of Martha Washington at Valley Forge in February 1778 revived the flagging spirits of her husband and, by extension, those of his troops.

Baron Friedrich Wilhelm von Steuben may have arrived at Valley Forge in February with a falsified résumé, yet he was credited by Washington with almost single-handedly transforming the Continental Army into a professional and powerful fighting force.

Despite a language barrier that forced Baron von Steuben to rely on translators to relay his curses-filled instructions, the Prussian's incessant drilling lessons quickly took hold.

When Gen. William Howe was recalled to England, it was Sir Henry Clinton who reluctantly took command of all British forces in North America and oversaw the near disastrous retreat from Philadelphia to New York.

A former Boston bookseller and one of George Washington's closest confidants, the autodidact General Henry Knox led the nascent Continental Army's artillery corps that so devastated the British at the Battle of Monmouth Court House.

At a critical moment during the Battle of Monmouth Court House in June 1778, Gen. Washington galloped along the front lines, demanding of his troops, "Will you fight?" They answered his call with a renewed strength.

TWENTY:
"HOWE'S PLAYERS"

By late January 1778, the Pennsylvania campaign of the American Revolution had reached an awkward impasse. At Valley Forge, what one historian describes as "a sense of inaction, restlessness, and drift" continued to fester among the men, particularly the officer corps. Washington continued to field a succession of plaintive petitions from idle subordinates of all ranks, the bane of any active military force with no immediate antagonist. The commander in chief prided himself on being the "common guardian" of each soldier's interests no matter how trivial the complaint, and personally dealt with these eruptions as best he could. Yet even his powerful personality found the restiveness difficult to quell.

Several New England generals who felt their honor besmirched by the failed invasion of Canada two years earlier now found the time to demand that Washington open public hearings on their conduct in order to clear their names. At the other end of the spectrum, a clique of artillery officers delivered a searing letter to the Potts House protesting the promotion of a French captain within their ranks.* A substantial contingent of troops from upstate New York, officers and enlisted men alike, asked to be transferred back to Albany, an appeal the commander in chief summarily denied without comment. His reaction was softer when a group from Virginia's 13th Regiment, having been promised service closer to home upon their enlistment, applied to be relocated to Fort Pitt. Washington, perhaps feeling more sympathy for his fellow Old Dominion regulars, went out of his way to visit their officers' quarters and patiently outline his reasons for retaining them at Valley Forge. When this kind of reasoning proved ineffective, he relied on courts-martial. Washington's daily General Orders reveal that military trials nearly tripled that winter, for offenses ranging from desertion, conduct unbecoming a gentleman,

* That the artillery officers agreed on anything was quite remarkable, as historians generally concur that the feuding among the Continental Army's squabblesome and brooding Artillery Division — a self-designated elite who occupied their own isolated "park" within the winter cantonment — encapsulated the willfulness, rancor, and fractious contentions of the greater whole at Valley Forge.

drunkenness on duty, theft, disobeying orders, dueling, and even the playing of cards and dice, "shameful vices" that Washington abhorred.

Although daily lashings became a regular occurrence on the camp's parade grounds — usually in accordance with the biblical "forty stripes save one" — divisional and regimental commanders charged with maintaining discipline also devised innovative punishments to break the monotony. Some offenders found guilty of minor crimes were sentenced to level to the ground the stumps of trees felled to build huts. More egregious transgressors were dismissed from the service in an elaborate ceremony that involved turning the offending soldier's coat inside out, tying his hands behind his back, and literally drumming him out of camp. While a rotation of generals and sometimes colonels presided over the daily courts-martial, Washington insisted on reviewing sentences of death for crimes including murder and trading with the enemy. In the latter case it was not unusual for the commander in chief to concur with the verdict before, at the last minute, commuting a hanging to lashes and banishment. Such was his universally respected integrity that even the most insurrectionist troops came to consider him a fair and balanced arbiter.

As with foot soldiers from the beginning of time, the fractious Continentals at Valley

Forge felt it their God-given right to grouse about how their superiors were botching the war. It was not unusual for platoons and even companies to descend on an officer's tent or hut and demand to know why they were not taking the offensive. The oft-voiced sentiments invariably involved preferring to die on a battlefield as opposed to wasting away in a disease-riddled hellhole. The clamor for some kind of military action intensified when word began to spread through the cantonment that Gen. Gates had persuaded Congress to mount a northern military expedition. His plan called for no less than the occupation of Canada, with the Marquis de Lafayette at the head of the conquering army.

The scheme must have struck Gates as a potential threefold triumph. First, a successful midwinter campaign would establish a political precedent for the Board of War's involvement in future military directives. This in turn would lead to a personal triumph, as a successful Canadian "irruption," as he phrased it, would scratch the congressional itch to take the offensive somewhere, anywhere, against the British. That this would polish his own strategic bona fides, particularly when placed in relief to his rival's inactivity at Valley Forge, would not go unnoticed. Finally, in a sort of *coup de grâce,* his sly appointment of Lafayette to lead the invasion would shunt offstage one of Washington's key personal and political allies. Gates had convinced Congress that the Catholic Frenchman was the perfect vehicle to inspire his many coreligionists in the would-be fourteenth state to rise in rebellion. Naturally, such a Canadian embrace of the American cause was also certain to catch the attention of the court at Versailles, still livid at having had to cede New France to the hated British. Gates knew that if he was to eventually ascend to the post of commander in chief, good relations with the French were imperative.

When the mail packet arrived at the Potts House from York on January 24, it contained the congressional ratification of Gates's invasion plan as well as orders for Lafayette to depart immediately for Albany, where the invasion force was to be gathered. To twist the knife, the marquis was informed that his second in command on the expedition would be none other than Gen. Thomas Conway. It was a wily maneuver. Enduring the harrowing misery of Valley Forge had only strengthened the bond that Lafayette and Washington had formed during the fall campaign. Their mutual affinity was evident to anyone who watched Washington's famous hauteur fall away when the two interacted. Washington had even taken to gently chiding Lafayette for his failure to bring his family to America, teasingly inquiring if the reason for his wife Adrienne's absence might be the Frenchman's fear that she might throw him over for a certain older gentleman who happened to command an entire army.

Gates's letter to Washington, written on "War Office" stationery, incorporated the customary courtesies due a commander in chief, including an overture to Washington to suggest any tactical components of the invasion strategy. "Should your Excellency think any Steps are wanting or any Directions omitted which may be necessary upon this important Enterprize," Gates wrote, "the Board will be happy on this, as well as every other occasion, to receive your Opinion and Advice." In other words — please do give us your thoughts about *my* operation. In his Judas kiss, Gates had refrained from informing Washington about the route of the offensive or the number of troops involved, although he hinted that new recruits from New England would make up the bulk of the invading army.

Yet again, John Laurens was among the first to see through the ploy. Four days after Gates's letter arrived at Valley Forge, he penned a short note to his father. In it he derided the very idea of attempting to occupy Canada while the British fleet still controlled the eastern seaboard. He also argued that to rely on volunteer New England militiamen to swell the invasion ranks was mad. Even if a few towns or enemy fortifications across the border were to initially fall, he wrote, there were not enough Continental troops to hold them. He then turned to the subject of Conway, doubtless seeing the appointment through Washington's eyes. "It is feared that the ambition and the intriguing spirit of Conway will be subversive of the public good," he told his father. "While he will proceed securely behind the shield of his commanding officer, taking to himself the merit of everything praiseworthy and attributing every misfortune to [Lafayette]."

Like Laurens, the visiting delegates at Valley Forge considered the Canadian campaign the height of recklessness. They voiced their vehement objections in a letter to their colleagues in York, specifically citing the twin debacles of America's first attempt on Quebec as well as Gen. Burgoyne's failed expedition "across the inhospitable wilderness" of northern New York in comparatively milder weather. Washington, on the other hand, took no public stance other than to approve the board's request to dispatch north a regiment of largely Canadian troops from the rolls at Valley Forge. It was a prudent measure, removing from camp not only nearly 500 mouths to feed, but an equal number of potential headaches. He was sorry to see Lafayette depart, but the invasion was not scheduled to kick off for several weeks, which he knew bought him enough time to adjudge exactly where Gates's new adventure might lead, both militarily and politically.

Meanwhile, in contrast to the tumult at the Continental Army's winter cantonment, some 20 miles to the southeast events were playing out in a much more serendipitous manner.

With Gen. Howe having convinced himself that he would make quick work of Washington's common ruck come spring, a sense of aristocratic complacency had settled over the British army's winter billet. As a precaution, Howe had ordered a score or so of houses on Philadelphia's periphery burned lest they provide cover for Continental sharpshooters. And he occasionally sent small companies of dragoons galloping through the city's near suburbs as a pro forma measure to protect Loyalist civilians on their way to and from the marketplace. But only when it became apparent that American control of the sweeping area east of the Schuylkill had greatly deteriorated did Howe direct larger parties of Redcoats and Hessians into Bucks County to harass the few remaining Whigs.

At first these were probing affairs. Doors were smashed, windows were broken, and John Bull and Herr Fritz would be back at the Man Full of Trouble tavern in time for a supper of cornmeal stew and spotted dick, or bratwurst and sauerkraut. But as mass desertions continued to plague the already paltry force of Pennsylvania militiamen under Gen. Lacey's command, the British raids became more blatant. Mounted units of Redcoats — guided along back roads by local Tories whom Washington and his staff sneeringly dubbed "royal refugees" — succeeded not only in kidnapping several Whig lawyers and politicians but also in capturing a large herd of cattle being driven from Massachusetts to Valley Forge. The enemy also seized a crucial mill responsible for turning tons of cloth into uniforms destined for the Continentals' winter camp.

It was as if Gen. Howe was toying with his antagonist. Though ice floes on the Delaware had begun to hamper the movements of his brother's supply ships, the massive forage foray into Derby over the Christmas week had sufficiently stocked his storehouses for the moment. And what few provisions his troops might have otherwise lacked were furnished by the uptick of merchandise flowing into the city from Montgomery County and Bucks County. This allowed him to avoid the risk of hit-and-run guerrilla ambushes farther afield on the west side of the Schuylkill, where, unlike the ragged Pennsylvania militia, Dan Morgan and "Light Horse Harry" Lee had proved estimable enemies.

With a serious effort to move on the Continentals' winter encampment itself out of the question, Howe and his senior officers settled into a lazy routine of enjoying the warmth, comfort, and urbane charms of the American capital city. As Dr. Franklin had predicted, Howe had not so much captured Philadelphia as Philadelphia had captured him.

Unlike his more austere older brother Adm. Lord Howe, the married Sir William was an avowed voluptuary. As he had in Boston and New York City, he enjoyed several mistresses from among Philadelphia's Loyalist upper crust, as noted in Francis Hopkinson's facetious composition. And it was said that his fervor for a bottle of port was superseded only by his well-known taste for other men's wives.

Moreover, Howe encouraged his officers to emulate his licentiousness. Those who could not afford the affections of high-end courtiers discovered a plethora of complacent servant girls in need of "protection" after their Whig employers had abandoned the city. And if by hard chance an unfortunate officer found himself momentarily shut out of the carnal revelry, all he needed to do was place an ad in a Tory newspaper soliciting a "housekeeper who can occasionally put her hand to anything" in exchange for "extravagant wages . . . and no character required." Howe's deputies — with or without "housekeepers" — enjoyed regular Thursday evening balls held at private homes and assembly halls, and Philadelphia's famous City Tavern — where Washington's officers once dreamed of dancing victory minuets — was turned into a private club. It was not unusual for its backroom faro bank to see the equivalent of today's $50,000 change hands in a night.

Similarly, the occasional escort patrols, raids on Whig strongholds, and routine garrison duties could not long occupy the 15,000 troops billeted in the city. Following their superiors' example, the rank and file were no less prone to a wide variety of leisure-time indulgences. If war was hell for a civilian population forced to quarter foreign soldiers prone to drunkenness, brawling, and petty thievery, it was a boon to the owners of the city's less sophisticated taprooms, gambling dens, and bawdy houses. Junior officers, trapped in the no-man's-land between the pageantry of *bals masqués* and the grime of venereal hotbeds serving watered-down ale, occupied themselves arranging elaborate dinner parties, organizing horse races and cricket matches, and staging amateur theatrics. These last, with the performers dubbing themselves "Howe's Players," were held each Monday night from January through May and included a variety of pantomimes, ballad operas, and dramatic productions such as *Hamlet* and *Julius Caesar.* Their venue of choice was South Street's cupola-topped Southwark Theater, America's first permanent playhouse.

Chief among the *bon vivants* capturing the hearts of Philadelphia's distaff society was the boyish and debonair John André. André, 27, was the wealthy son of a Parisian mother and a Swiss merchant based in London, and in his seven years of service to the Crown he had proved himself on the battlefields of the New World from Quebec — where he was captured and spent 13 months as a prisoner of war before being exchanged — to the cold steel charge at Paoli. A prolific writer fluent in French, German, and Italian, Andre was one of Howe's favorite secretaries. Further, André's artistic bent and dazzling eloquence made him equally at home in the salons of Philadelphia and in musty campaign tents. André had acted in several dramatic productions while stationed in New York, although in Philadelphia his experience with "Howe's Players" was apparently limited to scandalizing local Quakers with the racy dramas he suggested and painting the elaborate backdrops at the Southwark.* But it was as a sketch artist that he excelled, and he was

---

* André's last stage backdrop remained in place at the Southwark Theater until 1821, when it was destroyed in the fire that burned the playhouse to the ground.

rarely seen without his sketchbook and pencils protruding from his rucksack. The patrician ladies of the city vied to sit for him, among them the charming and alluring Margaret "Peggy" Shippen.

Peggy Shippen was the daughter of a prominent Philadelphia shipping magnate who was managing to survive the British occupation by proclaiming his "neutralist" leanings despite the fact that his brother was a Continental officer. Peggy had been tutored in the usual music, needlework, and drawing that were commonplace for upper-class girls of the era. But in contrast to most of her female peers, she was also an avid student of finance and politics. Her father indulged the indelicate curiosity of the youngest Shippen child and "family darling" by discussing the subjects in depth with her.

In keeping with their political interests and station, the Shippens hosted numerous social gatherings, and Capt. André, as stoically sensual as a Cézanne, was a frequent guest. It was said that André's eyes possessed a hypnotic quality, and though it is unclear whether he and Peggy were lovers, she was certainly drawn to what one biographer described as the captain's air of "subdued melancholy." The two were seen together enough to invite the usual gossip, particularly as Peggy was known to venture without a chaperone to the house that André had seized from Benjamin Franklin, and to pose there for his sketches.*

General Howe no doubt viewed his protégé's *affaire du coeur* with one of Philadelphia's leading ladies through a lens of pride and envy. But despite the profusion of amusements at his fingertips, Howe was concerned. Shortly after occupying Philadelphia he had written to George Germain officially requesting relief from "this very painful service wherein I have not the good fortune to enjoy the necessary confidence and support of my superiors." This was in reference to a string of criticisms that had begun with his abandonment of Boston and had reached fever pitch following the defeats at Trenton and Princeton. The latest, and most stinging, were the savage accusations that seeped from the halls of Parliament into London newspapers asking if he had sacrificed "Gentleman Johnny" Burgoyne and Burgoyne's army in his zeal to take the American capital. Howe had promised Whitehall that the capture of Philadelphia would tap a wellspring of Loyalist sentiment whose torrent, in the form of a

---

* André would later steal Franklin's electrical equipment, musical instruments, and books, and a portrait painted in 1759 by Benjamin Wilson. The portrait was not returned to American hands until 1906, and now hangs on the second floor of the White House.

newly established Provincial Corps, would submerge the Continental Army. Instead, not only did the fall of the city lack the political and psychological impact of the capture of a European capital, but its occupation had seemingly inflamed the rebels while swelling Howe's ranks by no more than a few hundred Tory volunteers.

Germain may have been imbued with a bleak worldview concerning his fellow man, but he was nothing if not calculating. For weeks he had contrived to force the resignation of both Howe brothers. Not only was he apoplectic over their failure to have put down the rebellion by now, he also sensed that King George and his military brain trust were moving in a softer direction against the insurgent Americans. The spark for this strategic realignment had been the Crown's dismay over the defeat at Saratoga. England's war planners suspected that the American victory there would hasten France's entry into the conflict, thus turning a colonial rebellion into a world war. In an effort to forestall this outcome, or at least reduce the number of fronts on which Britain would have to fight, Parliament was currently assembling a peace commission to cross the Atlantic to negotiate a treaty whose favorable terms toward the colonies mirrored the envoy Wentworth's proposal to Franklin and Deane. As the two American diplomats had discovered during their dinner with Wentworth in Paris, the most surprising overture was England's renunciation of the right to direct taxation. In essence, the king was proffering to the colonials an informal independence from London in all but name. Even if the rebels rejected this generous olive branch, the British were prepared to detach troops from the United States in order to confront France in Europe, Canada, and the French Caribbean.

In either case, to Germain the Howe brothers represented all that had gone wrong since the war's onset, and both needed to be ushered offstage before the introduction of England's new priorities. Now that Sir William's request for retirement had landed in his lap — the Admiralty had initially refused to accept a similar tender from Lord Howe — he viewed it as an opportunity. Although Germain was a favorite of George III, as secretary of state for the Americas he had not been immune to the defamatory whispers when the conflict dragged into its third year. He understood that the king's patience was not inexhaustible, and Gen. Howe's request to be relieved was an ideal way to shift blame for the British setbacks, particularly at Saratoga, from himself to the commander in the field. He immediately began laying plans to replace Howe with Gen. Clinton.

Germain's plan came to fruition in early February, when the king ordered his prime minister Lord Frederick North, first lord of the treasury and George III's principal adviser, to sack either Germain or Gen. Howe. Lord North chose the latter. As an unexpected bonus, the prime minister also acceded to an appeal from Adm. Richard Howe's wife that he be allowed to return home and retire. The well-connected Lady Howe had read the writing on the walls of Whitehall, and wanted her husband's departure from the campaign to at least appear voluntary.

What Germain did not know, however, was that the rather morbid and extremely sensitive Gen. Clinton, wintering over in New York City with barely 6,000 troops under his command, was also beginning to view his position as career-crushing. "I renewed my solicitation for leave to return home," Clinton wrote in his memoirs. "As I plainly saw that my continuance in America was not likely to contribute to the service of my country or the advancement of my own honor. But the Commander in Chief being of the opinion that my services could not be dispensed with for the present . . . I was obliged to submit to the mortification of enduring my situation somewhat longer."

What attitude either British commander might have taken had he been aware of the state of treaty negotiations an ocean away in Paris, no one can say. The same holds true for Washington, who as recently as December 29 had published one of America's earliest State of the Union addresses, warning his fellow patriots that, for all intents and purposes, the revolution was now America's alone to win or lose. "We may rest assured that Britain will strain every nerve to send from home and abroad, as early as possible, all the Troops it shall be in her Power to raise or procure," he wrote in his *Circular to the States.* "Her views and schemes for subjugating the States and bringing 'em under her despotic rule will be unceasing and unremitted. Nor should we in my opinion, turn our expectations to, or have the least dependance on the intervention of a Foreign War. Our wishes on this Head have been disappointed hitherto, and I do not know that we have a right to promise ourselves from any intelligence that has been received, bearing the marks of authority that there is any certain prospect of one.

"Be that as it may," the *Circular* concluded, "our reliance should be wholly on our own strength and exertions."

Given the vagaries of ocean travel in the eighteenth century, when a transatlantic crossing of five weeks was considered expeditious, it would be some time before any of the opposing generals discovered that the owner of the Philadelphia home which Capt. André had commandeered was at the moment concluding a pact that could well change the entire course of the war.

TWENTY-ONE:
FRANKLIN'S MIRACLE

On February 8, 1778, Benjamin Franklin took quill in hand at his residence in Passy. With Silas Deane at his side, he addressed a letter to the president of the Continental Congress, Henry Laurens, in York.

"Honourable Sir," he began, "We have now the great Satisfaction of acquainting you and the Congress, that the treaties with France are at length compleated and signed. The first is a Treaty of Amity and Commerce, much on the plan of that projected in Congress; the other is a treaty of Alliance, in which it is stipulated that in Case England declares War against France, or occasions War by attempts to hinder her commerce with us, we should then make common cause of it, and join our forces and Councils."

Franklin went on to praise King Louis XVI's "Magnanimity and Goodness," and clarified that the treaties required that neither France nor the United States agree to any future separate peace with Great Britain without recognition of the United States as an independent country. And with that, the world from Europe to India to Africa to the Caribbean was plunged into the war for American independence. It had not come easily. In truth, that it had ever come at all is a wonder.

Despite Franklin's celebrity and popularity across the spectrum of French society, obstacles to a Franco-American alliance arose nearly from the moment he stepped off the *Reprisal* in Nantes. The memory of France's defeat in the Seven Years' War remained molten, and since the conclusion of overt hostilities the court at Versailles had pursued an anti-British foreign policy, instituted major military reforms, and ordered the country's naval construction expanded in preparation for what the French foresaw as the next, inevitable engagement. This was all of a piece with the lessons learned in the wake of Britain's victory. Further, with the tacit assent of the king, the French Foreign Ministry and the Ministry of War had set to harassing the British by funding the occasional smuggling operation to deliver arms and supplies to the American revolutionaries.

The foreign minister, the Comte de Vergennes, had even dispatched the occasional military "volunteer" to enlist in the Continental Army and secretly report back on the rebels' dedication and fortitude. But France was not yet prepared to take on its rival in a declared war, and when it came to provoking England closer to home, de Vergennes trod a fine line. Thus Franklin had agreed to abide by a clause in the 1763 Treaty of Paris forbidding the two European nations to harbor privateers. Any American ships putting into French ports were thus proscribed from sailing against the Royal Navy. Yet only weeks after Franklin disembarked at Nantes, the *Reprisal*'s captain, Lambert Wickes, went hunting.

Cruising off the coast of Spain and along the mouth of the English Channel, Wickes captured six British merchantmen within a month. After refitting at the French port of L'Orient (later Lorient), he set sail for the Irish Sea, where the *Reprisal* was met by two smaller Continental Navy vessels. Together they formed a squadron, which sank or took another 18 prizes, including two warships and nine brigs. Despite his assurances to de Vergennes, French spies discovered Franklin actively encouraging the raids. When in July 1777 the English ambassador to France lodged formal protests with Louis XVI against abetting American "piracy" — clearly a thinly disguised warning of military retaliation — an irritated de Vergennes wrote to Franklin and Deane reminding them of France's treaty obligations. To drive home the point, he jailed the Irish-born American sea captain Gustavus Conyngham — the first American to be imprisoned in the Bastille. Conyngham promptly escaped, set sail, and continued to attack British shipping, capturing 24 vessels.*

Franklin, weighing the seizing or sinking of a few enemy vessels against future comity with the French, sent a letter of apology to the foreign minister and cautioned the raiding American captains — including John Paul Jones, awaiting a new ship in the Brittany port of Brest — against "giving any cause of complaint to the subjects of France, or Spain, or of any other neutral powers." Nonetheless, the dispute had taken its toll on the fragile Franco-American relationship, and never had the court at Versailles appeared so ill disposed toward the United States. Amid this intrigue, the French were also at a loss as to what to make of the enmity that Franklin and Deane held toward the third American peace commissioner, Virginia's Arthur Lee.

Lee, the youngest son of one of the state's most politically connected families, had

---

* Rarely commented upon in histories of the American Revolution was the efficacy with which the much-reviled "Washington's navy" disrupted British merchant shipping. Between May 1777 and January 1778, for instance, Continental privateers boarded 733 English merchantmen and captured close to £5 million worth of goods.

preceded Franklin's arrival in Paris by six months. Portraits depict the 35-year-old Lee as a gruff, stone-faced man with a broad forehead accentuated by his receding hairline and a pointed, jutting chin that reached its destination long before the rest of him. What does not come through in the images is Lee's intellectual versatility. Lee was a polymath who had attended England's Eton College and studied medicine and law at the University of Edinburgh before passing the bar exam and opening a law practice in London. He was also a vociferous critic of slavery who, when revolution broke out, abandoned his legal career to become the United States' first foreign secret agent. He may have been under the misguided impression that an American victory would validate the first sentence of the second paragraph of the Declaration of Independence regarding the equality of "all men."

Writing under a roster of pseudonyms, Lee produced endless tracts distributed throughout Europe extolling American independence while simultaneously developing a profusion of political and social connections to pry out information on the motives and movements surrounding George III and Parliament. As his older brother William had only recently been elected high sheriff of London, the only American ever to hold the position, Arthur Lee's cover was, for a time, unassailable. Yet in the spring of 1776, with the British authorities growing increasingly suspicious of a "pestilent traitor" in their midst, both Lees fled to the European continent. There, at Congress's behest, William argued the American cause to the Hapsburg monarchy in Vienna while Arthur unsuccessfully lobbied the courts at Madrid and Berlin before joining Deane in Paris.

Lee and Deane locked horns from the outset. Lee had little truck with Deane's habit of conveying across the Atlantic a string of unqualified foreign parvenus to bedevil Washington and, more important, drain the congressional coffers. He was apparently particularly annoyed when Deane wrote to Congress suggesting that he might be able to persuade the soldier turned diplomat Comte Charles-François de Broglie to join the revolution, but only as commander in chief of the Continental Army, a clear insult to Washington. Lee was also leery of Deane's blue-blooded coterie of French aristocrats. He feared that Deane's words to his wife, Elizabeth, upon departing the United States for France — "I am about to enter the great stage of Europe" — had gone to his head. Despite Lee's enthusiasm for breaking the chains of British colonization, there still resided in him what John Laurens described as "our ancient hereditary prejudices" against the French. France had been England's chief international antagonist since long before Jamestown or Plymouth, and Lee's suspicion that Deane had succumbed to the sirens of Versailles led him to publicly question not only his fellow diplomat's ability to secure French aid, but his commitment to the enterprise now that he was in fact a player on the European stage.

Deane, who had only recently learned from a newspaper article of his wife's death back in Connecticut, was quick to return fire. He noted Lee's long and deep connection to England, particularly his brother's political career, and pondered aloud where his true allegiance lay. Franklin's arrival in France merely exacerbated the animosity, and the Continental Congress was soon bombarded with a series of letters from Lee slandering Deane and the high-living Franklin as "thieves and potential traitors."

Lee had nurtured an intense dislike for Franklin since making his acquaintance during the latter's frequent prewar trips to London as a colonial agent for Pennsylvania. Despite his cosmopolitan accomplishments, Lee was something of a prig, and criticized Franklin's extravagant lifestyle as well as his apparently congenital flirting. In France, that flirting had culminated in what may or may not have been a platonic relationship with the renowned French musician and composer — and very much married — Anne Louise

Brillon. Madame Brillon, 38 years Franklin's junior, was known to refer to the rambunctious old American as *"mon cher papa,"* and wrote him over 100 letters. Lee was appalled when news spread of a chess match Franklin had held with the chemist, physician, and mayor of Passy, Louis-Guillaume Le Veillard, in Madame Brillon's bathroom. It was not the venue that consternated him so much as the fact that Madame Brillon watched the competition while soaking in her tub. Lee wrote to Samuel Adams that no diplomat with Franklin's libertine habits would ever convince Louis XVI to ally with the United States. This alone stood as proof of how little he understood the French.

Franklin did his best to ignore Lee's "Magisterial Snubbings and Rebukes," explaining sensibly, "I do not like angry letters. I hate Disputes. I am old, cannot have long to live, have much to do and no time for Altercation." Franklin did, however, find it prudent to warn Lee that he had best "cure your self of this Temper [or] it will end in Insanity."

As the summer of 1777 rolled into autumn, the internecine warfare in the American legation combined with a progression of dispiriting reports reaching French shores to take an obvious emotional and physical toll on Franklin. As Burgoyne marched on Albany, Howe threatened Philadelphia, and Washington appeared to be in continual retreat, both French and English spies reported a distinct transformation in his appearance and disposition. In public Franklin still exuded a confident air, championing the revolutionaries' values to anyone who would listen. When within earshot of those same secret agents, he was particularly vociferous in his belief that it was only a matter of time before France came to America's assistance. Yet in private he despaired. De Vergennes was refusing to respond to his pleas for meetings, the French finance minister had turned down his request for a substantial loan to the United States, and he seemed a house prisoner at Passy.

The news from Saratoga, of course, changed everything.

On Thursday morning, December 4, 1777, Benjamin Franklin watched as the 30-year-old Massachusetts revolutionary, spy, and sometime diplomat Jonathan Loring Austin, just arrived from the United States, galloped into Passy. Before Austin could dismount, Franklin called out, "Sir, is Philadelphia taken?"

When Austin said yes, the aging diplomat clasped his hands behind his back and turned away. But Austin was not finished. "But, sir," he said, "I have greater news than that. General Burgoyne and his whole army are prisoners of war."

Franklin clapped, and replied, "Oh, Mr.

Austin, you have brought us glorious news."

In the days following, the roads between Passy, Paris, and Versailles were crowded with a stream of coaches and carriages, more than a few carrying anxious British emissaries. They were suddenly more solicitous of finding a way to end the rift between England and its American "cousins." The parleys culminated in the visit from the official envoy Paul Wentworth. The gathering with Wentworth set two balls in motion. Less than 24 hours after Franklin's and Deane's noncommittal response to his overtures, the panicked British ambassador Lord Stormont informed London that he suspected a French treaty with the United States was already en route to the American Congress. Nearly simultaneously, Louis XVI — convinced that Wentworth was close to persuading the Americans to accept the British Crown's generous terms — instructed his foreign minister, de Vergennes, to conclude a commercial and military alliance with the American legation as soon as possible.

On January 18, 1778, drafts of the treaties were presented to Franklin, Deane, and Lee. Much to the French court's annoyance, the Americans spent days reviewing them. They still had not returned their annotated drafts when, on January 22, Lord Stormont called on de Vergennes demanding to know if there was an alliance. Stormont's agents had picked up rumors that the French and Spanish were about to launch an attack on Gibraltar. Vergennes was evasive; Stormont sullen.

Finally, in late January, the American representatives reached a general agreement on the terms of the pacts with the French. Louis XVI shrugged off Spain's official reluctance to participate, and on the evening of February 6 the documents were signed in de Vergennes's office in the Foreign Ministry. Later that night Franklin and Deane shared a carriage back to Passy carrying the two treaties. Once there, they asked an assistant named Edward Bancroft whom Deane had hired as the American legation's secretary to write copies of the accords while they composed their letter to Congress. That Franklin omitted Arthur Lee's name from the announcement is indicative of their mood. It would be more than a century before it came to light that Bancroft was a British spy who took the liberty of also making copies of the treaties for himself to send off to Whitehall the next day.*

The Spanish throne was far from alone in having misgivings about the efficacy of allying with the Americans. Several influential French officials were also wary of the unintended consequences of throwing their coun-

* On Lee's behalf, it must be noted that his early and deep mistrust of Bancroft was amply borne out.

try's lot in with a colonial rebellion. Louis XVI's minister of finance warned the king that a successful American war of independence would only inspire France's own colonies to follow suit — a prediction that reverberated from Port-au-Prince in 1804 through Dien Bien Phu 150 years later. And a few forward-thinking aristocrats, horrified by France's depleted treasury, noted that diverting precious *livres* from the country's own downtrodden peasant class in order to fund a foreign uprising could lead to violent repercussions.* Whether they had the Bastille and the guillotine specifically in mind is not recorded. In the end, however, the French recognition of the United States was perhaps no more of an anomaly than a revolution against the British monarchy sparked by a circle of affluent, conservative planters and businessmen.

Some argue that France's true recognition of the United States did not occur until April 1778, when Franklin visited the Academy of Sciences in Paris and was introduced to Voltaire, the titan of Enlightenment *philosophie.* One witness likened the two hugging and kissing each other on the cheek to "Solon embracing Sophocles." But in fact the

---

* France would eventually spend more than a billion in today's dollars on behalf of the rebelling Americans.

Franco-American alliance became semi-official on March 20 when, with throngs gathered outside the gates of Versailles shouting, "*Vive* Franklin," the king received the American diplomats at his court as official ambassadors. It would take another six weeks for the treaties to reach the United States. Until then, the paramount question of the revolution continued to loom — would the Continental Army still exist by that time?

TWENTY-TWO:
"THOSE DEAR RAGGEDY CONTINENTALS"

On February 7, 1778, the skies above Valley Forge darkened to an ominous pall, bringing early night to what had been noonday. There followed a rare cyclonic blizzard so heavy with pearly flakes that within hours the white-domed roofs of the log huts sagged and creaked as if calling for quarter beneath several feet of snow. The winter squall raged for two days, a horizontal blur washing in from the west, before suddenly soaring temperatures ushered in a rainfall of biblical proportions. Melting snow swelled rivers and streams that washed out fords and overran their banks. Roads and trails turned into impenetrable quagmires, and the camp itself was inundated with a welter of floating debris that leaped and dived through the widening runnels like schools of flying fish.

Dozens of teamsters whom Pennsylvania's governor Thomas Wharton had finally managed to contract to deliver food from the state's interior refused to slog through the morass. Other wagon masters, having already begun their journeys to Valley Forge, simply unhitched their teams, abandoned their drays in the knee-deep bog, and returned to their farms on foot, leaving their cargo to rot. Drivers who had reached the winter camp before the storms began found themselves stranded with no shelter but their overturned carts. Soon their horses, deprived of hay and grain, began toppling to the ground. They died where they dropped, their carcasses silent witness to the shuddering catastrophe.

When the rains ceased another ferocious cold front moved in, entombing the encampment in ice so thick that water parties gingerly picking their way to the Schuylkill had to hack at the river with axes and tomahawks before filling their pails. Movement became so parlous that on February 11 the congressional committee warned Washington not to hazard the two-mile journey from the Potts House to Moore Hall. And in the absence of mail riders, cabin fever stimulated rumors that bounced through the cantonment like hailstones, including one bizarre report that Dr. Franklin had been murdered in his French lodgings by a professional assassin. The Continental Army, already reeling from December's food and clothing shortages, was suddenly pitched into an even more precipitous spiral.

As the dismal days passed, strung together

like beads, the fear of riot increased exponentially. Washington was forced to deny Gen. John Sullivan's request for a brief furlough to visit his family, as he needed Sullivan close at hand to help quell what he feared was an incipient "Mutiny for want of Victuals." And when the congressman Francis Dana defied the weather and ventured out to visit a regiment from his home state, Massachusetts, he was astounded to arrive at the commander's hut at the same time as scores of his malnourished soldiers threatening to desert en masse. They were mollified only when issued certificates of credit and allowed to leave camp on foot to purchase food. It is likely that John Laurens had this and similar insurrections in mind when he wrote to his father, "The soldiers [are] scarcely restrained from mutiny by the eloquence and management of our Officers."

Laurens went on to fill his letter — carried to York in a sledge driven by Thomas Paine — with forlorn reports that echoed Washington's earlier grievances. He described an army "reduced almost to the point of disbanding." At best, he hoped, Valley Forge would be abandoned and the troops divided into smaller winter bivouacs. For the second time in weeks, the Continental Army found itself on the verge of dissolution.

A surviving commissary checklist for the previous month, January, illuminates the roots of the disaffection. In retrospect the inventory roster, specifying the provisions on order, serves as a sort of black joke. Of the requisitioned quantities of flour, pork, beef, veal or mutton, fish, butter, peas, turnips, potatoes, cabbages, wheat, lard, molasses, cider, rum, whiskey, vinegar, rice, and salt, less than 10 percent was on hand at Valley Forge. Even absent the miserable weather, few supplies would be forthcoming from local sources. During the Christmas food shortage, the farms surrounding Valley Forge had been stripped clean — "plundered for three miles in every direction" according to an unusually blunt Continental Army memorandum. General Varnum was more descriptive. "We are situated in a place that abounds with nothing but poverty and Wretchedness," he wrote to a fellow general officer stationed in the north. "Sickness and deaths are somewhat common."

When the worst of the weather cleared, Washington summoned Nathanael Greene to his headquarters and instructed him to lead a foraging party of over 1,500 men — close to a third of the able-bodied and adequately clothed soldiers left in camp — across Chester County as far west as Brandywine Creek. A withered Alexander Hamilton was placed in charge of confiscating horses and wagons from civilians in the area to turn over to Greene. Hamilton, still not fully recovered from his debilitating bout of pneumonia, was at a low ebb. For the first time since embracing the revolution, he was beginning to doubt its efficacy. As he rode through camp he saw nothing but gaunt, shivering men hunched over small campfires. The questioning eyes that peered up at him from those sallow faces reflected his own apprehensions — with one difference. Most of the troops were not quite certain who or what to blame for their cursed conditions. Hamilton had no doubts. It was Congress, "a degeneracy of representation in the great council of America," as he described the body to Gov. George Clinton of New York, that deserved censure. "Their conduct," he told Clinton, "with respect to the army especially is feeble and indecisive and improvident — insomuch that we are reduced to a more terrible situation than you can conceive."

Washington was undoubtedly of a similar mind, for at long last he was forced into a decision he had tried hard to avoid. He told Greene that his foragers were to seize any foodstuffs in their path — as always, giving the by now dubious certificates of seizure for all supplies confiscated. But he startled the general by failing to append his usual precaution: to leave the farmers and residents enough food to sustain their families. When Greene pressed him about the omission, Washington remained silent. Instead, he was vehement about his anger at war profiteers who placed their own acquisition of what he would call "a little dirty pelf" above the fate of the revolution. If Greene should catch any of these "stock jobbing" civilians trading with the enemy, Washington said, they were to be shown no mercy, and might even be summarily executed.

Washington undoubtedly recognized the dark implications of these imperious decrees, not least because they were diametrically opposed to the very philosophy from which the revolution was born. He himself, upon being named commander in chief, had directed every soldier in the Continental Army to sign a copy of regulations intended to limit the abuse of civilians and ensure that the soldiers' conduct respected what he called "the rights of humanity." This restraint, he wrote at the time, "justly secured to us the attachment of all good men." Now he was breaking his own commandment, forced to compromise the moral demands he had made of his own troops, in order to ensure their very survival. As he told Greene, "Our present wants will justifie any measures you take."

But Greene discovered that six months of dealing with marauding armies had transformed the local populace into sophisticated hoarders. They had cached provisions in nearly every thicket of trees or earthen defile through which Greene's men slogged, and at the first whisper of scavenging troops they drove their cattle deep into the country's marshes. There was even an elusive Tory freelance spy named Jacob James who, in the manner of the Doan Gang of Bucks County, had gathered 100 or so Loyalists into a Provincial Corps of dragoons determined to help Chester County farmers move their goods to the Philadelphia market.

Rapidly undoing "Light Horse Harry" Lee's more discriminating policies toward the inhabitants, Greene dutifully followed his commander in chief's orders. He arrested more than a score of collaborators and seized their carriages and carts. Any American mills suspected of provisioning the enemy were destroyed, their spindles removed and their waterwheels sawed off. Greene even ordered the lashing of two women whom he intercepted on the road transporting foodstuffs toward the city. "I determine to forage the country very bare," he informed Washington. "The inhabitants cry out and beset me from all quarters, but like Pharoh I harden my heart."

To that end Greene and his troops cut a swath that stretched for nearly 20 miles west of the Schuylkill, combing the area farmstead by farmstead. But even their haul fell short, as recorded by the diarist Joseph Plumb Martin, whose company had been assigned to operate a relay checkpoint delivering

Greene's spoils to Valley Forge. Theoretically, he and his fellow freighters should have been the first to benefit from the scavenging. But as he observed with his usual wryness, "Here we continued to fast; indeed we kept a continual Lent as faithfully as any of the most rigorous Roman Catholics did."

In desperation, Washington fired off orders to the commanders of both the southern and the northern divisions of the army to send supplies immediately. He beseeched the governors of Pennsylvania, New Jersey, New York, and Maryland to the same effect while detaching two more foraging companies even farther afield from Valley Forge. Anthony Wayne, who had accompanied Greene, was instructed to lead nearly 800 troopers into New Jersey to extend the supply search across an arc from Salem County in the southwestern corner of the state all the way north to Trenton. Whatever provisions Wayne could not drive before him or carry with him were ordered burned. But New Jersey was also fertile ground for British provisioners' thrusts.

When Gen. Howe learned of Wayne's expedition he sent close to 4,000 troops across the Delaware to find him and destroy his regiment. Wayne turned the tables, however, throwing his outnumbered troops against the enemy expedition with such ferocity that the British commander, Col. Charles Mawhood, was convinced he was being attacked by a much larger force and signaled retreat. Wayne's Pennsylvanians, flanked by Gen. Pulaski and some 50 dragoons, pursued the enemy nearly back to the Delaware River before disappearing into the wild. When an embarrassed Mawhood learned of the true size of Wayne's command, he turned and gave chase. Wayne managed to elude him.*

While Wayne traversed New Jersey, "Light Horse Harry" Lee was charged with leading another 500 Continentals south into Delaware. This was a risky enterprise. If the territory east of the Schuylkill had devolved into a virtual no-man's-land, Lee's horsemen in conjunction with Dan Morgan's riflemen on the river's west bank had at least constituted

---

* Wayne's skirmish with Mawhood inadvertently sparked a conflagration that burned at the southern end of the Garden State for months. When Mawhood could not find Wayne's regiment, he took out his frustration on the area's Whig population. Defeated New Jersey militiamen were bayoneted as they surrendered while their homes and farms were burned to the ground. Mawhood left a trail of butchery specifically intended, he wrote, "to reduce them [and] their unfortunate Wives & Children to Beggary & Distress." (http://www.revolutionarywar newjersey.com/new_jersey_revolutionary_war_sites/ towns/hancocks_bridge_nj_revolutionary_war_sites .htm.)

something of a firewall protecting Chester County from similar ravages. But as Gen. Greene had only just learned, despite Lee's best efforts to deal fairly with the locals, the lower reaches of Chester County remained tinged with Tory red. Moreover, from a tactical viewpoint the absence of Lee's dragoons would leave a gap in Valley Forge's defenses in the event that Gen. Howe decided to seize the opportunity for a full-scale attack. Though Morgan's small, mobile units continued to patrol the countryside west of the river, theirs was primarily an observational mission. They could not in reality be tasked with pacifying the region, much less enforcing American jurisdiction.

One beleaguered officer among Morgan's scouts who understood this perfectly was the company commander John "Silverheels" Marshall of the 11th Virginia. The 21-year-old Marshall, a sharpshooter from the state's western frontier, was nicknamed "Silverheels" for his speed and leaping ability, and would go on to write a comprehensive contemporaneous biography of Washington and serve as the United States' secretary of state before becoming the nation's most distinguished interpreter of the Constitution during his 34 years as the fourth Chief Justice of the Supreme Court. "The real condition of Washington was not well understood by Sir William Howe," Marshall wrote in the second volume of his *Life of Washington*. But in fact Gen. Howe was receiving steady reports of the deprivations at Valley Forge from deserters and local Loyalists. That he eschewed an assault on the camp to wipe out the rebels once and for all represented less an intersection of his timidity and confusion regarding instructions from Whitehall as his hauteur and an ingrained habit of avoiding winter battles. Besides, if what he was learning was true, nature would do his work for him. He had not counted on what Capt. Marshall called Washington's characteristic attention "to the lives and comfort of his troops [which] saved the American army."

What Marshall meant was that Washington understood better than most that without an immediate influx of supplies, hunger would crush his army without the enemy's having fired a shot. Thus when Capt. Lee reported the deficiencies of his march through Delaware, the commander in chief took the perilous step of ordering him to tap the food magazines from storehouses not only in that state, but in Maryland as well. These provisions had been earmarked to sustain his spring campaign, and some of the commander in chief's subordinates argued that he was mortgaging his future as a fighter. Washington's answer was succinct — there would be no future campaigns without food right now. These measures of "temporary

421

relief," as John Laurens called them, had barely edged the army back "from the brink of ruin."

As most at Valley Forge recognized, the modicum of provisions borne into the camp by Greene, Wayne, and Lee constituted no more than a stopgap. As famine and disease beset the winter cantonment, more than a few enlistees decided to take matters into their own hands.

Sometime around mid-February a British agent stationed along the heights overlooking the Hudson River near West Point dispatched an enigmatic message to his handler in New York City. Nearly daily, he had spotted dozens of Continentals snaking through the thick wood on the west side of the river. By night they would cross to the east bank, often in small craft operated by smugglers. Where these men disappeared to, he could not say. But he worried that they were massing for an operation behind Gen. Clinton's lines. He needn't have. The soldiers he had seen were in fact New Englanders deserting Valley Forge to return home. They were far from alone.

Farther south, the civilian teamsters and wagon masters may have considered the Schuylkill impassable, but the raging high waters did not prevent hundreds of Pennsylvania enlisted men from simply abandoning their posts, swimming the frigid river, and evaporating into the night. Many, upon finding their farmsteads ravaged and abandoned, continued on to Philadelphia to surrender in the hope of being fed. One of the rumors spreading through the winter camp was that Gen. Howe had finally bowed to pressure from Washington's repeated written protests and agreed to provide his American prisoners with blankets and food. In addition, Tory newspapers had begun posting notices promising Continental bounty jumpers free passage to England or Ireland.* When a foraging patrol of nearly two dozen men of Irish descent under Gen. Greene's command simply vanished in western Chester County, the general concluded that their officer had been forced at gunpoint to lead them into the enemy-held city for precisely this purpose.

* In fact, the American soldiers who fell for this ruse were forced to serve as seamen on British ships or in garrisons far from the revolution's battlefields. Like the British counterfeiting operation, the false promises in the newspaper postings enraged Washington, who wrote to the Virginia congressman Richard Henry Lee, "The enemy are governed by no principles that ought to actuate honest men." (From "George Washington to Richard Henry Lee, 15 February 1778," in *The Papers of George Washington,* Revolutionary War Series, Vol. 13, ed. Lengel, pp. 549–50.)

One Continental officer noted that during the worst of the February food crisis more than half the soldiers at Valley Forge had been apprehended attempting to slip away. This number is undoubtedly exaggerated — a starving, barefoot Rhode Islander or Virginian would have had to be taken in by delusion to imagine he could survive a winter journey of hundreds of miles without succumbing to either the elements or enemy patrols. Yet British records indicate that in the month of February alone an average of six Continentals per day walked into Philadelphia to surrender.

While penned up in the Potts House during the peak of the blizzard, Washington had complained to the ineffective commissary general, William Buchanan — the "present Gentleman" he had disparaged to the Camp Committee — "The spirit of desertion among the soldiery never before rose to such a threatening height as at the present time." His men needed food, he told Buchanan, and they needed it now. And it was not only enlisted men who were euphemistically categorized as being on "self-granted furlough." One regular-army brigade of Pennsylvanians found themselves so bereft of junior officers that their commander was reduced to placing ads in local newspapers ordering them to return to camp or face courts-martial. Rhode Island's Gen. Varnum, writing to Gen. Greene to inquire about the success of his forage expedition, cut to the nub of the matter. "The love of freedom," he observed, "is controlled by hunger."

Washington's correspondence from these weeks — actually written by Hamilton, Laurens, and Tench Tilghman, who shared not only their commander's growing dismay but the cornmeal mush that constituted most meals at the Potts House — expressed the frustration the commander in chief had to keep hidden from his soldiery. It was only his enormous self-control that allowed Washington to publicly suppress, as he put it, "a tendency to resignation." That his inspirational leadership, serene dignity, and sheer physical presence held the Continental Army together throughout this desperate month is no less than astounding.

Upon reflection, however, the near-catastrophe that befell his army at Valley Forge in February 1778 did result in two counterintuitive blessings. The first was its effect on the squabbling officer corps. Although the matter was poorly understood by most of his subordinates, the commander in chief had but limited power over decisions of rank and promotion. These were ultimately decided by Congress, and Washington had earlier beseeched the representatives on the Camp Committee to help him overcome this handicap. Now that their collective survival was at stake, however, the officers were forced to put aside their feuds in order to work together for the army's greater good. Their revolutionary credentials tested, they were destined to become, in John Laurens's description, "those dear ragged Continentals whose patience will be the admiration of future ages."

And if, as Laurens predicted, those future ages "would glory in bleeding with them," it was only because of the amazing spirit of self-sacrifice that the commander in chief had instilled in those who remained by his side. It took an anonymous French officer stationed at Valley Forge to encapsulate the impression that Washington's "imposing countenance" made on others — "grave yet not severe; affable without familiarity." He went on, describing the American general's "calm dignity, through which you could trace the strong feelings of the patriot and discern the father as well as the commander of his soldiers."

Many before, most notably Henry Knox, had referred to Washington as the spiritual father of the revolution. But it took the hardships of February 1778 for a soon to be commonplace phrase to be codified in print for the first time. For that was the month when the cover of a German-language almanac published in Lancaster described him as *Des Landes Vater* — "Father of the Country."

TWENTY-THREE:
THE POLITICAL MAESTRO

Except for the previous December's brief delegation to Whitemarsh, the storm-scoured February of 1778 marked the first occasion that any members of the Continental Congress were personally forced to confront the army's broken supply system. It was one thing to pace the floor of the county courthouse in York listening as Henry Laurens read aloud Washington's desperate appeals for succor. It was quite another for the five delegates who constituted the Camp Committee to witness the trauma inflicted upon the troops at Valley Forge. The effect was driven home viscerally by the stench from the rotting carcasses of starved army horses that had been corralled not far from Moore Hall. Although there is no proof, a skeptical observer might fairly wonder if this was the intent of the decision to house the delegates so near the stockade. In any case, the foul air wafting from the horse yard may have influenced a subtle if powerful shift in the committeemen's attitude toward their main purpose — the reorganization of the entire American military.

Since their initial meetings with Washington weeks earlier, the visiting congressmen had resolved several of the less contentious proposals contained within *A Representation to the Committee of Congress.* They had agreed to recommend to their parent body that a company of Indians be recruited to match those in the employ of the British. They had also acceded to Washington's suggestion that political considerations be eliminated in promoting officers, and bowed to his request to increase the current limit of lashes as corporal punishment — those convicted of the most heinous crimes could now receive over 100. The Camp Committee had also succeeded in sanding down some of the report's rougher edges that it sensed might encounter objections within the larger body. Given the sick and absent ghost soldiers still *technically* assigned to their units, for instance, Washington had wanted to recombine his battalions and reduce the current number from 97 to 80. But few delegates back in York wanted their respective states' contributions minimized. Congress, upon the committee's recommendation, eventually settled on 88.

More important, at Washington's urging the five congressmen insisted on inspecting the personnel rosters of the departments of the commissary general and forage master general. They were flabbergasted to find that these key support systems were larded with so many civilian purchasing and issuing agents as to create a corkscrew effect in the provisions pipeline. Although the delegates kept few written minutes of their early deliberations, they were doubtless also struck by the most obvious anachronism of the procurement process: while an entire country's political course could be debated and set by a mere 56 members of the Continental Congress — many of whom were not even in session in York during the early months of 1778 — the army's lifeblood depended upon a bureaucracy that required literally hundreds of civilian employees.

It took the Camp Committee less than two days to begin trimming what Washington called this "extravagant rage of deputation." It began from the top down. First the delegates recommended that Gen. Schuyler — Washington's old friend whose position Gen. Gates had usurped prior to Saratoga — be recruited to fill the quartermaster general position vacated by Gen. Mifflin in November. The proposal of Schuyler, sworn blood enemy of Gen. Gates and anathema to every New Englander sitting in Congress, was virtually covered with Washington's fingerprints. This was followed by a recommendation to sack the commissary general, William Buchanan, and replace him with the seasoned Connecticut sea trader Jeremiah Wadsworth. The choice of Wadsworth was telling. A patriot not averse to also pursuing a profit, Wadsworth had, through a combination of intelligence and guile, worked his way from common deck hand to captain of his own ship. He subsequently accrued a fortune trading in the West Indies, and when war broke out he volunteered to serve on several procurement committees obtaining supplies for the Continentals ranging from stockings to tin kettles. If anyone could wrangle the bureaucracy of the Commissary Department, it was Wadsworth.

Not all of the Camp Committee's efforts proved as productive. The panel recognized, for instance, that Washington's proposal of pensions on half pay would be an abomination to a substantial subset of congressional hard-liners skeptical about even the hint of a postwar standing army. Indeed, when weather permitted toward the end of February, the delegates Francis Dana and Nathaniel Folsom journeyed to York and argued in person for the pension plan. Their colleagues were not moved, and merely voted to table the matter indefinitely.* Similarly, Washington's

* After much haggling, a compromise was finally reached on May 15, 1778, when, in lieu of a half-

dual request for funds to procure extra horses and saddles for his cavalry corps and to streamline the army's clothing procurement process also disappeared into a bottomless bureaucratic maw.* And though it took less than a week of deliberations for the Camp Committee to recommend a military draft within the state militias, the formal enactment process would eventually take months.

After the initial flurry of activity, moreover, the Camp Committee's progress was increasingly sidetracked by the worsening food crisis. Some officers addressed the delegates directly. "Pray Use your Influence with the [Congress] to get our Soldiers clothed," begged the Massachusetts general John Patterson, who counted 450 of the 756 men

---

pay pension for life, Congress voted on a half-pay stipend to last for seven years after the war's end, provided that the recipient remained in the army through the conflict's conclusion.

* Though the Camp Committee's recommendation that Congress approve the cavalry realignment was submitted in February, the full body did not vote in favor of purchasing the additional horses until late May. The clothing procurement question lasted even longer; on August 3, and again five months later in January 1779, Washington was still petitioning Henry Laurens for a reorganization to deal with the army's "worsening" clothing shortage.

in his command as "unfit for Duty for want of Shoes and other clothing." Others were like Connecticut's acerbic Jedediah Huntington, who was just glad of the "happy Circumstance that the Com of Congress happen to be Eye Witness of our Condition." Similar mutterings and Washington's dramatically descriptive reports of his empty commissaries — "the present dreadful situation of the army for want of provisions and the miserable prospects before us" — were initially met with a measured skepticism by the delegates at Valley Forge. Their reaction was to suspect some form of accounting fraud.

But after a personal inspection of the camp's storehouses and larders, they faced the withering truth — there was no food. Each and every regiment, they noted, had been "destitute of fish or flesh" for days and the soldiers were barely surviving on maggot-infested firecakes. As an aside in the National Park Service's official history of Valley Forge drolly notes, "If the army had been able to subsist on magazines of flour or herds of cattle voted into existence with the summary ease and authority with which the new arrangements of battalions could be decreed, the committee could have completed its work and returned to York within a fortnight."

Instead, the specter of an army near disintegration galvanized the individual members of the Camp Committee to demonstrate an independence that in effect upended their political relationship with their parent body. What, after all, was the point of reorganizing a force teetering on the brink of starvation? They thus saw no need to consult with their peers in York before, as Washington had already done, officially imploring Gov. William Livingston of New Jersey and Gov. Thomas Johnson of Maryland to provide emergency provisions. The New York delegate Gouverneur Morris also wrote privately to his state's governor, George Clinton, pleading for cartloads of food. Morris warned Clinton "that an American Army in the Bosom of America is about to disband for want of something to eat."

This newfound autonomy in the Camp Committee bore the undeniable imprint of Washington and his circle of young aides working behind the scenes, cajoling the representatives to accept most of the arguments put forth in *A Representation to the Committee of Congress.* Hamilton in particular, the author of the report and still disgusted with the "glut of mediocrities" who had succeeded the First Continental Congress, saw the five delegates as the last best chance to hold the army together.

Such was Washington's canny ability to influence the panel that in several communiqués to York the task force adopted his report's language verbatim. The delegates' self-determination also empowered them to scuttle a harebrained proposal put forward by a clique of Pennsylvania congressmen clamoring once again for a full-bore assault on Philadelphia. The small delegation's new boldness and its alignment with Washington were not lost on the members of the Board of War. General Gates in particular took the nomination of Gen. Schuyler as a shot across his own bow. But ambition and bluster were Gates's stock-in-trade, and he was too shrewd to be out-flanked without a fight.

From the outset of his elevation to the reconstructed Board of War, Gates had been far from satisfied with what he considered the mundane tasks of the position. Overseeing recruiting and arms production, particularly now that the French were surreptitiously supplying most of the new weapons distributed throughout the American army, was a chore beneath his eminence. He and his closest ally Thomas Mifflin were even less enamored of having to arbitrate the disputes that arose between Washington and the individual states, especially the commander in chief's continual rifts with the Pennsylvania state assembly. Goading the likes of Thomas Wharton into collecting and transferring clothing and foodstuffs to Valley Forge was not what Gates had ridden south to do. He set his sights on grander accomplishments, the Canadian campaign being but one. So it was that the board, having already convinced Congress, first, to let it establish its own parallel commissary systems and, second, to bless its plan to invade Canada, now played its third card.

Washington and the delegates composing the Camp Committee had no idea that on the day before they tendered Gen. Schuyler as a candidate to fill the vacant post of quartermaster general, the Board of War had proposed to Congress an alternative plan, which would in effect hand Gen. Gates control of the Continental Army's quotidian operations. In the board's scenario, the quartermaster general would be relieved of his hands-on procurement duties, with those functions devolving to several regional superintendents who would be subordinate to the board.

Abolishing the traditional function of the quartermaster general as the unfettered guardian of the army's purse strings would effectively reduce him to a figurehead. It would also drastically undermine Washington's authority. As either a sop or a slap in the face to the commander in chief — no one was certain which — the board's overture did deign to leave the quartermaster general in control of mundane affairs regulating encampment sites and when and how to march into battle. In essence, the proposal would allow the generals Gates and Mifflin to dictate military strategies while graciously allowing Washington to devise the tactics to carry them out. It was the hauteur of the Canadian campaign writ large, and effectively amounted to a bloodless coup. The delegates in York adopted it in early February.

Why Congress would cooperate with the board's ploy to sabotage its top commander in the field remains something of a mystery. An obvious speculation touches upon that favorite congressional hobbyhorse, fiscal prudence. This pecuniary obsession was ingrained and had even influenced the appointment of Washington as commander in chief — as a wealthy planter married to an even wealthier widow, Washington had volunteered to forgo any salary when he accepted the post. Now, nearly three years later, the civil authorities could point to Washington's own testimony regarding the incompetence and waste pervading the Quartermaster Department as a rationale for handing the Board of War such power. General Gates, after all, had argued that under his new system the department's profligacy would magically vanish when all military expenditures were contingent upon his new implementation of proper checks and balances.

Another hypothesis regarding Congress's acquiescence was apparently more personal. At any given moment there were never more than 21 delegates sitting in York during the winter session of 1777–1778. The majority of these had replaced the deceased, retired, or enlisted congressmen who had taken part in the unanimous vote to appoint Washington to lead the Continental Army in June 1775. These new delegates had no personal investment in his selection, nor in his continuing service. Few of them had even met him, and most relied for their knowledge of him largely upon the legends that had sprung up. Further, in York Congress convened on the second floor of a nondescript brick county courthouse by day and congressmen slept in cramped rooms, often shared, that reeked of the stench from the city's half-frozen open sewers. Unlike Washington some 80 miles away, Gen. Gates took quarters in the city, ensuring that he was but a short stroll from lobbying individual delegates, particularly the New England contingent, over warm fires in cozy taprooms. A veteran back-channel operator dating back to his service in the British military, Gates had developed an ambitious friendship in particular with John Adams, whom the newer delegates held in awe. York was a small town of just 2,000, and it would be asking much for a cranky, sulky politician trapped in a squalid and overcrowded backwater to resist a bit of massaging from the "Hero of Saratoga."

In the end, the disappointing outcomes of Washington's autumn campaigns as well as the vortex of intrigue surrounding the Conway affair had chastened politicians. The fortunes of war had finally convinced the delegates, particularly the more vociferous armchair generals, to tread lightly through the minutiae of military comportment. For months these same statesmen had either completely misread or ignored the depths to which the army's broken supply arteries had collapsed. Now their commander in chief's own insistent warnings about the failure of his support systems had grown ever blunter. It would not have taken much persuasion to convince a majority of delegates that Gates was the officer to relieve them of the burden of cutting through these knotty conflicts.

There was, however, a flaw in Gates's strategy — the catastrophic mid-February food crisis at Valley Forge had proved a double-edged sword. For with each report arriving from the Camp Committee, it became more apparent to Gates and his allies that Washington's masterly handling of the visiting delegates was eroding the board's own backroom manipulations at York. Coincidentally, as the weather continued to worsen across the northeast, the same swollen rivers and impassable roads that had prevented supplies from reaching Valley Forge for two solid weeks had also cut off all communications between York and the cantonment. Thus were Washington, his young and devoted staff, and the Camp Committee initially insulated from any knowledge of Gen. Gates's putsch. The information blackout also provided the five delegates at Moore Hall a bit of breathing room to reconsider their nomination of Gen. Schuyler to the quartermaster general's post as perhaps too inflammatory. It was during this interlude that the Camp Committee, with an assist from Washington, recognized that an alternative candidate for the position was right under their noses. They turned their attention to Nathanael Greene.

The night before Greene had led his foraging party into eastern Chester County, the Camp Committee corralled him in an informal meeting at Moore Hall to gauge his interest in the quartermaster general's post. Greene knew how crucial the position was to the war effort, but also expressed reluctance to be pulled from the front lines. He dreaded the idea of his colleagues in the field "immortalizing [themselves] on the golden pages of history" while his own reputation would be "confin'd to a series of druggery." He nonetheless promised the delegates to give the matter more thought during his provisioning expedition, and rode off the next day.

Twenty-four hours later, on February 13, a mail rider from York finally made it through to Valley Forge. He carried a letter from Henry Laurens outlining Congress's decision to accept the Board of War's scheme to co-opt the Quartermaster Department. The elder Laurens also requested that the delegates at Valley Forge submit the names of officers they felt were best qualified to serve as Quartermaster Department superintendents in Gen. Gates's new arrangement. Congress, Laurens wrote, would whittle from this list its final nominees. Once confirmed they would report directly to the board. The delegates were stunned. That they waited several hours before informing Washington of this turn of events strongly hints at their fear that the commander in chief might resign on the spot.

Washington did not step down, of course. But the Camp Committee nevertheless still faced an impasse. The most effective riposte to the board's maneuvering would be to counter with their own qualified candidate for quartermaster general. To that end Washington made certain to keep them apprised of how effectively Greene was performing on his forage mission. He also talked up the Rhode Islander's nimble mind, his round-the-clock work ethic, and the indomitable courage he had displayed in battles from Long Island to Brandywine Creek. Finally, Washington also tacitly reminded them of Greene's early enthusiasm for the revolutionary cause — Greene was one of the first out-of-staters to reach Massachusetts and volunteer his services in the wake of Lexington and

Concord.

Were these not precisely the qualities the Continental Army needed in a quartermaster? Washington made plain that he was in no way attempting to lobby the distinguished gentlemen. He was merely offering his services, providing facts and commensurate recommendations that, he hoped, would buttress their decision-making. If these happened to guide the outcome of the committee's thinking, he was happy to be of service. Though Washington kept few written records during this period, there is no doubt that his backstage manipulations steered the panel toward the outcome he desired.

If the men on the Camp Committee had not been convinced of Greene's worthiness before his departure, they now were. But there remained two major obstacles: Greene was not due back in camp for another nine days, and no one was certain that he would accept the position. The delegates had no choice but to stall for time. They drafted a reply to Henry Laurens that effectively ignored the news of the Board of War's plans and instead devoted their report to describing Valley Forge's deprivations in lurid and alarming detail. Desertions were rampant, they wrote, and morning collections of the bodies of men who had died silently in the night had become routine. Those who still survived — "Naked from the Crown of their

Heads to the Soles of their Feet" — faced unimaginable "tryals and Sufferings of Body & mind." Not the least of these was an outbreak of scabies stemming from the lack of soap and the dearth of cisterns, pans, and buckets in which to wash. Joseph Plumb Martin relates a particularly gruesome home remedy that he undertook to relieve himself of "that delectable disease the itch" — inundating the scabies pustules on his body with burning-hot sulfur acquired from an artillery unit. He added that he could not have withstood the pain without also having acquired a jug of whiskey.

The members of the Camp Committee laid the entire "shameful Situation" at the feet of their fellow civil authorities. As they hoped and suspected, upon receipt of their doleful description, Henry Laurens convinced Congress to act immediately. In the interest of rectifying the food crisis as rapidly as possible, he wrote back that the delegates at Valley Forge were now empowered to immediately fill the Quartermaster Department's superintendent offices themselves. At some point in the future, he added, Congress would review their selections.

Still playing for time, the Camp Committee responded by acting as if the Board of War's takeover plot was not a *fait accompli* but still up for debate. Without mentioning Gen. Greene by name, they informed Henry Laurens that they had someone new in mind to fill the quartermaster general's position, but would need a few more days before "we shall do ourselves the Honor of laying our Sentiments before Congress on the material Alteration proposed in this Office." When this communiqué reached York, Laurens convinced Congress to again acquiesce. Ever so subtly, the five elected officials at Valley Forge were making their parent body subservient on this issue — the tail was wagging the dog. All the while Washington continued to lay the groundwork for a political counterattack against what Hamilton labeled "the traits of the monster" and their "secret machinations."

As the weather eased, the commander in chief rode off to Moore Hall daily to assist the delegates in shaping their job offer to Greene. Upon Greene's return the delegates began their campaign of persuasion immediately. Greene was as alarmed as his commander in chief at the prospect of subservience to Gates, Mifflin, and their accomplices, and Washington assured him that his reputation was enough to cow Congress into backing away from the board's designs. Playing on Greene's patriotism, his considerable ego, and especially his antipathy toward Gen. Mifflin, Washington convinced the proud Rhode Islander that he alone was the man on whose shoulders rested not only the Continental

Army's independence, but quite possibly its very survival. He also dangled a monetary plum — henceforth, Greene and those he selected as his deputies would be allocated a percentage of all official payments as salaries, in Greene's case a healthy one percent of all moneys handled by the department.

It took 72 hours for Greene to allow his name to be submitted for the post. He had but two stipulations — his elevation would be temporary until the immediate supply crisis was solved, and he would conduct all Quartermaster Department business from the front lines. He also asked to work with two familiar assistants. He wanted Col. John Cox, currently a deputy quartermaster stationed at Reading, as his chief procurement officer, and the scrupulous New Jersey iron merchant Charles Pettit as his head bookkeeper.

That night the members of the Camp Committee, emboldened by their formidable candidate, drafted a letter to their fellow congressmen critiquing the Board of War's plan as a waste of money that would divide the American army into clashing camps. The five delegates contended that the proposal to hand power to a gaggle of superintendents, as opposed to one controlling officer, could only increase "the Chance of Frauds." As their prime example they noted that a paucity of wagons had contributed mightily to the supply shortages at Valley Forge. The long list of civilian teamsters who had shirked their duty to the country in order to rent their services to private parties was damning. Under Gates's new operation, they argued, this practice would undoubtedly continue, given how easy it would be for the Board of War's superintendents to lay any blame for "Ignorance, Indolence, or Iniquity" on each other. Finally, in perhaps their most savvy counterpunch, the delegates questioned the wisdom of having those very superintendents report to an oversight board that included one member — Gen. Mifflin — whose neglectful tenure as quartermaster general could be construed as the root cause of the army's succession of supply misfortunes.

In Gen. Greene, the committeemen stressed, they had found an officer of impeccable character who knew firsthand the military's wants and needs, its strengths and weaknesses. Only Greene and his two hand-picked seconds could streamline the army's bloated, overwrought support systems. There would be no need for far-flung superintendents operating through a chain of command resembling a hedge maze.

The delegates' arguments were strong, clear, and effective. On March 2, five days after receiving their recommendation, Henry Laurens convinced Congress to withdraw its support for the Board of War's overhaul. Nathanael Greene was simultaneously elevated to the post of quartermaster general. The rapidity with which the parent body yielded to the committee's proposal must have surprised even the wily Washington. To pour salt into the wound, Gen. Mifflin was also ordered to hand over to Greene any preparations the board might have already made for the army's spring campaigns.

Washington had conducted the perilous political concerto like a maestro. He had used the confluence of the Camp Committee's journey to Valley Forge, February's catastrophic food shortages, and the Board of War's blunted coup to forge a greater cooperation between America's civil and military branches. Moreover, with eyes on the ground at the winter camp, the Congress in York now had a more practical vantage point from which to view, and appreciate, the commander in chief's many complex problems. In turn, Washington's personal outreach to the delegates at Moore Hall and his artful outmaneuvering of his political enemies provided him with deeper insight into the obstacles a nascent Continental Congress continually faced.

On the last day of February 1778, Washington encapsulated the entire episode in a letter to his fellow Virginian, Lt. Col John Fitzgerald. Eschewing his usual dictation, he took quill in hand to inform Fitzgerald that

"Matters have, & will, turn out very different to what the party expected. G[ate]s has involved himself in his letters to me, in the most absurd contradictions — M[ifflin] has brought himself into a scrape he does not know how to get out of . . . & C[onway], as you know, is sent upon an expedition which all the world knew — & the event has proved, was not practicable. In a word, I have a good deal of reason to believe that the Machinations of this Junto will recoil upon their own heads."*

Washington proved himself a fair prognosticator. For the final nail in the coffin of Gen. Gates's plan to usurp the commander in chief's position was driven by a hammer some 300 miles to the north of York and Valley Forge.

* In Washington's original letter, Gates was written as "G — s," Mifflin as "M —," and Conway as "C —."

Twenty-Four:
Martha

It was a disaster portended.

Despite his lust for battlefield glory, when Lafayette learned of his appointment to lead the Canadian expedition he was torn. When news of his achievements reached his homeland, there would not be enough stonemasons between the Pyrenees and the Rhine to carve the statues exalting him for liberating "New France" from the vile Roast Beefs. Typically, the young Frenchman never considered the possibility that he might fail. Yet he also saw through Gen. Gates's seductive ploy as easily as John Laurens, and recoiled at the idea of being manipulated to undermine his cherished commander in chief.

When the marquis approached Washington to voice his concerns, his mentor urged him to accept the assignment — as long as he understood the battle plan. General Gates's original orders were rife with ambiguities, and Washington advised the young Frenchman to visit York before leaving for Albany in order to learn the precise details of the campaign. In private, Washington considered the entire premise of an invasion of Canada foolhardy — "the child of folly," he wrote to the Virginia congressman and militia officer Gen. Thomas Nelson. He also doubted that the plan would ever come to fruition, but it would not be fair to dampen Lafayette's enthusiasm. In turn, Lafayette was perhaps naively confident that, on the strength of his reputation, he would be able to thread his way between battlefield laurels and loyalty to Washington. Lafayette thus departed Valley Forge for York with a list of carefully calculated demands.

He met first with Henry Laurens. Proclaiming himself "flattered and honored" by Congress's confidence in a 20-year-old foreigner's readiness to command an army, he nonetheless stipulated that he could not accept the position unless $200,000 in gold or silver to finance the expedition was immediately shipped to Albany. In addition, he demanded that "sixty days [worth of] provisions and all the necessary Baggage, Artillery, and Ammunition for an army of three Thousand men" also await his arrival. Mindful of the fine line he was treading, he then insisted that the civil authorities jettison Thomas Conway as his second in command. "I know that Conway will sacrifice honor, truth, and every thing respectable to his own ambition and desire of making a fortune," he told Henry Laurens. "What engages me to despise him more is that he is with me as submist, as complaisant, and low than he is insolent with those he do'nt fear."

There were also political ramifications to consider. Despite Conway's service in the French army, Lafayette intuited that Louis XVI and his ministers would take a dim view of an Irishman accruing any credit for liberating a French-speaking nation, even as a deputy commander. An American second in command, or even a volunteer officer from the European continent, would be more acceptable to French sensibilities. To that end, he suggested to Henry Laurens that replacing Conway with either Washington's confidant Gen. Alexander McDougall or his own fellow traveler Johann de Kalb might seem more accommodating. In either case, he reiterated, unless Conway was dismissed, he and every French officer currently in service to the United States would be prepared to quit the war and return home.

Henry Laurens was fully aware of the importance of the Gallic presence on American soil, as well as what disastrous reverberations such a mass exodus would send through the mirrored halls of Versailles. He agreed to each prerequisite. General Conway, already in Albany prepping for the offensive, was eventually posted to Peekskill where, for all intents and purpose, he disappeared from the pages of history until he was shot in the face during his duel with Gen. Cadwalader. As McDougall was too ill to undertake such an arduous adventure, de Kalb was soon tabbed to replace Conway.

Emboldened by Congress's submission, Lafayette next sought out Gen. Gates at his lodgings above a local tavern. Over a dinner attended by the entire Board of War, he told the gathering that he required detailed marching orders before his departure, and informed Gates that any subsequent instructions he received while stationed in the north country must arrive, per military protocol, via the commander in chief's headquarters at Valley Forge. In turn, all his own reports would be filed directly to Washington, with the board merely copied on their contents. Gates was trapped. He had painted himself into a corner with his fulsome praise of the Frenchman's military expertise in touting him to Congress to lead the expedition. There was nothing to do but accede. The evening turned even glummer for the host and his guests when, after what each thought was the final round of after-dinner toasts, Lafayette stood and insisted that they raise a final goblet to the health of George Washington. They did, Lafayette later recalled, "but not with much exuberance of feeling."

The marquis rode from York the next morning, stopping at Valley Forge to collect his battle gear and say good-bye to Hamilton and John Laurens before departing for Albany. Showing his unfamiliarity with the territory, along the journey he wrote to Washington with some wonderment that the farther north he traveled, the more he found the torrential downpours that had beset the Pennsylvania cantonment gradually freezing into the whiteout snowstorms to which upstate New Yorkers were so accustomed. He added that he much preferred the latter.

Oddly, almost 250 years of legend have left an impression of the Valley Forge winter of 1777–1778 as perpetually snowbound, with bone-chilling temperatures. In fact, although snowfall was relatively common at the camp, it was by historical standards a fairly mild winter for southeast Pennsylvania. Only twice did the mercury drop into single digits, on both occasions during the month of February. It had been consistently colder at the previous winter camp at Morristown, and would be more polar still the following year.

Counterintuitively, this meteorological variability only added to the Continental Army's suffering. Pining for the crisp New England winters of his youth, Rhode Island's Gen. James Varnum bemoaned the fact that the Pennsylvania weather "frequently changes five times in Twenty four Hours." And when it snowed, he added, "the snow falls only to produce Mire & Dirt." Washington himself noted that working or drilling in fortifying, below-freezing temperatures was preferable to slogging through an endless morass of half-frozen mud stippled with putrefying animal carcasses. Although details were formed to bury dead horses, the graves were so shallow that each lashing rainstorm reexposed the turgid remains. Whenever the mercury edged above freezing the stench of escaping gases made the atmosphere seem almost opaque and assaulted and lingered in the noses, eyes, and throats of an already sullen and febrile army.

Lafayette, blessedly free from this fetor and galloping hard, arrived in Albany on February 17, eight days earlier than he was expected. After conferring with New York's Gov. Clinton — a supporter of Washington who harbored grave doubts about the wisdom of a midwinter Canadian campaign — he set off to inspect his invasion force. As John Laurens had predicted, not only were there too few men to mount a successful "irruption," but the appalling lack of food and supplies cast the entire enterprise into so foul a light that many of the officers with whom he conferred considered the plan madness. Gates's old opponent Benedict Arnold, still recovering from the leg wound he'd received near Freeman's Farm, warned the young marquis that he would be daft to proceed with the operation.

Arnold noted that the Board of War's instructions to attack Montreal by crossing the frozen Lake Champlain would require some 800 sleds. There were 50 on hand. Further, of the 1,200 or so officers and enlisted men assembled in Albany — about half the promised number — most had no winter overcoats, wool uniforms, snowshoes, or gloves or mittens. Nor, as Lafayette discovered, were they in any mood to fight. Even with the distribution of the $200,000 promised and delivered by Congress — as well as some $50,000 of Lafayette's personal funds — the majority were still owed more than $400,000 in back pay. More harrowingly, word of the Continentals' "secret" assault had leaked to such an extent that British forces across Quebec were already strengthening their defensive redoubts in preparation for it.

Discouraged and frustrated perhaps for the first time in his life, Lafayette wrote to Henry Laurens detailing the hellish state "of blunders, madness, and deception I am involved in." Whether this had resulted from "a piece of folly or a piece of villainy" made little difference. He was embarrassed, and in a private communiqué to Washington he lamented that he had been "shamefully deceived by the board of war." Worst of all for the would-be conquering hero was his anguish over the slapdash plan; his rapidly deteriorating prospects for any invasion at all, much less a victory; and the possibility of becoming a laughingstock in France. He therefore begged a favor of Washington in order to save face. Might the commander in chief concoct a raid on New York City, with him in command, perhaps in conjunction with the main army's assault on Philadelphia?

Washington, having predicted the entire Canadian calamity, must have chuckled darkly at the idea of his emaciated troops attacking Philadelphia. Nor was he about to order a half-cocked offensive against Gen. Henry Clinton's New York defenses that, in the end, would be likely to fulfill Lafayette's foreboding of being an object of mockery. Instead, in an attempt to assuage his young friend's fragile ego, he replied that the mere fact of Lafayette's appointment to head an American expedition into Canada was proof enough to French and European observers of the Continental Congress's "good opinion and confidence" in him." As for the news of an aborted invasion reaching Paris and Versailles, he added that he was "persuaded that everyone will applaud your prudence in renouncing a Project, in pursuing which you would vainly have attempted Physical Impossibilities." Finally, regarding the prospect of an assault on New York, he assured Lafayette "that your Character stands as fair as it ever did, and no new Enterprise is necessary to wipe off this imaginary stain."

Meanwhile, during the last week of February, Henry Laurens made plain to his fellow delegates the sorry state of affairs in Albany. In response, Lafayette was instructed by Congress to delay the entire *folie de grandeur* until more militiamen could be recruited. When that goal faltered, and with an eye toward Lake Champlain's thinning ice, a second mail rider subsequently arrived from York informing the marquis that the invasion was canceled, thanking him for his efforts, and recalling him to Valley Forge. One needn't be a code breaker to detect that the politicians, recognizing a potential fiasco, thought it best to put the entire undertaking behind them as quietly as possible. But Washington, sensing an opening, was too shrewd for that.

The commander in chief had foreseen in the Canadian offensive the possibility of a political triumph even before the campaign reached its opera buffa denouement. Now he felt the time right for the whip hand to extend an olive branch. With the war far from over, it would serve no military purpose to completely embarrass and alienate the "Hero of Saratoga." General Gates, monitoring the situation in Albany, had in fact already put out feelers to Henry Laurens about returning to Washington's good graces. He had even written a strained letter to Washington disowning Gen. Conway. In his reply, Washington set aside what he considered the assaults on his dignity as well as his resentment against the plotters of the Conway Cabal. He would carry those feelings through the rest of the war and beyond, but now was not the time to air them. Instead, he wrote to Gates, "My temper leads me to peace and harmony with all men. And it is particularly my wish to avoid any personal feuds or dissensions."

The letter's nominal purpose was to suspend the discord between the two proud, prickly, and — despite the politesse of their written communiqués — ruthless generals. Washington had triumphed. Gates, Mifflin, Conway, and their allies were defeated. Now it was time for all involved to return their attention to the common enemy occupying Philadelphia and New York. At least a convalescing Conway had the grace to apologize to Washington for his behavior before resigning and sailing back to France nine months later. Gates, on the other hand, continued to disparage the commander in chief in his personal correspondence right up until his humiliating performance during the Battle of Camden in South Carolina two and a half years later. While the heroic de Kalb stood and fought to his last breath, Gates abandoned his troops and fled the battlefield in panic. The dishonorable act would finally end his military aspirations. Yet until that ultimate disgrace, he was far from the last of George Washington's burdens.

If a diffuse glint of light penetrated the darkest month of the darkest winter of the American Revolution, it was the arrival at Valley Forge of Martha Washington in the first week of February 1778. Washington had grown accustomed to having his wife join him at the Continental Army's winter billets — at Cambridge in 1775 and at Morristown in 1776 — and he had sent for her soon after settling into the Potts House.* But her departure from Virginia was delayed several weeks because of the recent death of her younger and favorite sister, Anna Maria Basset. It was not until January 26, after Martha settled her sister's affairs, that she and her cortege of indentured servants and slaves finally stepped into the carriages that would carry them the 160-odd miles north over rutted roads, across ice-choked rivers, and into increasingly inclement weather. It was a long and tedious journey, and not a little dangerous despite her military escort. But, as usual, her arrival seemed to transform the man she referred to as "the general."

* All told, before the eight-year war ended, Martha Washington would spend close to four years by her husband's side in the field.

Throughout their courtship and 19 years of marriage, Martha's natural aplomb had served as a balm to her husband, salving his many complicated inner torments. Some gossips sniped that Washington had married the plump, dowdy widow Custis, née Dandridge, with an eye toward the not inconsiderable fortune she inherited after the death in 1757 of her first husband, the elderly Daniel Parke Custis. It was true that physically, the two could not have been further apart. Few people who encountered the tall and imposing Washington failed to be struck by the sheer gravitas and silent authority he projected, an aura strong enough to penetrate the farthest corner of any room he entered. Martha, on the other hand, though at 45 only a year younger than her husband, could have been taken for a doting aunt, or the wife of the local vicar come to call, as imagined by the portraitist Gilbert Stuart.

Yet all who engaged with the couple discerned that the woman known to the era as "Lady Washington" was one of the few people granted total and unfettered access across the virtual moat that Washington had constructed around himself to forestall nearly every hint of intimacy. Martha somehow managed to open an emotional spigot in the decorous Washington, her presence turning the "the general's" stony persona soft as starlight. This was particularly true at Valley

Forge, where her bright recollections of their lives together back at their beloved Mount Vernon broke through the gray reality of the winter camp. Washington doted on her in return, and treated her only surviving child, the 22-year-old John "Jacky" Parke Custis, as his own.

Martha had traveled little before the war, and whenever she joined Washington he attempted to make her lodgings as familiar as possible. At Valley Forge he had his private baggage, including the family tableware and cutlery, released from storage and shipped to the Potts House. These possessions must have struck Martha as talismans — or as islands in a gale, crammed as the quarters were with tides of arriving and departing aides-de-camp, Continental officers, mail riders and messengers, and visiting dignitaries with their own retinues in train. Even after the addition of a new great room — its floor, walls, and roof hewn from the same trees as the huts — the Potts House afforded little privacy. Though secretly dismayed by the cramped living conditions, Martha never complained, and instead slipped naturally into her familiar role of convivial lady of the manor. She bustled about the household with a casual industriousness, acted as official hostess, organized social functions with the wives of other officers, and brought a semblance of decorum to the headquarters' fraternity house ambience.

Among the women in camp attracted to this good-humored woman were the ravishing Catharine "Caty" Greene, a dozen years her husband Nathanael's junior and a notorious flirt; the cosmopolitan Sarah Stirling and her 22-year-old daughter Lady Kitty; and the down-home Lucy Knox, as round as one of her husband Henry's cannonballs. The women were often at each other's throats — the swaggering Gen. Wayne's conspicuous attraction to Caty Greene caused his wife, Polly, to banish him from their home; Lucy Knox's catty remarks about the Greenes' marriage sparked a lifelong feud between the two; and the Stirling women's proclivity for putting on airs of Scottish nobility in the midst of a war fought to attain equality hardly endeared them to the proletariat. They nonetheless coalesced into Martha's inner circle. Together they herded a slew of junior officers' wives to the Potts House to participate in sewing bees arranged by Martha to mend soldiers' garments, stitch shirts, or, when materials were unavailable, simply roll bandages as they sang to keep up their spirits. A trait Martha shared with her husband was his work ethic, and during the rare interludes in her dawn-to–late night schedule — including overseeing multiple shifts of suppers, served before dusk in order to conserve candle wax — she would find a quiet corner in her sitting room and break out her needles and yarn to knit stockings for the troops.

Although with the outbreak of war Washington had insisted that Martha be inoculated against smallpox — he would otherwise never have allowed her to set foot near his camps — scant evidence exists to support the now popular myth that she was a figure always in motion at Valley Forge, flitting from hut to hut delivering food when there was any, good cheer when there wasn't, or even her knitted socks. She did reportedly visit dying soldiers on occasion, pausing to kneel and pray by their pallets. But more important than her prayers, particularly to her husband, were the homespun determination and common sense she returned to Washington's orbit. These were the same qualities she had shown in dealing with multiple London "factors," or purchasing agents, in the years between Daniel Custis's death and her remarriage. It was during this period that she had gained respect not only for her assertiveness in setting the price of the tobacco shipped across the Atlantic from the 18,000 acres that constituted the Custis plantations, but for her attention to detail concerning the clothes, perfumes, and exotic comestibles she imported. She would need every drop in her deep well of resolve to counterbalance the fatigue and anxiety she had never before seen in her husband.

One legendary tale in particular limns Washington's emotional state during that February, poetically throwing his near-despair into relief. Perhaps, skeptics charge, a bit too poetically. As the story is told, one night the young Quaker Isaac Potts was riding near the house his sister-in-law had rented to Washington, when he spied a solitary figure kneeling in a glade of crooked timber. Potts dismounted, tied his horse to a sapling, and quietly approached the scene. In the pale moonlight he recognized the obeisant man as Washington. The general's sword lay in the snow to one side, his cocked hat to the other. He was praying aloud, Potts reported, "to the God of the Armies, beseeching [him] to interpose with his Divine aid, as it was ye Crisis, & the cause of the country, of humanity & of the world."

The scene so struck the Tory-leaning Potts that he galloped home and told his wife that if the Continental Army's commander in chief could conduct himself as both a soldier and a Christian, he could too. He declared for the Whig cause on the spot. The fact that Potts's revelation came to light only some 38 years after the fact, when his family's pastor passed on the description of the incident to Washington's biographer Parson Mason Weems, has led most historians to view the recollection with suspicion. It was Weems, after all, who invented the fable of a young

Washington unable to lie about chopping down a cherry tree.

Washington was known to instruct his troops to attend religious ceremonies after military victories "to praise to the supreme disposer of all events who has granted us this signal success."* Similarly, on certain special occasions — as in the case of the thanksgiving on the Gulph Road — he would order his chaplains to perform divine services. But he himself was not overtly religious. Like many of his contemporaries, the avowed deist Thomas Jefferson perhaps most famously, he paid lip service to an amorphous Almighty. And though his public and private correspondence was liberally sprinkled with references to "God," "Providence," and "Heaven," he refused to be confirmed as a member of any one denomination. He was known to attend Episcopal services, although he usually left during the Communion ceremony.

Given the circumstances and timing of the incident Potts allegedly witnessed, some scholars are inclined to give the anecdotal version at least the benefit of the doubt. As

* Washington's General Orders for October 20, 1781 — the day after Gen. Cornwallis surrendered at Yorktown and effectively ended the war — encouraged his troops to commemorate the occasion by attending church services.

464

the historian and Revolutionary War chronicler Thomas Fleming observes, "In the agony of those two mid-February weeks, with his army dissolving into mutiny, with Generals Mifflin and Gates doing their utmost to ruin him, and with Lafayette about to invade Canada with unforeseeable but potentially ruinous consequences to Washington's prestige, could this man, alone in the wintry woods, have sunk to his knees? Perhaps." On the other hand, the most damning testament to what his biographer Ron Chernow views as a fraudulent attempt "designed to meld religion and politics" is Washington's well-cited aversion to kneeling before any god or man. It is indeed difficult to believe that the general would venture into the forest to so ostentatiously ask God to bless and protect his force. An even farther-fetched version of the story began to circulate in the late 1870s when a government pension agent published a remembrance from a Valley Forge veteran. This variant had the Marquis de Lafayette and the Virginia pastor turned general Peter Muhlenberg stumbling upon a "sorrowful" Washington on his knees in a barn near his Valley Forge headquarters.

Yet such was the impact of these stories, particularly Isaac Potts's version, that Arnold Friberg's painting *The Prayer at Valley Forge* — created in celebration of the United States' bicentennial in 1976 — remains a best-selling print today. This despite the fact that, in 1918, the National Park Service, which maintains and operates Valley Forge National Historical Park, refused a request to erect a monument to "Washington's prayer" after examining thousands of pages of Revolutionary War–era correspondence and diaries as well as manuscripts held by the Library of Congress. "In none of these [was] found a single paragraph that will substantiate the tradition of the 'Prayer at Valley Forge,'" reported the Park Service commission assigned to investigate.

Whether or not there is any veracity to the stories of Washington's prayer, there was no question that at this low point in the war he was certainly in need of guidance. And even if, as seems likely, the scene in the woods did not actually occur, the emotions it portrayed as swirling within and around the commander in chief of a rapidly deteriorating Continental Army were genuine. As for guidance, divine or mortal, Washington needed to look no further than to his wife, Martha, his polestar during the most melancholy days of the revolution as he turned a year older.

Sunday, February 22, 1778, dawned dank and chill. It was George Washington's 46th birthday; there was little to celebrate. One week earlier the commissaries at Valley Forge had run out of food, and seven days with no rations had again raised the prospect of famine in a cantonment that had taken on the trappings of a refugee camp. Having already issued a General Proclamation to "the virtuous yeomanry of the States of New Jersey, Pennsylvania, Delaware, Maryland, and Virginia" pleading for cattle in exchange for a "bountiful price," the commander in chief turned toward the sick in his General Orders for the date. The orders stressed that if rice could not be distributed in the "flying hospitals," sepawn, or "Indian meal" — boiled cornmeal ground from maize — was to be substituted. There followed an unmistakable warning to the infirmary administrators. "As [Indian meal] is an article that can at all times and under all circumstances be had, no excuse will be admitted for the neglect." It was all an angry and frustrated Washington could do. His ire would have surely risen had he been aware that earlier that morning a herd of 150 cows bound for Valley Forge had been captured by a British patrol mere miles from the Schuylkill, a dark precursor to the seizure of 2,000 yards of Continental cloth by Tories the next morning. As it was, he did not learn of either misadventure for days.

Even as Washington was dashing off another urgent letter to New York Governor George Clinton pleading for emergency provisions, Martha had arranged to purchase enough supplies from local farmers to constitute a veritable feast in honor of her husband's birthday. Using his personal account, she had managed to scrounge a meager quantity of veal and fowl as well as a small supply of vegetables and eggs. On this occasion, no one at the Potts House had to share a tin plate. As the celebratory after-dinner toasts came to an end the Washingtons and their guests heard stirrings outside on the Gulph Road. The next instant, from atop a hill just east of headquarters, the fife and drum corps from Pennsylvania's Philadelphia regiment burst into an impromptu concert. Though Washington retired without acknowledging the players — perhaps he felt the tribute too reminiscent of the British custom of military bands honoring the king on his birthday — Martha emerged and handed the bandleader 15 shillings. It was the first public recognition of George Washington's birthday in the history of the United States.

The melodies had barely ceased to echo off the eastern flank of Mount Joy when Gen. Greene and his foraging party trudged into camp with several wagonloads of food. Though the commander in chief's mood may have been black enough to match the day, Greene's return to camp foreshadowed the arrival of another visitor on his way to Valley Forge, a man who would transform the entire tenor of the Continental Army.

■ ■ ■ ■

PART III

■ ■ ■ ■

I rejoice most sincerely with you on the glorious change in our prospects. Calmness and serenity seems likely to succeed in some measure those dark and tempestuous clouds which at times appeared ready to overwhelm us. The game, whether well or ill played hitherto, seems now to be verging fast to a favourable issue, and I cannot think be lost, unless we throw it away by too much supineness on the one hand, and impetuosity on the other. God forbid that either of these should happen at a time when we seem to be upon the point of reaping the fruits of our toil and labour.

— GEORGE WASHINGTON TO
ROBERT MORRIS,
MAY 25, 1778

A portrait of General George Washington painted by James Peale, based on an earlier painting by his older brother, Charles Willson Peale, during the Valley Forge encampment.

Twenty-Five:
Prussian Spring

When Baron Friedrich Wilhelm Ludolf Gerhard Augustin von Steuben arrived at Valley Forge on the cold, dreary afternoon of February 23, he did so with panache. This was only fitting. For the corpulent Prussian nobleman's journey to the United States, like the man himself, had been as colorful as it was circuitous.

George Washington was not certain what to expect when he rode out of camp that afternoon to greet Steuben and his cortege as they emerged from the soft fronds of fading daylight that dappled the road from York. Twenty years earlier the Virginia planter had ordered from London a series of busts depicting history's renowned military figures, including the likenesses of Alexander the Great, Julius Caesar, and Friedrich II of Prussia — Frederick the Great. Now, a protégé of the exalted Hohenzollern warrior-king himself was arriving. The man whom Washington encountered was a plump officer

471

ensconced in a grandiose sleigh adorned with 24 jingle bells and pulled by a team of well-muscled, coal-dark Percheron horses stepping in sync, as if dancing a ponderous waltz. Steuben, as cheerful as Pickwick's precursor, had imported the horses from western France to enhance his entrance. As he introduced himself to Washington he stroked an Italian greyhound curled by his side. Azor was the dog's name.

It is not recorded what the American commander in chief made of his visitor's fur-trimmed silk robe, black beaver bicorne cocked in the French style, and double-holstered belt holding two enormous horse pistols. However, one teenage Continental private would, years later, remember the Prussian entering Valley Forge as the very "personification of Mars." For Steuben's part, Washington's towering personal bodyguard must have reminded him of the hand-picked grenadiers known as the "Potsdam Giants" with whom King Frederick routinely surrounded himself.

Washington had, of course, been briefed on Steuben's background. Some of what he had been told was even true. Steuben was indeed the grandson of one of Germany's most prominent theologians and the son of a career military engineer in Frederick's renowned army, then the most advanced and efficient force on the European continent. His childhood had been a nomadic blur as he, his mother, and his siblings followed their father from station to station across what today constitutes Poland, western Russia, and the Baltic States. At Breslau, on the banks of the Oder, Steuben, reared as a Calvinist, was granted the rare opportunity to study under Jesuit priests. And at the age of 14 he began his military apprenticeship by accompanying his father to Bohemia, where the elder Steuben directed the Prussian engineers executing the siege of Prague during the Second Silesian War. As decreed by Prussian law, at 17 Steuben formally enlisted in the army. Eschewing his father's "technical" branch of engineering, he opted instead for a career in the more glamorous infantry.

After a decade as a peacetime soldier, including five years living with the common enlisted men as an officer in training, Steuben received his first taste of fire in 1756 when Prussia allied with England upon the outbreak of the Seven Years' War. He saw action on the Austrian frontier, where he was seriously wounded. Upon his recovery he volunteered for a command post in Frederick's light infantry battalion, a new unit which the king was standing up to conduct reconnaissance and lightning raids. Both his superb war record and his family connections — Frederick the Great's father, Friedrich Wilhelm I, was one of Steuben's four godfathers

— led to an appointment on Frederick's staff. During this time he attended the Prussian king's personal classes on the art of war. Despite being dwarfed by its neighbors, Prussia was eighteenth-century Europe's great military success story — an army with a country, as the saying went, and not the other way around. And its king was already a mythic figure, an atheist as famous for his religious tolerance and Enlightenment values as for his martial prowess.

Frederick was also an admirer of Washington, and had followed the events of the American Revolution with interest. He described the engagements at Trenton and Princeton as among the most brilliant surprise attacks in the annals of warfare, and his unprecedented respect and fondness for commoners — epitomized by the soldiers of the Continental Army — influenced the young Steuben. As did Frederick's homophile fetishes. The king's summer palace in Potsdam included a "Friendship Temple" where the homoerotic attachments of Greek antiquity were celebrated. It was there that Frederick's younger and more openly homosexual brother, Prince Henry, took a particular interest in the ruggedly handsome — and inordinately lucky — young Lt. Steuben.

Incredibly enough, Steuben's good fortune reached its apex when he was captured by Russian forces in 1761 and marched off to

Saint Petersburg as a prisoner of war. As a child, he had lived for a time in the canal-crossed city and picked up the rudiments of the Russian language. It was the nature of the age to treat captive officers more as guests than as prisoners, and Steuben used his rough facility with the Cyrillic alphabet to cultivate a friendship with a Russian nobleman who, a year later, ascended to the czar's throne as Peter III. Despite allying with France and Austria in their war against Prussia and England, Peter had an undisguised admiration for all things Prussian, and he idolized King Frederick. Aware of this, Steuben suggested that the czar employ him as a go-between to initiate a separate peace between the two rulers. The idea could not have come at a more opportune time; Prussia was surrounded by much larger armies, and even its martial exceptionalism could not forestall its otherwise inevitable collapse. With the signing of the peace treaty between Prussia and Russia, the former was spared and Steuben was hailed as a hero in Berlin and promoted to captain. And then his inherent good luck turned.

With the Seven Years' War drawing to a close, Steuben and 12 other officers were invited to attend a special school for strategic warfare initiated by King Frederick with an eye toward grooming a new generation of generals. There he ran afoul of one of Frederick's favorite senior officers. Nothing in the annals records precisely why or how Steuben's star fell, although anonymous rumors of liaisons with teenage boys soon spread. Homosexuality may have been tolerated if not encouraged at Frederick's court, but pederasty overstepped the bonds. After being demoted to a backwater post on the far edge of the kingdom, Steuben was dismissed from the army altogether. That begat over a decade of wandering in Europe, forsaking his country's *Blut und Boden* to solicit the French, the English, the Spanish, and even his old archfoes the Austrians for an army posting. But Europe was at peace, and opportunities for freelance mercenaries were scarce. To survive he returned home and drifted from court to court among the scores of Germany's quasi-independent territorial states, seeking employment from a succession of princes, dukes, and margraves.

Finally, the ruler of the small principality of Hohenzollern-Hechingen engaged him as a court chamberlain and bestowed upon him the title *Freiherr,* or baron. By June 1777, however, the 47-year-old Steuben was again on the move, and this time his peregrinations took him to Paris. There the French foreign minister de Vergennes and the playwright turned arms dealer Beaumarchais somewhat enigmatically helped him to wangle an audience with Benjamin Franklin and Silas

Deane.*

Conversing with Steuben in French — the Prussian spoke no English — over the course of several meetings, a wary Franklin only reluctantly came to recognize that his country's interests dovetailed with those of this seasoned soldier seeking adventure across the sea. What differentiated Steuben from the hordes of foreign officers clamoring for service in North America was his background. Of all the armies of Europe, only Prussia's had vested in its officer corps the duty to personally instruct and tend to the physical and emotional welfare of the rank and file, a task invariably left to noncommissioned officers in other countries. Frederick led by example, and expected his officers to do the same. Such was his solidarity with his officers that he wore the same plain blue uniform and unadorned regimental jacket as they did while leading enlisted men in the unending tactical drills that characterized his army's Spartan efficiency. It was not unusual to see the king timing with a stopwatch the number of shots his infantrymen fired per minute or personally demonstrating the cor-

* There were rumors, never substantiated, that Steuben had made a side agreement with the French to secretly provide intelligence on the Continentals in exchange for a commission in the French army upon his return to Europe.

rect formation of a line of battle. For a regal general and his officers to muddy their uniforms teaching technique to troops of the line was unheard of. Except in Prussia.

Unaware of the gossip dogging Steuben, Franklin and Deane slowly warmed to the Prussian with the receding hairline, ample nose, and budding second chin. They were no less intrigued by his stint at Frederick's war college than by his description of spending five years in the ranks before obtaining his lieutenant's commission. That this included sharing the hardships and perils of the enlisted men he would one day command was a not inconsiderable skill to possess in a Continental Army lacking a history of expertise in military logistics and training. Moreover, aside from his military service, Steuben's curriculum vitae also included his turn as an amateur diplomat — while a prisoner of war, no less. The Americans also recognized that Steuben's broad intellectual interest in ancient Greek and Roman history, the arts, and literature would stand him well with the sophisticated Continental officers whom he would need to convince that he was not just another freebooting foreigner. Even the most famous character, Don Quixote, of his favorite writer Cervantes could be seen as a metaphor for the American Revolution. There was, however, a complication. It was clear to all who met him, particularly fellow military men, that Steuben possessed the qualities and credentials of a Renaissance soldier. But Franklin and Deane wrestled with the notion of recommending to Washington and Congress an officer who, for all his laurels, had never advanced past the rank of captain.

Thus, with the assistance of de Vergennes and Beaumarchais, the two Americans set out to tweak Steuben's résumé. His captain's bars were miraculously replaced by the three stars of a lieutenant general, and his brief interludes at Frederick's court were extended to two decades at the great warrior's side as both an aide-de-camp and the Prussian army's quartermaster general. His character now came recommended not only by King Frederick, but by a flock of respected European dignitaries including de Vergennes and his counterpart at the French Ministry of War, Comte Saint-Germain. Moreover, Franklin wrote that it was neither fame nor fortune that was driving Steuben to the shores of the United States, but a burning "Zeal for our good Cause." In their letters of introduction he and Deane hinted that Steuben had turned down several lucrative military posts in Prussia in order to fight under Washington. Further, that he had not simply retired to his vast estates in southwestern Germany — invented out of whole cloth by Deane — exhibited his revolutionary ardor. As a final hedge against anyone's requiring documentation of Steuben's credentials, they intimated that he had been in such haste to reach America that he had inadvertently left all his papers behind in his home country.

Summoning Steuben to Passy for one final meeting, Franklin stressed that he would be undertaking his overseas enterprise strictly as a volunteer, with no promise of rank. Should his services prove useful, perhaps after the war he would be rewarded with a land grant in the American wilderness. But even this was not guaranteed. One can imagine the two pear-shaped personages conversing in French in Franklin's pretty little garden cottage, their faces set in speculative half smiles at the irony of concocting tall tales for the now repackaged *Comte de Steuben* to buff the bona fides he most certainly already possessed.

In late September 1777 Steuben boarded a merchantman in the port city of Marseille allegedly bound for the French Caribbean. Its cargo manifest listed wine, sulfur, and vegetables. In reality, it was transporting to New England thousands of small arms, hundreds of barrels of gunpowder, and dozens of mortars and cannons. With money borrowed from Beaumarchais, Steuben had purchased his Percherons and — unfamiliar with the color of Continental uniforms — outfitted his entourage in dazzling scarlet jackets and black bicornes sporting plumes and cockades. The horses and stylish retinue would serve as a sign of "Gen." Steuben's importance, and the entourage included his tall, lanky 17-year-old military secretary Pierre Étienne du Ponceau, rumored to be Steuben's lover and the only member of the party who spoke English. Also traveling with the baron were his personal French chef, his African servants, and his chief aide-de-camp, the former French army lieutenant Louis de Pontière.

When Steuben and his company stepped onto the pier at Portsmouth, New Hampshire, on the first day of December they were momentarily mistaken for Redcoats and surrounded by gun-wielding patriots. Once the misunderstanding was cleared up, they journeyed on to Boston, where Steuben was extravagantly entertained by the likes of Samuel Adams and John Hancock. Steuben had written to Washington from Portsmouth, enclosing Franklin's and Deane's letters of introduction and ostentatiously reiterating his intention to serve only as an unpaid volunteer. The object of his "greatest ambition," he wrote, "is to render your country all the services in my power and to deserve the title of a citizen of America by fighting for the cause of your liberty." A cautious if cordial Washington redirected Steuben's application to the Continental Congress, and before long the Prussian was in York to formally introduce himself and press his case.

The congressional delegates were well

aware of Washington's disdain for most of the foreigners who had landed in America seeking battlefield honors. Steuben's circumstances differed in one major aspect that immediately ingratiated him with the cost-conscious delegates — he was willing to fight without pay. He had but two requests — that Congress recall several disaffected French officers whom he had befriended in Boston and who planned on returning to France; and that du Ponceau and de Pontière be awarded honorary captains' commissions.* He also asked that when the British were finally defeated and American independence was gained, if Congress deemed his sacrifice worthy, it would compensate him with retroactive pay and a pension.

Within days the delegates voted nearly unanimously to accept Steuben's offer of service as well as his nominal conditions. In the interest of military protocol — and in a delicate irony that no congressman could have been aware of — he was also assigned the rank of volunteer captain. Henry Laurens was so taken with the Prussian's spirit of cooperation and formidable *je ne sais quoi* that he personally provided Steuben with effusive

* Among the French officers Steuben met in Boston was the 23-year-old engineer Pierre Charles L'Enfant, who 13 years later was selected to design the city plan for Washington, D.C.

letters of introduction to his son John as well as to Washington. Over the course of their conversations the elder Laurens was also candid about the squalid conditions at Valley Forge, which may have influenced Steuben's decision to tarry in York for nearly two weeks before setting off for the winter camp.

Despite his foppish appearance, Steuben was warmly greeted at Washington's headquarters, particularly by John Laurens. The two had a conversation in French long into Steuben's first night at camp, the beginning of a series of deep discourses between the young American and the worldly soldier of fortune. Laurens was so impressed that he wrote to his father that after but a few brief interactions he already considered Steuben "a man profound in the Science of war, and well disposed to render his best services to the United States." Young Laurens pressed Steuben to look past the horrendous conditions at Valley Forge, which, he said, masked the innate discipline that the Continentals had demonstrated throughout the fall campaign. Even amid the deprivations of the February food crisis, he added, morale among the Continentals who had not deserted had barely slackened. "Our men [remain] the best crude materials for Soldiers I believe in the world," he wrote. He also noted that Steuben "seems to understand what our Soldiers are capable of."

John Laurens had reasons for his optimism. He had watched the emaciated and half-naked soldiers engage in such frivolities as sleigh races, snowball fights, and ice-skating competitions even during the most disastrous weeks at Valley Forge. He had also no doubt heard of, if not contributed to, the collection of 50 pounds a group of Virginia officers had raised for a widowed Pennsylvania camp follower who had tended to American prisoners in Philadelphia. Did this reflect the behavior of a beaten army? In the same correspondence with his father he cited the patience that the winter soldiers had shown in the face of desolation, and concluded with an upbeat assessment. "With a little more discipline," he wrote, "we should drive the haughty Briton to his ships."

Establishing discipline would be Steuben's primary hurdle, a task for which he was well suited. For perhaps the first time, there was an experienced officer at hand who could instill a dedicated professionalism in the Continental Army. Neither Prussian nor American soldiers simply sprang from the earth fully formed, and Steuben's years developing the clockwork efficiency of an unremarkable group of German peasants and serfs had enabled him to provide the leadership the average American soldier required. The would-be drillmaster would take on the task of molding the raw material the colonies had provided to George Washington into effectives with a distinctly martial enthusiasm. But first he found himself attending to more quotidian details.

Steuben spent his initial weeks at Valley Forge on an informal inspection tour during which he personally interviewed scores of officers and soldiers in their huts. Most were shocked when the eminent foreigner crossed their dingy thresholds to inquire about their rations, their arms, their sanitary habits. Steuben was equally astonished. His first report detailed a list of shortcomings including rusty muskets and ammunition tins, a dearth of bayonets, and — incredible to a former officer serving under Frederick the Great — both officers and enlisted men standing guard duty "in a sort of dressing gown made of old blankets or woolen bed covers." The camp's overall squalor offended not only his European sensibilities but his Teutonic sense of order. Particularly distasteful was the haphazard disposition of the open latrine trenches that snaked through the cantonment with no thought to their placement. Though officers had been instructed to ensure that all enlisted men used these "vaults" for bowel movements, this was more easily ordered than carried out, particularly under cover of darkness. Some men never even left their huts to urinate. In their ignorance of or indifference to personal hygiene, Steuben wondered, did the American soldiers not realize that the "foul airs" that enveloped the encampment were a virtual invitation to the diseases spreading among the soldiery?

In one of his first memorandums that John Laurens passed on to Washington, the Prussian suggested filling in the existing trenches and replacing them with new privies dug on a downhill slope at the far end of the camp from the cooking facilities. These vaults, he added, should be filled with dirt and new ones dug after every four days. He also worked with the French engineers on improving the breastworks, and laid out plans for a familiar arrangement of company and regimental rows and lanes to crisscross the plateau, a standard morale-boosting procedure in European armies. These hands-on instructions alone distinguished him from the more theoretical military maunderings the Americans were accustomed to receiving from foreign "experts." Steuben had not been in camp four full days before the young Laurens was touting him for the office of inspector general. This in spite of the fact that at the time Thomas Conway still technically held the post and Steuben had mastered only one word of English — "Goddamn."

"We want some kind of general tutoring in this way so much," Laurens wrote, "[Steuben] will not give us the perfect instructions, absolutely speaking, but the best which we are in a position to receive."

John Laurens was closer to the mark than he knew. For as February 1778 unwound, Washington recalled all his foraging parties in order to ready his army for war. Any supplies too unwieldy to be hauled back to Valley Forge were ordered burned lest they fall into enemy hands, and all boats remaining on the New Jersey banks of the Delaware were to be sailed or portaged north to Trenton. Just below that city the river dropped off the rocky Piedmont Plateau and into New Jersey's sandier coastal plain. With the ice floes soon to melt, this geological fault line, aptly named the Trenton Falls, created a natural barrier to British ships attempting to ride the strong flood tides upriver. With that, the commander in chief had taken every defensive precaution he could. It was now time to concentrate on turning the 8,000 troops who remained at Valley Forge into a force diligent enough to avoid the previous autumn's mistakes.

Since the engagement at Germantown, Washington had reluctantly accepted the resignations of nearly 300 officers. This left a void not only in the Continental Army's leadership, but in its training regimen. In that sense, Steuben's arrival proved a godsend. One of Washington's treasured books was Frederick the Great's *Instructions to His Gen-*

erals, a detailed army manual admired the world over. If the baron could replicate on the Valley Forge parade grounds even a semblance of the guidance sprung from the plains of Mecklenburg, there was hope for a successful spring campaign.

Like Washington, Steuben was also prone to taking the long view. Sensing the martial stirrings invigorating the Potts House and reverberating through camp, he plunged into his new duties determined to prove his worth, as well as to set the stage for his transformation from a volunteer captain into a salaried general officer. As he wrote to an old friend in Prussia, he could envision but two paths beckoning to him in the coming fighting season — one led to hell, the other to the head of a regiment.

TWENTY-SIX:
THE RAINS NEVER CEASE

In London, it was not Prussians crossing the Atlantic who alarmed British war planners. It was the French. As a result, in anticipation of the long-rumored Franco-American alliance, King George III and his ministers were in the process of drawing up an entirely new strategy for the colonial campaign.

Over the preceding months the generals Howe and Clinton had held decidedly differing views regarding the Continental Army's travails at Valley Forge. Washington's spies and double agents in Philadelphia repeatedly attempted to inflate the number of troops stationed at the winter encampment in order to discourage an attack. But the honeycomb of Loyalists reporting from counties surrounding the cantonment made it clear to British authorities that the slew of desertions and detachments had combined with the dearth of supplies to drastically reduce the Americans' effectiveness. When Clinton's agents informed him that the Continental

Congress was so concerned about the loyalty of its soldiery that it planned to administer an army-wide oath of allegiance, he viewed this as an invitation for Howe to overwhelm the rebels and force them to the negotiating table. "Now is the time to press them hard and offer them terms," he wrote to his uncle, the Duke of Newcastle. Clinton's hawkish exhortations, however, were met with less enthusiasm by his superior in Philadelphia.

The Howe brothers were in the peculiar position of fighting a war as well as acting as semiofficial peace commissioners. They thus commanded, in Gen. Howe's words, "with the sword in one hand and the olive branch in the other." This placed them in conflict with both George III and the hawkish George Germain, whose inclinations were to destroy the Continentals much as the king's uncle, the Duke of Cumberland, had crushed the Scottish Jacobite rebellion 30 years earlier. As such, Gen. Howe couched his reservations to London about attempting a winter offensive in both military and political rhetoric. His men and horses, he wrote to Germain, lacked sufficient food and forage to take the field for any extended period. On a broader, more strategic plane, he also argued that he had come to better understand and even appreciate the Continental mind-set. A full-out assault on Valley Forge, even if it ended in victory — a result he was certain of — would serve only to harden their resistance.

As noted, to this point Gen. Howe had limited his winter expeditions primarily to minor probes no farther afield than southern New Jersey and lower Bucks County. These somewhat haphazard excursions were aimed at collecting forage, disrupting American recruiting efforts, and — in the case of New Jersey — sowing terror among the Whig populace after the failure to destroy Anthony Wayne's command. Despite his triumphs at Brandywine and Germantown, Howe sensed that Lord Germain had lost confidence in him, and was resigned to the fact that the king would accede to his multiple requests to return to England — a certitude that would be confirmed to him in April.

For even the previous autumn's tactical victories had failed to tamp the savage treatment he was receiving in Parliament and in London newspapers for the loss of Burgoyne's army. He did not relish the idea of arriving home with the stain of another major defeat on his record. And as his excuses piled up, it became evident to Germain that the general did not have the stomach for one last major engagement. In the event, affairs in London to which neither Howe nor Clinton was yet privy would render their contrasting military strategies irrelevant.

In mid-February Lord North had introduced

proposals in the House of Commons suggesting some form of "conciliation" with the rebels. By early March these peace overtures had crystallized into specific instructions directed to Gen. Clinton, who had been selected to succeed Gen. Howe as commander in chief of British land forces in North America. Though Whitehall had yet to officially learn of the Franco-American treaty signed a month earlier, the tone and content of Germain's communiqué to Clinton strongly hinted that he and the king's war counselors considered the alliance a *fait accompli.* To counter this development, Clinton was to be informed that a new Peace Commission was being organized to present the Americans with terms similar to those the British agent Wentworth had offered to Franklin in Paris — most important, the modifications to the numerous parliamentary acts the colonists found so onerous and a restoration of normal trade. In short, nearly everything the Americans desired save formal independence.

There were various reasons behind the concessions. Several British MPs, sympathetic to the colonials' loathing of taxation without representation, had taken to wearing blue-and-buff clothing to Parliament in *homage* to Washington's uniform. Their spiritual leader, whom even the king could not ignore, was the renowned Irish statesman, philosopher, and essayist Edmund Burke, who in a speech before the House of Commons equated the American cause with every Englishman's civil birthright. Burke's ally Charles Pratt, Earl of Camden, went further, arguing that the conflict stemmed from a consistent effort by British ministers to drive the colonists into rebellion. "America never entertained any intention of rendering themselves of this country," Camden told Parliament, "till they were forced to it by a series of the most unjust, arbitrary, and cruel measures."

Less idealistic critics took a more pragmatic view. The British stock market had plunged on rumors of a two-front conflict with both France and the Americans, and William Wildman, Viscount Barrington — the nobleman charged with the manning, training, and equipping of the British Army — warned Lord North that though the Royal Navy might contain and constrict the rebellion along the North American coastline, the idea of subduing the entire continent while simultaneously preparing for a possible French invasion was madness.* There were, however, only so many compromises the king and his

* In eighteenth-century England the Secretary of War post had yet to be established and Viscount Barrington held the title of Secretary at War, a non-cabinet level position somewhat analogous, the military historian John J. Patterson explains, to

ministers were willing to make. Should the Peace Commission's terms be rejected, Clinton would be instructed, the war would now be "prosecuted upon a different plan." Specifically, if upon taking command Clinton could not decisively defeat Washington's army come the onset of spring, he was to "relinquish the idea of carrying on Offensive Operations against the Rebels within land" in the northern colonies. Instead, Britain's emphasis would move to the sea, where Clinton and Adm. Howe would be charged with shattering New England's maritime economy with a summerlong harassment of its seacoasts and ports.

Germain also planned to notify Clinton that he could expect reinforcements from England, with the provision that the bulk of these troops be used to strengthen the garrisons protecting British holdings in Canada — particularly Nova Scotia and Newfoundland — and East and West Florida, the two Loyalist colonies ceded by Spain after the French and Indian War, which had declined to send representatives to the First Continental Congress. Finally and if need be, Clinton was also authorized to abandon Philadelphia and lead his army north to New England in

Chairman of the Joint Chiefs of Staff in the current United States system.

order to clear staging areas for Adm. Howe. The summer thrust against New England was to be followed by an autumn campaign to subdue rebel activity in Georgia and the Carolinas. Central to this second phase was the notion that Loyalists in the deep south would, unlike those in the middle states, rise to fight alongside British regulars and the Florida militiamen.

With America's southern breadbasket thus defeated and occupied, its export economy — the primary source of its foreign credit — would crash. This would set the stage for a final, inexorable drive north into Virginia and Maryland, harassing the coastlines there in much the same manner that had (theoretically) beleaguered New England. If all went according to plan, these three tactical movements would coalesce into a strategy leaving the few remaining patriots in the northeast to wither on the vine.

It was a sound blueprint while it lasted — which it did for approximately 13 days. For on March 21 — eight days after the French formally announced their alliance with the Americans — an infuriated George III issued a new set of secret instructions to be relayed to Gen. Clinton. Abandoning the three-pronged campaign devised less than two weeks earlier, in a fit of pique the British monarch now ordered Clinton to immediately detach 5,000 of his troops to invade the

French island colony of Saint Lucia while preparing another 3,000 to be deployed to bolster Crown holdings in the Floridas. To Clinton's dismay, the king was effectively signaling that England would now assume a strictly defensive posture in North America. To erase any doubt, the Admiralty Board informed Adm. Howe, "The contest in America being a secondary consideration, our principal object must now be distressing France." The new orders included a coda — once Clinton had dispatched the nearly 8,000 troops from Philadelphia, he was to quit the city and lead his rump force back to New York. It was left to his discretion whether to remain there or, if he thought himself too vulnerable, to withdraw farther north to Rhode Island or even all the way to Halifax.

Needless to say, none of these instructions would reach the British commanders in America until late the following month. Meanwhile, the Howe brothers and Clinton were left to their own devices regarding a spring campaign that would never be. Not so George Washington.

As the most continuous cold rains in memory continued to lash Valley Forge, Washington and his aides nearly wore through the oaken floorboards of the cramped rooms of the Potts House on the bend of the Schuylkill. They were drafting plans for a spring offensive. Although Nathanael Greene had yet to completely settle into the job of quartermaster general — and Jeremiah Wadsworth had not yet informed Congress of his acceptance of the offer to replace William Buchanan as commissary general — for the moment the commander in chief was unburdened of the political intrigues that had consumed him for months. He was finally free to devote his full attention to the enemy.

True to Washington's lifelong impulses, his designs revolved around an offensive, slated for no later than June. But where to strike? Although he was not yet ready to summon his general officers to a formal Council of War, he shared his thoughts with his closest confidants. He had narrowed his thinking to two preliminary targets. The first, unsurprisingly, was Philadelphia. This in itself involved two options — whether to pursue a massed attack on the British bulwarks north of the city, or set in place a stranglehold blockade completely encircling it, intended to starve Gen. Howe and his troops into either surrender or retreat. The second objective under consideration was a stealth assault on New York City. If 6,000 able-bodied and well-equipped Continentals could be surreptitiously marched north from Valley Forge and ferried across the Hudson above New York — an optimistic projection at best — they could combine with troops stationed in the

Highlands to fall on Clinton.

While Washington mulled these alternatives, he was certain of one thing. In either battle scenario, the Hudson Highland garrison remained the key to keeping open his supply lines from New England. To that end he also recognized that he needed an officer he could trust commanding those heights. This, in his mind, was not Gen. Israel Putnam. Putnam had made his name as a fierce Indian-fighter, and though his personal courage and energy had never been questioned, he had proved a disappointment as a tactician. Eighteen months earlier, Putnam's inability to plan and coordinate large troop movements had allowed the British to outflank the Continental Army during the Battle of Long Island. Since then his reputation had only further eroded. "Old Put's" loud complaints over having to detach troops to reinforce the Pennsylvania campaign were still recalled with bitterness among some in Washington's inner circle. But the final indignity had occurred the previous October, when Fort Montgomery and Fort Clinton, the western anchors for the precious Hudson River antishipping chain, had fallen. During that campaign Putnam had been embarrassingly outmaneuvered by Gen. Clinton, whose feints had Putnam leading his troops in circles while the British overran the forts' paltry defenses.

So it was that, in early March, Washington relieved Putnam of command and appointed as his successor his own old friend Maj. Gen. Alexander McDougall, one of the original Sons of Liberty currently stationed in Morristown, New Jersey. McDougall, still recuperating from the illness that had prevented him from joining Lafayette in Albany, nonetheless agreed to travel from Morristown to the Hudson Highlands, where Washington tasked him with two directives. His first was to ensure that the same fate that befell Fort Montgomery and Fort Clinton would not occur at the new American redoubt rising some eight miles farther up the river at West Point. He was also, on congressional instructions, to convene a court of inquiry to investigate Putnam's responsibility for the loss of the Hudson River forts. Putnam was eventually exonerated of any wrongdoing when the court found that a lack of manpower, and not the actions of any one commander, was responsible for the loss. But the demotion and taint of dishonor seemed to break the 60-year-old veteran. Within a year he suffered a debilitating stroke and retired from the military.

Meanwhile, as a relentless mixture of rain and snow fell on the encampment for each of the first 17 days of March, Washington continued to wrestle with ways and means of raising his troop strength. Baron Steuben had already submitted his preliminary plans for the training of 15,000 effectives — the number Washington estimated he would need for an assault on either Philadelphia or New York, or even an impelling blockade of the former. This was perhaps twice as many able bodies as Washington now had under arms despite the fact that, as of March 1, 1778, the Continental Army's muster master listed 22,283 men in Washington's command. This optimistic number counted troops too ill to fight, others too ill-clothed to participate in combat, and still more on furlough or special assignment.*

To remedy this appalling lack of manpower, Washington pulled and prodded incessantly, dispatching messengers from headquarters nearly daily to exhort the states to fulfill their seasonal recruiting commitments, and sending riders to collect the hundreds of recovering convalescents who had wintered over in Continental hospitals. In addition, the regular-army detail guarding the storehouses at Lancaster was instructed to turn over its duties to local militiamen and report to Valley Forge, and a detachment of North Caro-

---

* Close to 5,000 Valley Forge soldiers had been detached from their battle units to serve as teamsters, bakers, blacksmiths, and carpenters, and as all-purpose valets to nearly all officers above the rank of lieutenant.

lina regulars Washington had lent to the Continental Navy for service on the Delaware River was recalled. Finally, with the Camp Committee delegation having acceded to his request for an Indian regiment, he wrote to Lafayette in Albany asking that at least 400 Oneida be pressed into service and hurried south. He then turned his attention to logistics.

A squad of officers was dispatched to Virginia with credit vouchers to purchase remudas with which to expand Gen. Pulaski's cavalry, and the governor of Pennsylvania, Thomas Wharton, was pressed to deliver to Quartermaster Greene all the wagons and dray horses that the state could appropriate. Henry Knox was ordered to Boston to collect as many field pieces as possible, including those that had been sent to Albany for the mismanaged Canadian campaign. Washington even tweaked the Board of War, expressing to Gen. Gates his "apprehensions" over the state of the armories and reminding him how "mortifying and discouraging" it would be if the board were unable to provide each of his soldiers, veteran and new recruit alike, with the appropriate weapons and ammunition.

In early March "Light Horse Harry" Lee had returned to Valley Forge with the contents of the Delaware and Maryland food magazines, which temporarily allayed the immediate threat of starvation. And by the middle of the month there were reports of herds of cattle being driven from New England and wagonloads of flour and salted meat en route from western Pennsylvania. Nonetheless, Washington's deputy commissary general warned him that the "Badness of the Roads, & high waters makes it impossible to say when they will arrive in Camp," and those charged with meting out provisions recognized that it was only a matter of days before their larders would again be depleted. In one of his first official acts as quartermaster general, Nathanael Greene responded to his chief wagon master's complaint that the army was "Near being totally undone for want of Forage" by ordering the Continental storehouses in Reading and Pottsgrove tapped and their contents shipped to Valley Forge. This was of small solace to American units in Trenton and Wilmington, which continued to face serious shortages of staples such as meat and bread.

The loud grievances that ensued from these shortages did not go unnoticed at the Potts House. Washington, stalling for time and hoping to check further unrest, disseminated a public proclamation offering his "warmest thanks to the virtuous officers and soldiery . . . for that persevering fidelity and Zeal [and] uncomplaining Patience during the scarcity of provisions." This was accompanied by the issuance of a gill of rum or whiskey to every man in the cantonment. Notably, in that same General Order the commander in chief also castigated "the few individuals who disgrace themselves by murmurs [and] unmanly behavior." John Laurens, ever the melancholy idealist, showed more sympathy for "the number of men unfit for duty by reason of their nakedness [and] the number of sick in hospitals." While Laurens agonized over the misery the fates had directed toward the Continental Army, the more gimlet-eyed Hamilton saw Congress's inaction as "the chief antagonist to our future prosperity, and with this idea I cannot but wish that every gentleman of influence in the country should think with me."

The lack of forage cited by Greene's wagon master was particularly acute in Trenton, where Casimir Pulaski was forced to relocate his three regiments of cavalry yet again after running through all the supplies to be had in the towns of Flemington and Pennington. Pulaski informed Washington that he was moving the horsemen even farther northwest, to the village of Chatham, where his unit commanders would undertake a rigorous regimen of drilling while awaiting the promised arrival of new men, animals, and equipment. Pulaski, however, would not be with them. He was riding to York in a sulk. Offended by the Continentals' lack of the deference traditionally shown to dashing cavalry officers throughout Europe, he had decided to resign his post — a resignation, Washington drily noted, "founded on reasons which I presume make you think the measure necessary."

Pulaski hoped to convince Congress to stand up under his command a legionary corps of some 70 lancers and 200 light infantry that would act as a guerrilla force operating separately from both the regular army and the militias. He suggested that the delegates allow him to recruit from the Indians fighting with the Continentals as well as any soldiers being held in custody for minor crimes. In theory, the unit would be, as Pulaski's sympathizer John Laurens envisioned, "perpetually scouring the interval between the two armies and embracing every opportunity for a stroke of partisanship." Laurens may have been "persuaded from [Pulaski's] intelligence and enterprising spirit" that yet another headstrong commander striking out on his own was precisely what the revolutionary cause needed at the moment. Cooler minds, less taken with the Polish count's self-reverence and sharp tongue, were skeptical. As it happened, what came to be known as the Pulaski Legion would later play a crucial role in the fight for American independence. But, for now, Pulaski's prickliness and pouting merely lent further credence to the idea of an American army in chaos.

Amid these seemingly unrelenting struggles, a messenger from York arrived at Valley Forge. He carried news that, per Washington's agreement with the Camp Committee, not only had new and larger state recruiting quotas gone into effect, but the first smattering of draftees from southern state militias had begun trickling through the town. This was in addition to a company of 130 black soldiers moving south from Rhode Island to join Gen. Varnum's brigade. Even the most morose congressional delegates were buoyed by the high-stepping soldiers marching down York's main street on their way to the winter encampment. Washington was similarly sanguine, and decided to postpone an official review he had ordered detailing the calamities the army had faced since December. Though his work ground on, wearying, wild, and certain to be bloody, he managed to find time to write to his confidant Gen. Cadwalader, "As our prospects begin to brighten, my complaint shall cease."

General Greene, charged with feeding and clothing the new troops soon to be pouring into Valley Forge, was not nearly so blithe.

TWENTY-SEVEN:
A TRIM RECKONING

Nathanael Greene preferred center stage to the wings. Despite his initial trepidation over abandoning the battlefield — "No body ever heard of a quarter Master in History as such or in relate-ing any brilliant Action," he fretted to Washington midway through his tenure — by early March he had thrown himself into the thankless assignment with the ardor of a bull eyeing a billowing red cape.

His first order of business was to demand an audit of his predecessor Thomas Mifflin's expenditures in order to determine just how corrupted the supply system had become. This led him to a flock of unpaid creditors who had vowed to never again do business with the Continental Army. In response, he informed Henry Laurens that he expected Congress to authorize "a large and immediate supply of cash" to lure these merchants back into the fold. In the meanwhile he dispatched teams of scouts to comb Pennsylvania and Delaware for any wagons and horses that Thomas Wharton's state agents had overlooked. Per Washington's instructions, the identifying details of all confiscated animals — age, size, color, distinguishing marks — were noted and their owners were allowed to negotiate a fair price before being issued certificates of seizure. Greene next took out advertisements in local Whig newspapers admitting that Mifflin's department had been rife with agents who had inappropriately appropriated cattle, hay, and grain without fair remittance. He promised to remedy this by paying going rates — and overpaying, if necessary — to win back the confidence of wary farmers.

Greene was barely a week into his tenure before he had discovered, and had transported to Valley Forge, thousands of shovels, spades, tomahawks, and bolts of tent cloth that had lain moldering in forgotten warehouses and barns. He also activated plans to store nearly 800,000 bushels of grain "and as much hay as can be procured" in strategic magazines at roughly 15-mile intervals along what he and Washington calculated would be the northern route of the spring campaign. In the interim, with the weather breaking and the roads improving, he agreed to pay sometimes exorbitant prices in order to direct emergency deliveries of food, forage, and clothing to Valley Forge; shipments that in mid-March began as a slow drip would by

May and June constitute a wellspring. The gills of rum and whiskey that Washington meted out in celebration of the army's perseverance had been made possible by Greene's organization of local sutler booths established across the Schuylkill on the outskirts of camp.

Greene also instituted a transport system to streamline the movement of French arms, ammunition, tools, and uniforms — including crates of the highly prized .69-caliber *Charleville* muskets — from New England's ports. With the assistance of Jeremiah Wadsworth — who had finally accepted the position of commissary general — he made certain that ships arriving from France were now met on quays by wagons leased by the Quartermaster Department and unloaded by commissary personnel. Whereas once the cargoes had languished in northern warehouses or, more perniciously, simply vanished at Continental chokepoints like Peeksville and Trenton, the materials were now hauled south via a network of protected inland roads that bypassed both major population centers and American base stations.

Given the continual vicissitudes since the very establishment of the cantonment at Valley Forge, not all of Greene's projects proceeded apace. A herd of cattle being driven south along one of the secret routes Greene had charted was captured in Connecticut by a company of Tories surreptitiously drilling in a secluded field. And a Massachusetts company ordered to unload a wagon train at a forage yard adjacent to the encampment elected to instead pilfer the wagons and desert as a body. Though several men and teams of horses drowned attempting to swim the Schuylkill, the majority made their escape and were never seen again. Washington may have required the faith described by Paul in Hebrews — the substance of things hoped for and the evidence of things unseen — but for the most part the commander in chief was elated by the electricity running through his reformed procurement department.

On March 17, Saint Patrick's Day, the commander in chief's mood was further lifted by the news that every man in camp had been inoculated against smallpox. That same afternoon he watched a group of soldiers celebrate the arrival of a shipment of eight-pound cannonballs from Rhode Island by taking part in a competition to see who could roll the munitions farthest. The game, called "Long Bullet," was a fitting metaphor. Over Washington's own long bullet of a winter, his army had overcome a season of logistical nightmares that would have brought a European force to its knees. Like pig iron stripped of its impurities and annealed into steel, his remaining regiments were emerging stronger for their ordeals. They were, as so eloquently described by the historian and Washington biographer Joseph Ellis, "the chosen few who preserved and protected the original ethos of 1775–76 after it had died out among the bulk of the American citizenry."

Coping with the privations of Valley Forge had indeed become so routine for Washington's troops that the influx of provisions, whether cannonballs or rum, constituted something of a divine dispensation. It also infused both his officers and his soldiery with a cautious optimism that was nowhere better reflected than in the manner with which they took to the tender ministrations of the ambitious and blustering Baron Steuben.

George Washington was not a man to let emotions, much less strained personal relationships, stand in the way of a good idea. When Thomas Conway had approached him with a plan to train a core of instructors who would then fan out among the regiments to impart their newfound knowledge, he had immediately grasped the efficacy of the Irishman's model. He just did not view Conway as the man to implement it. Now he revisited the strategy with Steuben.

Among the mythical images of the American Revolution is that of the musket-wielding Minuteman crouched behind a tree or a boulder firing into the squared ranks of the red-coated "Lobsters," as if picking off so many crustaceans in a barrel. In fact, it was the Continentals' utter disregard for the linear tactics employed by successful eighteenth-century armies that nearly doomed their cause. What military experts of the era called "fire discipline" required three rough components. First, infantry battalions on the march had to be able to change formations while maintaining cohesion. Then, upon meeting the enemy, each soldier required the discipline to stand and hold fire when so ordered even if the man next to him was torn to pieces by cannon fire. Finally, in engaging, the ability to load, fire, and reload rapidly and efficiently through the noise and smoke of a battlefield had to become second nature.

Washington recognized that the loosely conjoined brigades of the Continental Army required not so much a refresher course in the rudiments of tactical maneuvers as a complete overhaul. Thus was a grand experiment born. The commander in chief expanded his personal guard of 50 Virginians by 100 men selected from each state in camp, and lent them to Steuben to constitute a version of Conway's model company. They were joined by 14 majors — one from each of the infantry brigades — to serve as teaching inspectors who reported to Steuben's hand-picked subinspectors. Two days after the Saint Patrick's Day celebrations, Steuben resumed the soldier's life he had abandoned some 15 years earlier.

Each morning and afternoon, in fair weather and foul, the Prussian assembled his small troop on the vast parade ground in the center of camp. Circulating among the soldiers and barking instructions like a rabid drill sergeant, he preached the dual discipline of mind and body. Woe betide the soldier who was late to a training session or handled his weapon clumsily on what John Laurens took to calling "our Campus Martius." Steuben's face would turn crimson and contort into a mask and his arms would flail as he hollered in his guttural French for his translator: "Come over here and swear for me!" This was invariably followed by a cataract of German and French curses and oaths interspersed with the occasional "Goddamn!" The scene had the unintended effect of reducing the Americans to fits of laughter. Yet as the historian Wayne Bodle notes, Steuben's training regimen was "a difficult one: specialized, tedious, and in no way glamorous."

Without ever having seen them fight, Steuben intuited that the resiliency the Americans had exhibited to this point in the war was offset by their professional limitations. At less than three years old, the Continental Army lacked an institutional memory; its soldiers were no more adept at fighting a practiced, dedicated foe than its commissary officers were at feeding and clothing them. What few drills the army practiced were a mélange of the whims of individual state commanders whose influences, such as they were, ranged from bits of French, English, and Prussian field guides to homegrown backwoods fighting techniques. It was only the Americans' spirited tenacity that had prevented them from being completely swept away by polished British and Hessian soldiers at Brandywine and Germantown. Such hardiness had even been responsible for the surprise victories in Boston and at Trenton and Princeton. But Steuben knew that the Continentals' tendency to expose the flanks of their long files of Indian-style marching columns, for instance, or their inability to form swiftly into disciplined lines of fire, would ultimately lead to catastrophe.

His commitment to even the most mundane-seeming disciplines was personal and intense, leaving nothing to chance. His training, for instance, began with the most basic concept — standing at attention. Breaking his gaunt combatants into 10- and 12-man squads, the tallest in the rear, he demonstrated for each trooper how "to stand straight and firm upon his legs, with his head turned to the right so far as to bring his left eye over the waistcoat buttons; the heels two inches apart, the toes turned out; the belly drawn in a little, but without constraint; the breast a little projected; the shoulders square to the front and kept back; and the hands hanging down the sides, close to the thighs." In time he progressed from close-order drill to maneuvering from column to fire line and back again to column, to wheeling in compact formation with machinelike precision, to shouldering, firing, and swiftly reloading flintlocks while attacking and retreating in unison.

Unlike the imperious Conway — or, for that matter, unlike most American officers who felt it beneath their station as gentlemen to personally lead drills — Steuben was not afraid to literally get down on his hands and knees in the mud and muck to instruct his charges on such quotidian lessons as small-arms maintenance or how to read and exploit terrain — in short, everything he had learned under Frederick the Great, contoured for an American audience. He was aghast that the Continental soldier who even possessed a bayonet — about half of the troops did not own one — treated it as nothing more than a utensil "to roast his beefsteak." The bayonet had evolved into a powerful tool in European armies, and it was not unusual to see the portly baron doff his blue regimental coat, hand his silver-tipped swagger stick to an aide, and demonstrate over and again the correct manner of wielding and thrusting the weapon. By the end of his first week, Steuben — "exerting himself like a lieutenant eager for promotion" — and his drillers were surrounded by crowds of fellow soldiers whooping and clapping to their choreographed maneuvers.

Concurrently, in an effort to codify his methods, Steuben began compiling his legendary "Blue Book" of military regulations. At night he would return to his rented farmhouse at the south end of camp to compose his short chapters, subsections, and sub-articles in French for his military secretary du Ponceau to translate into textbook English. John Laurens and Alexander Hamilton, who had taken to doting on Steuben like a brace of Prince Hals orbiting Fat Jack Falstaff, would then polish the manual by adding a colloquial flourish easily digested by the common American soldier. Chapter and verse were subsequently copied longhand into regimental orderly books by the brigade inspectors for distribution to each of their commanders. Steuben's rules of war addressed subjects as disparate as the gathering and interpretation of intelligence; the proper arms and accoutrements to be carried by all officers and enlisted men; the marching formations and exercises of brigades, regiments, companies, and platoons; the instruction and inspection of new recruits; and even the correct method for executing an about-face.

By now Washington had ordered the cessation of all drilling not overseen by Steuben or his subinspectors, and that spring the resulting *Regulations for the Order and Discipline of the Troops of the United States* would be circulated among Gen. Smallwood's troops in Delaware as well as Continental regiments in New Jersey. The work eventually constituted the United States Army's primary field guide for decades. Its unique rationale — that European military methods could be integrated into a thoroughly independent-minded army — may be Steuben's greatest gift to his adopted country. It was also a metric that set him apart from his would-be predecessor Conway. Even Washington took notice when reports began trickling back to him that the German viewed the Continental soldier through a prism different from most European officers'.

Unlike his foreign-born peers, Steuben had experience with what would today be called unconventional warfare. He had cut his teeth commanding an ill-disciplined Magyar light infantry that served as Frederick the Great's shock troops, and realized that much like the wild Hungarians, the iconoclastic Americans had over generations lost their ingrained deference to authority for authority's sake. The Continentals required an understanding of why a particular order might mean the difference between victory and defeat, between life and death. "You say to your soldiers, 'Do this,' and he doeth it," he wrote to an acquaintance in the French army. "But I am obliged to say, 'This is the reason why you ought to do that,' and then he does it. Your army is the growth of a century, mine of a day."

Instead of recoiling from this singular American trait, he worked it into his training, patiently explaining the tactical and strategic logic behind each move and countermove he required of his students. As with the Magyars — who were known to turn on and kill officers they did not like — he found that once he had justified his premise to the rank and file, Washington's soldiers would run through flames for him. Conversely, Steuben's respect for the resiliency of the tattered rebels and their imposing commander in chief grew far greater than he could ever have imagined while plotting his journey with Benjamin Franklin in Paris. "No European army could have been kept together under such dreadful deprivations," he once mused. Not many would dispute that.

So meticulous was Steuben's process, so indefatigable his diligence, and so burgeoning his influence that Washington was soon issuing a series of General Orders suitable for, and nearly indistinguishable from, the Prussian army's boot camp directives. Soldiers whose arms and equipment were not maintained in proper fashion were subject to arrest. Brigade and regiment commanders were instructed to ensure that their men marched in step, even within camp and no matter how small the party, "in order to preserve order, regularity, and discipline." Noncommissioned officers who failed to adhere to "a conduct and example which ought to distinguish them from privates" were threatened with a reduction in rank. Each waking hour in camp, the diarist Joseph Plumb Martin complained, "was a continual drill."

In the meantime, even as Steuben remained officially classified as a "volunteer," he was already fulfilling John Laurens's prophecy by assuming the de facto role of the army's inspector general. This posed a problem. For despite his banishment to seeming obscurity in upstate New York, having his position usurped was not an insult Thomas Conway was willing to absorb. He was, after all, technically still the congressionally appointed inspector general of the Continental Army, and it galled him that Steuben had apparently stolen his training ideas and methods. It also puzzled him that during his years of service in France he had never heard of the famous lieutenant general who was allegedly such a cog in Frederick the Great's mighty Prussian war machine. It would not have been unusual for American generals such as Washington, Greene, Wayne, and Knox to be unaware of a Prussian officer's battlefield accomplishments. But foreigners occupying high ranks in the Continental Army such as Conway, de Kalb, and Lafayette — the latter two having yet to return from Albany — would surely have taken note of someone arriving on American shores with such a glorious reputation. Even enemy commanders such as the Howe brothers and Clinton were certain to grow suspicious. That this notion had also dawned on Steuben was reflected in the subtle manner in which he went about correcting his counterfeit record.

It began with a hint dropped to John Laurens. During one of their many late-night discussions, Steuben told the young aide that he had really not been Frederick the Great's quartermaster general, but merely a deputy quartermaster general with the rank of colonel. One supposes he just could not bring himself to admit that he had risen no higher in rank than captain. He also disclosed to Laurens that his lieutenant generalship and his noble title had not been conferred upon him until he was in the employ of the Margrave of Baden, after his retirement from the Prussian army.

Certain that these new fabrications would find their way from Laurens to his father, Henry, and from there to Washington, he explained that the misunderstandings must have arisen from errors in translation during his meetings in Paris with Franklin. Now, having been made aware of the inconsistencies, he felt it best to set the record straight. A few days after revising his résumé in conversation with the younger Laurens, Steuben apparently forgot that he had concocted the post in Baden. He wrote to Henry Laurens that he had been appointed a lieutenant general while in service to the Holy Roman Emperor in the province of Swabia. Yet by this point Steuben's reputation at Valley Forge was already such that the elder Laurens apparently decided to let the contradiction pass. He was no doubt influenced by his son's lavish praise for the Prussian.

In the same letter to his father subtly adjusting Steuben's biography, young Laurens also let it slip that after a proper period as a volunteer, "The Baron" expected to be rewarded with a major general's post and all the pay and perks that came with it, including an eventual command. After all, Laurens wrote to his father, "All the genl officers who have seen him are prepossessed in his favor and conceive highly of his abilities." Washington, he added, "seems to have a very good opinion of him, and thinks he might be usefully employed in the office of inspector general." Reading between the lines, Henry Laurens took his son's point, and began referring to Steuben as a former lieutenant general in some vague "foreign service." As if anyone on his side of the Atlantic would know, or even care to know, the difference between

Baden and Swabia.

Laurens *père et fils* were not alone in falling under Steuben's spell. The Caribbean-born Hamilton also viewed himself as something of a "foreigner" serving in an army of flinty New Englanders and rustic southerners, and fell easily into Steuben's circle. Linked by their language skills and their keen interest in military history, they delighted in discussing subjects ranging from Spartacus's strategy in the Third Servile War to Inaros II's successful guerrilla tactics against the Persians. The normally circumspect young scribe gushed to John Jay, " 'Tis unquestionably due to [Steuben's] efforts that we are indebted for the introduction of discipline in the army." The Prussian also made allies of lesser-known junior officers by hosting a series of dinners that only majors, captains, or lieutenants whose breeches were torn to rags were allowed to attend. Steuben himself presided over these events *sans-culotte,* sharing his allowance of "tough beef steaks," moldly potatoes, and hickory nuts. Similarly, enlisted men vied to be posted as sentries outside his quarters when word spread of his habit of sharing his nightly meals with his guard. And on the several occasions when Steuben was invited to dine at Washington's headquarters, his suave European manners charmed the French-speaking officers' wives; his aide du Ponceau noted that the flirtatious

Caty Greene and Lady Stirling's daughter Kitty were particularly enchanted.

Equally important, Steuben's general sense of order and discipline proved contagious. Cleanup crews were suddenly scurrying across the cantonment digging new latrines, filling in old vaults, and hauling away several months' worth of accumulated "Filth and nastiness" that included the foul-smelling offal from the carcasses of dead horses. Washington took notice, and even issued a General Order stating that despite a few remaining pockets of "intolerable smell," he was "very much pleased in a ride through the lines . . . to see what attention some of the Brigadiers had paid to his orders respecting the Neatness and Purity of their camp."

By late March, Steuben's original coterie of brigade inspectors from his model company had spread through the entire army to impart their balletic lessons. It was not long before each regiment was marching in double rank or in columns of four to either a "common" cadence of 75 steps per minute or a "quickstep" cadence of 120. Steuben made certain that officers, not sergeants, became responsible for leading their troops in advances against an imaginary enemy, and at the sound of regimental drums — "beating the long roll" — wheeling them into uniform lines for bayonet charges. The Prussian was pleased. "My enterprise succeeded better than I had dared to expect," he wrote to a friend. "I had the satisfaction, in a month's time, to see not only a regular step introduced into the army, but I also made maneuvers with ten and twelve battalions with as much precision as the evolution of a single company."

Washington was no less appreciative. By the end of the month he was discreetly lobbying Congress to consider Steuben for the inspector general's post. There was, however, still the matter of the man technically occupying the position. In the wake of the Canadian fiasco, Conway had at the direction of Congress reported to Peeksville. He had barely arrived before the new commander of the Hudson Highlands, Gen. McDougall, ordered him to the tiny outpost at Fishkill. Offended and confused, he wrote to his former mentor Gen. Gates complaining, "Boxing me about is not the usage which I ought to expect as a Gentleman, and as an officer." He was apparently the last to understand that Gates's tide was at a low ebb, for in the same letter he again threatened to relinquish his commission and return to France. Much to his surprise, this time Congress accepted his resignation. Flummoxed, he scrambled to assure the delegates that they had misunderstood his intent, and asked to be reinstated. They voted 23 to 4 to table his request without motion. Henry Laurens was quite succinct when Conway traveled to York from upstate New York to personally plead his case. "The door is shut," he told the Irishman.

At the same time, far to the east, the martial tempo of camp life that Steuben had helped introduce to Valley Forge combined with the warming weather to gradually dissipate the aura of doom that had infested the cantonment since December. As the branches of chestnut and oak blanketing Mount Misery and Mount Joy burst into green, this new aura of optimism had an intoxicating effect on both the officer corps and the rank and file. It was as if the army's metabolism was accelerating in preparation for the battlefield. "If Mr. Howe opens the campaign with his usual deliberation," John Laurens wrote to his father, "we shall be infinitely better prepared to meet him than ever we have been."

For once he was not accused of being a hopeless idealist.

Twenty-Eight:
A Rumor of War

On March 20, the very day that Washington's rider departed the Potts House with his sunny missive to Gen. Cadwalader about the army's prospects, American river watchers in the north were dispatching their own messengers to Valley Forge. The communiqués contained ominous news. Scouts along the Hudson in New Jersey had observed large numbers of Redcoats, perhaps as many as 2,500, boarding over 40 troopships in New York Harbor. No one knew their design or objective, but one destination stood out as the most logical — Philadelphia.

With this, Washington's tactical focus immediately swung from offense to defense. Despite Steuben's constant drilling and the wisps of confidence it engendered, he knew well that the scant number of effectives he had in camp were in neither shape nor position to receive an advanced blow from the enemy. Howe was thought to have some 10,000 troops in Philadelphia, while a combination of disease, desertions, and detachments had reduced the Continental force to barely 8,000 men, with perhaps half of that number considered able-bodied. If British columns buttressed by reinforcements from New York were to march on Valley Forge before Washington could concentrate his far-flung resources, the war for independence might very well be strangled in its crib on that cold and muddy plateau in southeastern Pennsylvania. Over the next several days his strategy sessions with his kitchen cabinet were dominated by questions of immediate survival.

Sensing the tension emanating from headquarters, the cantonment was suddenly galvanized into activity. Steuben and his sub-inspectors escalated their drills to battle-ready maneuvers. Battalion commanders ordered all extraneous equipment piled near campfires, the easier to set it ablaze should the army be forced to retreat. Commissary officers were ordered to convert their ovens to prepare travel-ready hardtack, what the soldiers called sea bread. And from northern New Jersey, Washington recalled his cavalry regiments, now commanded by Pulaski's replacement, Col. Stephen Moylan, one of the commander in chief's former aides-de-camp. But Moylan's horses were too sickly to be of much assistance, and in the end Washington decided to keep them out of harm's way. General Smallwood, on the other hand, was alerted to prepare to evacuate Wilmington in an instant to rejoin the main force. Where that rendezvous might take place, no one could say. On Gen. Greene's instructions Conestoga wagons creaking under the weight of emergency provisions rolled out of camp daily to bury caches of supplies in a series of depots laid along trails and roads leading west and north. In some instances, the ground was so frozen that holes had to be blasted out of the earth with precious gunpowder. In others the tides of flowing mud and drifting snow necessitated the use of surveying tools to mark where the stores had been sunk.

A few enthusiasts appeared to welcome, if ever so warily, an imminent British assault. John Laurens wrote that even if the army was forced to burn its huts and survive a fallback in tents, this would serve to make it a more elusive target. And upon hearing rumors that Gen. Howe had petitioned to be recalled to England, Anthony Wayne — the bloodbath at Paoli still fresh in his mind — informed his fellow Pennsylvanian Thomas Wharton that he could only hope that this did not occur, "untill we have an opportunity to Burgoyne him."

Such buoyancy, however, was clearly a minority opinion. For if it was indeed to be the enemy who choreographed the opening sequences of the spring campaign, even

Washington's most seasoned fighters feared the worst. "We could hardly wish Gen. Howe in a more convenient situation to attack than he is in now," Connecticut's Jedediah Huntington wrote in a sneering letter to his brother. Huntington also bewailed his state's meager contribution of reinforcements: "If every state had done like Connecticut, we would in all probability have shared the fate of Gen. Burgoine long before this."

The mood of the Continental Congress in York similarly vacillated. Yet again the delegates' anxiety over a British offensive overrode their adherence to the young country's core principle of civilian control of the military. After brief deliberations, they voted to grant Washington the power to bypass state authorities and call up some 5,000 soldiers from the New Jersey, Maryland, and Pennsylvania militias. Washington accepted this responsibility without comment, but did not act on it. His hesitance was as much philosophical as practical. He viewed the United States not only as a physical nation but as an idea "cleanly if not tightly defined." Even if Congress had decided to renege on the grand bargain it had struck with its citizenry, he knew better than to abet its momentary panic. Moreover, noting the threadbare ranks of the Pennsylvania militia patrolling east of the Schuylkill, he reminded Henry Laurens that in the past it had been difficult to muster

100 men from the state, let alone several thousand. He also told Laurens that it was not militiamen he needed, but regular-army troops, and he feared that the congressional decree would interfere with their recruitment. His dour assessment added to the bleak, tense mood that suddenly permeated Valley Forge during the last ten days of March.

Then, on March 31, the threat overhanging the camp burst like a frozen pipe. It was midmorning when an odd message arrived from Gen. Smallwood's headquarters in Wilmington. Smallwood's detachment had originally been conceived as a buffer between British-held Philadelphia and the American storehouses in Maryland. But the garrison had become so bereft of food, horses, equipment, and wagons that it had virtually ceased to exist as a military component. What it could do, however, was continue to monitor the enemy's shipping on the lower reaches of the Delaware. In that capacity several of Smallwood's scouts observed that newly arrived British vessels appeared to contain far fewer Redcoats than had been reported departing from New York. The number was sketchy, but Smallwood informed Washington that it was certainly nowhere near the reputed 2,500. When coast watchers in southern New Jersey reported similar findings, Washington reevaluated his position. Though he was baffled by the seemingly vanished regiments

— one Continental officer ventured a guess that they had been diverted to enemy-held territory in Rhode Island — his thoughts returned to the offensive.

Later that same afternoon he wrote to Gen. McDougall on the Hudson Highlands seeking advice. If his northern scouts had been anywhere near accurate in their reports, a subtraction of 2,500 troops from Clinton's rolls would have left him with a force of some 4,000 garrisoning New York City. "What is to be done?" Washington asked McDougall. It was a rhetorical question, for he was already formulating his options. "We must either oppose our whole force in this quarter," he continued, meaning Philadelphia, "or take advantage of [the enemy] in some other. Which leads me to ask your opinion of the practicability of an attempt upon New York."

As he awaited McDougall's reply, Washington was unaware that the playing field was again about to shift beneath him.

While George III's new instructions to his commanders in America made the slow journey across the wintry Atlantic, Washington and Congress had no idea that their fears of an imminent assault on Valley Forge stood in direct contradiction to Britain's new strategy of conciliation with the Americans and total war against the French. Given the imperfect intelligence he was receiving,

Washington's defensive preparations for an attack had been merely the default position of military commanders from time immemorial reacting to worst-case scenarios. By early April, however, with his spies and scouts reporting no unusual troop movements in or around Philadelphia, he conceded to Henry Laurens that the state of emergency that had descended on the winter encampment over the final ten days of March "had been founded on conjecture, and by some degree misinformation." This, however, was only a short respite.

Washington also stressed how fortunate both he and by extension the country had been to have avoided a confrontation with Gen. Howe. Regarding the Redcoats reported to have boarded the vessels in Manhattan, he confessed, "I know not certainly where they are gone." But had the enemy moved on him in strength, he added, Pennsylvania, Delaware, and Maryland might now be in British hands. He also chided the delegates for their continued delay in acting on some of the major principles to which he and the congressional Camp Committee had agreed back in February. Where were the thousands of fresh troops he had been promised? Of equal importance, why had he received no answer regarding his proposed half-pay pensions?*

* Incredibly, a full 70 years before Karl Marx and

Despite Steuben's near-magical achievements, Washington's most experienced officers remained restless. "Scarce a day passes," he wrote, "without two or three threatening to resign their commissions." These included the two brigadiers from his home state, the generals George Weedon and Peter Muhlenberg, as well as 90 of their officers. Even Rhode Island's James Varnum had requested a furlough, which Washington had declined to grant for fear that Varnum might not return. If he could not retain leaders such as these and was forced to settle for "low and illiterate Men void of capacity," all the raw recruits in the world would stand no chance against Howe's professionals. He concluded the communiqué with a dark flourish. The

---

Friedrich Engels published their *Communist Manifesto,* John Laurens was advocating that Congress enact a luxury tax "which would be felt only by the rich" in order to fund the military pension program. "I would wish the burthens of society as equally distributed as possible," he wrote to his father on April 11. "That there may not be one part of the community appropriating to itself the summit of wealth and grandeur, while another is reduced to extreme indigence in the common cause." ("John Laurens, Letter to Henry Laurens, 11 April 1778," in Simms, *The Army Correspondence of John Laurens 1777–1778,* p. 156.)

politicians would do well to keep in mind that if they failed to move forward on the military pension plan, they might well consider again relocating the capital city, this time as far south as Virginia. "Let Congress determine what will be the consequences."

This was of course not the first time Washington had resorted to exaggerated scare tactics in the face of congressional intransigence. For in reality the atmosphere at Valley Forge told a different story. Once the panic of late March subsided and April's first temperate breezes carried with them the scent of spring, the Continental Army's priorities shifted from mere survival to preparing for battle. This prompted a raft of charming missives that would have been unthinkable only weeks earlier.

A Rhode Island physician, noting that the last of the troops inoculated against smallpox had finally recovered, whimsically complained that the most urgent hardship his unit now faced was an acute shortage of grog. A lieutenant colonel from the same state, pining for his newlywed bride, described the solace he took traversing the "beautiful meadows" along the banks of the Schuylkill on his twice-daily constitutionals. Even the chronically vexed Albigence Waldo was moved to commit to his diary a bit of doggerel that began, "The day serene — joy sparkles round; Camp, hills and dales with mirth resound." And a Virginia officer assigned to Steuben as a brigade inspector captured the martial spirit animating the encampment when he wrote to his brother that the Continentals "were 50 times in better order this spring than we were last to receive the Enemy."

There existed of course more cynical souls whose tactile instincts left little room for either whimsy or wishful thinking. General Greene in particular held little hope that Congress would accede to Washington's half-pay pensions, and predicted that the delegates would slough off this responsibility to the individual state legislatures. It would be in the state capitals, he wrote, where the proposal would "dye and sink into forgetfulness."* Greene also chafed at the sluggish arrival of regular-army reinforcements, and wondered if news of the American victory at Saratoga had left his fellow patriots too complacent to bother to meet the quotas set by the Camp Committee. Greene's evident consternation was shared by a cadre of officers who, unaware of Washington's private deliberations with his inner circle, muttered over the lack of planning for a spring cam-

---

* Greene was almost correct; an attempt by Congress to defer the question of half-pay pensions to state politicians was narrowly voted down by the delegates at York.

paign. Their grumblings, however, were soon to be answered when, in mid-April, the Crown's tentative new Bills of Conciliation reached Valley Forge.

Washington was instantly suspicious. When they sent the Bills of Conciliation to Valley Forge and York under flags of truce, the British had simultaneously also published the contents in several Philadelphia newspapers and handbills. This was accompanied by a direct address from Lord North imploring the rebellious colonists to cease their "disorders" and return to the British fold where, in essence, all would be forgiven. The prime minister promised that the repressive Coercive Acts would be repealed, Parliament would abandon any right to tax the colonies, the Continental Congress would be recognized as a legal body, and the Americans might even be allowed to elect representatives to the House of Commons. Washington sensed that the concessions, particularly the renunciation of direct taxation, would have a "malignant influence" on the Continental will to continue fighting.

Lord North's peace overture, Washington wrote to Henry Laurens, "is certainly founded in principles of the most wicked and diabolical baseness, meant to poison the minds of the people & detach the wavering from our cause." He urged the delegates to counter the enemy's disingenuous feint with a strong political dismissal of North's propositions, and to unequivocally reject any hint of a negotiated settlement. "Nothing short of Independence can possibly do," he wrote. Much to his satisfaction, Congress replied that its stance had not changed — it would welcome the arrival of the Crown's representatives as soon as every British soldier and sailor had withdrawn from American shores and England officially recognized the independence of the United States. In the meantime, the delegates added, any person seeking to strike a bargain with the British would be labeled a traitor.

On the military front, Washington recognized that the clearest sign to any vacillating soldiers that the revolution would continue was to finally share his plans for the upcoming campaign. On April 20 he summoned the 11 general officers then in camp as well as Baron Steuben, still technically a foreign volunteer, to an unofficial meeting at the Potts House. The generals included Lafayette, only just returned from Albany and back in command of his division of Virginians. The marquis remained embarrassed and exasperated by the foolishness of the stillborn Canadian excursion, and wrote to Henry Laurens that while he was delighted to be back on Pennsylvania territory, "I wish I had never seen the northern ones. By that expedition (besides what disagreement it brings in itself) I have only got many enemies [and] much trouble." He was nonetheless excited to be joining his fellow general officers to plan for a real fight.

As the field commanders filed into the Potts House that morning, a few noticed the absence of Charles Lee, who had been returned several days earlier in exchange for a British general virtually kidnapped from his mistress's bed in Rhode Island. The British had held Lee in custody in comfortable Manhattan quarters, where they had treated him as military royalty, plying him with fine food and drink. There were in fact suspicions, not proved until decades later, that Lee had collaborated with the enemy by sharing Continental strategies and suggesting countermeasures. Pending his release, he had been transferred to Philadelphia, and Washington had sent a guard to greet him on the Germantown Highway with the pomp customarily extended to a conquering hero.

It took Lee less than 24 hours to wear out his welcome at Valley Forge. After a celebratory supper at the Potts House, he was given his own bedroom behind Martha Washington's sitting room. The next morning he arrived for breakfast late, unwashed, and noticeably disheveled. It was subsequently discovered that he had used a back door to smuggle in his mistress, the wife of a British sergeant. Martha Washington was not amused. Lee subsequently found it expeditious to leave for York to meet with Congress before heading home to his Virginia tobacco plantation for several weeks of "recuperation" from his ordeal as a prisoner. It is doubtful that he was now missed as Washington addressed his senior officers.

In his opening remarks the commander in chief couched his call to arms as a response to the "injustice, delusion, and fraud" of the British peace terms. He assured his guests that the enemy's offer represented nothing so much as a sign of desperation. Congress was of a similar mind, he continued — the proof was the delegates' acceding to Gen. Gates's request to return to a field command. Even as they met here at Valley Forge, Washington said, Gates was preparing to ride to Fishkill to place the northern army on a war footing.

Washington also disclosed that his spy network in Philadelphia had uncovered interesting information — the same packet ship that had carried the Bills of Conciliation to America had also delivered to Gen. Howe a letter stating that his resignation had been accepted. He guessed — correctly as it would happen — that Howe would be succeeded by the more bellicose Gen. Clinton. With this in mind he then presented to his subordinates the alternative campaigns he had been pondering for weeks — Philadelphia or New

York. If they leaned toward the latter, he asked, should it occur "by a coup de main, with a small force? Or shall we collect a large force and make an attack in form?" He then put forth a third option for consideration — to remain at Valley Forge until all the states had met their recruitment commitments. He asked his generals for written responses. He received them within a week.

Four of the officers — Massachusetts's John Patterson, the Ulster-born New Jerseyan William Maxwell, Anthony Wayne, and Lord Stirling — voted for a siege of Philadelphia, with Lord Stirling adding in a footnote to his comments that his first preference was simultaneous expeditions against Philadelphia from Valley Forge and against New York City from the Hudson Highlands. Four others — Rhode Island's James Varnum, Enoch Poor of New Hampshire, Massachusetts's Henry Knox, and Virginia's Peter Muhlenberg — were keen to fall in with the Highlanders and march on New York. The three New Englanders, no doubt weighing the outcome at Saratoga against the engagements at Brandywine and Germantown, all noted the assistance Washington could expect from the northern militias should he opt to move the theater of war to the Hudson.

Finally, of the remaining four, two of the three foreigners — Steuben and the French engineer Louis Duportail — joined Gen.

Greene in expressing a preference to bide their time at Valley Forge until a refortified army was strong enough to move on either target. Curiously, Lafayette was the only general officer to withhold an explicit opinion. In a long letter to Washington that constituted his response, he called the three options "the most difficult to resolve" since he had landed in America. He did evaluate each one in detail, but the closest he came to offering a solid suggestion was his recommendation that a move on either Philadelphia or New York would require at least 25,000 troops. This large number, he had determined, would be needed to counteract the reinforcements that Adm. Howe's vessels would be sure to rush from British strongholds in Rhode Island, Canada, and perhaps even the Floridas.

It crossed no one's mind that the elder Howe's ships might be otherwise engaged. For not a man in the room that morning could have been aware that only days earlier, on April 13, a French war fleet had sailed west from the port of Toulon. The armada, under the command of Lafayette's dashing 48-year-old cousin-in-law Adm. Comte Jean-Baptiste-Charles-Henry-Hector d'Estaing, consisted of four frigates carrying 4,000 French soldiers and 12 ships of the line, including the 90-gun *Languedoc*. It had been

540

provisioned for nine months. Its destination was the United States.

Twenty-Nine:
"Long Live
the King of France"

To the British it was a bold ambush. To George Washington, it was yet another war crime. In the event, there was little doubt that what came to be known as the Battle of Crooked Billet was designed as a harbinger — these were the consequences facing the upstart Continentals who had the temerity to decline the Crown's generous peace terms.

The engagement was conceived in the waning hours of the final night of April 1778, when Gen. Howe summoned Capt. John Graves Simcoe and Lt. Col. Robert Abercrombie to his headquarters at the Masters-Penn House in Philadelphia to order their light infantry units into the field. Despite his reluctance to initiate a full-scale engagement with Washington's regulars, Howe was quick to recognize, and to take advantage of, the Pennsylvania militia's tenuous hold on the townships and farmsteads that lay between the Schuylkill and Delaware Rivers.

Earlier that day, Loyalist spies had passed

along the precise location of the young militia leader Gen. John Lacey's camp on the border of Bucks County and Montgomery County. Simcoe, whose regiment had been fighting in the area for months, knew the place well. The British-born Simcoe's green-coated Queen's American Rangers, as they had been dubbed, were a particularly brutal band of Tories who had earned the description "partisan hunters" for their search-and-destroy missions against civilians thought to be sympathetic to the rebels. They rarely took prisoners. Simcoe's orders were, in cooperation with Abercrombie's regulars, "to secure the country and facilitate the inhabitants bringing in their products to market." If in the process of "securing the country" the Rangers managed to stage a sneak attack on Lacey's bedraggled force, so much the better.

Over the first months of 1778 reports of British incursions and depredations across southern New Jersey had streamed into Washington's headquarters. More recently — and more worrisomely — enemy movements into Pennsylvania east of the Schuylkill had also grown more flagrant. Since assuming command from Gen. Armstrong in January, Lacey had been handicapped by — and complained loudly about — a hostile populace and, not coincidentally, a lack of accurate intelligence. The allotment of 1,000 troops promised to him by the Pennsylvania state legislature had never arrived, and by early spring a combination of desertions and decommissions had reduced his strength to little more than 400 men to patrol an area larger than Rhode Island. Of these troops, the majority had arrived in-theater only within the past week. Most were without guns; none had ever seen combat.

By both necessity and their instructions, Lacey and his irregulars were constantly on the move, either seeking (with little success) to intercept farmers hauling goods into Philadelphia or avoiding the more frequent and larger British patrols. Added to their woes were the well-armed gangs of Loyalist vigilantes that had lately sprung up in imitation of the Doan Gang. These mounted cohorts lived off the plunder looted from Whig-owned farms and mills, and had given themselves semiofficial-sounding names such as the Independent Dragoons and the Pennsylvania Volunteers. So undermanned and ill-equipped was Lacey's company that it could not even interdict a committee of Quakers openly traveling to Philadelphia earlier that month for their annual meeting under the protection of these armed guards.

On the night of April 30, Lacey had made camp along Pennypack Creek near the Crooked Billet Tavern, about midway between Valley Forge and Trenton and just over 20 miles from Philadelphia. He ordered pickets to patrol the surrounding roads, but the officer in charge of the sentries fell asleep before assigning the manpower.* Simcoe's Rangers and Abercrombie's Redcoats, totaling some 850 men, encountered no resistance as they crept to the edge of the encampment in a pincer formation. As dawn broke on May 1, they attacked.

Surrounded and outnumbered, the groggy Americans took heavy casualties as they stumbled out of their tents into sheets of musket fire. Lacey at last managed to mount his horse and whip into place a tenuous battle line that repelled a subsequent bayonet charge. Then, while the British regrouped, he led a small company of troops into a nearby brake of wood. Employing the thick copse of oak and chestnut to defensive advantage, he and his surviving militiamen repulsed a cavalry charge from Abercrombie's dragoons before engaging in a running, four-mile firefight. Then, inexplicably, the British broke off the engagement despite having suffered only seven men wounded and two horses killed. When Lacey and his little company returned to the original battleground they understood why. While they had been fending off Abercrombie, Simcoe's Rangers had turned their campground into a charnel house. Nearly

* That officer, Lt. William Nielson, was subsequently court-martialed and cashiered from the army.

half of Lacey's command had been wiped out, with civilian witnesses reporting that surrendering Continentals were run through with bayonets and cutlasses while the American wounded were heaved onto pyres of buckwheat straw and burned alive.

The atrocity at Crooked Billet in effect rendered moot the entire Continental presence in Pennsylvania east of the Schuylkill. Many of the militiamen who had managed to flee the slaughter never returned to duty. Even as his company commanders took roll call in the blood-soaked fields, Lacey recognized that those who remained were now too psychologically damaged to constitute a professional force. As Simcoe himself noted in his journal, the savagery of the massacre "had its full effect of intimidating the militia, as they never afterward appeared but in small parties and like robbers." It was with a bittersweet melancholy that Washington would within the week relieve Gen. Lacey of command. He told Lacey that he recognized that he had done his best with the "fatiguing" task he had been assigned, "considering the smallness of your numbers and the constant motion which you have consequently obliged to be in." He also understood that the inexperienced Lacey through no fault of his own was in over his head, a quandary all too common in every state's militia.

For Washington, the similarities between

the Battle of Paoli and the Battle of Crooked Billet were palpable — with one striking difference. In the wake of the debacle at Paoli eight months earlier, the American commander in chief had been left to ponder, yet again, the futility of asking amateur citizen-soldiers to stand and fight against trained professionals. Then, with a weakened army and no hope for reinforcements, he had been left to merely watch from across the Schuylkill as Gen. Howe moved on Philadelphia. Now, however, some 24 hours before the news from Crooked Billet had even reached Valley Forge, a breathless courier had arrived at the Potts House with a message that would break over the winter encampment like a mustering thunderclap. France had entered the war.

Rumors that Louis XVI would formally recognize the United States had been circulating in America since at least the previous November. In the middle of that month Washington had even dropped an apocryphal hint in the last paragraph of a long letter to his stepson Jacky Parke Custis: "War expected every moment between France & Britain." Over the interim similar unfounded reports had abounded, with at least two Whig newspapers publishing stories asserting that France and Spain had agreed to aid "the Independence of the American States." But it was not until April 13 that the wishful fantasy became fact when Simeon Deane, Silas's older brother, disembarked from the fast French frigate *Sensible* at the docks of what is now Portland, Maine. He carried with him copies of the Treaties of Alliance.

As Simeon Deane made his way to York, he paused at his home in Bethlehem, Pennsylvania, to entrust a friend to convey the news to Valley Forge. The courtesy call to Washington had been the idea of his brother, who was preparing to relinquish his Parisian diplomatic assignment to John Adams later in the year. The commander in chief received Simeon Deane's letter on the evening of April 30, the same night that Howe, Simcoe, and Abercrombie were plotting to assail John Lacey's little company. Though exultant at the "glorious News" certain to set "all Europe into a flame," Washington thought it prudent to refrain from disclosing the pact, except to a few close members of his staff, until an official announcement from Congress.

When he shared the news with John Laurens, the young aide reacted with his typical brio, calling the alliance "the most humiliating stroke that the national pride of Britain ever suffered." On a more personal level, Laurens also fretted that "France might give a mortal blow to the English" before he had an opportunity to achieve battlefield glory. Lafayette, on the other hand, was so overcome by his nation's *beau geste* that he flung open the door to Washington's study without knocking, smothered the aloof general in a bear hug, kissed him on both cheeks, and burst into tears. The young marquis's emotion was understandable. The same courier who had delivered the announcement from Simeon Deane also carried a letter from Lafayette's wife, Adrienne, informing him that their 22-month-old daughter Henriette had died of pneumonia.

The following morning, Washington's communiqué to the delegates in York betrayed no small sense of relief. "With infinite pleasure I beg leave to congratulate Congress on the very important and interesting advices brought by the frigate *Sensible,*" he wrote to Henry Laurens. "I believe no event was ever received with more heartfelt joy." And though he still kept the news hidden from his troops, his General Orders for May 1 instructing the camp's chaplains to perform special services the next day at 11 a.m., with compulsory attendance of officers of all ranks, hinted that something momentous was afoot.

The whispers grew louder when word spread through camp that Steuben had been summoned to the Potts House and instructed to prepare the army for a "Grand Review." Deciphering the extra jaunt to Steuben's step, the jubilant Continentals erected maypoles decorated with spring flowers before each regimental headquarters hut and rushed back from their drills to congregate in the brigade lanes to toast each other with free-flowing spirits purchased from the suddenly pro-republican sutlers' stocks. It was always the civilians who were the first to sense a change in the wind.

At the same time in York, Henry Laurens was summoning the delegates to a special Saturday session at which the treaties were read aloud. The following days were a blur of giddy festivity. After attending a thanksgiving service on Sunday, the South Carolina congressman William Henry Drayton hurriedly dictated and had printed 100 copies of a broadsheet hailing the alliance. These were for distribution in and around Valley Forge. On Monday, May 4, the delegates unanimously ratified the treaties and sent couriers galloping off in all directions to announce the triumphant news. That evening, upon learning of the vote in York, Washington journeyed from the Potts House to dine at the artillery park with Henry Knox and his senior officers.

Although Drayton's official notices had yet to reach the encampment, Washington confided to Knox that the following morning's General Orders would contain the announcement along with his grand good thanks "to the Almighty ruler of the Universe [for] raising us up a powerful friend among the princes of the earth, to establish our liberty and independence upon a lasting foundation." As Washington was returning to his headquarters he noticed a group of Knox's young cannoneers gathered in the gloaming for a raucous game of wickets, an Americanized form of cricket. The commander in chief dismounted, and much to the artillerymen's amazement, deigned to take several swings with the bat. Perhaps he felt that his prayers in that snowy glade had indeed been answered.

It had been a celebratory French tradition since the fourteenth century, when the Mongols and their Chinese mercenaries introduced gunpowder to Europe. Now it was crossing the Atlantic. George Washington eagerly seized upon Lafayette's suggestion of the *feu de joie,* or "fire of joy," as a most apt tribute to commemorate the official notice of France's alliance with the United States. At just past nine on the morning of May 6 a booming cannon report summoned all troops to the parade ground in the center of camp. There the Treaties of Alliance were read aloud before Steuben and his subinspectors marched the entire Continental Army, brigade by brigade, to the middle of the drilling fields. Steuben had spent the preceding days literally diagramming the movements of each brigade, regiment, company, and platoon, and now, their thousands of flintlocks polished to a gleam, the troops were arranged into two long, parallel columns by the generals de Kalb, Lafayette, and Lord Stirling.

Washington, astride his white Arabian and surrounded by mounted aides, watched from beneath an arbor erected atop a small hillock as each of the three spectacular discharges from the 13 assembled field pieces was followed, at Steuben's signal, by a cascade of musket fire that roared sequentially down the forward battle line from right to left and then up the rear line from left to right. The rapid symphony of fire and smoke was accompanied by full-throated huzzahs from nearly 10,000 men.

"Long live the King of France."

The cannons boomed again as the entire procedure was repeated.

"And long live the friendly European powers."*

And, finally, a third demonstration.

"To the American States."

As the Continentals grounded their weapons, wheeled, and re-formed into their regiments, the consequences of Steuben's six weeks of drilling and training were more than evident. "The admirable rapidity and precision," young Laurens told his father, had been "executed to perfection. Through it all,"

* This in honor of Spain and Prussia, which most expected to join the fight.

he added, Washington "wore a countenance of uncommon delight." Though many of the soldiers remained half-clad, and not a few were still shoeless, these troops resembled nothing so much as an army.

If, as Washington had always believed, survival was the father of success, then here before him was made manifest the projection of his own steely reserve. Whatever the depths of his personal despondency over the previous months, he had never failed to maintain a facade of serene determination that had in turn inspired the men under his command to persevere. Before him on the Valley Forge parade grounds were the fruits of his labor. When the soldiers were dismissed their commander in chief ordered a gill of rum ladled into every man's canteen.

The "Grand Review" was followed by an outdoor reception in the center of the artillery park attended by the army's entire officer corps and their wives, including Martha Washington. Long plank tables arranged beneath a bower of tent marquees groaned under the weight of a profusion of meats and cheeses requisitioned by Quartermaster Greene, and enough barrels of wine and spirits were tapped to slake the thirst of 1,500 men.

Before the festivities began, Washington summoned Steuben to his side and asked for a moment of quiet. A week earlier he had surreptitiously written to Henry Laurens "with regards to the merits of the baron de Steuben" and importuned Congress to appoint the Prussian to the post of inspector general. Now he announced to thunderous cheers that earlier that morning a courier from York had arrived with news that the delegates had acceded to the request. Steuben was now officially a major general in the Continental Army. Steuben, smothered in bear hugs, seemed to swell with pride at his elevation — and not least at the prospect of the salary that accompanied the rank. He did his best to hide his greatest trepidation. For like John Laurens, he was conflicted over the idea of France stealing his glory, and brooded to Henry Laurens "that I may not, perhaps, have the opportunity of drawing my sword in your cause."

In reply the elder Laurens, having spent time in London and being better acquainted with the British character, assured the Prussian, "It is my opinion that we are not to roll down a green bank and toy away the ensuing summer. There is blood, much blood in our prospect."

Meanwhile, as his subordinates clanked tin cups and drank in their newfound circumstances, Washington retired early. When he and his guard cantered to the top of a rise overlooking the artillery park, the commander in chief wheeled his horse, waved his hat, and shouted one final "Huzzah" to the officers whose spirit and morale he had kept buoyant through looming crisis after crisis. It was a telling gesture from the sober Virginian, as it masked a sense of gnawing doubt. The cold pragmatist in Washington was already looking ahead to the potential ramifications of Louis's XVI's profoundly consequential decision.

The man who only two days earlier had lost himself if only for a moment in the revelry of a game of wickets now worried that an infectious overconfidence "shall relapse [us] into a state of supineness and perfect security." He well knew that despite the professional precision his soldiers had demonstrated during the *feu de joie,* it would take more than Steuben's histrionic oaths to transfer that discipline from the parade ground to the battleground. This was particularly salient now that France would be watching with a much more critical eye. Moreover, what of the British? Rumors were already circulating that Gen. Clinton planned to quit Philadelphia for New York. But Washington had to consider that the engagement at Crooked Billet might have been not just an isolated incident but the opening foray of an all-out assault on Valley Forge. He could not put it past the bellicose Clinton to attempt to foreclose the conflict before French reinforcements even reached American shores. It was the savvy strategy; it was what he himself would do.

That night Washington ordered Dan Morgan's riflemen to supplement the pickets patrolling the camp's perimeter.

THIRTY:
THE MODERN CATO

The sun had barely crested the eastern horizon when Gen. William Maxwell's chestnut mare loped across the temporary bridge spanning the Schuylkill. Maxwell reined to the side of the trail on the river's eastern bank and watched as four regiments of New Jersey regulars, some 1,200 men, crossed behind him. Soon they had disappeared into the demilitarized zone that arced all the way to Trenton. It was May 7, the day after the Grand Review, and Maxwell's orders were succinct — to succeed where John Lacey's militia had failed. Maxwell was to rendezvous with what was left of the militiamen, now under the command of Gen. James Potter, incorporate them into his force, and take the fight to the enemy. George Washington was tired of running.

Washington liked and trusted the Irish-born Maxwell. The two had served together as junior officers during the Braddock campaign in the French and Indian War, and at 45 the

557

general remained as hardy as a Connemara pony. Maxwell's hollow cheeks and rose-red nose studded with gin blossoms were a testament to his reputation as a man who drank as hard as he fought. Yet Washington had enough faith in his old companion to place him at the head of a select regiment of hit-and-run shock troops during the fights at Trenton and Brandywine. A week before the latter, Maxwell had led his light infantry deep into enemy-held territory to form an advance skirmish line along a height named Iron Hill. There his undermanned infantry had held off an early British advance until the Continentals "had shot themselves out of ammunition" and were forced to retreat. His present task was equally unenviable.

On the very morning that Maxwell and his troops forded the Schuylkill, news reached Valley Forge that a battalion of British infantry had sailed up the Delaware and disembarked on the New Jersey side of the river at Bordentown, just below the Trenton Falls. They had encountered no resistance, and destroyed a number of Continental storehouses and burned some 40 American vessels to the waterline. Maxwell sent word to Washington that he was racing the 50 miles to the scene. Perhaps the Redcoats were not finished raiding along the New Jersey side of the river. The commander in chief immediately recognized that the move would open a large and undefended gap in the eastern cordon between Philadelphia and Valley Forge. Yes, there were rumors that the British were preparing to evacuate Philadelphia — for what purpose, no one knew. But if they marched on his winter camp, their path was now clear.

That night Washington again redoubled his sentries and pickets and carried those burdensome thoughts to bed as he prepared to convene the next morning's Council of War.

During the informal war conference held nearly three weeks earlier, it had been Gen. Greene who argued most vociferously against an impulsive flight into combat. Even now, with the French alliance transforming the chemistry of the war, Greene continued to advise against an offensive. It was his position that the troops who had survived the winter, as well as the new recruits drifting into camp, needed more training. Further, his procurement department may have been running efficiently enough to supply a stationary army with a modicum of food, clothing, and arms. But it was not nearly prepared to provision an entire army on the move. Washington did not need to be told that while tactics win battles, logistics win wars. Yet he also recognized that at the very least he needed a contingency plan in place.

Since his April meeting with his brigadiers,

Washington had put to paper, in order of desirability, the proposals discussed at that assembly as well as his officers' reaction to them. He'd entitled his private manifesto "Thoughts upon a Plan of Operation for Campaign 1778," and shared it with only his closest aides. Now, anticipating that the conflict was about to enter a new and perhaps ultimate stage, he intended to present these priorities to his general officers for "mature consideration."

The first was an assault on Philadelphia, or at the very least a strangling blockade. As much as it pained him to relegate an attack on New York to a lower rung — his inglorious retreat from that city was never far from his mind — he was nothing if not a realist. Any attempt to surreptitiously move 15,000 troops north was doomed to failure. Now, as then, his third alternative was the least enticing — "to lay quiet in a secure Camp and endeavor by every possible means to train and discipline our Army." Like Greene, Washington understood well the difficulties posed by the choices. The first two, he wrote, would "be attended with considerable expense — great waste of Military Stores, and Arms." A retrenchment at Valley Forge, on the other hand, "would be giving the Enemy time to receive their reinforcements, spread their baneful influence more extensively — and be a means of disgusting our own People by our apparent inactivity." To sift through these options was precisely why he had summoned his most senior officers to the formal Council of War.

Though Greene, Lord Stirling, Steuben, Knox, and the Frenchmen Lafayette and Duportail were again present, excluded were six of the brigadiers who had taken part in the earlier meeting — Anthony Wayne, James Varnum, Enoch Poor, John Patterson, Peter Muhlenberg, and the departed Maxwell. In their stead stood the major generals Mifflin, de Kalb, and Armstrong — the last having left his sickbed to journey the 100 miles from his home in Carlisle. General Gates, who had postponed his journey north to attend at Washington's request, was also present. This was the first meeting between Washington and Gates and Mifflin since what the commander in chief euphemistically described as "the cloud of darkness [that] hung heavy" over the so-called Conway Cabal. Yet as was his wont, in both his written invitations and his physical welcome he betrayed no outward enmity toward the colluders. He "was determined out of respect for congress," he wrote to his ally Gouverneur Morris, "to treat the New members with civility." The former conspirators, in turn, acted as if the entire affair had never occurred.

Washington was brisk in his opening statements. His spy network in Philadelphia placed between 15,000 and 20,000 enemy troops in the city, he said, "exclusive of marines and seamen." Another 4,000 were thought to occupy New York, and somewhere in the neighborhood of 2,000 were scattered about Rhode Island. He could only guess if enemy reinforcements were on their way from England, but he suspected that with France's intentions now public, Whitehall would at the very least look to buttress its holdings in Canada and perhaps in the Floridas as well. He told the council that over the past month the dribble of returning convalescents and new recruits signed "for the duration" into his own army's ranks had held at a steady if languorous level. When all was said and done, he was still unlikely to have more than 17,000 regulars under his command by the end of the month. At their core would be some 5,000 battle-hardened veterans. These included all troops not only at Valley Forge, but scattered about upstate New York from Fishkill to Albany.

No matter what future course of action they decided upon, he went on, some 2,000 Continentals would need to remain on the Hudson in order to keep open the supply lines from New England. That left about 15,000 effectives at his disposal. He was not certain if his Commissary and Quartermaster Departments could provision such a force for an extended campaign, much less feed and clothe the supplementary militia detachments he required. This was the unvarnished, bleak picture.

This time Washington did not invite his general officers to state a preference for a specific plan of action. Instead, before yielding the floor he merely asked each man to present his own written assessment for a broad-based spring campaign. Although he emphasized that the speed of their reckonings was of the essence, he was surely shaken not only by their feedback, but by the rapidity with which it was reached. The next day the participants, forgoing Washington's request for individual responses, replied with a *per curiam* written recommendation. The written consensus was that the army required more provisioning and training, and for the time being it "should remain on the defensive and wait events." This was the very option that had garnered the least support in the balloting three weeks earlier.

Washington might have expected Gates, Mifflin, Patterson, and de Kalb to stand with the previous dissenters Greene, Steuben, and Duportail against an immediate assault on the British. Just as his quartermaster general, his new inspector general, and his chief engineer had now voted twice for the natural priorities of their respective departments, so the more experienced men present were content to deliberate the *when* of an opening salvo as opposed to the *where*. Moreover, in electing to keep the army bivouacked at Valley Forge, the Pennsylvanians Mifflin and Armstrong were probably displaying the same geographical bias as the New England brigadiers had expressed during the earlier poll, only in this case in the form of a defensive posture for their home state.

But Lord Stirling and Henry Knox? Only 20 days earlier they had been vociferous proponents of attacks on Philadelphia and New York City. Now, like Lafayette, they had endorsed a wait-and-see approach, "put[ting] nothing to the hazard," while the army grew in strength. The announced alliance with France, the generals wrote, "may oblige the enemy to withdraw their force, without any further troubles to us." There also seems to have been an underlying agreement among them that the ramifications of a failed spring offensive could redound all the way to Versailles. In truth, we will never know, as the dearth of minutes recording the Council of War's deliberations over those 48 hours leaves much room for speculation. Even the single document proffered to Washington includes few notes on any officers' individual thought processes, much less hints of competing views. The attendees were, however, unanimous in one other aspect — each considered 15,000 soldiers an inadequate force for either an assault on or a siege of Philadelphia or for an attack on New York.

As it happened, even as Washington's general officers were urging caution, the tempo of activity at Valley Forge increased dramatically. Work began anew on the fortifications and palisades left half-completed owing to the months of horrid weather, ill health, and frozen ground; and the sounds of banging hammers, scraping shovels, and grunting men echoed through camp. The labor gangs restoring the redoubts competed for the use of the few horses, wagons, and building tools with crews charged with the construction of more huts to house the camp's growing rosters. And the Commissary Department was ordered to install more bread ovens to feed the new troops. For a brief moment in mid-May a beef shortage appeared imminent, and the cantonment was momentarily racked by memories of the December and February food crises. In the end, however, Jeremiah Wadsworth alleviated the scare by rushing several droves of cattle south from New England.

General Steuben, meanwhile, took advantage of the mild weather and drying mud to step up his twice-daily training regimen. He boasted to Henry Laurens that the Continentals "have made a more rapid progress than any other Army would have made in so Short a time," and his enthusiasm proved contagious even beyond the camp's boundaries. Articles began to appear in Whig broadsheets lauding not only the surging morale of Washington's soldiery but also its newfound professionalism. Perhaps nothing reflected the citizenry's changed attitude as dramatically as the sudden about-face of the local populace. Once-empty sutlers' stalls on the outskirts of camp now overflowed with early spring vegetables and freshwater shellfish gathered from thawed rivers and streams. Even among the cantankerous men in the artillery park, one officer took note of "the great change in this state since the news from France — the Tories all turned Whigs; as eager now for Continental money as they were a few weeks ago for [British] gold."

This shift in mood naturally engendered an eagerness to strike at the enemy immediately among Washington's more precocious junior officers, not least John Laurens. Laurens was fully aware of the outcome of the commander in chief's war council. That did not mean he had to like it. Still brooding over the possibility that the French would end the conflict before he had earned his martial glory, he wrote to his father, "It gives me concern that there is no immediate prospect of closing the war with brilliancy. A successful general action, or some happy stroke upon one of the important points of which the enemy are at present in possession would be very desirable, as it would clearly establish the military reputation of our country, render us more independent of our allies, raise the character of our General, and give all young soldiers one more opportunity of distinguishing themselves in the dear cause of their country."

For Washington, however, there remained one major piece of unfinished political business before he could turn his full attention to the battlefield — Congress's reluctance to adopt his proposed half-pay pension. Although the pension plan had been endorsed by the Camp Committee, the majority of delegates in York refused to budge. They had floated several alternatives, including interest-free loans to veterans, tax exemptions, and the sale of federal lands, with the profits to be placed in a sort of pension escrow. None of these schemes satisfied either Washington's officer corps or the commander in chief himself. In an attempt to calm the disquiet that he sensed was resurfacing, on Monday, May 11, Washington ordered a performance of the play *Cato,* which had for years been the most popular drama in America.

Addison's narrative of a patriot prepared to make the ultimate sacrifice for the cause of liberty was performed in a hastily constructed open-air theater on the banks of the Schuylkill. Washington and Martha both attended, as did Nathanael Greene and his coquettish wife, Caty, and Henry and Lucy Knox. By all accounts it was a soft spring night, with a gentle breeze off the river keeping at bay the fetid smells of thousands of dilapidated huts. Officers in their best uniforms crowded around the little stage while enlisted men, though not within earshot of the actors' lines, milled in the shadows beyond the firepits serving as footlights. Following the dramatic depiction, four more officers tendered their resignations.

Whether word of this embarrassment reached York remains unrecorded. What is known is that, one week later, Congress finally agreed to a compromise on the pension pay conundrum that proved acceptable to both the soldiers and the most parsimonious of the politicians. In addition to granting each noncommissioned officer and private a onetime payment of $80, the delegates would appropriate funds for each officer's half-pay pension for the period of seven years following the war's end. "Joy," wrote one artillery officer, "sparkles in the Eyes of our whole Army."

Not a moment too soon, he might have added. For just as news of the pension agreement reached Valley Forge, rumors from Philadelphia had the British again stirring.

THIRTY-ONE:
KNIGHTS AND FAIR MAIDENS

If truth is the first casualty of war, Gen. Sir William Howe was Louis XVI's second victim. On the same day that Washington convened his Council of War, a British packet ship sailed up the Delaware carrying official notice to the general that France had entered into a military alliance with the United States and that the Crown had named Gen. Clinton to replace him. These were not hail-fellow communiqués; there was a distinct undertone that his dawdling was to blame for the French perfidy. Howe was ordered to immediately effect the transition of power to his successor, whose frigate had arrived from New York only hours earlier. His brother Richard — Adm. Lord Howe — was also being recalled as soon as a replacement arrived from England.

If Gen. Howe was relieved to be finally returning home, Clinton was far from feeling empowered. He was in fact mortified upon receiving the instructions from George Germain to abandon Philadelphia without a fight and to detach a third of his army, nearly 8,000 troops, to defend the Floridas and attack French holdings in the Caribbean. Citing his "regard for his professional fame," in his journal, a clearly irritated Clinton concluded that his appointment was nothing more than a "hopeless" footnote "to the unfortunate contest we were engaged in."

The portraitists of the era were not kind to the short, bowlegged 48-year-old Clinton. Most depictions emphasized his outsize jaw, crooked nose, and thick black eyebrows that resembled nothing so much as a brace of sleeping fruit bats. We will never know if this was the artists' retaliation for Clinton's vain and quarrelsome personality. Morbidly sensitive to even perceived slights, the new commander of all British forces in North America had bided his time for three years in the muddy backwaters of the New World awaiting this opportunity. Now, in a series of letters to confidants in London, he carped that his order to retreat from a rabble of American rebels was "beneath the dignity of a British officer." Clinton was, nonetheless, a soldier loyal to king and Crown. But even here he faced a quandary.

The ship that had borne the announcement of the Franco-American alliance had also brought rumors of a French armada sailing for America. When and where it would make land no one knew. As Adm. Howe's fleet was too dispersed up and down the eastern seaboard to undertake the immediate troop movements requested by Whitehall, Clinton saw only two options. He could tarry in Philadelphia and hope that the French were no closer to Chesapeake Bay than the Royal Navy's wayward craft. Or he could consolidate his forces within the relative safety of New York. He chose the latter. The army's baggage, provisions, and armory, he decided, would be shipped north aboard all available vessels while he marched the bulk of his troops up through New Jersey. For the time being, he declined to share his evacuation plans with Philadelphia's civilian population, and even attempted to mask his intentions by assigning work gangs to expand the fortifications around the city. This facile "shew of a design to remain," as John Laurens sneered, fooled neither Washington's network of double agents nor the panicked Tory population. If the crates piling up on Philadelphia's quays were not evidence enough, the die was notably cast when the heavy cannons that had anchored the defensive line to the north of town were disassembled and replaced by field pieces.

The members of the Pennsylvania state assembly in Lancaster had made no secret of their plans to hang any American civilian who had cooperated with the British during the occupation of Philadelphia. They had even debated the notion of seizing the property of each such traitor's surviving family members. With this proverbial "rope about [our] necks," as one frightened Loyalist put it, the fate of the city's Tories became a bone of contention between Clinton and his former superior. After the transition ceremony on May 11, Clinton informed Gen. Howe that he would find room either on the cargo ships or in his overland train for the thousands of "Friends of Government" seeking sanctuary from the rebels. Yet this still left a great many of His Majesty's loyal subjects outraged over the prospect of abandoning their homes, stores, and property to a band of brigand rebels. They begged Howe to intervene, and the genial general, having grown fond of his hosts, agreed. He gathered on his brother's flagship most of the men who had formed the backbone of the city's civil government and advised them to send a delegation to Valley Forge to broker a truce.

When word of this reached Clinton, he sputtered an enraged oath. Not only was such a decision no longer Howe's to make, but any third-party overture to the Continentals would undercut the role of the official peace commissioners scheduled to arrive from London within the month. Clinton was also watching his flank — colonial subjects negotiating a separate peace in Philadelphia would set a dangerous precedent for the Tory population of New York City.

In the end, Clinton was a much savvier political animal than either Howe. Despite the tarnish on the Howe brothers' military reputation, their family crest still carried weight back in England. Cognizant of this, Clinton hit upon a compromise with his former commander. In lieu of having a citizen's board journey to Valley Forge, he would deliver a general outline of the Bills of Conciliation to the Continental Congress in York as a sort of gambit before the parley, to buy time to better organize the evacuation of the city. General Howe was confused. The contents of the bills were already well known among the American delegates. They had been quite vocal in rejecting them.

When Washington learned of the ploy he was equally flummoxed. "The Enemy are beginning to play a Game more dangerous than their efforts by Arms," he wrote to his fellow Virginian John Banister, an attorney serving as a lieutenant colonel in their state's militia. "They are endeavoring to ensnare the people by specious allurements of Peace." It was as if he and his adversaries were engaged in an existential chess match whose rules changed by the moment. Washington instructed Dan Morgan to intercept the British officer traveling under a flag of truce and turn him back. More positively, he recognized that each day that he could forestall the enemy's withdrawal from Philadelphia was that much more time for Steuben and his drillmasters to sharpen the soldiery. Finally, on May 18, he moved his first pawn.

Notwithstanding his aborted misadventures at Albany, in the third week of May the Marquis de Lafayette was given his first field command. Washington entrusted him to lead some 2,200 seasoned troops — nearly a fifth of the effectives available at Valley Forge — across the Schuylkill to gather intelligence about the enemy's evacuation plans. The British were obviously preparing to abandon Philadelphia. But for where? New York? Halifax? Or would they quit the American continent altogether to face the French in either the West Indies or Europe? He hoped that a deserter or prisoner falling into Lafayette's hands might make their destination less opaque.

One can only speculate as to why the commander in chief felt he needed such a large and vulnerable force to perform a task just as easily assigned to a scouting unit. Some guessed that Washington was attempting to salve his surrogate son's Gallic sense of honor in the wake of the Canadian debacle. Others suspected that given the makeup of the detachment — it included Enoch Poor's respected New Hampshire brigade, a company of 50 of Dan Morgan's riflemen, and about an equal number of Oneida Indians — the mission was actually the vanguard of a secret assault on Philadelphia. The first notion is unprovable. The second was implausible.

What is recorded is that Washington warned the young Frenchman against splitting his divisions, and stressed that he should keep his party moving at all times "to guard against a surprise." The British might be teetering in Philadelphia, but the city still housed close to 20,000 enemy troops. Any "severe blow" to the expedition, he wrote to Lafayette, would result in the most "disastrous consequences" not only to the upcoming campaign, but perhaps to the entire revolution. It was sage advice. For barely had Lafayette's column reached the east bank of the river before it was being stalked by British patrols specifically dispatched to deter American attempts to disrupt Gen. Howe's extravagant farewell party.

General Howe may have been awaiting censure upon his return to London, but in Philadelphia his recall was already engendering an air of nostalgia among his status-conscious junior officers. From Jamestown to Calcutta to Hong Kong, the English who had colonized the globe carried with them the powerful class echelons attendant on hide-bound Albion. The bedrock of this cultural system was the entwined concepts of aristocratic privilege and prestige — bespoke tailors, membership in the right clubs, a plummy accent, riding to hounds. Whatever their personal differences, this shared sense of bloodlines had spawned a robust bond between Howe and his officer corps. Moreover, unlike the humorless Clinton, Howe had proved a guileless and, in the eyes of his troops, competent general. He had, after all, won a string of resounding victories on his way to capturing and occupying two of America's three largest cities. London magazines and newspapers pillorying Howe for the loss of Burgoyne's army were readily available in Philadelphia, and to the general's subordinates the perception of their longtime commanding officer skulking home to public opprobrium was decidedly unsporting.

All this convinced a number of them, led by the ubiquitous Capt. André, to pool their private funds to send Howe off with a festival of the likes of which America had never seen. The gala was scheduled for May 18, the same day that Lafayette and his troops marched east. What André dubbed, with typical British military understatement, his *Meschianza* — from the Italian *mescolanza,* meaning a "mixture" or "medley" — kicked off with 400 officers joining the elite of Philadelphia's Tory society on a regatta down the Delaware. The gaudy fleet of beribboned boats and barges sailed to the accompaniment of a military band playing "God Save The King." Alighting at Walnut Grove, the confiscated estate of the wealthy rebel merchant Joseph Wharton — Thomas Wharton's uncle — the guests were escorted into a temporary amphitheater that overlooked the estate's manicured lawns. From tiered bleachers they watched a mock jousting tournament in which costumed medieval "knights" bearing lances and shields contested to honor "fair maidens" clad in Turkish gowns.* At dusk, what the British called the "lighty-dark" time of day, all the participants formed a procession that passed beneath a pair of triumphal arches erected in honor of the Howe brothers to a formal ball, which included a fireworks display that could be seen for miles.

At one point the bacchanal was disrupted by distant gunfire. The commotion was the brainchild of the Continental captain Allan McClane, who had succeeded "Light Horse Harry" Lee as the area's spymaster. McClane and a small unit of riders, drawn to the sight and sound of the fireworks, had ridden to the

* Captain André himself, attended by a teenage "squire" and resplendent atop a great gray charger, took part in the pageant as a "Knight of the Blended Rose" engaging in combat for Peggy Shippen.

edge of the city, dismounted, and stolen to the base of a makeshift defensive wall. They poured buckets of whale oil over the wooden abatis encompassing the barrier, and set it alight. Panicked British sentries were still firing wildly into the trees as McClane and his men galloped away.

With the disturbance, and the fire, quelled, Gen. Howe's guests adjourned to a candlelit midnight supper served in a cavernous mirrored tent by African American slaves clothed in turbans and sashes. Then the faro tables opened.

When reports of the farewell party reached England, the *London Chronicle* was far from alone in wondering what exactly Gen. Howe had accomplished in America to deserve such a "nauseous" sendoff. If through the long lens of history the baroque extravaganza of Capt. André's *Meschianza* stands in stark relief against the deprivations suffered by the Continentals at Valley Forge — the event was said to have cost over half a million in today's dollars — not all military matters were cast aside. For throughout the long day and night, the pageant's honoree, although no longer in command, was nonetheless receiving steady reports of Lafayette's whereabouts from Loyalist informers.

Across the Schuylkill, Lafayette had no way of knowing that such a fete was playing out in the city. Washington, however, had been prescient to be wary of the marquis's command inexperience. On his first night in enemy territory he had pitched camp on a treeless plateau called Barren Hill some 11 miles northwest of Philadelphia and less than three miles from the most northerly British pickets. There he would remain for the next 36 hours, using an abandoned limestone church on the crest of the rise as his headquarters. When his junior officers reminded Lafayette of Washington's admonition against remaining stationary, he promised to be on the move again as soon as a messenger he had sent to track down Allan McClane returned.

Meanwhile, he dispatched scouts to probe the British lines. Some of the troops grew confused over the Frenchman's alleged tactics, not least the acerbic diarist Joseph Plumb Martin, who was marching with Enoch Poor's New Hampshire unit. "We placed our guards, sent off our scouting parties, and waited for — I know not what," he recorded. By the following evening he was still waiting as Lafayette's entire brigade remained bivouacked atop Barren Hill. And the British knew it.

That night, with Gen. Clinton ceding one last courtesy to his former commanding officer, Howe sent a combined force of nearly 5,000 Redcoats and Hessians on a north-by-northwest trajectory with instructions to gird the Continentals from the north and west, cutting them off from the Schuylkill. He then ordered another 2,000 grenadiers and a troop of dragoons under the command of the butcher of Paoli, Gen. Charles "No Flint" Grey, directly up the Germantown road that looped around and approached Barren Hill from the east. To snap shut the trap, Howe and Clinton personally led a third column of 2,000 men on an easy lope up another road and across a series of cultivated fields south of the plateau. Lafayette, surrounded and outnumbered, would have no choice but to surrender. Howe was scheduled to sail home within the week, and the vision of his command ship tacking up the Thames with the most famous Frenchman in North America as his prisoner of war made the *coup de main* too tempting to pass up.

But there was a complication. An eerie, ground-hugging fog obscured the stars that night, hindering the advance of the largest British attack force across a route strewn with narrow pocket canyons and thick copses of oak, hickory, and yellow poplar. Howe had assumed these men would be in place by dawn. But the sunrise found them still struggling through the thick brake and brushwood. Before they could reach their ambush site, Lafayette's pickets spotted them and alerted him. In a testament to the discipline instilled by Steuben, the marquis rallied his troops quickly and silently into a marching column. Screened by Morgan's riflemen and the Oneida, the Continentals slipped through the gap the enemy had left them. They covered the three miles to the Schuylkill in quickstep, linked arms against the strong current, and were splashing back across the chest-deep river as Howe's column climbed the southern flank of Barren Hill only to meet Grey's grenadiers scrambling up the north face.

Howe was flabbergasted. Could these elusive Continentals be the same oafish provincials who had collapsed along the Brandywine and fallen upon themselves during the confusion of Germantown? A disdainful Clinton, on the other hand, refused to concede the professionalism of the retreat and concurred with the infamous Capt. Simcoe, who, citing the starless night and rugged terrain, attributed the incident to just another instance of inexplicable "good fortune" enjoyed by the rebels and their apparently bulletproof commander in chief. Neither man seemed to grasp that throughout his military career, Washington more often than not made his own luck. In any case, with the Americans seemingly vanished, there was nothing left for the British but to re-form and slink back to Philadelphia as Morgan's sharpshooters and the Indian cohort harassed their rear.

At Valley Forge, Lafayette's close-run

escape was greeted with encomiums. "A brilliant retreat," gushed John Laurens. And Henry Laurens urged the pamphleteering New Jersey delegate Francis Hopkinson — author of "The Battle of the Kegs" — to once more take quill in hand to commemorate the wily escape "that has done [the marquis] more honor than he would have gained by a drawn battle." Even Joseph Plumb Martin deigned to praise his field commander's "courage and conduct."

Washington, on the other hand, was more chastened, though relieved, and privately wondered if he had made a mistake in handing too much responsibility to a 20-year-old major general. He also realized that even the hint of a reprimand might not sit well with his new French allies, not to mention call into question his own judgment. Instead, he praised Lafayette's tactical skills while quietly marveling over the transformation Steuben had wrought in his army. He also vowed to send no more large-scale expeditions into no-man's-land until his entire force was prepared to fight. That moment was fast approaching.

Thirty-Two:
The Gauntlet Thrown

They watched from across the river. There was no need for an abacus. A cursory glance at the traffic on the Delaware told the American scouts that the British did not have enough ships to transport an army. This was confirmed in the last week of May, when Continental spies in Philadelphia reported the first of the vessels on hand departing under the cover of darkness, their holds bulging with crates of heavy equipment, their decks crammed with sick soldiers and Loyalist women and children. The round-the-clock procession of carts and wheelbarrows adding to the jumbled piles of baggage and armaments littering the wharfs pointed to the only conclusion possible. General Clinton would have to march his troops overland. But to where?

At least one of Washington's chief lieutenants suspected Delaware. This was Charles Lee, who had arrived back at Valley Forge on May 23. During his incarceration, Lee said, he had picked up loose talk about the enemy's next destination. He believed that after a series of feints toward New Jersey, the British were planning to seize the entire Chesapeake Bay area. There they would stand up a new center of operations in a last-ditch attempt to sever New England from the rest of the colonies. At the very least, he warned, Gen. Clinton was probably preparing to make a dash for Delaware's riverside city of New Castle to await the gathering of Adm. Howe's troop transports. Lee even suggested that he cleave a section of Washington's army to lead south to counter the threat. The commander in chief demurred.

Lee was as odd a duck as ever. His 16 months in British hands had done nothing to sweep away the nimbus of hauteur that enveloped him like a shroud. On his journey to Valley Forge from his Virginia estate he and his hounds had even tarried in York, where he publicly pressed Congress for a promotion to lieutenant general, which would have made him Washington's equal in rank. The delegates could only react with a collective head shake. Washington, aware of Lee's pretensions, nevertheless continued to treat him with the warmest cordiality. He retained Lee as his second in command, and gave him charge of Gen. Greene's old division. Perhaps part of this consideration was due to Washington's provincial insecurities, but he still valued Lee's military mind and, at least on the face of it, attributed the general's natural obstreperousness to a "fountain of candor."

The commander in chief also had to consider Lee's familiarity with his jailers — many of whom he had served with during the French and Indian War. For that reason, at least for the moment, he was forced to take seriously the prospect of Clinton's marching on Delaware or Maryland. Only when riders from New York reached Valley Forge with news that housing in Manhattan and Brooklyn was being appropriated for officers, and that larger New York City structures were being converted into barracks, did Washington know. Clinton would withdraw through New Jersey.

Washington had long been a student of international politics, and with the French now in the fight it was obvious that England faced a hard choice: "Relinquishing all pretensions to conquest in America," he predicted in a letter to Gouverneur Morris, or abandoning its lucrative West Indian islands. The latter, of course, would prove disastrous on the world stage. Yet, as he concluded, "what she *will* choose, I cannot say; what she *ought* to do, is evident. But how far obstinacy, revenge, & villainy, may induce them to persevere I shall not undertake to determine." Thus whether Clinton would linger in New York or use its harbor as a staging area to depart for Canada or the Caribbean was anyone's guess. One thing, however, was certain — his long and unwieldy column would be vulnerable as it traversed New Jersey.

From here events moved rapidly; Washington reacted instinctively. He ordered Gen. Maxwell, now camped in Bucks County, to recross the Delaware with his two regiments and fold the New Jersey regulars already there under Col. Israel Shreve into his command. They were to block the roads leading north with felled trees and destroy any bridges spanning creeks and streams. General Smallwood was instructed to remove the warehoused stores from Head of Elk, Maryland, and hand over the defense of Wilmington to local militiamen. Thereafter he was to split his command of 2,000 regulars, sending half to Valley Forge and leading the other half to Chadds Ford. From that location they could serve as a forward screen in the unlikely event that Gen. Lee's intelligence proved correct, yet still be within a day's march of Valley Forge. General Greene's quartermasters, already creaking under the strain of laying in caches of supplies approximately every 15 miles along the enemy's likely escape route through New Jersey, were pressed to double their efforts to acquire more horses and wagons. And Henry Knox was implored to somehow hasten the expected shipments of artillery and arms from Massachusetts and upstate New York, including 2,000 muskets and bayonets en route from Albany that had been waylaid by Gen. Gates at Peekskill. Finally, the camp's surgeons were advised to scour the flying hospitals for any hog lard and sulfur that could be made ready to move. The scabies epidemic had barely abated.

Amid this frenzied final week of May a succession of General Orders reminded regimental commanders to lighten their baggage and prepare their troops "to be ready to march at an hour's warning." Each soldier was issued 40 rounds of ammunition and two flints, and commissary officers were instructed to have hardtack and salted meat ready to be loaded onto wagons. The excitement at the prospect of renewed fighting was distinctly discernible as both officers and enlisted men, contravening Washington's long-standing injunction against gambling, circulated pools as to what day, down to the hour, the army would take the field. Those who had no money to wager staked their beaver hats. One Massachusetts colonel compared the British in Philadelphia to "a wounded dog, as malicious as ever." And even Alexander Hamilton took it upon himself to notify regimental commanders — under his own signature, no less — that they would be held personally responsible for wayward or furloughed troops who failed to rejoin their units.

Yet Washington remained torn. Heartened by his army's enthusiasm, he recognized that his brigadiers needed time to integrate the thousands of new recruits flocking into their ranks. He was also anxious about his support departments' ability to provision the 15,000 troops he now commanded over a prolonged campaign. Despite Greene's yeoman efforts, blankets remained in short supply, several companies of Massachusetts men were still awaiting a shipment of shoes, and an entire regiment had arrived from North Carolina without a single musket among them. He was also alert to the possibility that the British would make a final thrust toward Valley Forge before they quit the area.

Henry Laurens, unaware of Gen. Clinton's orders to abandon Philadelphia without a fight, urged the commander in chief to beware of Clinton's cunning. Transporting Loyalists from Philadelphia, he noted, was no assurance that the British would leave without a fight. And in an ominous message, a Continental agent reported Redcoats and Hessians queuing in the city center to draw three days of provisions and full canteens of rum. This was not enough to carry them to New York, but certainly adequate, as Washington observed, for them "to cross the Schuylkill and by a sudden and rapid march" strike at either Valley Forge or Wilmington. Though the information turned out to be erroneous, the cannon master Knox acknowledged these fears in a letter to his brother in which he brooded over the deficiencies of the cantonment's artillery redoubts, "for the Enemy threaten hard to fight bloodily before they depart."

On May 24, as rumors of a direct assault on Valley Forge peaked, Washington recalled two of Col. Stephen Moylan's three cavalry regiments, perhaps 200 men, from northern New Jersey to bolster his defenses. He also urged Martha and the other officers' wives to begin making their arrangements to depart the encampment.* Yet four days later he redirected the horsemen to Trenton and asked Martha to remain for at least another two weeks. In the interim it had become clear why the British were loitering in Philadelphia. It was not to stage an assault on Valley Forge. It was to await the arrival of George III's Peace Commission.

On Saturday, June 6, the three-man British negotiating team disembarked in Philadelphia. Led by Frederick Howard, the 30-year-

---

* Before her ultimate departure on June 8, Martha Washington visited the camp's deputy quartermaster to request several earthenware mugs specific to Pennsylvania's Amish country to carry back to Mount Vernon as souvenirs. The embarrassed man could not find any.

old Earl of Carlisle, the commission that bore his name was charged with presenting the formal terms of the Bills of Conciliation to the Continental Congress.* Carlisle immediately made clear that it would be the rebels who would be responsible for the "horrors, devastations, and calamities" to follow should they fail to accept the king's generous overture. "We call God and the world to witness that the evils which must follow are not to be imputed to Great Britain," he announced. The emissaries also employed the more subtle and emotional tactic of delivering private letters to prominent Americans from friends and relatives in England. Naturally these missives urged the recipients to help broker a cease-fire. Henry Laurens heard from his old Scottish trading partner, and John Laurens received a note from his father-in-law in London pleading with him to reject the "unnatural alliance" with France. Father and son both saw through the "awkward and disgraceful" ploy.

Two years earlier, a committee from the First Continental Congress had agreed to meet with Adm. Howe to discuss a rapprochement between England and its colonies. This time, however, Henry Laurens sent

* Perhaps auspiciously, one day earlier the missing crates of 2,000 muskets and bayonets finally found their way to Valley Forge.

word to Carlisle not to waste the delegates' time. The earl was not surprised. In the few days since he landed he had come to realize that the America of his expectations was a vanished world, all but erased by the war. He and his fellow commissioners had been chosen for a fool's errand, and had not even been informed of George Germain's instructions to withdraw from Philadelphia. Carlisle was flabbergasted at how far along Gen. Clinton's evacuation plans had come, and urged Clinton to delay his departure. Why, he asked, would the Americans deign to bargain with a retreating enemy? But Clinton had long ago read the tea leaves. Citing his orders, he refused.

From there Carlisle's mission rapidly descended into farce. Before the week was out one of his commissioners was accused of attempting to bribe several American delegates to sign the Bills of Conciliation.* The same

---

* Curiously, a Scottish lawyer well connected to the Crown suggested to George III that Washington be offered the title of duke in exchange for endorsing the peace overtures. The king instead endorsed a plan to have his colonial officials distribute forged documents contending that Washington was in fact a secret British agent bent on losing the war, with the defeats at Brandywine and Germantown and the horrors the Continental Army endured at Valley Forge merely the initial phases of this nefarious plot.

man was then challenged to a duel by Lafayette for publishing a broadsheet article denigrating the French. And the peace panel's secretary, the renowned Scottish philosopher and historian Adam Ferguson, publicly ruminated over which "Instruments of Terror" the Crown might employ to bring the traitorous rebels to heel. Ferguson was apparently not fully cognizant of the mores of diplomatic statecraft.

By this point there were few instruments of terror or of any kind that might have swayed Congress to accept the Crown's terms. The Americans, long schooled in self-government, were well past the stage where half measures — what Washington's aide Tench Tilghman called "This last effort to divide us" — would resolve their myriad grievances. Tilghman was quite obviously channeling his commander in chief's thoughts. Writing to his fellow Virginia planter Landon Carter, Washington described the offers put forward by the Carlisle Commission as "so strongly marked with folly and villany, that one can scarce tell which predominates." They were, he added, "an insult to common sense" that demonstrated "to what extremity of folly wicked men in a bad cause are sometimes driven."

On June 10, with Valley Forge near to bursting with recalled regulars, new recruits, and returning convalescents, Washington ordered the first of his troops across the Schuylkill to establish a temporary camp on the east bank of the river. The withdrawal was hastened by an unseasonable heat wave that caused nearly six months of effluvia to bubble up from the miles of trench latrines and haphazardly buried animal carcasses — "the unwholesome exhalations from the ground which we occupy," as perhaps only the young Laurens could describe it. As the beginnings of this duck-cloth tent city arose across the water, some 20 miles to the south Washington's actions were mirrored by Clinton, who each night employed a flotilla of flat-bottomed barges to ferry his own horses, wagons, and select units of soldiers across the Delaware to New Jersey.

Finally, on June 17, after three days of deliberations, Congress formally rejected the Crown's Bills of Conciliation, calling the proposals "derogatory to the honor of an independent nation." In a defiant coda, Henry Laurens denounced the British sovereign and his emissaries for "suppos[ing] the people of these states to be subjects of the crown of Great Britain" and reaffirmed his earlier demand that only "an explicit acknowledgement of the independence of these states or the withdrawing of [the king's] fleets and armies" would end hostilities.

By this time the British had all but abandoned Philadelphia, leaving behind only a small rear guard. When word reached Clinton of the Continental Congress's rejection, he withdrew that guard, too. Even as those last Redcoats were departing, American state and federal officials were arriving at the Potts House in anticipation of reclaiming the city. They were met by a contingent of uneasy Tories who had opted to stand fast in Philadelphia. With nothing to lose, they had defied Gen. Clinton's orders and traveled to Valley Forge to ask for terms. As the two sides bickered, Washington sensed the disorganization and confusion in the making, and saw a solution in the person of Benedict Arnold. General Arnold had only recently arrived at Valley Forge. Though the musket ball that had shattered his leg at Saratoga still left him barely able to walk, the more serious wound was to his fragile ego. He still chafed at what he considered the inadequate recognition of his battlefield heroics, and was eager for any assignment to salve his honor and, should fortune smile, replenish his empty pocketbook. After conferring with Henry Laurens, Washington placed Arnold at the head of a small occupying force to take control of the city until civil authority was restored. He also issued a General Order forbidding any Continental soldier not under Arnold's command to enter Philadelphia. He then turned his gaze north.

On the morning of June 18, two American

divisions consisting of some 8,000 men under Charles Lee assembled into six brigades, turned northeast, and began marching toward New Jersey. Those who remained at Valley Forge set to burning whatever the army could not carry. The jagged flames and greasy smoke from the pyres could be seen for miles.

At dawn the following morning — June 19, exactly six months from the day when the Continental Army staggered out of the Gulph and into its winter camp — Washington led his last three divisions away from the cantonment in quick time to the beat of fifes and drums. He left behind rows of crumbling huts, an ecologically despoiled landscape, and an enervated local populace. In the months to follow the winter encampment in the southeastern corner of Pennsylvania would become home to a logistical support center, a military hospital, and a temporary prisoner-of-war holding pen. But for now, it was abandoned. It is not recorded if George Washington stopped to look back.

Thirty-Three:
"You Damned Poltroon"

The column consisted of some 1,500 wagons, carriages, and carts, and stretched for 12 miles. Its wanton trail was not hard to follow, littered as it was by burned farmsteads and hayricks, dead cattle shot for sport or vengeance, and fruit trees in bloom hacked at the stump.

Composed of close to 20,000 British and Hessian troops and encumbered by 1,500 Loyalist Philadelphians, the procession slogged north at a languorous six miles per day, an unintentional metaphor for the British war effort through 1778.* It was slowed by a series of severe downpours interspersed with "melting hot" temperatures that dehydrated and felled scores of wool-clad Redcoats. Forced to halt intermittently to repair the bridges burned by Gen. William Maxwell's guerrilla cadre, it presented a fat target.

* An additional 3,000 civilian Tories had previously been evacuated from Philadelphia on Adm. Howe's ships.

General Clinton was certain that the Americans would attack somewhere along the road. He did not expect an all-out assault, not with Washington waiting on the French. The Americans would be likely to come away happy with "a little triumph of some partial blow," as he recorded in his journal. He was particularly protective of his baggage train, a meaty spoil of war he knew the underfed and underequipped Continentals eyed hungrily.

Maxwell and his Continental regulars, abetted by close to 1,000 New Jersey militiamen, had shadowed the convoy's every step from its onset, nipping at its flanks with musket fire from behind stone fences, farm sheds, and dense thickets of scrub pine. They were soon reinforced by Col. Stephen Moylan's dragoons as well as 600 sharpshooters under Dan Morgan's command. The accuracy of Morgan's Virginians only further inflamed an army already humiliated by its retreat from Philadelphia.

Clinton, eager for the dam to break, halted his caravan often enough to lure Washington into a larger provocation. He had stationed in the rear some 6,000 of his most experienced British troops under Gen. Cornwallis. He did not trust the Hessians, who were deserting in droves.

The final regiments of the Continental Army, 12,000 strong, crossed the Delaware and landed above Trenton in western New Jersey on June 22. After poring over maps of the state's eastern roads and compiling information gleaned from scores of enemy defectors, Washington convened a Council of War. He suspected that the British were making for Sandy Hook, a thin barrier peninsula on New Jersey's north-central coast about 100 miles northeast of Philadelphia. From there Royal Navy transports and hundreds of small boats, already gathering, would ferry them to Manhattan and Long Island. Reading the pulse of the suddenly invigorated American citizenry, the homegrown firebrands Anthony Wayne and Nathanael Greene pressed for a major attack. Their enthusiasm was shared by Baron Steuben, still eager to draw his sword; and of course by Lafayette, who was harrowed over the "disgrace" and "humiliation" of permitting the British to traverse New Jersey "with impunity."

Henry Knox and Lord Stirling were among the majority of general officers who disagreed. They held that Clinton's humbling withdrawal from Philadelphia was victory enough, at least until reinforcements from France arrived. They also pointed out that despite the abundant magazines of food, hay, and even straw bedding that Greene's quartermasters had cached along various New Jersey routes, horses and wagons remained scarce. A dash across the state would put the army in danger of outrunning its supply lines.

The strongest advocate for prudence was Gen. Lee. Not surprisingly, Lee had taken an intense dislike to Steuben, and refused to recognize the effects of his training regimen. His perception still moored in 1776, Lee cautioned that the ragtag American force stood no chance against a professional British army. His final contention struck a more practical chord — why sacrifice more lives against an enemy virtually certain to evacuate New York in flight from the French? Citing a Spanish military proverb, he suggested that "a Bridge of Gold should be built for a flying enemy." Then they would each raise a glass as they watched the British depart from the war. Lee's argument repulsed Alexander Hamilton, who noted that the general's hesitancy "would have done honor to the most honorable society of midwives, and to them only."

Privately, Washington agreed with Hamilton, partly because of his own natural aggressiveness, and partly because he too sensed the mood of their suddenly sanguine countrymen. But his initial inclination was to pursue a middle ground between a major assault and complete inaction. Inflicting a sharp if glancing blow on the rear of Clinton's train without risking his entire army would sate the more aggressive bloc of his officers as well as result in a wealth of political capital. To that end, on June 24 he dispatched another 1,500 Virginians to reinforce Maxwell, Morgan, and the New Jersey militiamen. He had not counted on Gen. Greene's powers of persuasion. That night Greene sent him a private communiqué. "If we suffer the enemy to pass through the Jerseys without attempting any thing on them I think we shall ever regret it," he argued. "People expect something from us & our strength demands it."

The quartermaster general, one of his most trusted and effective officers, also reminded Washington how his Fabian tactics had already resulted in defeat at Brandywine and the loss of Philadelphia. It was Greene's steady hand that had stayed Washington from attempting a harebrained Christmas assault on the city. But now, he advised the commander in chief, the war's momentum had turned. Was it not time, he prodded, to trust in his army despite the enemy's superior numbers? Plus, he added, with the British train so strung out, what were the chances that Gen. Clinton would be able to throw his entire force against an American assault? Washington was convinced, and that night summoned Greene to help him redraw his plan of attack. It was decided that Gen. Wayne's 1,000-man brigade would now join the nearly 4,000 Continentals already harassing the British. Together they would fall in force on the rear of the enemy line. Should

Clinton decide to stand and fight with a reinforced rear guard, Washington would sweep in with the bulk of the army. If the Redcoats ran for Sandy Hook, the American advance corps would devour whatever defensive screen they threw up.

Ironically, the honor of leading this vanguard would fall to his second in command, the suddenly pacific Gen. Lee. Who turned it down. Heading such a small force, Lee caviled, was beneath the dignity of his rank. Lafayette, "still burning to distinguish himself," leaped at the opportunity.

Lafayette insisted that he had learned his lesson at Barren Hill. There would be no more immature mistakes. Further, this was no cat-and-mouse scouting expedition. It was a full-on offensive calling for zeal and daring. It was not lost on Washington that these were the very qualities that made up for the marquis's tactical inexperience. The commander in chief was also secure in the knowledge that Gen. Wayne would be present and would provide a guiding hand. As insurance, he also freed the coolheaded Hamilton from his inkwell and assigned him to the Frenchman's personal guard. But Lafayette had not even drawn up his battle plan before Charles Lee had a change of heart. Fearing that the glory of a possible war-ending triumph would fall to another, he beseeched Washington to reconsider and reinstate him. This left the commander in chief somewhere between the tree and its bark.

On the one hand, a French expeditionary force — led by Lafayette's cousin, no less — was already somewhere on the high seas racing to America's relief. What might be the repercussions of withdrawing a laurel already bestowed on the flower of France? Moreover, taking the command from Lafayette and handing it to Lee broke a cardinal maxim of warfare — never place a man in charge of a mission whose heart is not in it. Yet both Lee's battlefield experience and his length of service eclipsed Lafayette's. By rights it was his expedition to command. Before Washington could commit, Lafayette himself broke the impasse by volunteering to serve under Lee "for the good of the service." It was a face-saving courtesy Washington would never forget.

By Friday, June 26, the Continental Army's most forward elements had closed to within six miles of the tail of the British column. That morning Washington dispatched Steuben, John Laurens, and the French engineer Louis Duportail to evaluate the terrain through which the enemy was traveling. The Prussian was delighted with what he found. The boggy, wooded countryside, laced with deep ravines and crosshatched by a series of fenced orchards, was splendidly suited for a surprise attack. The enemy would have neither room nor opportunity to arrange his rear guard for a pitched, European-style battle. In any case, the more muscular British regiments would surely be surrounding Clinton's supply train in the van of the column. By the time they responded to the raid the damage would have been done.

The next evening Gen. Clinton made camp some 30 miles from Sandy Hook, near the small crossroads village of Monmouth Court House. Another day's march, Steuben warned Washington, would place the enemy in the hills of Middletown, New Jersey, unassailable high ground, and thence at the seacoast. It was time. Washington showed no hesitation. He ordered Gen. Lee to launch his assault as soon as the Redcoats resumed their movements at daybreak. He told Lee that he would rejoin and lead his main force to support the assault as necessary while, given Lee's proximity to the field, he left the specifics of the attack to his second's discretion. This was an error.

That night, with torrential downpours battering his tent, Lee declined to ride through the heavy rains to conduct his own reconnaissance, leaving himself personally ignorant of both the terrain and the enemy's strength. He instead relied upon a crude map, which John Laurens had sketched while scouting with Steuben, as well as on incomplete reports from the New Jersey militiamen. But the latter had seriously underestimated Cornwallis's numbers. Lafayette and Wayne both came away perplexed from their final meeting with Lee. He had given them no coordinated instructions other than a vague order to prepare to advance in the morning. To where, he did not say. He preferred to wait and see.

A sultry summer wind had blown the rain clouds to sea as Sunday, June 28, dawned unbearably hot and humid. Among the Americans stalking the British that morning was the peregrine Joseph Plumb Martin, who compared traversing New Jersey's sandy tidal plains and airless woods to marching through "the mouth of a heated oven." By the time they received their orders to move out, he and many of his compatriots had already doffed their shirts.

General Lee's offensive proved a cavalcade of blunders from the onset. It took the various spokes of the Continental vanguard five hours to pick their way across the three miles of marshy, treacherous terrain. During the advance Lee had no communication with his flanking wings. When his central assault column finally broke out of a wood and onto a muddy plowed cornfield, he found himself facing not the expected 1,500 or so troops protecting the British train's tail, but Cornwallis's 6,000 grenadiers and Foot Guards. Lee, staring at these elite units of the British army, panicked. Before the majority of the Continentals had even reached their staging areas, he ordered a general retreat. Lafayette was aghast. Lee, wheeling his horse, scoffed at him, saying that the Frenchman did not know British soldiers. Steuben's training be damned; the British would annihilate his patchwork collection of shopkeepers and farmhands.

Cornwallis easily beat back the few disconnected skirmishers who managed to break forward under elements of Gen. Wayne's corps. Then, with Clinton rushing more troops to Cornwallis's side, the two organized a counterattack. If they were careful, a confident Clinton told Cornwallis, they might even turn the action into a rout. At his signal 10,000 red-coated soldiers shed their heavy packs and fixed bayonets.

Some five miles to the west, Washington's frustration climbed with the temperature, now cresting 100 degrees Fahrenheit. Earlier that morning he had received an assurance from Gen. Lee that he was about to encircle a small enemy rear guard. With that the commander in chief had dashed off a note to Henry Laurens informing Congress that an important clash was imminent. He then led his two divisions of 6,000 to 8,000 men in a march east toward Monmouth Court House.

Since that moment he had listened for the cascading sounds of artillery fire that would indicate a serious engagement. They never came. The occasional report of a distant field piece was all he had heard. As noon approached and with his patience running out, he ordered his aides Robert Hanson Harrison and John Fitzgerald to the front to survey the field. It was not long before they came upon the retreating Lee. Lee told them that he had had no communication with his flanking commanders, and was not quite certain of their whereabouts. When Harrison asked what message he should take back to Washington, a glassy-eyed Lee replied that "he really did not know what to say." The men stared at each other, sweat pouring from their brows.

It was a dramatic moment of honesty. John Laurens, riding with Lee, described the general's serial instructions as "one [succeeding] another with a rapidity and indecision calculated to ruin us." "All this disgraceful retreating," Laurens would write to his father, "passed without the firing of a musket, over ground which might have been disputed inch by inch."

By early afternoon Washington still had no idea that Lee's forces were falling back. He was two miles from Lee's position when he received his first inkling of the debacle in progress. As he interviewed a local resident who told him of spotting half-naked Continentals staggering helter-skelter through his fields, Hamilton rode up to confirm the news. He also urged Washington to cover his right flank, as the British were massing for a counterstrike. A moment later a terrified young fifer was brought before the commander in chief. The boy allowed that his fellow soldiers were retreating, although more in bewilderment than in panic. Washington had commanded troops for long enough to place great faith in the adage that one should never trust a deserter and rarely trust a straggler. Yet he also knew how rapidly the merest scent of impending defeat could permeate an army. With that, he threatened the lad with a horsewhipping should he repeat his story to anyone else, and arranged for the generals Greene and Lord Stirling to quick-march their divisions to the front. Greene, per Hamilton's suggestion, veered off to the right at the head of his smaller force. Washington then spurred the handsome white charger gifted to him the day before by the governor of New Jersey and galloped forward with his remaining aides in tow.

He had raced less than half a mile before he encountered the first signs of stragglers. Dozens became scores, scores became companies, companies became entire regiments. Many of the Continentals, felled by the searing heat, had simply slumped to the ground in exhaustion. Their officers appeared as mystified at their circumstances as the young fifer. One volunteered that they were "flying from a shadow." Washington ordered the junior officers to gather and re-form their companies, and pointed them toward a nearby wood to shade themselves and rest. A moment later, pushing forward, he crossed a small wooden bridge spanning a swampy culvert known as the West Ravine. As he crested its eastern slope, he spied a familiar sight — Gen. Lee's hunting dogs keeping pace with a rider darting directly toward him. Lee was still reining his frothing horse when Washington thundered, "What is the meaning of this, sir? I desire to know the meaning of this disorder and confusion!"

Lee's face betrayed a dazed bewilderment. He expected acclamation on the orderly nature of his retreat. Instead, perplexed and battered by what some witnesses described as a string of oaths coming from his superior, he initially responded with a slurred mumble that one of Washington's aides made out as, "Sir? Sir?" Finally, as his commander in chief towered over him, Lee gathered himself enough to manage a coherent sentence: "The American troops would not stand the British bayonets." He then blurted something to the effect that his brigade commanders were disobeying his orders.

Washington, who those same witnesses describe as trembling with rage, pointed to the confused mass of soldiers streaming to the rear. They had thrown down neither their muskets nor their cartridge cases. None appeared wounded, and there was no sign of powder-blackened hands or faces that would indicate that they had even fired their weapons. This was not a mob fleeing in terror. It was an army bereft of leadership, an army retreating because it had been ordered to retreat. In his memoirs, Lafayette recorded Washington turning to Lee and shouting, "You damned poltroon. You never tried them."

Another officer observing the exchange reported that Washington proceeded to aim yet more oaths at Lee "till the leaves shook on the trees." This is probably apocryphal, although what is certain is the astonishment the commander in chief's aides and nearest soldiers felt at his rare public display of temper. It was as if some internal bottle in which he had stored all the slights suffered at the hands of the pompous Lee had finally been uncorked. "No one," wrote Lafayette, "had ever before seen Washington so terribly excited; his whole appearance was fearful."

Lee, confused and distraught, stammered that he had advised against the attack in council, and had but reluctantly accepted its command. With that Washington turned his back to Lee and again pressed on.

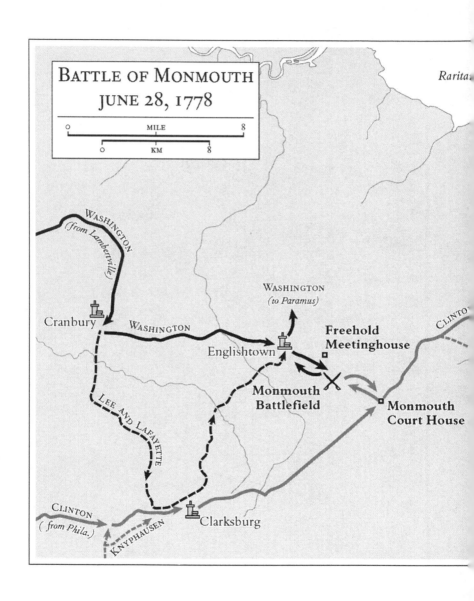

BATTLE OF MONMOUTH
JUNE 28, 1778

MILE   8

KM   8

Raritan

WASHINGTON
(from Lambertville)

Cranbury

WASHINGTON

WASHINGTON
(to Paramus)

Englishtown

Freehold
Meetinghouse

CLINTON

LEE AND LAFAYETTE

Monmouth
Battlefield

Monmouth
Court House

CLINTON
(from Phila.)

KNYPHAUSEN

Clarksburg

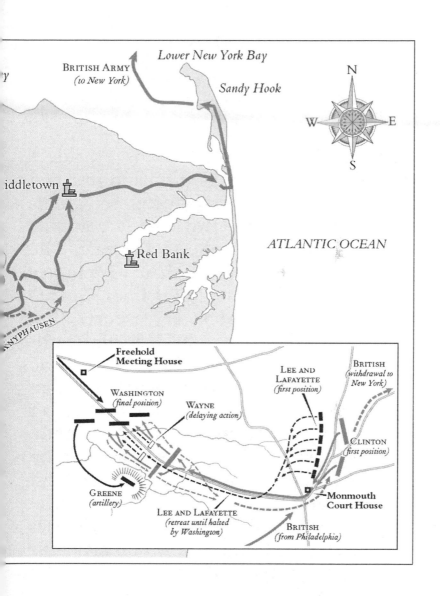

BRITISH ARMY
(to New York)

Lower New York Bay

Sandy Hook

N
W   E
S

iddletown

Red Bank

ATLANTIC OCEAN

KNYPHAUSEN

Freehold
Meeting House

LEE AND
LAFAYETTE
(first position)

BRITISH
(withdrawal to
New York)

WASHINGTON
(final position)

WAYNE
(delaying action)

CLINTON
(first position)

GREENE
(artillery)

LEE AND LAFAYETTE
(retreat until halted
by Washington)

Monmouth
Court House

BRITISH
(from Philadelphia)

THIRTY-FOUR:
"SO SUPERB A MAN"

By the time Washington and his outriders reached a rolling stretch of farmland bisected by yet another deep, marshy crevasse, Continental scouts reported two enemy columns advancing less than a mile to the east. The approaching force, no more than 15 minutes away, consisted of some 2,500 Foot Guards and grenadiers with a cavalry escort. That Gen. Clinton would throw his best and hardest fighters into the center of the fray was no surprise. But Washington also suspected that the enemy would at some point attempt to flank him from the north, the south, or both. He had already decided to make a stand on the high ground of the far rim of the West Ravine several hundred yards to his rear that he had crossed while searching for Charles Lee. But he needed time to form up his battle line. He then spied two threadbare battalions from Anthony Wayne's brigade falling back nearby and waylaid Wayne and their commanders.

Washington instructed them to take positions in a finger of forest that jutted into the field from the north. He could only hope that from this "Point of Woods," as it came to be called, Wayne and his 900 or so men could buy him enough time to organize a defensive line along the heights behind them. He then spotted Gen. Lee. Lee later testified that he believed he had been dismissed by Washington after his dressing-down, and some eyewitnesses reported hearing Washington order Lee to the rear. But Lee had not fallen back. Still dazed, and not certain what to do with himself, he had ended up skulking after Washington's party at some distance. Now the commander in chief waved him forward. He asked if Lee was prepared to muster as many retreating troops as possible to stand and fight. The humiliated general, sensing redemption, replied that he would be one of the last to leave the field. Washington nodded, and he and his coterie turned and rode back west.

John Laurens and Alexander Hamilton were among the 700 or so soldiers whom Gen. Lee positioned behind a hedgerow atop a small rise as the British column approached. Hamilton reined his horse next to Lee's, brandished his sword, and declared, "That's right, my dear general, and I will stay, and we will all die here on this spot." Some said that Lee then offered Hamilton a courtly bow and a pithy rejoinder. This is doubtful. The two hated each other.

While Hamilton and Lee played out their melodrama on the line's right flank, the implacable Gen. Wayne — seething at Lee for the retreat and refusing to speak to him — raced his regiments toward the Point of Woods to the left. They made the timberland without being spotted, and settled in amid the thick spinney of juniper and oak. There, with Wayne urging them to "pick out the king birds," they waited until a company of horsemen charging Lee's position through a narrow defile were at nearly point-blank range. The series of musket volleys emanating from the trees decimated the enemy cavalry and tore through Redcoats marching on either flank. Yet true to their training, the experienced British guards and grenadiers reformed rapidly. A portion charged the timber while the remainder, flanked by what was left of the dragoons, fell on Lee's wing. The close-quarters fighting that ensued was savage and swift. Both sides fixed bayonets that hacked and tore at human flesh. When Laurens's horse was shot out from under him, Hamilton — whose own steed had been killed earlier in the action — raced to his side with a spare.

The initial bloody clash was followed by an hour or so of heavy fighting. Through it, Lee and Wayne managed to lead their surviving troops west toward the bridge that crossed the ravine in front of Washington's line. A trail of bodies littered the field, red-coated, blue-clad. "A little skirmishing in the wood," Laurens, grazed by a musket ball, wryly called it. They had bought Washington his precious time.

As Washington dashed to and fro across the western heights, his white stallion leaping gullies and hedgerows, some of his veterans were reminded of an incident that occurred during the Delaware crossing 18 months earlier. Then, Washington's horse had stumbled climbing an icy slope and the commander in chief — shifting his balance in the saddle and gripping the animal's mane and lifting its head with his enormous hands — had kept the horse upright by dint of sheer "strength, skill, and timing." Now, as then, he seemed to appear everywhere and anywhere, a ghost with a drawn saber glinting beneath the pale sun. Impervious to injury, his mere presence breathed new life into the broken command.

By this time British cannons had moved into range, and the sky darkened with canister, grape, and solid shot. As he gathered his troops around him, Washington had to shout to be heard over the incessant din of soaring projectiles. "Will you fight?" he cried. The answer came in the form of three ringing cheers reverberating down the line, a verbal *feu de joie.*

Within the hour Washington and his division commanders had managed to organize a stout defensive position. Lord Stirling's column of men in particular, concentrated around their 10-gun artillery position on the left wing, had formed up with such discipline that had Steuben been present he might well have wept. At one point, Washington culled two regiments of New Englanders and led them to a fence line upon an eminence overlooking the meandering creek. Henry Knox and a company of light artillery had been joined by an exhausted Steuben, who earlier that morning had survived a hard chase after John Graves Simcoe and a unit of his Queen's American Rangers had recognized him and tried to ride him and John Laurens down.* Now Knox and Steuben were attempting to ford the stream in order to reinforce Gen. Greene and secure the high ground on the Continentals' right flank. It was apparent to Washington that Clinton and

---

* Simcoe had recognized the array of European medals on Steuben's chest. Laurens urged Steuben to spur his horse; the middle-aged Prussian, his blood rising as if he were back on the Austrian front, had demurred and taken the time to draw his brace of horse pistols and fire them at his pursuers before fleeing.

Cornwallis were attempting to envelop the Americans while simultaneously breaking through the center. At his command the New Englanders poured enough balls into the advancing Redcoats to allow Knox's cannoneers to splash across the knee-deep water and position their guns on the opposite rise. With Knox's guns in position, Steuben recrossed the creek and rode to Washington, who ordered him back to rally those of Lee's troops who had already left the field.

To Lafayette, the transformation in his commander in chief was astonishing. "His presence alone stopped the retreat," the marquis recalled in his memoirs. "His graceful bearing on horseback, his calm and deportment . . . were all calculated to inspire the highest degree of enthusiasm." In short, Lafayette concluded, "I thought then as now that I had never beheld so superb a man."

Through the shank of the afternoon Continental soldiers spotted Washington here shoring up a faltering line and there leading reserves into gaps in his defenses. His courage under fire was inspiring as he personally stationed a company of New Yorkers behind a defensive hedgerow looking down on a trail the advancing British would have to traverse; and, during propitious moments, he detached parties of light infantry into the teeth of the enemy advance. The impact made by the imposing Virginian's presence on the battle-field that day cannot be overstated. It is no exaggeration to state that wherever Washington made his stand on the bloody field, so stood the American Revolution. At one point, while he was gathering dragoons to counter an enemy cavalry charge, a cannon ball landed yards from his position, spooking his horse and throwing mud into his face. Washington never flinched. Hamilton, now back at his commander in chief's side, could not help seeing it as a metaphor in the making.

Citing Washington's "coolness and firmness," he later recalled, "I never saw the general to so much advantage, directing the whole with the skill of a master workman."

Not long afterward, as Washington galloped off to confer with Wayne, his steed staggered, slumped, and tumbled to the ground. It had died from heat exhaustion. Washington grabbed the reins of a chestnut mare tendered by his slave Billy Lee, leaped into the saddle, and rode on.

What would become known as the Battle of Monmouth Court House raged until dusk, the longest engagement of the American Revolution. The desperate British formed and re-formed for multiple charges with both bayonet and horse, a tide of scarlet flowing over green fields pocked by what was later described as the heaviest cannonade of any single day of the war.* "The dust and smoke . . . sometimes so shut the view, that none could form what was going on," wrote one American officer. Through it all, the Continentals never broke. As at Barren Hill, veteran British officers were astounded. Where had the Americans acquired such discipline?

It was closing on six o'clock when Gen. Clinton had his drummers beat a retreat. As the Redcoats faltered back through the gloaming their rear guard was harried by a company of Continental dragoons, and Lafayette pressed Washington for a final *coup de grace* to wipe the field clean. The commander in chief was tempted, and even instructed Steuben to gather three of Lee's brigades to move on the British right wing. He himself would lead an assault from the left, a pincer maneuver that would leave Clinton no escape.

As Steuben moved forward he passed Lee cantering aimlessly toward the rear. He described the general as slumped atop his horse, his eyes again glazed. Lee mentioned

---

* It was during one of these ferocious assaults that the legend of "Molly Pitcher" arose. Molly, whose real name may have been Mary Ludwig Hayes, was the wife of a Continental artilleryman. She had been fetching water for the troops, and when her husband fell dead, was said to have stepped in to man his cannon-swabbing post.

to Steuben that he was tired, and asked what the Prussian was doing. Steuben replied that he was preparing to run down the retreating Redcoats. Lee stiffened, his gaze suddenly focused. The British falling back? The motley Continentals running them down? This was impossible; he said Steuben's intelligence had to be faulty. He suggested that Clinton and Cornwallis were likely to be merely resting their troops for a final assault. He then proposed that he and Steuben form a defensive line where they stood to fend off the attack. The drillmaster ignored him and pressed on with his troops.

By the time Steuben reached the front, Washington had a change of heart. He sent word to all his commanders to stand down. Darkness was falling, water was scarce, and he recognized that, as Joseph Plumb Martin well put it, "Fighting is hot work even in cool weather." The Continentals, on the march since dawn through the sultry heat, had given all they had. The sun had nearly set when Washington instructed the entire army to spread their blankets where they stood. Tonight there would be no tents or cook fires beneath the canopy of stars. Just the living sleeping among the dead.

The commander in chief laid his own cloak on the ground beneath a spreading oak tree, where Lafayette joined him. British campfires flickered but a few miles away, and the occasional scream from a nearby surgery pierced the eerie stillness. Washington and his young protégé rehashed the events of the day — Lee's perfidiousness; Wayne's bold stand; Knox's industriousness; Steuben's professional polish. They talked well into the night of their plans to storm the enemy at first light. They were unaware that Clinton's army was already stealing away under cover of darkness. The fires were decoys, a ruse that Washington had employed many times himself. At sunup the Continentals discovered that the British had vanished.

Later that day Stephen Moylan relayed word that Clinton's army had reached the easily defensible hills that Steuben had noted. Washington understood, and instructed Moylan's cavalry and Dan Morgan's Virginians to follow from a safe distance. They were to ensure that the British did indeed sail from Sandy Hook, but to provoke no major action. Let them have New York. They would abandon it soon enough. At the end of the day the commander in chief was content in the knowledge that American soldiers could be made the equal — indeed, had been made the equal — of their British foes. It was time to tend the wounded and bury the dead.

Both sides attempted to gloss their "victory" on the plains, in the culverts, and in the woodlands encompassing the town of Monmouth Court House. According to the most reliable casualty estimates, the British could technically be considered vanquished, with Gen. Clinton reporting 64 men missing, 170 wounded, and 147 killed, among them what Anthony Wayne adjudged "the flower of their army." The Continentals buried some 106 dead (including 37 from heatstroke), treated 161 wounded, and reported 95 missing.* But it was the psychological defeat that stung the Crown forces most pointedly.

Early on that blistering June morning, with nearly half of the American army falling away in a confused and fatigued mass and the remainder still miles from the field, a rout by the British appeared inevitable. Yet within hours Washington had managed to check the retreat, form his troops, take and hold the high ground, and withstand a series of murderous assaults. It was beyond belief, as if Addison's Cato had survived. And Washington certainly realized it. In the hours to follow, the commander in chief set aside time

---

* Clinton's numbers apparently did not include casualties from the one German regiment at the scene of the battle. John Laurens and Alexander Hamilton, meanwhile, constructed a fiction that, with deserters included, the British had lost some 2,500 men between Philadelphia and Sandy Hook. Even in the immediate throes of celebration, few found the figure credible.

for his soldiery "to unite in thanksgiving to the Supreme disposer of human Events for the Victory which was obtained on Sunday."

Though Monmouth was perhaps less dramatically timed than the Battle of Saratoga, a valedictory note had been struck on what Washington described as that most "glorious and happy day" on the rolling green fields of central New Jersey. It was in fact the turning point in the War for American Independence. Though armed conflict would rage for another five years, the Battle of Monmouth Court House marked the end of the war's classic period. From there on the struggle would move to the southern states, and Washington would not personally participate in another engagement until the British surrender at Yorktown in 1781.

There can be nothing more *Washingtonian* than the lengthy after-action report the commander in chief sent to Congress in the wake of Monmouth. In it he described, in specific detail, the "brave and spirited conduct" of his subordinates without once mentioning his own contributions. "Were I to conclude my account of this days transactions without expressing my obligations to the Officers of the Army in general, I should do injustice to their merit, and violence to my own feelings," he wrote. "They seemed to vie with each other in manifesting their Zeal and Bravery. The Catalogue of those who distinguished themselves is too long to admit. The Behaviour of the troops in general . . . was such as could not be surpassed." And in a grandly satisfying letter to his brother soon after the engagement, he predicted that the outcome would reduce the likelihood of George III and his war counselors' deciding to send reinforcements to America.

Oddly, undoubtedly ironically, it was left to another colonist whose people had been ground under the British heel to foresee the essence of the American Revolution. Nearly two decades before taking up the cause of the 13 colonies in Parliament in 1776, the Irish statesman Edmund Burke published a treatise delineating the difference between the beautiful and the sublime. The beautiful, he posited, is smooth, polished, relatively small, and founded on pleasure. The sublime, by contrast, is vast and rugged, powerful and magnificent, and — most important — founded on pain. "The passion caused by the great and sublime in nature, when those causes operate most powerfully," Burke concluded, "is astonishment."

The world may have been astonished that the resilience shown by the Continental Army across the winter of 1777–1778 would culminate in the Battle of Monmouth Court House. Washington knew better. He recognized that there would have been no victory near New Jersey's sandy shores without the sublime sacrifice of Valley Forge, where over 2,000 American soldiers perished. No battle, no campaign of the war would take a higher toll. For those who survived, not least their inspired and inspiring commander in chief, the hardships they overcame had not so much transformed their innate character as revealed it.

The Valley Forge winter, the greatest and most costly symbolic victory of the rebellion, had been a cold season out of Revelation, less the city of gold with its walls of glistening jasper. And the massive responsibilities that George Washington had singularly borne on that windswept plateau became the seed for what the first governor of Massachusetts, John Winthrop, citing the Gospel of Matthew, had once foreseen as the creation of the mythic "shining city on the hill."

No other man, at no other time, in no other place, can boast of such an achievement.

EPILOGUE

Ten days after Gen. Clinton's army sailed from Sandy Hook to New York — and only weeks after British and French vessels exchanged gunfire in the English Channel, marking the official beginning of hostilities between their two countries — the Comte d'Estaing's 12 ships of the line carrying 4,000 French troops hove over the eastern horizon and dropped anchor in Delaware Bay. This event may not have been the precise beginning of the end for Great Britain's colonial rule in America. But it certainly represented, as a future British prime minister would put it, "the end of the beginning."

As noted, George Washington would not personally participate in another military engagement until Gen. Charles Cornwallis's surrender at Yorktown, Virginia, three years after the Battle of Monmouth Court House. There were two underlying reasons for this. One was his obsession with recapturing New York, the loss of which remained, to his mind, the most ignominious chapter of his military career. Equally important was the insistence by the French that, as the British carried out their "southern strategy," they be met with armed resistance at every turn throughout Georgia and the Carolinas. Washington, recognizing that the revolution relied on France's navy and expeditionary force, was in no position to argue the point.

Not surprisingly, Gen. Charles Lee's advice prior to the Battle of Monmouth Court House that the Continentals should construct for the withdrawing enemy a "Bridge of Gold" to hasten their flight from New York proved, once again, erroneous. In fact, the British would not abandon the city until the ratification of the 1783 Treaties of Paris in which a sullen King George III — who drafted an abdication notice but never delivered it — recognized an independent United States. Washington could and did take solace, however, in having turned the tables on the British in New York. As he wrote to the Virginia statesman and militia commander Gen. Thomas Nelson not long after Monmouth, "It is not a little pleasing, nor less wonderful to contemplate, that after two years of Maneuvering . . . the British are reduced to the use of the spade and pick axe for defense."

Over the eight years of America's Revolutionary War, including the five that followed the fateful winter at Valley Forge, George Washington was a paradox. He was a man of few words in person, but during the conflict he and the 32 aides he employed produced some 17,000 official documents, including 12,000 letters and orders. This coheres with the historian Garry Wills's observation, "Before there was a United States, before there was any symbol of that nation — a flag, a Constitution, a national seal — there was Washington." This was never more evident than at Valley Forge. The contrast between Washington's larger-than-life leadership, as shown during that horrid winter, and his verbal tendency toward the terse characterized him for the rest of his life. His second presidential inaugural address remains, at 135 words, the shortest in American history. But it was his valedictory speech of 1796, upon his refusal of a third term, in which he warned the country that the most serious threat to our democracy — "the most frightful . . . and permanent despotism . . . at the expense of public liberty" — could well come from within is not only relevant today, but was so at the time. One need look no further than to the fate of the British officers whom he vanquished.

Upon his return to England in July 1778 Gen. William Howe continued to receive public opprobrium over the loss of Gen. John Burgoyne's army, criticism that would hound him to his grave. He also faced censure for his actions, or, more specifically, the lack thereof, during the Pennsylvania campaign. To clear his name, Howe demanded a parliamentary inquiry into his and his brother Richard's conduct. Though the official probe was unable to confirm any charges of mismanagement or impropriety on either brother's part, conventional sentiment had already hardened. General Howe published a narrative journal defending himself, to little avail. After losing a bid for reelection to the House of Commons, he spent the next decade or so on the fringes of various branches of British public service — including an appointment to the king's privy council — until, in 1793, he was reinstated in the army as the French Revolutionary Wars swept the Continent. He saw no action. When his brother Richard died without leaving a male heir, he assumed the title, becoming the fifth Viscount Howe. As he was himself childless, the title died with him in 1814.

Admiral Richard Howe lived out his final years with his reputation somewhat more intact. Long out of favor with the government of Lord North — whom the admiral accused of failing to supply him and his brother with the matériel support to properly put down the rebellion — Adm. Howe was called back to England in September 1778, and spent the next three years campaigning against what he saw as the maladministration of the Royal Navy as the conflict with the Americans escalated into a world war. With the fall of North's government in the wake of the surrender at Yorktown, Howe returned to the Admiralty in 1782 and accepted command of the Channel Fleet. He distinguished himself during various engagements against the French, Spanish, and Dutch navies and, sailing with an outnumbered squadron, led a heroic relief mission to the besieged Gibraltar peninsula. The following year, Howe was appointed first lord of the admiralty, a post from which he spearheaded a naval arms race against France and Spain. In 1788 he resigned the position after a political rift with Prime Minister William Pitt the Younger, but he returned to duty two years later when a territorial dispute with Spain raised the threat of another war. When that conflict was averted, Howe continued to serve through the hostilities brought upon by the French Revolution before dying at the age of 73 in his London home in August 1799. For his lifelong service to the Crown he was posthumously honored with a monument at Saint Paul's Cathedral.

Though Gen. Henry Clinton remained the commander in chief of British forces in the Americas for three more years, his relationship with his subordinate Gen. Charles Cornwallis deteriorated steadily until it finally broke with Cornwallis's surrender at York-town. After that disaster, Clinton was recalled to England, where like Gen. Howe he published a defensive tract. His *Narrative of the Campaign of 1781 in North America* rather unsuccessfully attempted to blame the loss of the American colonies on Cornwallis, and the bitter diatribe exacerbated their feud. Cornwallis's star inexplicably rose while Clinton spent his final years serving in and out of Parliament before dying just as he was about to assume the governorship of Gibraltar in 1794.

John André's demise was a bit more abrupt. On October 2, 1780, he was hanged as a spy. General Clinton had promoted André from captain to major following the British retreat from Philadelphia, and charged him with organizing all British intelligence activities in America. In that capacity André used his ongoing friendship with Peggy Shippen, who had remained in Philadelphia, to ensnare Benedict Arnold in the most notorious case of espionage in American history. After entering Philadelphia, Arnold conducted a whirlwind romance with Shippen which ended in their marriage less than a year after he had taken over as temporary "governor" of the city. Corrupted by Philadelphia's high society, he lived well above his means and had accrued huge debts by the time he was transferred to command of the American fort at

West Point. He also remained bitter over the lack of recognition for his accomplishments at Saratoga.

With his new wife shuttling messages between him and André, in July 1780 Arnold offered to surrender West Point, the most strategic Continental outpost on the Hudson, to the British for a fee. At André's urging, Gen. Clinton reluctantly allowed his spymaster to sail up the Hudson to personally negotiate the turnover. On September 21, the two had a secret meeting during which Arnold handed over a sheaf of papers, including a map of West Point detailing how he had systematically weakened the stockade's defenses. André, wearing civilian clothes, was detained and questioned by a Continental patrol on his way back to his schooner. His captors discovered the papers in his boot — a British officer's boot, no less — and he was arrested.

When Arnold learned that André had been taken, he fled West Point on the very day that Washington arrived at the redoubt, leaving his wife to face the commander in chief. In a letter to John Laurens, Washington railed against Arnold's "villainous perfidy" while acknowledging André as "an accomplished man and gallant officer." He then ordered him tried by a military court. One week later André was hanged and buried beneath the scaffold from which he had swung. When confronted by Washington, Peggy Shippen Arnold feigned madness, and was eventually reunited with her husband in New York City. The two moved to London, where Arnold died in 1801. Peggy Shippen Arnold, whose Philadelphia family renounced her, outlived her husband by three years. They are buried in adjoining plots at Saint Mary's Church in Battersea. André's remains were disinterred in 1821, removed to England, and reburied beneath a marble monument among the kings and poets of Westminster Abbey's "Heroes' Corner."

No such splendid fate awaited the co-conspirator who lent his name to the so-called Conway Cabal. After recovering from the wounds received in his duel with John Cadwalader, the Irish-born Thomas Conway returned to France in November 1778. He was assigned to its army's colonial service, and thereafter assumed the governorship of the French holdings in India. He was called back to France following the overthrow of Louis XVI, and commanded a royalist army in the south of the country before his capture by French revolutionaries. Condemned to the guillotine, he was granted a last-minute reprieve under mysterious circumstances probably stemming from France's centuries-old solidarity with Ireland. From there Conway faded into the fog of history. He was rumored to have died in poverty somewhere in his home country around 1800.

Thomas Mifflin, by contrast, became a leading figure in the formation of the political system of the United States. Continually dogged by charges of corruption during his tenure as the Continental Army's quartermaster general, Mifflin resigned his military commission seven months after the Battle of Monmouth Court House in order to clear his name and return to politics. He never quite accomplished the first objective. He excelled at the second. Reelected to the Continental Congress as a Pennsylvania delegate in 1783, Mifflin, as the body's presiding officer, personally accepted Washington's resignation as commander in chief in December of that year. Six months later he appointed Thomas Jefferson as America's minister to France. Mifflin went on to represent Pennsylvania as a member of the Constitutional Convention in 1787 before being elected as the first official governor of the state in 1790. He served in that capacity until his death in Lancaster in January 1800.

Horatio Gates could only have wished for such a second act. After the American southern army's disastrous defeat at the Battle of Camden, South Carolina, in 1780 — arguably Britain's greatest victory of the Revolutionary War — Gates's reputation lay in tatters. His cowardly performance — he and several units of southern militiamen fled nearly 200 miles in three days while his 900 or so regular troops from the north stood fast to be slaughtered — was put in further relief by the heroism of his second in command Johann de Kalb. After Gates fled, it was Gen. de Kalb who attempted to rally the outnumbered Continentals in the face of successively more murderous bayonet charges. De Kalb fought hard to the end, receiving 11 wounds before finally falling. Like Casimir Pulaski, who died in his saddle after being riddled with grapeshot defending Charleston a year earlier, de Kalb's legacy lives on in the numerous American streets, monuments, bridges, and even a city in Illinois named in his honor.

Washington relieved Gates of command following Camden, and though the Continental Congress briefly reinstated him two years later, his tenure proved uneventful. He never again took the field. He retired from military service in 1783. History does not, but should, remember Gates for one sterling act — in 1790 he sold his Virginia plantation and, at the urging of John Adams, freed his slaves. He then moved to a farm in what are today the upper reaches of New York City's Manhattan Island and served a term in the New York state legislature. He died in April 1806 and is buried in an unmarked grave in New York City's Trinity Church cemetery.

Gates, it will be recalled, was merely the second pretender to Washington's position as commander in chief. The first, Gen. Charles Lee, remained a carbuncle of a creature until the end. Lee recovered rapidly from his stupor at the Battle of Monmouth Court House. Within days he was alternately bragging that his strategy and tactics had placed his force on the brink of total victory when Washington's arrival ruined all, and complaining that Washington had taken command in the field only when "victory was assured." He then wrote to Washington blaming the "stupid" and "wicked" generals and aides surrounding him for misrepresenting his battlefield actions. "The success of the day," he asserted," "was entirely owing" to his own martial maneuvering. This final insolence sealed his fate.

Washington accused Lee of misbehavior and a breach of orders during his "shameful retreat," and ordered the general arrested and brought before a court-martial presided over by Lord Stirling. Lord Stirling and 11 of his fellow officers listened to testimony for six weeks before finding Lee guilty of disobeying orders, permitting a disorderly retreat, and disrespecting the commander in chief. Lee's sentence, eventually certified by Congress, was a suspension from the army for one year. The verdict ended his military career. Not atypically, Lee labeled the proceedings a sham and soon thereafter published a self-vindicating tract that further insulted his former superior officer. This was too much for John Laurens.

In late December 1778, with Alexander Hamilton acting as his second, young Laurens challenged Lee to a duel. Whether Washington condoned his aide's action remains inconclusive, although he certainly could have stopped it. In any case, Lee accepted the ultimatum, and on the appointed morning a ball from Laurens's pistol pierced Lee's side, wounding but not killing him. Lee retired to his Shenandoah Valley farm to recover among his beloved dogs, and soon afterward sent to Congress a letter which so offended the delegates that they cashiered him from the army for good. Two years later, on a visit to Philadelphia, he was struck by a sudden fever. As he lay dying on the upper floor of a tavern, Lee requested that he be buried anywhere except a churchyard. Since throwing his lot in with the American cause for liberty, he wrote in a hastily dictated last will and testament, "I have kept so much bad company while living, that I do not choose to continue it when dead." Fittingly, Lee's final order was ignored. He was interred in the cemetery of Philadelphia's Episcopal Christ Church, not far from the graves of Benjamin Franklin and four other signers of the Declaration of Independence.

Seventy-five years later, in 1857, the official librarian of the New York State Historical Society was rummaging through a dusty file of Revolutionary War–era papers when he discovered a letter in what was later proved to be Charles Lee's handwriting. It was addressed to the commander of all British forces in America, Gen. William Howe, and contained Lee's detailed strategy for the subjugation of the colonial rebellion. That Charles Lee was a traitor surprised few. That he had refrained from boasting about it shocked many.

Just as there is no reliably precise figure for the number of troops who spent the winter of 1777–1778 at Valley Forge, so does the total number of men who fought for the Continental Army between April 19, 1775, and September 3, 1783, vary. The most accurate rolls indicate that some 232,000 men enlisted during those eight years, although those same rosters do not differentiate among the legions of multiple reenlistees. Historians generally agree that around 170,000 officers, noncommissioned officers, and privates took part in the conflict. In contrast to the many officers who published personal histories of their experiences, the unsung foot soldiers who fought for independence left little for posterity to ponder. Like the majority of warfighters from time immemorial, they marched or sailed into battle, served their country to the best of their abilities, and those lucky enough to return home went about their lives. With several notable exceptions.

Many of the survivors among the 5,000 or so African Americans who took up the cause of American liberty were left bitterly disappointed when denied citizenship upon the ratification of a United States Constitution in 1787. Incredibly, when that document formally incorporated slavery into the law of the land, hundreds of black men who had stood side by side with white Continentals from Bunker Hill to Yorktown were cast back into chains. This blight on the nation's founding was loudly protested by foreigners such as Lafayette and Kosciuszko, to no avail. The southern planters — including Washington and Jefferson — convinced the northern businessmen to continue to abide by the African Americans' chattel status in the peculiar institution. Equally galling is the gap in the postwar histories pertaining to black soldiers who enlisted to free the country from British rule. As the Rev. William Howard Day put it in 1852 while addressing a convention of black veterans who had fought in the War of 1812, "Of the services and sufferings of the colored soldiers of the Revolution, no attempt has, to our knowledge, been made to preserve a record. Their history is not written; it lies upon the soil watered with their blood."

By contrast, the same cannot be said for the ordinary and obscure diarists such as Albigence Waldo and Joseph Plumb Martin who did put their experiences to paper with such erudite panache. Subsequent to the war, the surgeon Waldo continued his medical practice throughout New England — there are recovered letters addressed to him in Plainfield, Connecticut; in Foster, Rhode Island; and in Worcester, Massachusetts — before his death in 1793. It is thanks to Waldo's journal that we can today envision the starving and half-naked Continental soldier at Valley Forge who "labors thro' the Mud & Cold with a Song in his mouth extolling War and Washington."

"The sufferings of the Body naturally gain the Attention of the Mind," the insightful Waldo wrote in that same diary entry. "And this Attention is more or less strong, in greater or lesser souls, altho' I believe that Ambition & a high Opinion of Fame, makes many People endure hardships and pains with that fortitude we after Times observe them to do."

It is hard to imagine any trooper enduring with such fortitude more hardships than the perspicacious Joseph Plumb Martin. He went on to serve admirably through the conclusion of the American War for Independence, rising to the rank of sergeant. True to his Zelig-like character, in 1781 he was one of the sappers and miners digging siege lines around the British fortifications at Yorktown. Regarding the signal to open the bombardment of Cornwallis's cornered army, he wrote that the sight of the American flag "waving majestically in the very faces of our implacable adversaries" evoked a spontaneous and continuous cheer from the nearly 8,000 French troops on hand, all shouting "Huzzah for the Americans."

Joseph Plumb Martin was honorably discharged in June 1783, and after several months wandering in New York state, he settled in Maine — then a northwestern province of Massachusetts — to take up farming in the frontier town of Prospect. Over his long life — he died in 1850 at the age of 89 — he served variously as a Prospect selectman, justice of the peace, and town clerk while fathering five children with the former Lucy Clewley. He published his war recollections anonymously in 1830 to little acclaim. It was only after his death that *A Narrative of a Revolutionary Soldier,* originally entitled *Yankee Doodle Dandy,* was recognized as one of the most extraordinary memoirs of the era. An odd sidebar to Joseph Plumb Martin's life story was a land dispute he engaged in with the Continental Army's former chief artillery officer Gen. Henry Knox.

After stepping down from his position as President Washington's secretary of war in 1794, Knox maintained that 100 acres of land to which Joseph Plumb Martin had laid claim were in fact part of a 600,000-acre land grant seized from his Loyalist in-laws that rightly belonged to him. Knox's argument was upheld in court, and Martin was ordered to pay Knox $170, over $3,200 in today's dollars. Martin did not have the money, and in several plaintive letters begged Knox to allow him to keep the land, particularly the mere eight acres that he actually tilled. Knox never acknowledged these appeals, but neither did he ever take any action to collect the fee before his death in 1806.

Before resigning from the army in 1784, Knox was the guiding force behind the establishment of a national naval academy and the Military Academy at West Point, where he was briefly commandant. He was also a vigorous proponent of a strong national government and a standing peacetime army, both concepts strongly opposed by political leaders like Thomas Jefferson, Samuel Adams, and John Hancock. When the latter forces prevailed, Knox left military service, returned to Boston, and engaged in sketchy land speculation deals, including the scheme to acquire the parcel upon which Joseph

Plumb Martin had settled in Maine. His business acumen, however, stood in stark contrast to his military mastery, and in hindsight Knox was probably fortunate to be plucked from civilian life in 1789 to serve as Washington's secretary of war.

During his early tenure in that office he argued that dispossessing the Native Americans from their traditional homelands on the western fringes of the United States violated the fundamental laws of God and nature. His rhetoric was largely ignored as the nation expanded west along a line from western Georgia to Kentucky to the Old Northwest Territories of the Ohio Country. Nonetheless, Knox's early calls for the benevolent treatment of the tribes could have been his lasting legacy. It was not to be. In time and at Washington's urging, Knox came around to side with and oversee the nascent country's "Indian Removal" policies of broken treaties, relocations, and exterminations. When Knox left government and returned to Maine, his attempts at cattle ranching, shipbuilding, brick making, lumber milling, and further real estate speculation as far west as the Ohio Valley all failed. He had fathered 13 children with his wife Lucy when, in 1806, he swallowed a chicken bone that lodged in his throat and became infected. He died three days later at the age of 56, leaving Lucy to sell off what remained of his insolvent estate to pay his creditors.

It was during Knox's Indian wars that Gen. Anthony Wayne capped his aggressive military career. In the aftermath of the Battle of Monmouth Court House, Wayne's daredevil personal heroics were encapsulated by the nighttime bayonet charge he personally led to capture what was considered an impenetrable British fort at Stony Point on the Hudson River north of New York City. Thereafter ordered south by Washington, he never forgot the lessons of the Paoli Massacre, and cut a bloody swath through the British lines across the deep south before the war's end. Such was his renown that the state of Georgia gave him a rice plantation for negotiating peace treaties — soon to be broken — with the Cherokee and Creek tribes who had been allies of the British. Along the way he acquired the sobriquet "Mad Anthony" Wayne, in part for the manner in which he put down mutinies by trying and executing the ringleaders on the spot in view of his entire force.

Hard living and hard charging, a bout of malaria, and the two musket balls lodged in his body had left Wayne in poor health. He retired from the Continental Army in 1783 and returned home to Chester County with the rank of major general. Upon his recovery he played an active part in the Pennsylvania state assembly as well as at the Constitutional Convention. Like Henry Knox, Wayne was an outstanding soldier and a poor business-man. He lost his Georgia plantation to financial mismanagement and was rescued from further malefactions when, in 1792, President Washington called him out of retirement and appointed him commander of America's fledgling professional army, the Legion of the United States. His first task was to extinguish the Northwest Indian War then raging across the territory destined to become the state of Ohio.

After a series of brutal skirmishes, in the summer of 1794 Wayne's forces crushed a combined American Indian army of Shawnee and Miami at the Battle of Fallen Timbers just south of present-day Toledo. After a two-year respite at his Pennsylvania home, in 1796 he again headed west on an inspection tour of the camps and outposts he had stood up during his Indian campaigns. These included the United States Army's first formal basic training facility at Legionville, just outside Pittsburgh. It was during this journey that Wayne took ill near Detroit. His subordinates managed to transfer him to better medical facilities at Fort Presque Isle, now Erie, Pennsylvania. For naught. He died there on December 15, 1796, at the age of 51 from a combination of severe gout and what may have been infected stomach ulcers. But "Mad Anthony" Wayne's eerie legend does not conclude at that frontier outpost.

In 1809 Wayne's son, Col. Isaac Wayne, journeyed to Fort Presque Isle to disinter his father and return his remains to the family plot in Pennsylvania. The physician whom Isaac Wayne hired to exhume the body found it in surprisingly good shape and, as embalming fluid was unavailable at the site, he decided to boil the flesh off the cadaver's bones for easier transport. Isaac Wayne then carted his father's skeleton some 300 miles across the state of Pennsylvania. It was interred with full military honors at Saint David's Episcopal Church in Radnor Township. According to legend, Isaac Wayne's wagon bounced so mightily across the state's rough frontier roads that many of his father's bones were jounced from the cart. Every January 1, on the anniversary of his birthday, Anthony Wayne's ghost is said to rise from his grave to ride along what is now U.S. Route 322 between Radnor and Erie in search of his lost bones.

Of all the strategic camps Wayne established across the Old Northwest Territories during his Indian campaigns, he may have been most attached to Fort Greeneville, where he had signed the final treaty with the defeated tribal confederacy. It was of course named in honor of his old friend and fellow Valley Forge survivor Nathanael Greene. Following Benedict Arnold's betrayal, Washington appointed

Greene as the commandant of West Point, where he oversaw the military court's decision to execute John André. After Gen. Gates's defeat at the Battle of Camden, Washington ordered Greene to take command of the southern theater of war, handing him total authority over all Continental troops from Delaware to Georgia. It was a splendid selection.

Greene, who arrived in the Carolinas in late 1780, rapidly brought order to the chaotic skeleton force that had lost Savannah, lost Charleston, and finally been devastated at Camden. General Gates's cowardice might well have opened the door for Gen. Cornwallis to execute Britain's "southern strategy" of recruiting Loyalists throughout the deep south and taking the war to Virginia. Only Greene's self-taught organizational and military skills stood in the way of that strategy. Greene's first move was to divide his own troops, forcing Cornwallis to do the same with his superior force. Greene then proceeded to elude the enemy with a series of feints and strategic retreats until, in January 1781, his grand design paid off when a portion of his army under the command of Dan Morgan, by now promoted to general, virtually wiped out a force of over 1,000 British soldiers led by the hated Banastre Tarleton at the Battle of Cowpens in South Carolina. Greene joined his forces with Morgan's soon afterward and, after four months of recruiting and refitting, finally thought the time right for a full-scale confrontation.

In mid-March 1781, Greene lured Cornwallis and his seasoned army of veterans to a hilly, forested battleground in the center of North Carolina far from the British supply depot on the state's southern coastline. There, at the Battle of Guilford Courthouse, rifle fire from the outnumbered Continentals so devastated Cornwallis's lines that at the height of the battle the British general ordered grapeshot fired into the mass of men fighting hand-to-hand, killing Americans and his own soldiers indiscriminately. At this Greene ordered a tactical retreat, and though the Americans were the first to leave the field, Cornwallis's bruised and battered forces were left with no choice but to make a run for Virginia via the North Carolina coast. While Cornwallis swerved north, Greene turned south to concentrate on reconquering South Carolina. Within two months the British were so weakened in both Carolinas that their occupation of Georgia became untenable. With the lower south in Continental hands, all that was left was for Cornwallis and his army to be bottled up at Yorktown.

At the war's end in 1783, the 40-year-old Nathanael Greene retired from the Continental Army. He returned briefly to his home state, Rhode Island, but, like Anthony Wayne, he had received as a gift from the state of Georgia a 24,000-acre expanse of choice bottomland along the Savannah River as a gesture of appreciation for his services. In 1785 Greene; his wife, Caty; and their six children relocated to their new plantation, which they dubbed Mulberry Grove. In June of the following year Greene visited a nearby plantation to learn the mechanics of growing rice. There, in no small irony, he was felled by the heatstroke that had taken the lives of so many Continentals at the Battle of Monmouth Court House. Five days later, on June 19, 1786, he was dead at the age of 43. A shocked nation mourned the passing of the general who was one of only three — the others were Washington and Henry Knox — to serve during the entire eight years of the Revolutionary War. Greene was buried in a cemetery outside Savannah until 1901, when his remains were removed and interred beneath a monument in his honor in what is now the city's financial district.

Naturally, as with so many other Valley Forge survivors, Greene's life story has a strange coda. Nearly a decade after the death of her husband, Caty Greene was introduced to a shipmate while sailing from New England to Savannah. The young man, a recent Yale graduate from Massachusetts named Eli Whitney, had agreed to take a job as a tutor in South Carolina in order to save money for law school. Caty Greene invited Whitney to visit her at Mulberry Grove, which he did when he left his tutoring position because of a dispute over salary. It was at the Greene plantation that Whitney invented the cotton gin, which not only solved the south's long-standing problem of speeding up cotton production, but not incidentally led to an almost immediate intensification of American slavery as the cotton crop became a profit machine. With the invention of the "gin" — short for "engine" — what little emancipation rhetoric that had existed below the Mason-Dixon Line was quickly drowned out by the roaring cataracts of money pouring into the southern states.

One southerner who did not live to partake of this "cotton rush" was Henry Laurens. The senior Laurens resigned from his position as president of the Continental Congress in December 1778 in order to return to South Carolina and restore his failing business empire. It is estimated that during the war years Henry Laurens accumulated losses of close to four million in today's dollars. These included the burning of his plantation outside Charleston by the British. The pull of public service proved too much for Laurens, however, and in the fall of 1780 he was named America's minister to the Netherlands with a brief to obtain loans from the Dutch republic. Days after setting sail from Philadelphia,

Laurens's packet ship was intercepted by a British frigate off the coast of Newfoundland. When Royal Navy officers discovered a cache of papers in his possession containing the outlines of trade agreements and a treaty between the United States and the Netherlands, Laurens was taken to England, charged with treason, and imprisoned in the Tower of London — the first and only American ever incarcerated there. While Laurens languished in confinement for 15 months, Britain declared war on the Netherlands. He was finally freed on the last day of December 1781, in a prisoner exchange for Gen. Cornwallis. Two years later he was again sent overseas, as a member of the American contingent negotiating the Treaties of Paris with the British Crown. Spurning entreaties to return to Congress and take part in the Constitutional Convention, he retired permanently from public life and died in December 1792 at the age of 68. It is reported that his was the first formal cremation to be performed in the United States. His ashes were scattered on the grounds of his rebuilt estate, parts of which are still in use today as a Trappist monastery.

While he was held in the Tower of London, Henry Laurens was visited often by his son John's wife, Martha, who was sometimes accompanied by his granddaughter Frances, the daughter John had never met. No doubt

Henry and Martha spoke often of Henry's meetings with John in Philadelphia. For while Henry was making his preparations to sail to Amsterdam, John had arrived in the capital city on parole after being captured by the British in May 1780. Neither father nor son suspected that their meetings in Philadelphia would be the last time they ever saw one another.

Following the Battle of Monmouth Court House, John Laurens sensed — perhaps even before Washington — that the conflict would now turn south. He badgered his commander in chief to be released from his duties as aide-de-camp in order to fight. After his duel with Charles Lee, Washington acceded to the young man's requests, and with Congress's blessing John Laurens was sent home to South Carolina with permission to raise a regiment of slaves who would be promised their postwar freedom. The state's governor and other local politicians, however, saw no good coming of that scheme, and forbade Laurens to even attempt the endeavor. Stymied at one turn, Laurens took another, and was easily elected to South Carolina's house of representatives where, he felt, he could argue his cause more authoritatively. Three times he would introduce a bill to fold a brigade of slaves into the Continental Army. Three times it would be voted down overwhelmingly.

While serving as a representative Laurens retained the rank of lieutenant colonel, and he fought with Continental forces in and around the Charleston area. In his thirst for glory Laurens foolishly disobeyed an order to retreat during an engagement in May 1779, and was wounded in the arm by shrapnel while another unlucky horse was blown out from under him. Upon his recovery he commanded an infantry regiment in the failed assault on Savannah, and in May 1780 he was taken prisoner after the fall of Charleston. He was paroled to Philadelphia on the gentleman's condition that he not leave the state of Pennsylvania.

Laurens was released from his parole in a prisoner exchange in December of that year. He chafed to return south, but was instead persuaded by Alexander Hamilton to join Thomas Paine on a special mission to France. He and Paine returned from Europe three months later with over one third of a promised French gift of six million livres of silver as well as an even larger loan guarantee from Versailles. Laurens was at Washington's side when the French fleet arrived in the waters off Yorktown in the fall of 1781, and along with Hamilton participated in the siege. Upon the ensuing British surrender, he was appointed by Washington to join Lafayette's brother-in-law the Vicomte de Noailles to negotiate terms with Cornwallis. He then returned to South Carolina, where he organized a spy network for Gen. Greene.

On August 27, 1782, mere weeks before the British withdrew from Charleston for good, Laurens — who had malaria — dragged himself from his sickbed to lead a platoon of light infantry against a British foraging party. His detail was ambushed along the Combahee River, and Laurens fell from his saddle mortally wounded at the first volley. He was 27 years old. Only a month earlier Alexander Hamilton had begged his good friend to "quit your sword, put on a toga, come to congress." But, as with Lear, all the power of John Laurens's wits had given way to his impatience. With him died the seeds of whatever vision he carried for the future United States.

John Laurens was interred on the grounds of the plantation where he had spent his last night alive. When Henry Laurens returned from Europe, he had his son's remains unearthed and laid to rest on his own estate outside Charleston. The elder Laurens was an educated man who surely knew his Cicero — "In peace, sons bury fathers; in war, fathers bury sons." One can only hope that he was equally familiar with, and took solace in, the words of Cicero's rediscoverer Petrarch, who observed that "a good death does honor to a whole life."

Following the Battle of Monmouth Court

House, Baron Friedrich von Steuben spent the winter of 1778–1779 in Philadelphia preparing and editing his military instruction manual. On March 29, 1779, the Continental Congress ordered published *Regulations for the Order and Discipline of the Troops of the United States.* Steuben's "Blue Book," a work of martial art, encompassed "drill instructions, tactical maneuvers, procedures for marches, the establishment and maintenance of encampments, roll calls, inspections, drumbeats, guard duty, care of arms and ammunition, treatment of the sick, military reviews, and duties of officers and men."

The following year Steuben served on the court-martial that convicted John André, and then accompanied Nathanael Greene to the south. From his post in Virginia he kept a steady stream of trained regulars flowing into Greene's ranks. He was briefly felled by a bout of malaria, but recovered in time to take command of one of the three American divisions besieging Yorktown. At the war's end he advised Washington on how to demobilize the Continental Army and also helped to draw up plans for the new nation's defense.

Steuben's tutelage proved the exception to the rule that actual war separates the parade ground from the battleground. Some respected revolutionary-era historians, Wayne Bodle in particular, downplay the Prussian's role in transforming the Continental Army.

They argue that, as the last major northern engagement, the Battle of Monmouth Court House was, in modern parlance, too small a sample size to truly gauge Steuben's influence. More sympathetic voices rise in Steuben's defense, pointing to the army's newfound professionalism displayed not only by the rank and file at Monmouth, but in the too often ignored battles that raged across the south in 1780 and 1781. Even Bodle concedes that Steuben's training regimen imbued Washington's troops with "a deeper identification with and pride in their craft." Further, the archivist and author John Buchanan cites several instances that make a strong case for Steuben's impact.

The first instance occurred in defeat, at the battle of Camden. Buchanan notes that after the Virginia and North Carolina militiamen fled with Gen. Gates, the outnumbered northern regulars from Maryland and Delaware who had drilled under Steuben remained to fight and die with Johann de Kalb. "In the old days the Continentals probably would have fled when they saw the militia desert them," writes Buchanan. Similarly, six months later during the victorious Battle of Cowpens, the tactics employed by Gen. Dan Morgan and Col. John Howard — including a crisply executed bayonet charge that turned the tide of the fight — were the very model of training and discipline that Steuben had instilled at Valley Forge and laid out in his Blue Book. Finally, at the crucial Battle of Guilford Courthouse, it was again regulars from Delaware and Maryland who stood stalwart against a wild charge from crack British and Hessian troops, holding their lines until the enemy was within 100 feet before unleashing a thunderous volley and counterattack that broke the British.

The greater weight of Steuben's training regimen might best be attributed to the man whose army he rebirthed in the mud and snow of Valley Forge. George Washington, in his last official act before tendering his resignation as the Continental Army's commander in chief, penned a note to Steuben to express his "Sincere Friendship and Esteem for you."

"Acknowledging your great Zeal, Attention and Abilities in performing the duties of your Office," Washington concluded, "I wish to make use of this Last moment of my public Life to Signify in the strongest terms, my intire Approbation of your Conduct, and to express my Sense of the Obligations the public is under to you for your faithful and Meritorious Services."

Steuben was discharged in March 1784, the same month he was granted his American citizenship. He settled in New York and moved with the seasons, spending winters in New York City and summering farther north in the Mohawk Valley, in a two-room cabin set on a tract of land, both gifts from the Empire State. The state of New Jersey also eventually deeded to him a 40-acre estate and gristmill across the Hudson River from Manhattan Island. Yet like so many of his Valley Forge compatriots, he fell on hard financial times. Expecting that his long-ago request for postwar financial compensation would be forthcoming from Congress, he borrowed heavily — accumulating debts he could repay only by selling his New Jersey farm and mill. Alexander Hamilton and a coterie of veteran officers stepped in to help when they could, but it was not until 1790 that the United States government granted Steuben a yearly pension of $2,500 — nearly $65,000 today.

Steuben never married, and died childless in 1794 at the age of 64. He was buried in a grove near his upstate New York log cabin in Oneida County. He left his estate to two junior aides, both presumed now to have been homosexual, whom he had met at Valley Forge and whom he adopted after the war. A third young "adopted son," also a former military aide, was named an heir to Steuben's library and collection of maps. Various statues, parades, social and charitable societies, county names across the United States, and even a city in Ohio honor Steuben. His grave, in what became the town of Steuben, New York, is now commemorated by a historical site that bears his name. Although he is most closely associated with his training techniques, as one biographer notes, "At heart [Steuben] was a soldier, not an administrator," with a desire to lead troops into battle, a desire honed since his childhood in northern Europe and fulfilled on the battlefields of the United States.

Not quite in the same league as Henry Knox's about-face on American Indian policy, but for all of Baron von Steuben's professed love of democracy, there was to his mind one fatal flaw in the ideals with which the signers of the Declaration of Independence had established their new nation. A republic, he felt, was only as virtuous as the men who led it. Perhaps owing to the lack of movement on his pleas for a pension, by the late 1780s he had grown increasingly disenchanted with many of the politicians replacing the men who had embodied the spirit of 1776. His proposed answer to this deficiency, discussed at length with Alexander Hamilton, was the notion of installing a constitutional monarchy in the United States. His choice for the throne was Frederick the Great's younger brother Prince Henry. Steuben even wrote to the cultured and liberal-minded — and wonderfully ostentatiously homosexual — prince to gauge his interest. With the onset of the Constitutional Convention, however, the scheme died so quick a death that it does not even merit a mention in the hit Broadway musical based on Hamilton's life.

It hardly needs to be said that what Lin-Manuel Miranda's reimagination of Hamilton's life, as well as the overall renewed interest in his biography, does emphasize is Hamilton's outsize roles in the nation's founding as a soldier, economist, political philosopher, constitutional lawyer, and abolitionist. During the war, Hamilton served for four years as George Washington's principal aide, in every sense lending his voice to the commander in chief's thousands of pages of writings. Washington finally granted Hamilton's request for a field command during the Battle of Yorktown in 1781. With Laurens by his side, he captured a critical redoubt held by the British, and this action was credited with accelerating Gen. Cornwallis's decision to surrender.

Hamilton relinquished his military commission after Yorktown and, in 1782, was appointed to the new Congress of the Confederation — the successor to the Second Continental Congress. He never lost his antipathy toward the decentralized leanings of both political bodies, however, and resigned that same year to open a law practice in Albany. When the British evacuated New York City at the war's end he moved south, and in 1784 founded the Bank of New York. The following year, in honor of his fallen friend John Laurens, he established the New York Society for Promoting the Manumission of Slaves.

Some contend that Hamilton never really recovered from Laurens's death. As mentioned, there have even been attempts to elevate their Damon and Pythias friendship into a love affair. The evidence is speculative. It is true that throughout their service together Hamilton and Laurens continued to pore over sources as disparate as Plutarch and Demosthenes and record passages from them to give as gifts to one another. But a rumored gay relationship sidesteps the fact that in 1780 — two years prior to Laurens's death — Hamilton married Elizabeth Schuyler, the daughter of Washington's old ally Gen. Philip Schuyler, and went on to father eight children with her. In this regard one must also contend with the fact that Hamilton was the first major American politician to become involved in a sex scandal when, in 1797, he admitted to having carried on a yearlong affair with a 23-year-old married woman some six years earlier.

Less salacious, but perhaps more pertinent, was Hamilton's composition of 51 of the 85 *Federalist Papers* — James Madison and John Jay were the other anonymous authors — which were published in 1787 and 1788. The arguments put forth in the documents were key to the ratification of the Constitution, and Hamilton took part in the Constitutional Convention in Philadelphia as a New York delegate. In 1789, President Washington tabbed Hamilton as the nation's first Secretary of the Treasury, a post he held for over six years. It was from this position that he formed and enacted the primary economic policies of the administration that we are so familiar with today — the establishment of a national bank, the funding of state debts by the federal government, and open mercantile relationships with Europe, most notably his old adversary England, to name a few. All this led to his leadership of the Federalist Party, which was created in great part to support his centralized monetary views. It also likely led to his premature death.

During the 1800 presidential election, Hamilton headed the successful Federalist Party campaign against John Adams. When Adams's support fell off and Thomas Jefferson and Aaron Burr amassed an equal number of electoral college votes, Hamilton broke with his party's orthodoxy by casting the tie-breaking vote for Jefferson on the thirty-sixth ballot. Burr never forgave him, and the enmity between the two escalated when Hamilton lobbied hard against Burr's 1804 run for the governorship of New York state. Burr, taking issue with what he felt was Hamilton's calumny in a series of letters and gossipy conversations, challenged him to a duel.

On July 11, 1804, atop a rocky ledge on the New Jersey side of the Hudson River — not far from where Hamilton's oldest son Philip had died in a duel three years earlier — the antagonists paced off their flintlock pistol range, turned, and fired. No one knows who pulled his trigger first. Hamilton's ball cracked a tree branch high above Burr's head. Burr's found its mark in Hamilton's abdomen, breaking several ribs and tearing through his liver and diaphragm before lodging in his spine. All present, including Hamilton, recognized it as a mortal blow. Hamilton, 49, was transported back to a friend's home in New York City where, anesthetized with heavy doses of laudanum, he died the following afternoon surrounded by family and friends. He was, and remains, entombed in the cemetery at lower Manhattan's Trinity Church.

Though Hamilton's biography has been recounted well and often in many venues, perhaps less well known to most Americans is the postwar fate of the Marquis de Lafayette. In the aftermath of the Battle of Monmouth Court House, Lafayette beseeched both Washington and Versailles to allow him to attempt another invasion of Quebec. The American commander in chief, taking his usual long view, privately questioned if the presence of a second "New France" on the United States' northern border might not potentially amount to simply trading one European master for another. Without disparaging Lafayette's motives, Washington diplomatically rejected the idea, noting that the war in the southern states was far from over, and Lafayette might be needed there. Louis XVI and his foreign minister the Comte de Vergennes, meanwhile, recognized that they had spread their troops far too thin fighting the British around the world to consider opening a Canadian front.

After his request was rebuffed, in late 1778 Washington granted Lafayette permission to return to France, where he lobbied to organize a French invasion of the British Isles. When the French king and his ministers dismissed that idea, Lafayette returned to America in April 1780 to act as a liaison for the additional 6,000-man force that Louis XVI had decided to dispatch to Washington's command. In the meanwhile, back in France, Adrienne gave birth to their first and only son, whom the couple named Georges Washington Lafayette.

In early 1781, while Lafayette awaited the arrival of the promised French troops, Washington sent him south with a division of Continentals to join Steuben in Virginia. Vastly outnumbered by Cornwallis, the marquis nipped at the British heels as best he could until, joined by Washington, Greene, and the French reinforcements, the Americans finally cornered the Redcoats at Yorktown. After Yorktown, Congress appointed Lafayette as an official adviser to its European diplomats — Benjamin Franklin in Paris, John Jay in Madrid, and John Adams at The Hague. He also eventually became part of the Paris delegation negotiating the British capitulation. Lafayette's parting with Washington at Mount Vernon in 1784 was a tearful affair, for despite the young Frenchman's protestations the commander in chief suspected that this would be the last time they would ever see each other. Again, Washington's premonition proved prescient. Returning to Paris a hero on two continents, feted by kings, statesmen, and generals at home and abroad, the world as Lafayette knew it came crashing down with the storming of the Bastille on July 14, 1789.

Lafayette was originally caught in the middle by the French Revolution. Viewed by the radicals as a royal ally, he had also fallen out of favor with Louis XVI for his efforts to provide the serfs and burgeoning middle class with a more potent voice in a French Assembly dominated by the nobility and the clergy. To that end he had stopped using his title of marquis. During the revolution's infancy he continued to attempt to thread this needle, but by mid-1791 he was being denounced by leading insurgents such as Maximilien Robespierre and Georges-Jacques Danton. Given command of an army when France declared war on Austria the following year, Lafayette saw firsthand the effects of the slow-rolling revolution when the common soldiers displayed more animosity toward their own officers than toward enemy troops. While he was in the field, the Jacobins took control of Paris, and Danton, the new Minister of Justice, issued a warrant for his arrest.

Lafayette attempted to flee to the United States, but was captured by the Austrians in present-day Belgium. Ironically, in the eyes of the Austrians and their Prussian allies, Lafayette's earlier, measured steps to steer a middle course between the French radicals and the nobility were proof of his antimonarchical tendencies. While he was held in various Prussian and Austrian prisons from September 1792 to September 1797, the Parisian radicals had also jailed his wife, Adrienne. She was spared the guillotine only by the impassioned pleas of the American minister to France, James Monroe, who managed to smuggle her son Georges Washington Lafayette to Connecticut. Similar American efforts to free Lafayette were futile, as the United States had no formal ties or treaties with Austria and Prussia. And though the Secretary of State, Thomas Jefferson, did manage to push an act through Congress awarding Lafayette back pay for his service to the country — the funds eased the severity of his imprisonment for a time — President Washington, despite his deep personal empathy, was determined to avoid any actions that could embroil America in intramural European affairs. Even a freelance escape attempt organized by Alexander Hamilton's sister-in-law went awry.

In October 1795, Ambassador Monroe managed to obtain American passports for Adrienne Lafayette and her two daughters on the basis of the many states that had granted her husband United States citizenship. With this, she and her girls traveled to Vienna, where she convinced Emperor Francis II to allow them to join Lafayette in confinement. The four lived together in his cell for the next two years until the young General Napoleon Bonaparte helped to negotiate their release.

Lafayette and Adrienne were reunited with their son, and they and their daughters were allowed to return to France upon Lafayette's promise to refrain from any political activities. Even when Napoleon held a memorial service in Paris for the recently deceased George Washington, Lafayette was not invited. Lafayette's relationship with Bonaparte remained icy even after the soon-to-be "emperor for life" restored his French citizenship in 1800. And when President Thomas Jefferson offered Lafayette the governorship of the newly acquired territory of Louisiana he declined, citing his determination to work quietly to build a democratic France in the shape of a constitutional monarchy.

In 1814 — seven years after Adrienne's death on Christmas Day, 1807 — the French monarchy was restored and the Comte de Provence, brother of Louis XVI, was placed on the throne. It is said that in their long exile the Bourbons neither learned anything nor forgot anything, and Lafayette reacted as coolly toward his country's autocratic new ruler as he had toward Napoleon. Ever the idealist, he kept hoping that he could in some way effect a more democratic ruling system by means of a strong and diverse National Assembly. When Napoleon escaped Elba a year later and regained power, Lafayette again refused any role in his government. Yet four months later, upon the emperor's abdication in the wake of Waterloo, Lafayette magnanimously arranged with President James Madison for Napoleon's retirement in America. The victorious British, having none of that, instead escorted him to Saint Helena. Over the ensuing years Lafayette stealthily threw his influence into causes ranging from Greek democracy to American abolitionism.

In 1824, at the age of 66, Lafayette returned to the United States to a hero's welcome as the only living general who had fought in the

Revolutionary War. Traveling with his son, he was feted in scores of cities and towns in all 24 states of the union. Over the course of his 14-month tour he dined with President James Monroe, traveled on the Ohio River and that modern marvel the Erie Canal by steamboat, took in Niagara Falls, visited with Gen. Andrew Jackson in Tennessee, witnessed the inauguration of President John Quincy Adams, and laid the cornerstone of the Bunker Hill Monument before scooping up a handful of dirt he wanted spread on his grave. Arriving at the foot of Manhattan, he is said to have steadied himself on his cane, taken in the rapturous throngs, and burst into tears.

Back in France, Lafayette spent the next decade promoting the same republican impulses he had always hoped to plant in his native soil. To little avail. France was still under the heel of an all-powerful king and noble class when, on May 20, 1834, Marie-Joseph-Paul-Yves-Roch-Gilbert du Motier de Lafayette died in Paris, felled by pneumonia. He was buried next to Adrienne in Picpus Cemetery in what is now the city's eighth arrondissement. The French king ordered Lafayette buried with full military honors in order to prevent mob riots, and toward the end of the ceremony Georges Washington Lafayette sprinkled the dirt from Bunker Hill over his father's grave. Each Fourth of July thereafter representatives and military attachés from the French and American governments join Lafayette's descendants in watching the American flag flying over his grave replaced by a new Stars and Stripes. One such commemoration in particular stands out.

On July 4, 1917, at the height of World War I, the initial 200 soldiers of the first American Expeditionary Force to land in Europe entered Paris. Among the delegation led by Gen. John "Black Jack" Pershing to Lafayette's tomb was Col. Charles Stanton, the nephew of Abraham Lincoln's Secretary of War, Edwin Stanton. "America has joined forces with the Allied Powers," Stanton pronounced, "and what we have of blood and treasure are yours."

Speaking in French, Stanton concluded, "Lafayette, we are here!"

When Victor Emmanuel united the warring principalities and city-states of the Italian peninsula into a consolidated nation some 85 years after the American Revolution, it was estimated that less than three percent of the population spoke standard Italian. "We have made Italy," the Piedmontese statesman Massimo d'Azeglio was said to have remarked, "now we must make Italians."

George Washington faced the opposite problem at Valley Forge. There, Americans understood each other perfectly but all too often worked at cross-purposes. Yet despite any technical limitations Washington may have had as a battlefield general, at Valley Forge he displayed a personal quality of steely leadership that is difficult to imagine being matched by any other soldier or statesman of the era.

On December 4, 1783 — almost precisely six years from the day he had led the Continental Army out of the dank, rugged Gulph and onto that bleak plateau in the southeastern corner of Pennsylvania — Washington acknowledged how far that army had come, during a private farewell address to some 30 of his commanding officers. Nine days earlier he had ridden into New York City at the head of a procession that reclaimed his long-lost prize even as the last of the British occupiers scurried onto transports in the harbor. Now, with Henry Knox and Friedrich von Steuben seated to either side of him at the head of the long banquet table on the second floor of Samuel Fraunces's tavern in Lower Manhattan, Washington — dressed in his finest blue-and-buff uniform — raised his glass with a trembling hand.

"With a heart filled with love and gratitude, I now take leave of you," he said, his voice catching in a rare show of emotion. "I most devoutly wish that your latter days may be as prosperous and happy as your former ones have been glorious and honorable."

He paused, and tears began to stream down his cheeks. He then concluded his toast: "I cannot come to each of you, but shall feel obliged if each of you will come and take me by the hand."

At this all the officers stood to embrace their commander in chief. When the last man had brushed his cheek with a solemn kiss, Washington crossed the room and lifted his hand in a gesture of farewell. He then turned and walked through the door without looking back.

AFTERWORD

It was not the first time he had revisited the former winter camp. That had occurred almost a decade earlier, during a recess in the Constitutional Convention in Philadelphia. Then, George Washington and his old friend Gouverneur Morris, both delegates at the convention, had decided to test the trout of Valley Creek on a sunny July afternoon. Tiring of the fishing, Washington had left Morris to his casting to, as he put it, "ride the old Cantonment," and take in the ruins. On his circuit he had reined his horse on Valley Forge's outskirts to speak to a passel of farmers about their planting methods and harvest yields. He took notes, planning to put their crop lore to good use at Mount Vernon as soon as he returned home.

Now, in the late summer of 1796, seven months shy of the end of his second and final presidential term, Washington had returned once again for a final look around. He loped out of Philadelphia by himself, clad in a simple black linen suit. The fields where the dilapidated huts had once stood were now in cultivation, and he spied a man tilling a plot near the French engineer Louis Duportail's decaying redoubts. The plowman introduced himself as Edward Woodman. He was originally from North Carolina, Woodman told the stranger, and said that he had been stationed here during the horrible winter of 1777–1778.

Farmer Woodman allowed that he had been honorably discharged from the Continental Army in 1782. He described how, on his way home from the Hudson Highlands, he had decided to pass by Valley Forge to visit a Quaker family whom he'd befriended lo those years ago. He'd taken sick while visiting his friends, and as they nursed him back to health he had fallen in love and married the family's eldest daughter. Woodman had not been a farmer before the war, but had since learned a few tricks. The stranger was eager to hear them. Come spring he would be heading home to his own Virginia farm, he told Woodman, and would be glad to experiment with any planting practices he could pick up.

It was likely that the mention of Virginia shook Woodman's memory. He stared for a moment, and then apologized profusely for not immediately recognizing his old commander in chief. George Washington but

678

smiled and tipped his hat. Then he spurred his horse and waved adieu. He still had business, he said, to attend to in Philadelphia.

ACKNOWLEDGMENTS

We could not possibly have written this book without the assistance and courtesy of archivists, curators, researchers, and historians at multiple organizations and institutions devoted to the American Revolution and the individuals who played significant roles in it. We especially want to recognize the help provided by Margaret Baillie at the Chester County Historical Society, Rose Buchanan at the National Archives and Records Administration, James Fleming at the National Archives of the United Kingdom, Sarah Myers at the Washington Library at Mount Vernon, and the staff at the Library of Congress.

In addition: William Adams at the University of South Carolina Press, Dawn Bonner at George Washington's Mount Vernon, Amanda Breen at the Gibbes Museum of Art, Seth Michael James at the Lilly Library at Indiana University, Tyler Love at the Independence National Historic Park, Michelle Moskal at the Museum of the American

Revolution, and the Prints Division of the New York Public Library.

A special thank-you goes to the National Park Service rangers, particularly the Interpretive Specialist William Troppman and the archivist Dona McDermott at Valley Forge National Historical Park. Moreover, the official National Park Service history of Valley Forge as compiled by Wayne K. Bodle and Jacqueline Thibaut proved invaluable to our research efforts. We are also grateful to Dr. William Crawley at the University of Mary Washington; Nancy and Lawrence Goldstone; Commander (Ret.) John J. Patterson, Dr. Paul Jussel, and Robert Martin at the U.S. Army War College; Michael Mannella; and John O. Thornhill of the Sons of the American Revolution. Once again, we appreciate the insights and suggestions of the underground editors David Hughes and Bobby Kelly.

From the onset of this project and through its completion we have benefitted from the enthusiastic support of our editor, Jofie Ferrari-Adler. Others we are happy to thank at Simon & Schuster are Jonathan Karp, Cary Goldstein, Julianna Haubner, Larry Hughes, Stephen Bedford, Nicole Hines, Kathy Higuchi, Susan Gamer, and David Lindroth. Scott Manning and Abigail Welhouse also deserve our appreciation. And as always, we survive to write another day thanks to Nat Sobel and his merry band of elves at Sobel-Weber Associates, particularly Adia Wright. Kudos, too, to the efforts on our behalf of Michael Prevett at the Rain Management Group.

As with any long writing project, we depended on the ongoing support and encouragement of family and friends. You know who you are, but let us single out Denise McDonald, Liam-Antoine DeBusschere-Drury, Leslie Reingold, Kathryn Clavin, and Brendan Clavin.

BIBLIOGRAPHY

Books

André, John. *Major André's Journal.* Scotts Valley, CA: CreateSpace, 2016.

Andrist, Ralph K. *George Washington: A Biography in His Own Words.* New York: Harper and Row, 1972.

Billias, George Athan. *George Washington's Generals and Opponents.* New York: Da Capo, 1994.

Bodle, Wayne. *Valley Forge Report, Volume 1: The Vortex of Small Fortunes, the Continental Army at Valley Forge, 1777–1778.* National Park Service, Washington, DC, 1980.

———. *Valley Forge Winter: Civilians and Soldiers in War.* University Park: Pennsylvania State University Press, 2002.

Boyle, Joseph Lee, Ed. *"Fire Cake and Water": The Connecticut Infantry at the Valley Forge Encampment.* Baltimore, MD: Clearfield, 2001.

———. *Their Distress Is Almost Intolerable:*

The Elias Boudinot Letter Book. Bowie, MD: Heritage, 2002.

———. *Writings from the Valley Forge Encampment of the Continental Army.* Bowie, MD: Heritage, 2000. *Volume II.* Bowie, MD: Heritage, 2007. *Volume III.* Bowie, MD: Heritage, 2007.

Brown, Lloyd A., Ed. *Revolutionary War Journals of Henry Dearborn 1775–1783.* Bowie, MD: Heritage, 2007.

Buchanan, John. *The Road to Valley Forge.* Hoboken, NJ: Wiley, 2004.

Burke, Edmund. *A Philosophical Inquiry into the Origins of Our Ideas of the Sublime and Beautiful: With an Introductory Discourse Concerning Taste, and Several Other Additions,* 1757. Harvard Classics, Volume 24, Part 2.

Burnett, Edmund, Ed. *Letters of the Members of the Continental Congress, Volume II.* Washington, DC: Carnegie Institute of Washington, 1921.

Busch, Noel F. *Winter Quarters: George Washington and the Continental Army at Valley Forge.* New York: Liveright, 1974.

Butterfield, L. H. *Letters of Benjamin Rush, Volume I.* Princeton, NJ: Princeton University Press, 1951.

Callahan, North. *Connecticut's Revolutionary War Leaders.* Chester, CT: Pequot, 1973.

Carrington, Henry Beebee. *Battles of the*

American Revolution, 1775–1781. Victoria, Canada: Promontory, 1974.

Chernow, Ron. *Alexander Hamilton.* New York: Penguin, 2004.

———. *Washington: A Life.* New York: Penguin, 2010.

Chesnutt, David R., and C. James Taylor, Eds. *The Papers of Henry Laurens, Volumes XII and XIII.* Columbia: University of South Carolina Press, 1990 and 1992.

Clary, David A. *Adopted Son: Washington, Lafayette, and the Friendship That Saved the Revolution.* New York: Bantam, 2007.

Clinton, Henry. *American Rebellion: Sir Henry Clinton's Narrative of His Campaigns, 1775–1782.* New Haven: Yale University Press, 1954.

Commager, Henry Steele, and Richard B. Morris, Eds. *The Spirit of 'Seventy-Six: The Story of the American Revolution as Told by Participants.* Edison, NJ: Castle, 2002.

Cox, Clinton. *Come All You Brave Soldiers: Blacks in the Revolutionary War.* New York: Scholastic, 2002.

Crane, Elaine Forman, Ed. *The Diary of Elizabeth Drinker: The Life Cycle of an Eighteenth-Century Woman.* Philadelphia: University of Pennsylvania Press, 2010.

Custis, George Washington Parke. *Recollections and Private Memoirs of Washington.* Bridgewater, VA: American Foundation

Publications, 1999.

Ellis, Joseph. *His Excellency: George Washington.* New York: Knopf, 2004.

Feist, David. *Lt. Colonel John Laurens, 1754–1782.* Finlayson, MN: Self-published, 2015.

Ferreiro, Larrie D. *Brothers at Arms: American Independence and the Men of France and Spain Who Saved It.* New York: Knopf, 2016.

Fischer, David Hackett. *Washington's Crossing.* New York: Oxford University Press, 2004.

Fitzpatrick, John C., Ed. *The Writings of George Washington from the Original Manuscript Sources* (39 Volumes). Washington, DC: U.S. Government Printing Office: 1931–1944.

Fleming, Thomas. *Washington's Secret War: The Hidden History of Valley Forge.* New York: HarperCollins, 2005.

Flexner, James Thomas. *George Washington: The Indispensable Man.* New York: Back Bay, 1994.

Ford, Washington Chauncey, Ed. *Journals of the Continental Congress.* Washington, DC: United States Government Printing Office, 1906.

Freedman, Russell. *Washington at Valley Forge.* New York: Holiday House, 2008.

Freeman, Douglas Southall. *Washington.* New York: Simon and Schuster, 1995.

(Originally published 1948–1954.)

Gaines, James R. *For Liberty and Glory: Washington, Lafayette, and Their Revolutions.* New York: W.W. Norton, 2007.

Ganoe, William A. *The History of the United States Army.* New York: D. Appleton-Century, 1942.

Gillis, Jennifer Blizin. *Mercy Otis Warren.* Minneapolis, MN: Compass Point, 2006.

Goldstone, Lawrence. *Going Deep: John Philip Holland and the Invention of the Attack Submarine.* New York: Pegasus, 2017.

Gruber, Ira D. *The Howe Brothers and the American Revolution.* New York: W.W. Norton, 1975.

Hamilton, Allan McLane. *The Intimate Life of Alexander Hamilton.* New York: Racehorse Publishing, reprint ed., 2016.

Hucklebridge, Dane. *The United States of Beer: A Free-Wheeling History of the All-American Drink.* New York: William Morrow, 2016.

Idzerda, Stanley J., Ed. *Lafayette in the Age of the American Revolution: Selected Letters and Papers, 1776–1790, Volume I.* Ithaca, NY: Cornell University Press, 1977.

———. *Volume II (April 1778–March 1780).* Ithaca, NY: Cornell University Press, 1979.

Isaacson, Walter. *Benjamin Franklin: An American Life.* New York: Simon and Schuster, 2003.

Jackson, Donald, and Dorothy Twohig, Eds. *The Diaries of George Washington, Volume 5: 1 July 1786–31 December 1789.* Charlottesville: University of Virginia Press, 1979.

Jackson, John W. *The Delaware Bay and River Defenses of Philadelphia, 1775–1777.* Philadelphia, PA: Philadelphia Maritime Museum, 1977.

————. *Valley Forge: Pinnacle of Courage.* Gettysburg, PA: Thomas, 1992.

Kapp, Friedrich. *Life of de Kalb: Major General of the Revolutionary Army.* London: Forgotten Books, 2017.

Lee, Henry. *Memoirs of the War in the Southern Department of the United States.* London: Forgotten Books, 2017.

Lefkowitz, Arthur S. *George Washington's Indispensable Men.* Mechanicsburg, PA: Stackpole, 2003.

Lender, Mark Edward. *Fatal Sunday: George Washington, the Monmouth Campaign, and the Politics of Battle.* Norman: University of Oklahoma Press, 2016.

Loane, Nancy K. *Following the Drum: Women at the Valley Forge Encampment.* Washington, DC: Potomac, 2009.

Lockhart, Paul. *The Drillmaster of Valley Forge: The Baron de Steuben and the Making of the American Army.* New York: HarperCollins, 2008.

Mackesy, Piers. *The War for America 1775–1783.* Lincoln, NE: Bison, 1993.

Marshall, Christopher, and William Duane. *Extracts from the Diary of Christopher Marshall.* Whitefish, MT: Kessinger Legacy Reprints. (Originally published 1877.)

Martin, Joseph Plumb. *Narrative of a Revolutionary Soldier.* New York: Signet, 2010.

Massey, Gregory D. *John Laurens and the American Revolution.* Columbia: University of South Carolina Press, 2015.

McCullough, David. *1776.* New York: Simon and Schuster, 2005.

McGuire, Thomas J. *The Battle of Paoli.* Mechanicsburg, PA: Stackpole, 2000.

————. *The Philadelphia Campaign, Volume II: Germantown and the Roads to Valley Forge.* Mechanicsburg, PA: Stackpole, 2006.

McHenry, James. *Journal of a March, a Battle, and a Waterfall.* Greenwich, CT: Helen and Henry Flynt, 1945.

Miller, John C. *The Triumph of Freedom.* New York: Little, Brown, 1948.

Milsop, John. *Continental Infantryman of the American Revolution.* Oxford, UK: Osprey, 2004.

Mowday, Bruce E. *September 11, 1777: Washington's Defeat at Brandywine Dooms Philadelphia.* Shippensburg, PA: White Mane, 2002.

Murray, Stewart. *Atlas of American Military History.* New York: Facts on File, 2004.

Nelson, Craig. *Thomas Paine: Enlightenment, Revolution, and the Birth of Modern Nations.* New York: Penguin, 2007.

Palmer, Dave Richard. *George Washington and Benedict Arnold: A Tale of Two Patriots.* New York: Regnery, 2010.

Palmer, John McAuley. *General von Steuben.* New Haven, CT: Yale University Press, 1937.

Papers of Henry Laurens, Volumes XII, XIII. Columbia: University of South Carolina Press, 1990–92.

The Papers of George Washington. Charlottesville, University of Virginia Press. (Volumes cited are listed chronologically by subject.)

Colonial Series, *Volume 1: 7 July 1748–14 August 1755,* ed. W. W. Abbot, 1983.

Revolutionary War Series, *Volume 1: 16 June 1775–15 September 1775,* ed. Philander D. Chase, 1985.

Volume 3: 1 January 1776–31 March 1776, ed. Philander D. Chase, 1988.

Volume 4: 1 April 1776–15 June 1776, ed. Philander D. Chase, 1991.

Volume 7: 21 October 1776–5 January 1777, ed. Philander D. Chase, 1997.

Volume 10: 11 June 1777–18 August 1777, ed. Frank E. Grizzard, Jr., 2000.

Volume 11: 19 August 1777–25 October 1777, ed. Philander D. Chase and Edward G. Lengel, 2001.

Volume 12: 26 October 1777–25 December 1777, ed. Frank Grizzard, Jr., and David R. Hoth, 2002.

Volume 13: 26 December 1777–28 February 1778, ed. Edward G. Lengel, 2003.

Volume 14: 1 March 1778–30 April 1778, ed. David R. Hoth, 2004.

Volume 15: May–June 1778, ed. Edward G. Lengel, 2006.

Volume 16: 1 July–14 September 1778, ed. David R. Hoth, 2006.

Volume 19: 15 January–7 April 1779, ed. Philander D. Chase and William M. Ferraro, 2009.

Confederation Series: *Volume 3: 19 May 1785–31 March 1786,* ed. W. W. Abbot, 1994.

Presidential Series: *Volume 1: 24 September 1788–31 March 1789,* ed. Dorothy Twohig, 1987. *Volume 5: 16 January 1790–30 June 1790,* ed. Dorothy Twohig, Mark A. Mastromarino, and Jack D. Warren, 1996.

Pappas, Phillip. *Renegade Revolutionary: The Life of General Charles Lee.* New York: NYU Press, 2014.

Pearson, Michael. *Those Damned Rebels: The American Revolution as Seen Through British Eyes.* New York: Da Capo, 1972.

Public Papers of George Clinton, First Governor

of New York. New York: Wynkoop Hallen-
beck Crawford, 1900.

Quincy, Josiah, Ed. *The Journals of Major
Samuel Shaw.* London, UK: Forgotten
Books, 2012.

Randall, Willard Sterne, and Nancy Nahra.
*Forgotten Americans: Footnote Figures Who
Changed American History.* New York: Da
Capo, 1999.

Reed, John Ford. *Campaign to Valley Forge.*
Union City, TN: Pioneer, 1980.

Rhodehamel, John, Ed. *The American Revolution: Writings from the War of Independence.*
New York: Library of America, 2001.

————. *George Washington: Writings.* New
York: Library of America, 1997.

Scheer, George F., and Hugh F. Rankin. *Reb-
els and Redcoats: The American Revolution
Through the Eyes of Those Who Lived It.*
New York: Da Capo, 1957.

Schiff, Stacy. *The Great Improvisation: Franklin, France, and the Birth of America.* New
York: Henry Holt, 2005.

Sedgwick, Theodore. *A Memoir of the Life of
William Livingston.* Whitefish, MT: Kessinger, 2010.

Showman, Richard K., Ed. *The Papers of
General Nathanael Greene, Volume I* and
Volume II. Chapel Hill: University of North
Carolina Press, 1976, 1980.

Simcoe, John Graves. *Journal of the Queen's*

Rangers. Ann Arbor, MI: Gale ECCO, 2010.

Simms, William Gilmore, Ed. *The Army Correspondence of John Laurens, 1777–1778.* London: Forgotten Books, 2015.

Smith, Jean Edward. *John Marshall: Definer of a Nation.* New York: Holt, 1998.

Smith, Paul H., et al., Eds. *Letters of Members of the Continental Congress.* Washington, DC: Government Printing Office, 1981.

Sparks, Jared, Ed. *The Diplomatic Correspondence of the American Revolution.* Boston: Gray and Bowen, 1829–1830.

Steuben, Frederick William von. *Baron von Steuben's Revolutionary War Drill Manual.* Dover, 1985.

Symonds, Craig L. *A Battlefield Atlas of the American Revolution.* National and Aviation Publishing Co. of America, 1986.

Syrett, Harold C., Ed. *The Papers of Alexander Hamilton, Volume I: 1768–1778.* New York: Columbia University Press, 1961.

Szymanski, Leszek. *Casimir Pulaski: A Hero of the American Revolution.* New York: Hippocrene, 1979.

Taylor, Alan. *American Revolutions: A Continental History, 1750–1804.* New York: W.W. Norton, 2016.

Tilghman, Tench. *Memoir of Lieut. Col. Tench Tilghman, Secretary and Aide to Washington.* SC: Nabu Public Domain Reprints.

Townsend, Joseph. *Some Account of the British Army Under General Howe.* Philadelphia, PA: T. Ward, 1846.

Trussell, John B. B. Jr. *Birthplace of an Army: A Study of the Valley Forge Encampment.* Harrisburg: Pennsylvania Historical and Museum Commission, 1998.

Twohig, Dorothy, Ed. *George Washington's Diaries (An Abridgment).* Charlottesville: University of Virginia Press, 1999.

Vowell, Sarah. *Lafayette in the Somewhat United States.* New York: Riverhead, 2015.

Waldo, Albigence. *Account of the Ordeal at Valley Forge.* Amazon Digital Services, 2013.

Watson, Robert P. *The Ghost Ship of Brooklyn: An Untold Story of the American Revolution.* New York: Da Capo, 2017.

Wick, Wendy C. *George Washington: An American Icon.* Washington, DC: Smithsonian Institution, 1982.

Willcox, William B., Ed. *The Papers of Benjamin Franklin.* New Haven: Yale University Press, 1986, 1987.

Wills, Garry. *Cincinnatus: George Washington and the Enlightenment.* New York: Doubleday, 1984.

Wirt, William. *The Life of Patrick Henry.* London: Forgotten Books, 2017.

Wood, Gordon S. *The American Revolution.* New York: Modern Library, 2003.

Articles

Americanrevolution.org, "Battle of the Kegs, 1778."

Blanco, Richard L. "American Army Hospitals in Pennsylvania During the Revolutionary War." *Pennsylvania History Journal,* 1981.

"Clement Biddle." Mountvernon.org, July 12, 2017.

Eastby, Allen. "Setback for the Continental Army." *Military History,* December 1998.

Fleming, Thomas. "Congress Does Not Trust Me. I Cannot Continue Thus." *Journal of the American Revolution,* 2015.

Gopnik, Adam. "Trump's Radical Anti-Americanism." *New Yorker,* February 13 and 20, 2017.

Jahromi, Neima. "Fraunces Tavern." *New Yorker,* January 29, 2018.

Milkofsky, Brenda. "David Bushnell and His Revolutionary Submarine." ConnecticutHistory.org, May 2012.

Segal, David. "The Diss Song Known as Yankee Doodle." *New York Times,* July 1, 2017.

Siebert, Wilbur H. "The Loyalists of Pennsylvania." *Ohio State University Bulletin,* Vol. 24, No. 23, 1920.

Vowell, Sarah. "Join the Army, Love the Constitution and Pray to Whomever You

Like." *New York Times,* August 14, 2016.

Williams, Keith. "Evacuation Day." *New York Times,* February 4, 2018.

http://www.ushistory.org/valleyforge/you asked/071.htm.

http://militaryhistorynow.com/2014/07/04/americas-first-soldiers-12-amazing-facts-about-the-continental-army/.

http://www.gwyneddmeeting.org/history/minutes1776.html.

http://mentalfloss.com/article/51899/7-john-adams-greatest-insults.

http://www.u-s-history.com/pages/h3996.html.

Parliamentary Register, 10:13, 30–33.

Collections

Alexander McDougall Papers, New-York Historical Society, New York.

Andre deCoppet Collection, Princeton University Library, Princeton, NJ.

Charles Stewart Collection, New York State Historical Association.

Clinton Papers, William L. Clements Library, Ann Arbor, MI.

Cornelius Hartnett Papers, University of North Carolina Library, Chapel Hill.

Dreer Collection, Members of the Old Congress, Historical Society of Pennsylvania, Philadelphia.

Dudley Coleman Papers, Massachusetts

Historical Society, Boston.

Ely Collection, New Jersey Historical Society, Newark.

Emmet Collection, New York State Library, Albany.

Germain Papers, William L. Clements Library, Ann Arbor, MI.

Gratz Collection, Historical Society of Pennsylvania, Philadelphia.

Jeremiah Wadsworth Papers, Chicago Historical Society, IL.

John Reed Collection, Valley Forge National Historical Park.

Joseph Trumbull Collection, Connecticut Historical Society, Hartford.

Knox Papers, Massachusetts Historical Society, Boston.

NARA Pension Papers, Washington, DC.

Newcastle MSS, Nottingham University Library, Nottingham, UK.

Papers of the Continental Congress, NARA, Washington, DC.

Pennsylvania Historical and Museum Commission, Harrisburg, PA.

Sackville-Germain Papers, William L. Clements Library, University of Michigan, Ann Arbor.

Sebastian Bauman Papers, New-York Historical Society, New York.

Ward Papers, Rhode Island Historical Society, Providence.

Weedon Papers, Chicago Historical Society, IL.

Williams Papers, Connecticut Historical Society, Hartford.

NOTES

Prologue

"What is the meaning of this, sir?": Chernow, *Washington: A Life*, p. 342.

"Sir?" he stammered. "Sir?": Lender and Stone, *Fatal Sunday: George Washington, the Monmouth Campaign, and the Politics of Battle*, p. 289.

"A gallant example": Josiah Quincy, Ed., *The Journals of Major Samuel Shaw, the First American Consul at Canton*, p. 48.

"Will you fight?": Chernow, *Washington: A Life*, p. 343.

"His presence": "Memoir of 1779," in Idzerda, *Lafayette in the Age of the American Revolution: Selected Letters and Papers, 1776–1790*, Vol. 1, p. 11.

"We are betrayed": Custis, *Recollections and Private Memoirs of Washington*, p. 219.

"Colonel Hamilton," he said: Ibid.

Part I: Epigraph

"The Enemy were routed": "From George Washington to Major General Israel Putnam, 8 October 1777," in *The Papers of George Washington,* Revolutionary War Series, Vol. 11, ed. Chase and Lengel, pp. 446–47.

Chapter One: A Sprig of Green

A "multiplicity of interests": James Madison, *Federalist Papers,* no. 51.

Now, this morning: Vowell, "Join the Army, Love the Constitution and Pray to Whomever You Like."

Despite his efforts, he could not prevent: http://www.hopkinsandcompany.com/Books/Revolutionary%20Mothers.htm.

Contemporary descriptions of the general: Townsend, *Some Account of the British Army Under General Howe . . . Which Came to the Knowledge and Understanding of Joseph Townsend,* p. 25.

Yet close observers also noted: Gruber, *The Howe Brothers and the American Revolution,* pp. 56–57.

It was not lost on the Americans: Vowell, *Lafayette in the Somewhat United States,* p. 195.

General George Weedon: Bodle, *Valley Forge Report,* Vol. 1: *The Vortex of Small Fortunes:*

*the Continental Army at Valley Forge, 1777–
1778,* pp. 48, citing "George Weedon to
John Page, 23 August 1777," Chicago
Historical Society.

He wrote to a subordinate: "From George
Washington to Brigadier General Thomas
Nelson, Jr., 2 September 1777," in *The
Papers of George Washington,* Revolution-
ary War Series, Vol. 11, ed. Chase and Len-
gel, pp. 128–30.

As it happened, this was what Washington:
Palmer, *George Washington and Benedict
Arnold,* p. 231.

They were even, incredibly: Bodle, *Valley
Forge Report,* Vol. 1, p. 3, citing "Supreme
Executive Council to the County Militia
Lieutenants, 6 September, 1777," Frames
0988–0990, Roll 12, PA, Pennsylvania
Historical and Museum Commission, Har-
risburg.

Chapter Two: To Crown the Brave

As the historian Wayne Bodle: Bodle, *Valley
Forge Report,* Vol. 1, p. 5.

In his letter to Whitehall: Ibid., p. 16, citing
"William Howe to Lord George Germain,
30 August 1777" (extract), Sackvill-
Germain Papers.

As Washington's biographer: Chernow, *Washington: A Life,* p. 331.

It frustrated Washington: "From George Washington to Major General Horatio Gates, 1 September 1777," in *The Papers of George Washington,* Revolutionary War Series, Vol. 11, ed. Chase and Lengel, pp. 107–8.

Washington publicly acknowledged: Ibid., "George Washington to Jonathan Trumbull, Sr., 8 September 1777," pp. 173–74.

privately entertained "little doubt": "From George Washington to Brigadier General John Cadwalader, 28 August 1777," *Founders Online,* National Archives.

The British, having shorn themselves: "General Orders, 7 September 1777," *Founders Online,* National Archives. Original source: *The Papers of George Washington,* Revolutionary War Series, Vol. 11, ed. Chase and Lengel, pp. 167–69.

A defeat of the British here: Ibid., "General Orders, 5 September 1777." Original source: *The Papers of George Washington,* Revolutionary War Series, Vol. 11, ed. Chase and Lengel, p. 148.

To emphasize the importance: Ibid., "General Orders, 6 September 1777." Original source: *The Papers of George Washington,* Revolutionary War Series, Vol. 11, ed. Chase and Lengel, pp. 157–58.

Now, with their "arms cleaned": Ibid., "General Orders, 26 August 1777."

the Continentals were, in the words: Bodle, *Valley Forge Report,* Vol. 1, p. 7.

Despite his lack of formal education: Chernow, *Washington: A Life,* p. 203.

Whenever possible, Washington instead intended: "From George Washington to Robert Dinwiddie, 10 June 1754," in *The Papers of George Washington,* Colonial Series, Vol. 1, *7 July 1748–14 August 1755,* ed. W. W. Abbot (Charlottesville: University Press of Virginia, 1983), pp. 129–40.

Now, however, the majority of Sullivan's soldiers: http://www.wtj.com/articles/brandy wine/).

This afternoon they made deadly use: Bodle, *Valley Forge Report,* Vol. 1, p. 10, citing Reed, *Campaign to Valley Forge,* p. 128.

"Fighting is a new thing": Billias, *George Washington's Generals and Opponents,* p. 111.

Washington's officers, grasping for: Bodle, *Valley Forge Report,* Vol. 1, p. 9.

That night, in a letter: "George Washington to John Hancock, 11 September 1777," in *The Papers of George Washington,* Revolutionary War Series, Vol. 11, ed. Chase and Lengel, pp. 200–201.

At least he could take solace: Vowell, "Join the Army, Love the Constitution and Pray to Whomever You Like."

Chapter Three: The French Connection

One night at a dinner party: http://www.history .com/news/10-things-you-may-not-know-about-the-marquis-de-lafayette.

The ambitious Lafayette: Ibid.

As the inestimable biographer of Lafayette: Vowell, *Lafayette in the Somewhat United States,* p. 50.

When Deane introduced him: "Benjamin Franklin and Silas Deane to the Committee of Secret Correspondence, 25 May 1777," National Archives.

Perhaps feeling last-minute pangs: Idzerda, *Lafayette in the Age of the American Revolution,* Vol. 1, p. 108.

He had given his word: Ibid.

Writing years later: Memoirs, Correspondence and Manuscript of General Lafayette, Vol. 1, Published by his Family, New York, Saunders and Otley Ann Street and Conduit Street London, Entered According to the Act of Congress in the Year 1837 by William A. Duer in the Clerk's Office in the Southern District of New York.

"The happiness of America": http://moland .org/lafayette/.

He also informed both Hancock: "Lafayette to John Hancock, 12 August 1777," National Archives.

"If Congress meant": "George Washington to Benjamin Harrison, 19 August 1777,"

Founders Online, National Archives. Original source: *The Papers of George Washington,* Revolutionary War Series, Vol. 11, ed. Chase and Lengel, pp. 4–5.

In this instance: Ibid.

But Lafayette's self-effacement: Vowell, "Join the Army, Love the Constitution and Pray to Whomever You Like."

Moreover, their ubiquitous demands: "George Washington to Benjamin Franklin, 17 August 1777," *Founders Online,* National Archives. Original source: *The Papers of George Washington,* Revolutionary War Series, Vol. 10, ed. Grizzard, pp. 647–49.

Although thankful for hardened warriors: Ibid.

He went so far: Ibid.

Although Lafayette lacked: Chernow, *Washington: A Life,* p. 296.

Chapter Four: Burned Forges

Their attitude was reflected: Syrett, *The Papers of Alexander Hamilton,* Vol. 1, p. 321 (September 1, 1777).

Nathanael Greene went even further: Bodle, *Valley Forge Report,* Vol. 1, p. 12, citing "Nathanael Greene to his wife, 14 September 1777," Andre deCoppet Collection.

Only 14 months earlier: http://militaryhistory now.com/2014/07/04/americas-first-soldiers-12-amazing-facts-about-the-continental-army/.

"Swarms of Officers": Declaration of Independence.

Instead they hoped to throw: http://military historynow.com/2014/07/04/americas-first-soldiers-12-amazing-facts-about-the-continental-army/.

By 1777, as reality set in: http://www.history.org/Foundation/journal/Autumn04/soldier.cfm.

Yet the civil authorities: Bodle, *Valley Forge Report,* Vol. 1, p. 56, citing "Samuel Hay to William Irvine, 14 November 1777," Draper MSS, Series AA, Irvine Papers, State Historical Society of Wisconsin (SHSW), Madison.

Even if an infusion of militiamen: Ibid., p. 63, citing "Louis Lebeque Duportail to St. Germaine, 12 November 1777" (copy), Andre deCoppet Collection.

It was well understood by combatants: Freeman, *Washington,* p. 356.

As the historian Ron Chernow: Chernow, *Washington: A Life,* p. 208.

The remaining 40 percent constituted: Taylor, *American Revolutions: A Continental History, 1750–1804,* p. 214.

Still, Washington sensed: "To Alexander Hamilton from George Washington, [21 September 1777]," *Founders Online,* National Archives. Original source: Syrett, *The Papers of Alexander Hamilton,* Vol. 1, pp. 330–31.

"I feel, and I lament": Ibid.

"The business you are upon": "To Alexander Hamilton from George Washington, 22 September 1777," in Syrett, *The Papers of Alexander Hamilton,* Vol. 1, pp. 332–33.

Chapter Five: Fix Bayonets

Although he had no formal: McGuire, *The Battle of Paoli,* p. 46.

As Grey's second in command: André, *Major André's Journal,* "20 September, 1777," p. 34.

Moments later, on the cry: McGuire, *Battle of Paoli,* p. 104.

This was accomplished by: Ibid., p. 115.

As Capt. André laconically: Commager and Morris, *The Spirit of 'Seventy-Six: The Story of the American Revolution as Told by Participants,* p. 621.

The American colonists: Major André's Journal, "20 September 1777," p. 50.

Describing the engagement: McGuire, *Battle of Paoli,* p. 144.

Perhaps deeming that euphemism: Ibid.

Chapter Six: A Perfect Scribe

Cornwallis's triumphal entry: McGuire, *Battle of Paoli,* p. 1.

While the rest of his mounted: Lee, *Memoirs of*

the War in the Southern Department of the United States, pp. 19–21.

"Aid de Camps are person's": From George Washington to John Hancock, 23 April 1776, in The Papers of George Washington, Revolutionary War Series, Vol. 4, ed. Chase, pp. 112–13.

As the biographer Joseph Ellis: Ellis, His Excellency, p. 12.

By the time the British marched: Chernow, Washington: A Life, p. 292.

Like the prickly John Adams: Vowell, Lafayette in the Somewhat United States, p. 125.

The great propagandist Paine: Ibid., p. 126.

"No," he quipped: Murray, Atlas of American Military History, p. 30.

Such were the perils: Bodle, Valley Forge Report, Vol. 1, p. 22, citing "Jedediah Huntington to Colonel Williams, 29 September 1777," Williams Papers.

But even this peace offering: Ibid., p. 23, citing "Samuel Holden Parsons to Jeremiah Wadsworth, 30 September 1777," Andre deCoppet Collection.

On September 28, Washington summoned: Ibid., p. 22, citing "Council of War, 28 September 1777," in Fitzpatrick, Writings of George Washington, Volume IX, p. 277–91.

It was often noted: https://www.gilder lehrman.org/history-by-era/age-jefferson-and-madison/resources/john-adams-describes-george-washington%E2%80%99s-ten-tale.

As the Valley Forge historian: Bodle, *Valley Forge Report,* Vol. 1, p. 25.

Chapter Seven: A Bloody Day

"The term of mercy": "General Orders, 3 October 1777," National Archives. Original source: *The Papers of George Washington,* Revolutionary War Series, Vol. 11, ed. Chase and Lengel.

Gen Howe, he added: Ibid.

It was later reported: Scheer and Rankin, *Rebels and Redcoats,* p. 245.

To Gen. Armstrong: Bodle, *Valley Forge Report,* Vol. 1, p. 56, citing "John Armstrong to Thomas Wharton, 5 October 1777," Gratz Collection, Case 4, Box 11, Historical Society of Pennsylvania, Philadelphia.

Armstrong himself later equated: Ibid.

Washington's old friend: Ibid., p. 29, citing "George Weedon to Washington, 4 October 1777," Weedon Papers.

His Virginians, he wrote: Ibid.

And Tench Tilghman: Tilghman, *Memoir of Lieut. Col. Tench Tilghman,* pp. 160–61.

One American surgeon wrote: Bodle, *Valley Forge Report,* Vol. 1, p. 30, citing "Jonathan Todd to his father, 6 October 1777," RG 15, M-804, Roll 1561, National Archives.

A New York company commander: Commager

and Morris, *The Spirit of 'Seventy-Six: The Story of the American Revolution as Told by Participants,* p. 631, citing "Lt. Will Heth to Col. John Lamb, October 12, 1777," Lamb Papers, New-York Historical Society.

Even Washington's chief intelligence officer: Bodle, *Valley Forge Report,* Vol. 1, p. 30, citing "Benjamin Talmadge to Jeremiah Wadsworth, 5 October 1777," Jeremiah Wadsworth Papers, Correspondence.

He had been in the thick: Ibid., p. 29, citing "Lord Stirling, 5 October 1777," Dealer's catalog, American Art Association, 1926.

Like the others: Ibid.

But in the aftermath: "From George Washington to John Augustine Washington, 18 October 1777," in *The Papers of George Washington,* Revolutionary War Series, Vol. 11, ed. Chase and Lengel, pp. 551–53.

To John Hancock he described: Ibid., "From George Washington to John Hancock, 5 October 1777," pp. 393–401.

He later sent an addendum: Ibid., "From George Washington to John Hancock, 7 October 1777," pp. 416–20.

And in a letter: Ibid., "From George Washington to Thomas McKean, 10 October 1777." pp. 478–79.

Putnam could only sputter: Ibid., "From George Washington to Major General Israel Putnam, 1 October 1777," pp. 363–64.

In a typical understatement: Wood, *The American Revolution,* p. 304–5.

As two historians of the American Revolution: Scheer and Rankin, *Rebels and Redcoats,* p. 253.

As the general pleaded: Ibid., p. 254, citing "William Duer to Philip Schuyler, June 19, 1777," in Burnett, *Letters,* Vol. II, p. 385.

"His manner was ungracious": Ibid.

Now, nine months later: Ibid.

"He behaved, as I then thought": Scheer and Rankin, *Rebels and Redcoats,* p. 281.

By nightfall nearly half: "George Washington's General Orders," in *The Papers of George Washington,* Revolutionary War Series, Vol. 11, ed. Chase and Lengel, pp. 512–14.

Chapter Eight: The Idealist

From as far away as Saint Croix: Syrett, *The Papers of Alexander Hamilton,* pp. 365–67.

Once integrated into Washington's main force: Bodle, *Valley Forge Report,* Vol. 1, p. 48, citing "Jedediah Huntington to Colonel Trumbull, 27 October 1777," Joseph Trumbull Collection.

Less than a month after: Ibid., p. 138, citing "Nathanael Greene to his wife, 2 November 1777," Manuscript Division, Princeton University Library.

Despite publicly urging his own: "General Orders, 15 October 1777," in *The Papers of*

George Washington, Revolutionary War Series, Vol. 11, ed. Chase and Lengel, pp. 512–14.

In the face of this dual burden: Gruber, *The Howe Brothers and the American Revolution,* p. 257.

At this Howe dug: Marshall and Duane, *Extracts from the Diary of Christopher Marshall,* pp. 133–34.

Marshall, a former Philadelphia chemist: Ibid.

Washington's chief artillery: "To George Washington from Brigadier General Henry Knox, 3 December 1777," in *The Papers of George Washington,* Revolutionary War Series, Vol. 12, ed. Grizzard, and Hoth, pp. 524–25.

In a bitter letter to John Adams: Butterfield, *Letters of Benjamin Rush,* Vol. 1, p. 137.

"I have heard several": Ibid.

Upon receiving news: Smith et al., *Letters of Members of the Continental Congress,* Vol. 8, p. 187.

When informed of the British victory: Flexner, *George Washington,* p. 294.

Adams's fellow Massachusetts congressman: Smith et al., *Letters of Members of the Continental Congress,* Vol. 8, p. 302.

And even Lafayette: Idzerda, *Lafayette in the Age of the American Revolution,* Vol. 1, p. 121.

By mid-October Henry Laurens: Chesnutt and

Taylor, *The Papers of Henry Laurens,* Vol. XII, p. 227.

Though Washington seemed to take: "From George Washington to Richard Henry Lee, 28 October 1777," in *The Papers of George Washington,* Revolutionary War Series, Vol. 12, ed. Grizzard and Hoth, pp. 40–42.

More overtly — and quite out of character: "From George Washington to John Hancock, 24 October 1777," in *The Papers of George Washington,* Revolutionary War Series, Vol. 11, ed. Chase and Lengel, pp. 596–97.

Washington had officially congratulated: "From George Washington to Major General Horatio Gates, 30 October 1777," in *The Papers of George Washington,* Revolutionary War Series, Vol. 12, ed. Grizzard and Hoth, pp. 59–60.

In a letter to his friend: Ibid., "From George Washinton to Richard Henry Lee, 28 October 1777," pp. 40–42.

And in his one public hint: "From George Washington to John Hancock, 24 October 1777," in *The Papers of George Washington,* Revolutionary War Series, Vol. 11, ed. Chase and Lengel, pp. 596–97.

"I can never": Willcox, *The Papers of Benjamin Franklin,* Vol. 26, *March 1 through June 30, 1778,* pp. 478–89.

Naturally, his decision: Massey, *John Laurens*

and the American Revolution, p. 72.

Henry made it clear: Ibid.

Yet what stirred Washington most: "George Washington to William Gordon, 8 March 1785," *Founders Online,* National Archives. Original source: *The Papers of George Washington,* Presidential Series, Vol. 1, ed. Twohig, pp. 1–5.

Washington preferred that: Massey, *John Laurens and the American Revolution,* p. 73.

As his biographer Gregory D. Massey: Ibid., p. 79.

"I would willingly risk": Syrett, *The Papers of Alexander Hamilton,* Vol. 1, p. 4. (Letter of November 11, 1769.)

"Every lad had a lover": Massey, *John Laurens and the American Revolution,* p. 81.

As he wrote to his father: "John Laurens Letter to Henry Laurens, November 5, 1777," in Simms, *The Army Correspondence of John Laurens 1777–1778,* p. 62.

In a postscript he added: Ibid.

Chapter Nine: An Eerie Foreboding

Every recruit was theoretically entitled: Martin, *Narrative of a Revolutionary Soldier,* p. 84.

The son of a prominent: Busch, *Winter Quarters: George Washington and the Continental Army at Valley Forge,* p. 57.

In a rare instance of public: McCullough, *1776,* p. 190.

"It gives me pain": "From George Washington to John Hancock, 13–14 October 1777," in *The Papers of George Washington,* Revolutionary War Series, Vol. 11, ed. Chase and Lengel, pp. 497–501.

The return Washington: Ibid.

"It is impossible": Ibid.

As he vowed: McGuire, *The Philadelphia Campaign,* Vol. II, *Germantown and the Roads to Valley Forge,* pp. 125–80.

"At the same time.": "From George Washington to Major General Horatio Gates, 30 October 1777," in *The Papers of George Washington,* Revolutionary War Series, Vol. 12, ed. Grizzard and Hoth, pp. 59–60.

At this, Hamilton slyly wrote: Syrett, *The Papers of Alexander Hamilton,* Vol. I, p. 353.

Chapter Ten: Blood on the Delaware

The fort's 10 cannons: Waldo, *Account of the Ordeal at Valley Forge,* entry of November 10, 1777.

The waterborne show: "From George Washington to Commodore John Hazelwood, 28 October 1777," in *The Papers of George Washington,* Revolutionary War Series, Vol. 12, ed. Grizzard and Hoth, p. 39.

"I have seen": Martin, *Narrative of a Revolutionary Soldier,* p. 75.

Martin witnessed: Ibid., p. 80.

while he himself: Ibid., p. 74.

This persistence eventually broke: "From George Washington to Henry Laurens, 1–3 November 1777," in *The Papers of George Washington,* Revolutionary War Series, Vol. 12, ed. Grizzard and Hoth, pp. 78–85.

Washington advised the senior Laurens: Ibid., "From George Washington to Henry Laurens, 26–27 November 1777," pp. 420–22.

Moreover, in the wake: Ibid.

"The Marquis," Washington added: Ibid., "From George Washington to Henry Laurens, 1–3 November 1777," pp. 78–85.

More impressive, Lafayette's own précis: Idzerda, *Lafayette in the Age of the American Revolution,* Vol. I, p. 157.

Sensing a final opportunity: "John Laurens Letter to Henry Laurens, 3 December, 1777," in Simms, *The Army Correspondence of John Laurens 1777–1778,* p. 90.

"We wished nothing": Martin, *Narrative of a Revolutionary Soldier,* p. 86.

"Two battles he has lost": Lender, *Fatal Sunday: George Washington, the Monmouth Campaign, and the Politics of Battle,* p. 27.

As Jedediah Huntington wrote: Bodle, *Valley Forge Report,* Vol. 1, p. 55, citing "Jedediah Huntington to his father, 11 November," Jedediah Huntington Letters, Connecticut Historical Society, Hartford.

Or, as the historian Wayne Bodle observed: Ibid., p. 51.

General Lord Stirling's was the lone voice: "From George Washington to Joseph Reed, 2 December 1777," in *The Papers of George Washington,* Revolutionary War Series, Vol. 12, ed. Grizzard and Hoth, p. 500.

On the other was the political reality: Bodle, *Valley Forge Report,* Vol. 1, p. 71, citing "Thomas Wharton to Elias Boudinot, 13 December 1777," Frame 0258, Reel 13, PA, Pennsylvania Historical and Museum Commission, Harrisburg.

As the French foreign minister: Carrington, *Battles of the American Revolution, 1775–1781,* p. 400.

He had personally journeyed: "John Laurens Letter to Henry Laurens, 3 December, 1777," in Simms, *The Army Correspondence of John Laurens 1777–1778,* p. 89.

Young Laurens was equally direct: Ibid.

As he wrote to his old friend Patrick Henry: "From George Washington to Patrick Henry, 13 November 1777," in *The Papers of George Washington,* Revolutionary War Series, Vol. 12, ed. Grizzard and Hoth, pp. 242–43.

"I am informed that it": Ibid., "From George Washington to Henry Laurens, 17–18 November 1777," pp. 292–96.

To drive home the point: Idzerda, *Lafayette in the Age of the American Revolution,* Vol. I, p. 165.

In this instance, one can assume: "John Laurens Letter to Henry Laurens, 3 December, 1777," in Simms, *The Army Correspondence of John Laurens 1777–1778,*" p. 90.

Without naming a specific location: Ibid.

Part II: Epigraph

"I am sick": Waldo, *Account of the Ordeal at Valley Forge.*

Chapter Eleven: The Relics of an Army

"A cavalcade of wild beasts": Martin, *Narrative of a Revolutionary Soldier,* p. 121.

Influenza, typhus, typhoid, dysentery: "Journal Entries of Albigence Waldo Regarding the Continental Army Moving to Valley Forge," December 12, 1777, in Waldo, *Account of the Ordeal at Valley Forge.*

"a good and loving wife": Ibid., December 31, 1777.

"pretty children": Ibid., December 12, 1777.

Waldo stretched the horizons: Ibid., November 10, 1777.

He could not help ruing: Ibid.

At night, gazing about: Bodle, *Valley Forge Report,* Vol. 1, p. 76.

Such a feast, he wrote: Martin, *Narrative of a Revolutionary Soldier,* p. 88.

As the commander in chief beheld: "From George Washington to John Bannister, 21

April 1778," in *The Papers of George Washington,* Revolutionary War Series, Vol. 12, ed. Grizzard and Hoth, pp. 291–92.

More important, the travelogue shone: Ellis, *His Excellency,* p. 7.

Thereafter he told friends: Plaque at Museum of the American Revolution, Philadelphia, PA.

As a Richmond newspaper editorial: Ellis, *His Excellency,* p. 23.

The company he recruited: Ibid., p. 24.

Three weeks earlier Henry Knox: The Papers of George Washington, November 26, 1777.

Chapter Twelve: Chaos in the East

As he wrote to Henry Laurens: "From George Washington to Henry Laurens, 11 November 1777," in *The Papers of George Washington,* Revolutionary War Series, Vol. 12, ed. Grizzard and Hoth, pp. 208–10.

To lighten their loads: Busch, *Winter Quarters: George Washington and the Continental Army at Valley Forge,* p. 54.

When they finally procured beef: "Brig. Gen. James Mitchell Varnum to George Washington, Dec. 22," George Washington Papers, Library of Congress.

Joseph Plumb Martin, now an 18-year-old: Martin, *Narrative of a Revolutionary Soldier,* p. 91.

The snake-rail fencing: Nelson, *Thomas Paine:*

Enlightenment, Revolution, and the Birth of Modern Nations, p. 121.

The commander in chief's General Orders: "General Orders, 20 December 1777," in *The Papers of George Washington,* Revolutionary War Series, Vol. 12, ed. Grizzard and Hoth, pp. 641–44.

The effort expended to assemble: "Jonathan Todd Jr. to Jonathan Todd Sr., December 25, 1777," Record Group 15, National Archives and Records Administration.

His regimental officers: "General Orders, 22 December 1777," in *The Papers of George Washington,* Revolutionary War Series, Vol. 12, ed. Grizzard and Hoth, pp. 662–65.

Even the strongest threats: Idzerda, *Lafayette in the Age of the American Revolution,* Vol. I, p. 170.

A colonel from New York's brigade: "Col. Henry Livingston to Gov. George Clinton, 24 December, 1777," in *Public Papers of George Clinton.*

"The Men must be Supplied": "Brig. Gen. James Mitchell Varnum to George Washington, Dec. 22," George Washington Papers, Library of Congress.

"Were soldiers to have": "Journal Entries of Albigence Waldo Regarding the Continental Army Moving to Valley Forge, 8 December 1777," in Waldo, *Account of the Ordeal at Valley Forge.*

Instead he was left: Ibid., "21 December 1777."

The French engineers grumbled: "Gen. Johann de Kalb to Count Charles Francis de Broglie, 25 December, 1777," in Kapp, *Life of de Kalb,* pp. 137–43.

Calling Washington: Ibid.

Writing years later, he observed: "Memoir of 1779," in Idzerda, *Lafayette in the Age of the American Revolution,* Vol. I, pp. 169–70.

Chapter Thirteen: Trenton Redux?

It was against this shortfall: "General Orders, 22 December 1777," in *The Papers of George Washington,* Revolutionary War Series, Vol. 12, ed. Grizzard and Hoth, pp. 662–65.

Only that morning he had informed: Ibid., "From George Washington to Henry Laurens, 23 December 1777," pp. 683–87.

As his longtime aide Tench Tilghman: Boyle, *Writings from the Valley Forge Encampment,* Vol. II, p. 3, citing John Reed Collection, Valley Forge National Historical Park.

The left wing of the shock corps: "Plan to Attack Philadelphia, 25 December 1777," in *The Papers of George Washington,* Revolutionary War Series, Vol. 12, ed. Grizzard and Hoth, pp. 701–3.

Even if Washington viewed: Ibid.

But he reminded Washington: Ibid., "To

George Washington from Major General Nathanael Greene, 24 November 1777," pp. 376–79.

In the end, Washington heeded their advice: Chernow, *Washington: A Life,* p. 208.

Still others, the usually sober: Bodle, *Valley Forge Report,* Vol. 1, p. 127.

The latter, "adapted to privation": Idzerda, *Lafayette in the Age of the American Revolution,* Vol. I, p. 170.

Chapter Fourteen: Starve, Dissolve, or Disperse

The delegates were still in fact: "To George Washington from Henry Laurens, 22 December 1777," in *The Papers of George Washington,* Revolutionary War Series, Vol. 12, ed. Grizzard and Hoth.

After reading Henry Laurens's missive: Ibid., "George Washington to Henry Laurens, 22 December 1777," pp. 667–71.

He then wrote, "Unless more": Ibid.

"It would give me infinite": Ibid.

He was, he wrote, "most sensible": Ibid.

Now, more than ever: Ibid., pp. 683–87.

When he learned that Howe: Ibid.

No man, he wrote: Ibid.

"I can assure those Gentlemen": Ibid.

He even resorted to stark: Ibid.

One such uprising, he wrote: Ibid.

He wrote that he was now convinced: Ibid.

More dispiriting was the sight: "John Laurens Letter to Henry Laurens, 23 December, 1777," in Simms, *The Army Correspondence of Colonel John Laurens in the Years 1777– 1778,* p. 96.

Chapter Fifteen: The Best Answer to Calumny

Lee may have been: "From George Washington to John Augustine Washington, 31 March 1776," in *The Papers of George Washington,* Revolutionary War Series, Vol. 3, *1 January 1776–31 March 1776,* ed. Chase, pp. 566–71.

His bewildered new father-in-law: Paul David Nelson, "Charles Lee," in *American National Biography,* http://www.anb.org/view/10.10 93/anb/9780198606697.001.0001/anb-9780198606697-e-0100506.

Lee was also taken: Buchanan, *The Road to Valley Forge,* p. 142.

Conversely — as the historian: Ibid., p. 143.

Upon receiving the "melancholy intelligence": "From George Washington to John Hancock, 15 December 1776," in *The Papers of George Washington,* Revolutionary War Series, Vol. 7, ed. Chase, pp. 344–45.

But as the lack of purposefulness: Ellis, *His Excellency,* p. 9.

Although technically against army regulations: "John Adams to Abigail Adams, 22 May

1777," in Smith et al., *Letters of the Members of the Continental Congress,* Vol. 7, p. 103.

It helped that the awestruck statesmen: "John Laurens Letter to Henry Laurens, 3 January 1778," in Simms, *The Army Correspondence of John Laurens 1777–1778,* p. 103.

Alexander Hamilton, less florid: Lefkowitz, *George Washington's Indispensable Men,* p. 152.

"The promotion of Gen. Conway": "John Laurens Letter to Henry Laurens, 1 January 1778," in Simms, *The Army Correspondence of John Laurens 1777–1778,* p. 100.

It was a warning borne out: Lefkowitz, *George Washington's Indispensable Men,* p. 152.

The concepts of reputation: Bodle, *Valley Forge Report,* Vol. 1, p. 202, citing "Officers of Artillery to Washington, 10 February 1778," George Washington Papers, Library of Congress.

As John Laurens added: "John Laurens Letter to Henry Laurens, 3 January 1778," in Simms, *The Army Correspondence of John Laurens 1777–1778,* p. 103.

Though he filed no formal protest: "From George Washington to Major General Thomas Conway, 30 December 1777," in *The Papers of George Washington,* Revolutionary War Series, Vol. 13, ed. Lengel, pp. 66–67.

"If there is any truth": "George Washington to Richard Henry Lee, 17 October 1777," in Fitzpatrick, *Writings of George Washington,* Vol. IX, pp. 387–89.

Washington also made it known: "From George Washington to Brigadier General Thomas Conway, 5 November 1777," in *The Papers of George Washington,* Revolutionary War Series, Vol. 12, ed. Grizzard and Hoth, pp. 129–30.

He wrote to his friend George Clinton: "Alexander Hamilton to Henry Clinton, 13 February 1778," in Syrett, *The Papers of Alexander Hamilton,* Vol. 1, p. 428.

Compared with Hamilton's diatribe: "From George Washington to Richard Henry Lee, 28 October 1777," in *The Papers of George Washington,* Revolutionary War Series, Vol. 12, ed. Grizzard and Hoth, pp. 40–42.

He finally penned another letter: "To George Washington from Major General Thomas Conway, 10 January 1778," in *The Papers of George Washington,* Revolutionary War Series, Vol. 13, ed. Lengel, pp. 195–96.

"Since you will not accept": Ibid.

Finally, he effortlessly deflected: "From George Washington to Brigadier General Thomas Conway, 16 November 1777," in *The Papers of George Washington,* Revolutionary War Series, Vol. 12, ed. Grizzard and Hoth, p. 277.

Tilghman surely spoke for Washington's inner circle: "Tench Tilghman to John Cadwalader, January 18, 1778," *Memoir of Lieut. Col. Tench Tilghman.*

Intimating a duel: "John Laurens Letter to Henry Laurens, 3 January 1778," in Simms, *The Army Correspondence of John Laurens 1777–1778,"* p. 103.

As he would explain: "From George Washington to William Livingston," in Sedgwick, *A Memoir of the Life of William Livingston,* p. 343.

"I fancy they don't like us": Bodle, *Valley Forge Report,* Vol. 1, p. 197, citing "Jedediah Huntington to Joseph Trumbull, 31 January 1778," Governor Joseph Trumbull Collection, Connecticut State Library, Hartford.

The young Frenchman wrote: "To George Washington, December 30, 1777," in Idzerda, *Lafayette in the Age of the American Revolution,* Vol. 1, p. 204.

The general's successes in the north: Ibid., letter of January 5, 1778, p. 215.

Thus the new year opened: "From George Washington to Major General Lafayette, 31 December 1777," in *The Papers of George Washington,* Revolutionary War Series, Vol. 13, ed. Lengel, pp. 83–84.

Patrick Henry forwarded an anonymous letter:

Butterfield, *Letters of Benjamin Rush,* Vol. 1, pp. 182–83.

Chapter Sixteen: Integration

When Washington took command: "General Orders, 4 July 1775," in *The Papers of George Washington,* Revolutionary War Series, Vol. 1, *16 June 1775–15 September 1775,* ed. Chase, pp. 54–58.

As the revolutionary historian John Milsop: Milsop, *Continental Infantrymen of the American Revolution,* p. 5.

An excited Laurens wrote: "John Laurens Letter to Henry Laurens, 14 January 1778," in Simms, *The Army Correspondence of John Laurens 1777–1778,* p. 108.

In an earlier letter: Ibid., "John Laurens Letter to Henry Laurens, 3 January 1778," p. 103.

"Habits of subordinations": Ibid.

Laurens even proposed a uniform design: Ibid., "John Laurens Letter to Henry Laurens, 9 February 1778," p. 120.

In a letter to John Hancock recommending: "From George Washington to John Hancock, 28 August 1777," in *The Papers of George Washington,* Revolutionary War Series, Vol. 11, ed. Chase and Lengel, p. 85.

Chapter Seventeen: Firecakes and Cold Water

Though bedridden by a nearly crippling attack: Bodle, *Valley Forge Report,* Vol. 1, p. 142, citing "Henry Laurens to William Livingston, 30 December 1777," PCC, RG 93, M-247, Roll 23, National Archives.

Within days of his lobbying campaign: "Thomas Jones and John Chaloner to Thomas Wharton Jr., December 24, 1777," Pennsylvania Historical and Museum Commission.

One of Wharton's fellow Pennsylvanians: Bodle, *Valley Forge Report,* Vol. 1, p. 142, citing "Daniel Roberdeau to Thomas Wharton, 26 December 1777," Frame 0364, Reel 13, PA, Pennsylvania Historical and Museum Commission.

The board also warned Wharton: Ibid., 135, citing "Francis Lightfoot Lee to Thomas Wharton, 30 December 1777," Autographs of Signers of the Declaration, Pierpont Morgan Library, New York.

"Either from my own particular": "From George Washington to Henry Laurens, 1 January 1778," in *The Papers of George Washington,* Revolutionary War Series, Vol. 13, ed. Lengel, pp. 103–6.

Within 10 days it had delegated: Bodle, *Valley Forge Report,* Vol. 1, p. 136, citing Ford, *Journals of the Continental Congress,* Vol.

IX, p. 1073.

The New Jersey delegate John Witherspoon: Ibid., citing "John Witherspoon to William Churchill Houston, 27 January 1778," in Burnett, *Letters,* Vol. III, p. 58.

Yet Henry Laurens praised: Ibid., p. 201, citing "Henry Laurens to John Rutledge, 30 January 1778," in Burnett, *Letters,* Vol. III, p. 58.

Anthony Wayne, the blunt general from Chester: "Anthony Wayne to Thomas Wharton, 28 December 1777," John Reed Collection, Valley Forge National Historical Park.

"We live from Hand to Mouth": Bodle, *Valley Forge Report,* Vol. 1, p. 206, citing "Jedediah Huntington to his father, 7 January 1778," John Reed Collection.

A year earlier, before the victories: "America's First Soldiers: Twelve Remarkable Facts About the Continental Army," Military History Now.

"Notwithstanding the orders": "General Orders, 27 December 1777," in *The Papers of George Washington,* Revolutionary War Series, vol. 13, ed. Lengel, p. 16.

Once, when a scrawny cow: "Journal Entries of Albigence Waldo Regarding the Continental Army Moving to Valley Forge, 14 December 1777," in Waldo, *Account of the Ordeal at Valley Forge.*

"There comes a Soldier": Ibid.

Concludes the account: Ibid.

If they survived the journey: Loane, *Following the Drum: Women at the Valley Forge Encampment,* p. 119.

While at the time the death toll: Blanco, "American Army Hospitals in Pennsylvania During the Revolutionary War," p. 355.

In the same letter in which he detailed: Bodle, *Valley Forge Report,* Vol. 1, p. 161, citing "Enoch Poor to Mesech Weare, 21 January 1778," Force MSS, Series 7-E, New Hampshire Council, Library of Congress.

Chapter Eighteen: Civil War

Still, even if the Drebbel submarine: Goldstone, *Going Deep,* p. 12.

Years later Washington hailed his pet: "From George Washington to Thomas Jefferson, 26 September 1785," in *The Papers of George Washington,* Confederation Series, Vol. 3, ed. Abbot, pp. 279–83.

He wrote to one militia commander: "From George Washington to Colonel Joseph Kirkbride, 20 April 1778," in *The Papers of George Washington,* Revolutionary War Series, Vol. 14, ed. Hoth, pp. 568–69.

Pulaski was in essence: "Circular to Brigadier General Casimir Pulaski and the Colonels of the Continental Light Dragoon Regiments, 25 October 1777," in *The Papers of George Washington,* Revolutionary War

Series, Vol. 11, ed. Chase and Lengel, pp. 619–20.

But a string of outraged General Orders: "General Orders, 26 December 1777," in *The Papers of George Washington,* Revolutionary War Series, Vol. 13, ed. Lengel, pp. 1–2.

He was flattered by the offer: "To George Washington from Captain Henry Lee, Jr., 31 March 1778," in *The Papers of George Washington,* Revolutionary War Series, Vol. 14, ed. Hoth, pp. 368–69.

Moreover, Gen. Howe had offered: Marshall and Duane, *Extracts from the Diary of Christopher Marshall,* February 23, 1778 entry, p. 169.

As the historian Wayne Bodle observes: Bodle, *Valley Forge Report,* Vol. 1, p. 173.

The farmhouse had more windows: Ibid., p. 176, citing "Henry Lee to Washington (two letters), 20 January 1778," *George Washington Papers,* Library of Congress.

John Laurens was naturally agog: "John Laurens Letter to Henry Laurens, 23 January 1778," in Simms, *The Army Correspondence of John Laurens 1777–1778,*" p. 111–12.

And a 19-year-old New Jersey captain: http://patch.com/california/brentwood/letter-valley-forge-1778-0.

Washington personally congratulated Lee: "From George Washington to Captain Henry Lee, Jr., 20 January 1778," in *The*

Papers of George Washington, Revolutionary War Series, Vol. 13, ed. Lengel, p. 294.

"his warmest thanks to": Ibid., "General Orders, 20 January 1778," pp. 286–88.

General Poor, for instance, having: Bodle, *Valley Forge Report,* Vol. 1, p. 160, citing "Enoch Poor to Mesech Weare, 21 January 1778," Force MSS, Series 7-E, New Hampshire Council, Library of Congress.

His starving and half-naked soldiers: Ibid.

Some 90 of his soldiers: Ibid., p. 175, citing "Samuel Carlton to William Heath, 28 January 1778."

"If they had any idea": http://patch.com/california/brentwood/letter-valley-forge-1778-0.

Instead, they found themselves: Ibid.

The 26-year-old Massachusetts lieutenant colonel: Bodle, *Valley Forge Report,* Vol. 1, p. 156, citing "John Brooks, 5 January 1778," Miscellaneous Collection, Massachusetts Historical Society, Boston.

Chapter Nineteen: An American Army

These men had watched friends: Bodle, *Valley Forge Report,* Vol. 1, p. 278, citing "John Patterson to Colonel Marshall, 23 February 1778," Ely Collection, New Jersey Historical Society.

More than one bitter patriot: Ibid., p. 156, citing "John Brooks, 5 January 1778," Miscellaneous Collection, Massachusetts Historical Society, Boston.

Perhaps more chillingly: Ibid., p. 314, citing "James Varnum to Mrs. William Greene, 7 March 1778," John Reed Collection.

The hostile interactions between Continental troops: Ibid.

The Hessians in particular: Ibid., p. 156, citing "John Brooks, 5 January 1778," Miscellaneous Collection, Massachusetts Historical Society, Boston.

Two days after the battle of Germantown: http://www.gwyneddmeeting.org/history/minutes1776.html.

Not the least of these events was a 1775 decree: Siebert, "The Loyalists of Pennsylvania."

In defiance of the legislation: Ibid.

While most Quakers fled: Crane, *The Diary of Elizabeth Drinker.* (See also http://www.gwyneddmeeting.org/history/minutes1776.html.)

This practice eventually led: Mowday, *September 11, 1777,* p. 57.

Yet whatever his private feelings: "From George Washington to the Society of Free Quakers, c. 8 April 1790," in *The Papers of George Washington,* Presidential Series, Vol. 5, ed. Twohig, Mastromarino, and Warren, pp. 296–99.

That the thoughts: http://mentalfloss.com/

article/51899/7-john-adams-greatest-insults.

In his 1910 biography of his paternal grandfather: Hamilton, *The Intimate Life of Alexander Hamilton,* p. 245.

Laurens, with his odes: "John Laurens Letter to Henry Laurens, 23 January 1778," in Simms, *The Army Correspondence of John Laurens 1777–1778,* pp. 111–12.

If the men who had journeyed: Flexner, *George Washington: The Indispensable Man,* p. 251.

He and his staff had spent: Bodle, *Valley Forge Report,* Vol. 1, p. 202.

Composed in the baroque vernacular: "From George Washington to a Continental Congress Camp Committee, 29 January 1778," in *The Papers of George Washington,* Revolutionary War Series, Vol. 13, ed. Lengel, pp. 376–409.

Fashioned in the form of a legal indictment: Ibid., "To George Washington from Henry Laurens, 27 January 1778," pp. 364–66.

In an attached note he suggested: Ibid.

But it wasn't burned: Ibid., "From George Washington to Henry Laurens, 31 January 1778," pp. 420–21.

In his report to the delegates: Ibid., "From George Washington to a Continental Congress Camp Committee, 29 January 1778," pp. 376–409.

He singled out the Maryland militia's . . . In his

conclusion Washington drove home: Ibid.

Chapter Twenty: "Howe's Players"

At Valley Forge, what one historian: Bodle, *Valley Forge Report,* Vol. 1, p. 255.
Washington's daily General Orders reveal: Jackson, *Valley Forge: Pinnacle of Courage,* p. 178.
Although daily lashings: 2 Corinthians, 11:24.
This in turn would lead: "To George Washington from Major General Horatio Gates, 24 January 1778," in *The Papers of George Washington,* Revolutionary War Series, Vol. 13, ed. Lengel, pp. 329–32.
"Should your Excellency think": Ibid.
"It is feared that the ambition": "John Laurens Letter to Henry Laurens, 28 January 1778," in Simms, *The Army Correspondence of John Laurens 1777–1778,* p. 113.
Mounted units of Redcoats: Ibid., "John Laurens Letter to Henry Laurens, 17 February 1778," p. 128.
And if by hard chance: Fleming, *Washington's Secret War,* p. 40.
the youngest Shippen child: Willard Sterne Randall and Nancy Nahra, *Forgotten Americans: Footnote Figures Who Changed American History.* New York: Da Capo, 1999, p. 83.
It was said that André's eyes possessed: Fleming, *Washington's Secret War,* p. 37.

Shortly after occupying Philadelphia: Scheer and Rankin, *Rebels and Redcoats,* p. 320.

"I renewed my solicitation": Clinton, *American Rebellion,* p. 84.

"We may rest assured": "Circular to the States, 29 December 1777," in *The Papers of George Washington,* Revolutionary War Series, Vol. 13, ed. Lengel, pp. 36–39.

"Be that as it may": Ibid.

Chapter Twenty-One: Franklin's Miracle

"Honourable Sir," he began: "Franklin and Silas Deane to the President of Congress, 8 February 1778," in Willcox, *The Papers of Benjamin Franklin, Vol. 25, October 1, 1777, through February 28, 1778,* pp. 634–35.

Franklin, weighing the seizing or sinking: Sparks, *The Diplomatic Correspondence of the American Revolution,* Vol. I, p. 361.

Yet in the spring of 1776: http://www.stratford hall.org/ meet-the-lee-family/arthur-lee/.

He feared that Deane's words: Connecticut Historical Society Museum, Document 18.

Despite Lee's enthusiasm for breaking: Vowell, *Lafayette in the Somewhat United States,* p. 205.

He noted Lee's long and deep connection: Fleming, *Washington's Secret War,* p. 98.

Madame Brillon, 38 years Franklin's junior: http://articles.chicagotribune.com/1990-05-06/features/9002070773_1_command

ments-18th-century-love-papa.

Franklin did his best to ignore: "From Benjamin Franklin to Arthur Lee, 3 April 1778," in Willcox, *The Papers of Benjamin Franklin,* Vol. 26, p. 223.

Franklin did, however, find it prudent: Ibid.

Before Austin could dismount: Isaacson, *Benjamin Franklin: An American Life,* p. 343.

"But, sir," he said: Ibid.

Franklin clapped, and replied: Ibid.

One witness likened the two: https://www.laphamsquarterly.org/foreigners/miscellany/voltaire-and-benjamin-franklin-share-sweet-embrace.

Chapter Twenty-Two: "Those Dear Raggedy Continentals"

Washington was forced to deny: "From George Washington to Major General John Sullivan, 14 February 1778," in *The Papers of George Washington,* Revolutionary War Series, Vol. 13, ed. Lengel, pp. 541–42.

It is likely that John Laurens: "John Laurens Letter to Henry Laurens, 17 February 1778," in Simms, *The Army Correspondence of John Laurens 1777–1778,* pp. 126–27.

He described an army: Ibid.

During the Christmas food shortage: Bodle, *Valley Forge Report,* Vol. 1, p. 252, citing "Anonymous memorandum specifying criteria for honoring civilian claims for payment for goods seized by the army near Valley Forge, January 1778," George Washington Papers, Library of Congress.

We are situated in a place": J. M. Varnum to Major General Alexander McDougall, Feb. 7," Alexander McDougall Papers, New York Historical Society.

It was Congress: "Alexander Hamilton to George Clinton, 13 February 1778," in Syrett, *Papers of Alexander Hamilton,* p. 425.

When Greene pressed him: "From George Washington to James Warren, 31 March 1779," in *The Papers of George Washington,* Revolutionary War Series, Vol. 19, ed. Chase and Ferraro, pp. 673–75.

If Greene should catch any: Ibid.

He himself, upon being named commander in chief: Fitzpatrick, *Writings of George Washington,* Vol. IX, p. 443.

This restraint, he wrote: Ibid.

As he told Greene: "From George Washington to Major General Nathanael Greene, 16 February 1778," in *The Papers of George Washington,* Revolutionary War Series, Vol. 13, ed. Lengel, pp. 556–57.

"I determine to forage": Bodle, *Valley Forge Report,* Vol. 1, p. 287, citing "Nathanael Greene to Washington, 15 February 1778," George Washington Papers, Library of Congress.

But as he observed: Martin, *Narrative of a*

Revolutionary Soldier, p. 85.

"The real condition of Washington": Smith, *John Marshall: Definer of a Nation,* p. 63.

He had not counted on: Ibid.

These measures of "temporary relief": "John Laurens Letter to Henry Laurens, 17 February 1778," in Simms, *The Army Correspondence of John Laurens 1777–1778,"* pp. 126–27.

Yet British records indicate: "From George Washington to William Buchanan, 7 February 1778," in *The Papers of George Washington,* Revolutionary War Series, Vol. 13, ed. Lengel, pp. 465–66.

While penned up in the Potts House: Ibid.

And it was not only enlisted: Bodle, *Valley Forge Report,* Vol. 1, p. 265.

"The love of freedom": Commager and Morris, *The Spirit of 'Seventy-Six: The Story of the American Revolution as Told by Participants,* pp. 650–51.

It was only his enormous self-control: "From George Washington to William Gordon, 15 February 1778," in *The Papers of George Washington,* Revolutionary War Series, Vol. 13, ed. Lengel, pp. 545–46.

Their revolutionary credentials: "John Laurens Letter to Henry Laurens, 9 March 1778," in Simms, *The Army Correspondence of John Laurens 1777–1778,* p. 134.

And if, as Laurens predicted: Ibid.

It took an anonymous French officer: Gilbert Chinard, *George Washington: As the French Knew Him,* p. 13.

For that was the month: Wick, *George Washington: An American Icon,* p. 9.

Chapter Twenty-Three: The Political Maestro

It took the Camp Committee less: Bodle, *Valley Forge Report,* Vol. 1, p. 208, citing "Committee of Conference, 'Minutes,' 29 January 1778," in Burnett, *Letters,* Vol. III, p. 62.

"Pray Use your Influence": "Brig. Gen. John Patterson to Thomas Marshall, 23 February," Ely Collection, MG 14, New Jersey Historical Society.

Others were like Connecticut's acerbic: "Jedediah Huntington to Gov. Jonathan Trumbull, 20 February, 1778," Trumbull Papers, Vol. 6, No. 4, Connecticut State Library, Hartford.

Similar mutterings and Washington's dramatically: "From George Washington to George Clinton, 16 February 1778," in *The Papers of George Washington,* Revolutionary War Series, Vol. 13, ed. Lengel, pp. 552–54.

Each and every regiment: Bodle, *Valley Forge Report,* Vol. 1, p. 249, citing "Francis Dana, 16 February 1778," Dreer Collection, Members of the Old Congress, Historical

Society of Pennsylvania, Philadelphia.

As an aside in the National Park: Ibid., p. 210.

Morris warned Clinton: Ibid., p. 215, citing "Gouverneur Morris to George Clinton, 17 February 1778," Emmet Collection, No. 4190, New York State Library, Albany.

Hamilton in particular: Chernow, *Alexander Hamilton,* p. 108.

He dreaded the idea: Bodle, *Valley Forge Report,* Vol. 1, p. 315, citing "Nathanael Greene to Alexander McDougall, 28 March 1778," Alexander McDougall Papers, New-York Historical Society.

Those who still survived: "Brig. Gen. John Patterson (of Massachusetts) to Thomas Marshall, Feb. 23," Ely Collection, MG 14, New Jersey Historical Society.

"tryals and Sufferings": "Thomas Jones to Charles Stewart, Feb. 18, 1778," Charles Stewart Collection, New York State Historical Association.

The members of the Camp Committee laid: "Jedediah Huntington to Gov. Jonathan Trumbull, Feb. 20," Trumbull Papers, Vol. 6, No. 4, Connecticut State Library.

Without mentioning Gen. Greene: Bodle, *Valley Forge Report,* Vol. 1, p. 202, citing "Committee of Conference to Henry Laurens, 20 February 1778," Papers of the Continental Congress, NARA, Washington, DC, RG 93, M-247, Roll 40, NA.

All the while Washington continued: "Alexander Hamilton to Gov. George Clinton," in Syrett, *The Papers of Alexander Hamilton,* Vol. I, p. 428.

The five delegates contended: Bodle, *Valley Forge Report,* Vol. 1, p. 241, citing "Committee of Conference to Henry Laurens, 25 February 1778," PCC, RG 93, M-247, Roll 40, NA.

Under Gates's new operation: Ibid.

Eschewing his usual dictation: "From George Washington to Lieutenant Colonel John Fitzgerald, 28 February 1778," in *The Papers of George Washington,* Revolutionary War Series, Vol. 13, ed. Lengel, pp. 694–95.

Chapter Twenty-Four: Martha

In private, Washington considered: "From George Washington to Brigadier General Thomas Nelson, Jr., 8 February 1778," in *The Papers of George Washington,* Revolutionary War Series, Vol. 13, ed. Lengel, pp. 480–82.

Proclaiming himself "flattered": Idzerda, *Lafayette in the Age of the American Revolution,* Vol. I (18 February 1778), p. 288.

In addition, he demanded: Ibid.

"I know that Conway": Ibid. (26 January 1778), p. 253.

They did, Lafayette later: Ibid. (27 January

1778), p. 255.

Pining for the crisp New England: "James Mitchell Varnum to Mrs. William Greene, March 7, 1778," John Reed Collection, Valley Forge National Historical Park.

Gates's old opponent Benedict Arnold: Fleming, *Washington's Secret War,* p. 193.

Discouraged and frustrated: Idzerda, *Lafayette in the Age of the American Revolution,* Vol. I (19 February 1778), pp. 295–96.

Whether this had resulted: Ibid.

He was embarrassed: Ibid., p. 300.

Instead, in an attempt to assuage: "From George Washington to Major General Lafayette, 10 March 1778," in *The Papers of George Washington,* Revolutionary War Series, Vol. 14, ed. Hoth, pp. 132–33.

As for the news: Ibid.

Finally, regarding the prospect: Ibid.

Instead, he wrote to Gates: "From George Washington to Major General Horatio Gates, 24 February 1778," in *The Papers of George Washington,* Revolutionary War Series, Vol. 13, ed. Lengel, pp. 654–55.

He was praying aloud: http://ushistory.org/valleyforge/washington/prayer.html.

Washington was known to instruct: "General Orders, 18 October 1777," in *The Papers of George Washington,* Revolutionary War Series, Vol. 11, ed. Chase and Lengel, pp. 541–42.

And though his public: Ibid., "From George Washington to John Augustine Washington, 18 October 1777," pp. 551–53.

As the historian and Revolutionary War: Fleming, *Washington's Secret War*, p. 191.

On the other hand, the most: Chernow, *Washington: A Life,* p. 326.

This variant had the Marquis: http://ushistory.org/valleyforge/washington/prayer.html.

"In none of these": http://www.ushistory.org/valleyforge/ washington/prayer.html.

Having already issued: "Proclamation on Cattle, 18 February 1778," in *The Papers of George Washington,* Revolutionary War Series, Vol. 13, ed. Lengel, pp. 577–78.

The orders stressed that: Ibid., "General Orders, 22 February 1778," pp. 637–39.

Part III Epigraph

"I rejoice most sincerely": "From George Washington to Robert Morris, 25 May 1778," in *The Papers of George Washington,* Revolutionary War Series, Vol. 15, ed. Lengel, pp. 221–22.

Chapter Twenty-Five: Prussian Spring

However, one teenage: http://www.smithsonianmag.com/history/baron-von-steuben-180963048/.

The king's summer palace: https://www .spectator.co.uk/2015/10/frederick-the-great-king-of-prussia-is-a-great-read/.

Moreover, Franklin wrote that it was: Lockhart, *The Drillmaster of Valley Forge,* p. 45.

The object of his "greatest ambition": Scheer and Rankin, *Rebels and Redcoats,* p. 320.

Laurens was so impressed: "John Laurens Letter to Henry Laurens, 28 February 1778," in Simms, *The Army Correspondence of Colonel John Laurens 1777–1778,* p. 131.

"Our men [remain]": Ibid., p. 112, letter of 23 February 1778.

He also noted that Steuben: Ibid.

"With a little more discipline": Ibid.

His first report detailed: Buchanan, *The Road to Valley Forge,* pp. 303–4.

"We want some kind": "John Laurens Letter to Henry Laurens, 28 February 1778," in Simms, *The Army Correspondence of John Laurens 1777–1778,* p. 132.

As he wrote to an old friend: Lockhart, *The Drillmaster of Valley* Forge, p. 1.

Chapter Twenty-Six: The Rains Never Cease

"Now is the time to press": Bodle, *Valley Forge Report,* Vol. 1, p. 336, citing "Sir Henry Clinton to the Duke of Newcastle, 22 March 1778," Newcastle MSS, Nottingham University Library.

They thus commanded: Plaque at Museum of

the American Revolution, Philadelphia, PA.

His men and horses: Bodle, *Valley Forge Report,* Vol. 1, p. 337, citing "William Howe to Lord George Germain (extract), 19 April 1778," Germain Papers, William L. Clements Library.

"America never entertained": Parliamentary Register, 10:13, 30–33.

The British stock market: Bodle, *Valley Forge Report,* Vol. 1, p. 333, citing "Lord George Germain to Sir Henry Clinton, 8 March 1778," Secret Dispatch Book, Germain Papers, William L. Clements Library.

Specifically, if upon taking command: Ibid.

It was a sound blueprint: Bodle, *Valley Forge Report,* Vol. 1, p. 334, citing "George III, 'Secret Instructions for Our Trusty and Wellbeloved Sir Henry Clinton, K.B. and General & Commander in Chief of Our Forces in North America or the Commander in Chief of Our Forces for the time being,' 21 March 1778," Clinton Papers, William L. Clements Library.

To erase any doubt: Bodle, *Valley Forge Report,* Vol. 1, p. 335, citing "Admiralty Board to Lord Richard Howe, 22 March 1778," quoted in Mackesy, *The War for America,* p. 186.

The new orders included a coda: Ibid., p. 334, citing "George III, 'Secret Instructions,' 21 March 1778," Clinton Papers, William L.

Clements Library.

Washington even tweaked: "From George Washington to Major General Horatio Gates, 6 March 1778," in *The Papers of George Washington,* Revolutionary War Series, Vol. 14, ed. Hoth, pp. 77–79.

Nonetheless, Washington's deputy commissary: Ibid., "General Orders, 1 March 1778," pp. 1–4.

In one of his first official acts: "James Thompson to Clement Biddle, March 2, 1778," Washington Papers, Roll 47, Library of Congress.

Washington, stalling for time: "General Orders, 1 March 1778," in *The Papers of George Washington,* Revolutionary War Series, Vol. 14, ed. Hoth, pp. 1–4.

Notably, in that same General: Ibid.

John Laurens, ever the melancholy: "John Laurens Letter to Henry Laurens, 9 March 1778," in Simms, *The Army Correspondence of John Laurens 1777–1778,* p. 135.

While Laurens agonized over: "Alexander Hamilton to Gov. George Clinton, March 12, 1778," in Syrett, *The Papers of Alexander Hamilton,* Vol. I, p. 441.

Offended by the Continentals' lack: "From George Washington to Brigadier General Casimir Pulaski, 3 March 1778," in *The Papers of George Washington,* Revolutionary War Series, Vol. 14, ed. Hoth, pp. 49–50.

In theory, the unit would be: "John Laurens Letter to Henry Laurens, 14 March 1778," in Simms, *The Army Correspondence of John Laurens 1777–1778*, p. 142

Though his work ground on: "From George Washington to John Cadwalader, 20 March 1778," in *The Papers of George Washington*, Revolutionary War Series, Vol. 14, ed. Hoth, pp. 234–35.

Chapter Twenty-Seven: A Trim Reckoning

Despite his initial trepidation: Curtis F. Morgan, Jr., *Journal of the American Revolution*, Yardley, PA: Westholme, 2016.

In response, he informed: "Nathanael Greene to Henry Laurens, 26 March 1778," in Showman, *The Papers of Nathanael Greene*, Vol. 2, p. 321.

He also activated plans: "From George Washington to Major General Nathanael Greene, 31 March 1778," in *The Papers of George Washington*, Revolutionary War Series, Vol. 14, ed. Hoth, pp. 367–68.

They were, as so eloquently: Ellis, *His Excellency*, p. 114.

Woe betide the soldier: "John Laurens Letter to Henry Laurens, 1 April 1778," in Simms, *The Army Correspondence of John Laurens 1777–1778*, p. 152.

"Come over here": http://gayinfluence .blogspot/2011/12/baron-von-steuben.html.

Yet as the historian Wayne Bodle notes: Bodle, *Valley Forge Report,* Vol. 1, p. 350.

Breaking his gaunt combatants: Frederick William von Steuben, *Regulations for the Order and Discipline of the Troops of the United States* (published by the Continental Congress, 1779), p. 10.

He was aghast: New England Historical Society, http://www.newenglandhistorical-society.com/baron-von-steuben-shows-the-army-is-not-a-grilling-tool/.

By the end of his first: "John Laurens Letter to Henry Laurens, 18 April 1778," in Simms, *The Army Correspondence of John Laurens 1777–1778,* p. 160.

"You say to your soldiers": Lockhart, *The Drillmaster of Valley Forge,* p. 104.

"No European army": Joseph R. Conlin, *The American Past: A Survey of American History,* (Belmont, CA: Wadsworth, 2013), Vol. 1, p. 15.

Brigade and regiment commanders: "General Orders, 9 April 1778," in *The Papers of George Washington,* Revolutionary War Series, Vol. 14, ed. Hoth, p. 431.

Noncommissioned officers: Martin, *Narrative of a Revolutionary Soldier,* p. 118.

After all, Laurens wrote to his father: "John Laurens Letter to Henry Laurens, 9 March

1778," in Simms, *The Army Correspondence of John Laurens 1777–1778*, p. 137.

The normally circumspect young scribe: Syrett, *Papers of Alexander Hamilton,* Vol. I, p. 588.

Cleanup crews were suddenly: "General Orders, 13 March 1778," in *The Papers of George Washington,* Revolutionary War Series, Vol. 14, ed. Hoth, pp. 166–67.

Washington took notice: Ibid., "General Orders, 14 April 1778," pp. 508–9.

"My enterprise succeeded": Scheer and Rankin, *Rebels and Redcoats,* p. 320.

Offended and confused: The Papers of Henry Laurens, Vol. XII, 22 April 1778.

"The door is shut": Ibid.

"If Mr. Howe opens": "John Laurens Letter to Henry Laurens, 1 April 1778," in Simms, *The Army Correspondence of John Laurens 1777–1778,* p. 152.

Chapter Twenty-Eight: A Rumor of War

And upon hearing rumors: Bodle, *Valley Forge Report,* Vol. 1, p. 357, citing "Anthony Wayne to Thomas Wharton, 10 April 1778," Wayne Papers, William L. Clements Library, Ann Arbor, MI.

"We could hardly wish": "Jedediah Huntington to Jabez Huntington, 13 March 1778," Huntington Papers, Connecticut Historical Society, Hartford.

He viewed the United States: Gopnik,

"Trump's Radical Anti-Americanism," *New Yorker,* p. 29.

"What is to be done?": "From George Washington to Major General Alexander McDougall, 31 March 1778," in *The Papers of George Washington,* Revolutionary War Series, Vol. 14, ed. Hoth, pp. 369–70.

"We must either oppose": Ibid.

By early April, however: Ibid., "From George Washington to Henry Laurens, 10 April 1778," pp. 459–64.

Regarding the Redcoats: Ibid., "From George Washington to Major General Alexander McDougall, 8 April 1778," pp. 426–27.

"Scarce a day passes": Ibid., "From George Washington to Henry Laurens, 10 April 1778," pp. 459–64.

If he could not retain leaders: Ibid.

The politicians would do well: Ibid.

A lieutenant colonel from: Bodle, *Valley Forge Report,* Vol. 1, p. 359, citing "Samuel Ward to Phoebe Ward, April 1778," Ward Papers, Rhode Island Historical Society.

Even the chronically vexed: "Valley Forge" (poem), *History Magazine,* September 1863, p. 272.

And a Virginia officer assigned: Bodle, *Valley Forge Report,* Vol. 1, p. 358, citing "Gustavus B. Wallace to Michael Wallace, 28 March 1778," University of Virginia Library, Charlottesville.

It would be in the state: Ibid., citing "Nathanael Greene to Alexander McDougall, 16 April 1778," McDougall Papers, New-York Historical Society.

This was accompanied by a direct: "From George Washington to Henry Laurens, 18 April 1778," in *The Papers of George Washington,* Revolutionary War Series, Vol. 14, ed. Hoth, pp. 546–48.

Washington sensed that the concessions: Ibid.

Lord North's peace overture: Ibid.

"Nothing short of Independence": Ibid.

The marquis remained embarrassed: Idzerda, *Lafayette in the Age of the American Revolution,* Vol. II (April 14, 1778), pp. 25–26.

In his opening remarks: "From George Washington to Henry Laurens, 18 April 1778," in *The Papers of George Washington,* Revolutionary War Series, Vol. 14, ed. Hoth, pp. 546–48.

If they leaned toward: Ibid., "From George Washington to the General Officers, 20 April 1778," p. 567.

In a long letter to Washington: Idzerda, *Lafayette in the Age of the American Revolution,* Vol. II (25 April 1778), p. 28.

Chapter Twenty-Nine: "Long Live the King of France"

in cooperation with Abercrombie's regulars: https://www.myrevolutionarywar.com/

battles/780501-crooked-billet/.

As Simcoe himself noted: Bodle, *Valley Forge Report,* Vol. 1, p. 424, citing Simcoe, *Journal of the Queen's Rangers,* p. 60.

He told Lacey that he recognized: "From George Washington to Brigadier General John Lacey, Jr., 11 May 1778," in *The Papers of George Washington,* Revolutionary War Series, Vol. 15, ed. Lengel, pp. 101–2.

In the middle of that month: "From George Washington to John Parke Custis, 14 November 1777," in *The Papers of George Washington,* Revolutionary War Series, Vol. 12, ed. Grizzard and Hoth, pp. 249–50.

Over the interim similar: Pennsylvania Gazette (York), April 11, 1778; and *Pennsylvania Packet* (Lancaster), April 8, 1778.

Though exultant at the "glorious News": "From George Washington to John Augustine Washington, 1 May 1778," in *The Papers of George Washington,* Revolutionary War Series, Vol. 15, ed. Lengel, pp. 285–87.

"all Europe into a flame": "From George Washington to Brigadier General William Smallwood, 30 April 1778," in *The Papers of George Washington,* Revolutionary War Series, Vol. 14, ed. Hoth, pp. 684–86.

When he shared the news: "John Laurens Letter to Henry Laurens, 12 May 1778," in Simms, *The Army Correspondence of John*

Laurens 1777–1778, p. 171.

On a more personal level: Ibid., "John Laurens Letter to Henry Laurens, 1 May 1778," p. 166.

"With infinite pleasure": "From George Washington to Henry Laurens, 1 May 1778," in *The Papers of George Washington,* Revolutionary War Series, Vol. 15, ed. Lengel, pp. 4–5.

Although Drayton's official notices: Ibid., "General Orders, 5 May 1778," pp. 38–41.

"Long live the King of France": Ibid.

"And Long live the friendly European powers": Ibid.

"To the American States": Ibid.

"The admirable rapidity": "John Laurens Letter to Henry Laurens, 7 May 1778," in Simms, *The Army Correspondence of John Laurens 1777–1778,* p. 169.

A week earlier he had surreptitiously: "From George Washington to Henry Laurens, 30 April 1778," in *The Papers of George Washington,* Revolutionary War Series, Vol. 14, ed. Hoth, pp. 681–83.

For like John Laurens: Kapp, *Life of de Kalb,* p. 138.

In reply the elder Laurens: Ibid.

The man who only two days: "From George Washington to Major General Alexander McDougall, 5 May 1778," in *The Papers of George Washington,* Revolutionary War

Series, Vol. 15, ed. Lengel, pp. 47–48.

Chapter Thirty: The Modern Cato

He'd entitled his private: "Washington's Thoughts upon a Plan of Operation for Campaign 1778, 26–29 April 1778," in *The Papers of George Washington,* Revolutionary War Series, Vol. 14, ed. Hoth, pp. 641–47.

Now, anticipating that: Ibid.

Now, as then, his third: Ibid.

A retrenchment at Valley Forge: Ibid.

This was the first meeting: "From George Washington to Gouverneur Morris, 18 May 1778," in *The Papers of George Washington,* Revolutionary War Series, Vol. 15, ed. Lengel, pp. 156–57.

His spy network: "Washington's Thoughts upon a Plan of Operation for Campaign 1778, 26–29 April 1778," in *The Papers of George Washington,* Revolutionary War Series, Vol. 14, ed. Hoth, pp. 641–47.

The written consensus: Bodle, *Valley Forge Report,* Vol. 1, p. 401, citing "John Armstrong et al., 'Summary of Opinions of the Council of War,' 8 May 1778," George Washington Papers, Library of Congress.

Now, like Lafayette: "Continental Army War Council, 8 May 1778," George Washington Papers, Library of Congress.

The announced alliance: Ibid.

He boasted to Henry Laurens: Bodle, *Valley Forge Report,* Vol. 1, p. 407, citing "Friedrich Steuben to Henry Laurens, 15 May 1778" (typescript), Laurens Papers, Long Island Historical Society.

Even among the cantankerous: Ibid., p. 411, citing "George Fleming to Sebastian Bauman, 14 May 1778," Sebastian Bauman Papers, New-York Historical Society.

Still brooding over the possibility: "John Laurens Letter to Henry Laurens, 12 May 1778," in Simms, *The Army Correspondence of John Laurens 1777–1778,* p. 172.

"Joy," wrote one: Bodle, *Valley Forge Report,* Vol. 1, p. 411, citing "George Fleming to Sebastian Bauman, 14 May 1778," Sebastian Bauman Papers, New-York Historical Society.

Chapter Thirty-One: Knights and Fair Maidens

Citing his "regard": Clinton, *American Rebellion,* p. 85.

Now, in a series of letters: Bodle, *Valley Forge Report,* Vol. 1, p. 437, citing "Sir Henry Clinton, 6 June 1778," Clinton Papers, William L. Clements Library; "Sir Henry Clinton to the Duke of Newcastle, 16 June 1778," Newcastle MSS, Nottingham University Library.

This facile "shew of a design": "John Laurens

Letter to Henry Laurens, 12 May 1778," in Simms, *The Army Correspondence of John Laurens 1777–1778,* p. 172.

With this proverbial: "Journal of Ambrose Serle, 21 May 1778," in Rhodehamel, *The American Revolution,* p. 429.

After the transition ceremony: Bodle, *Valley Forge Report,* Vol. 1, p. 422, citing "Henry Clinton, 'Minutes of Conversation with Lord Howe and Joseph Galloway,' May, 1778," Clinton Papers, William L. Clements Library.

"The Enemy are beginning": "From George Washington to John Banister, 21 April 1778," in *The Papers of George Washington,* Revolutionary War Series, Vol. 14, ed. Hoth, pp. 573–79.

What is recorded: "From George Washington to Major General Lafayette, 18 May 1778," in *The Papers of George Washington,* Revolutionary War Series, Vol. 15, ed. Lengel, pp. 151–54.

Any "severe blow": Ibid.

When reports of the farewell: Fleming, *Washington's Secret War,* p. 271.

"We placed our guards": Martin, *Narrative of a Revolutionary Soldier,* p. 103.

A disdainful Clinton: Bodle, *Valley Forge Report,* Vol. 1, p. 417, citing Simcoe, *Journal of the Queen's Rangers,* pp. 60–61.

"A brilliant retreat": "John Laurens Letter to

Henry Laurens, 27 May 1778," in Simms, *The Army Correspondence of John Laurens 1777–1778*, p. 174.

And Henry Laurens urged: Papers of Henry Laurens, Vol. XIII, pp. 345–47 (27 May 1778).

Even Joseph Plumb Martin: Martin, *Narrative of a Revolutionary Soldier,* p. 106.

Chapter Thirty-Two: The Gauntlet Thrown

Perhaps part of this: "From George Washington to Major General Charles Lee, 15 June 1778," in *The Papers of George Washington,* Revolutionary War Series, Vol. 15, ed. Lengel, pp. 406–8.

"Relinquishing all pretensions": Ibid., "From George Washington to Gouverneur Morris, 29 May 1778," pp. 260–62.

Yet, as he concluded: Ibid.

Finally, the camp's surgeons: "General Orders, 25 May 1778," *Founders Online,* National Archives, last modified November 26, 2017. Original source: *The Papers of George Washington,* Revolutionary War Series, Vol. 15, ed. Lengel, p. 213.

Amid this frenzied final: "General Orders, 23 May 1778," in *The Papers of George Washington,* Revolutionary War Series, Vol. 15, ed. Lengel, p. 194. See also "General Orders, 28 May 1778," pp. 241–44; "General Orders, 29 May 1778," pp. 249–50.

Each soldier was issued: Ibid., "General Orders, 28 May 1778."

One Massachusetts colonel: Bodle, *Valley Forge Report,* Vol. 1, p. 419, citing "Dudley Coleman to his wife, 30 May 1778," Dudley Coleman Papers, Massachusetts Historical Society, Boston.

And even Alexander Hamilton: Syrett, *The Papers of Alexander Hamilton,* Vol. I (29 May 1778), p. 491.

This was not enough: "From George Washington to Brigadier General William Smallwood, 23 May 1778," in *The Papers of George Washington,* Revolutionary War Series, Vol. 15, ed. Lengel, pp. 206–7.

Though the information turned: Bodle, *Valley Forge Report,* Vol. 1, p. 419, citing "Henry Knox to William Knox, 27 May 1778," Knox Papers MHS (Massachusetts Historical Society).

Carlisle immediately made clear: Commager and Morris, *Spirit of 'Seventy-Six,* pp. 696–97.

Henry Laurens heard from: Massey, *John Laurens and the American Revolution,* p. 105.

Father and son both: "John Laurens Letter to Henry Laurens, 11 June 1778," in Simms, *The Army Correspondence of John Laurens 1777–1778,* p. 184.

And the peace panel's secretary: https://blog.oup.com/2013/08/carlisle-commission-us-congress-part-1/.

The Americans, long: "Tench Tilghman to James Tilghman, April 24, 1778," in Tilghman, *Memoir of Lieut. Col. Tench Tilghman,* p. 165.

Writing to his fellow: "From George Washington to Landon Carter, 30 May 1778," in *The Papers of George Washington,* Revolutionary War Series, Vol. 15, ed. Lengel, pp. 267–70.

The withdrawal was hastened: "John Laurens Letter to Henry Laurens, 9 June 1778," in Simms, *The Army Correspondence of John Laurens 1777–1778,* p. 182.

Finally, on June 17: Bodle, *Valley Forge Report,* Vol. 1, p. 444, citing "Circular Letter to the States," in Ford, *Journals of the Continental Congress,* Vol. XI, pp. 583–84. See also "Henry Laurens to George Washington, 14 June 1778," William L. Clements Library, University of Michigan, Ann Arbor.

In a defiant coda: Henry Laurens, in Ford, *Journals of the Continental Congress,* Vol. XI, p. 615; Commager and Morris, *Spirit of 'Seventy Six,* p. 698.

Chapter Thirty-Three: "You Damned Poltroon"

It was slowed by: Marshall and Duane, *Extracts from the Diary of Christopher Marshall,* (27 June 1778), p. 190.

The Americans would be likely: Wood, *The American Revolution,* pp. 89–90.

Their enthusiasm was shared: Lafayette, "Memoir of 1779," in Idzerda, *Lafayette in the Age of the American Revolution,* Vol. II, pp. 5–7.

Citing a Spanish: Ibid., pp. 50–52.

Lee's argument repulsed: "Hamilton to Elias Boudinot," in Syrett, *The Papers of Alexander Hamilton,* Vol. II, p. 510.

"If we suffer the enemy": "To George Washington from Major General Nathanael Greene, 24 June 1778," in *The Papers of George Washington,* Revolutionary War Series, Vol. 15, ed. Lengel, pp. 525–26.

Lafayette, "still burning": "Journal of James McHenry, 25 June, 1778," in Rhodehamel, *The American Revolution,* p. 462.

Before Washington could commit: Idzerda, *Lafayette in the Age of the American Revolution,* Vol. II, p. 90.

Among the Americans stalking: Martin, *Narrative of a Revolutionary Soldier,* p. 110.

If they were careful: Pearson, *Those Damned Rebels,* p. 310.

When Harrison asked: Lender, *Fatal Sunday: George Washington, the Monmouth Campaign, and the Politics of Battle,* p. 270.

It was a dramatic moment: "John Laurens Letter to Henry Laurens, 30 June 1778," in Simms, *The Army Correspondence of John*

Laurens 1777–1778, p. 196.

"All this disgraceful": Ibid.

One volunteered that they: "Testimony of Lt. Col. Richard Harrison at Gen. Henry Lee's court-martial," New-York Historical Society Collection, Vol. VI, pp 71–75, cited in Commager and Morris, *Spirit of 'Seventy-Six,* p. 712.

Lee was still reining: Chernow, *Washington: A Life,* p. 342.

Instead, perplexed and battered: Ibid.

"The American troops": Ibid.

In his memoirs: Chernow, *Alexander Hamilton,* p. 114.

Another officer observing: Lockhart, *The Drillmaster of Valley Forge,* p. 160. See also Clary, *Adopted Son,* p. 196.

"No one," wrote Lafayette: Idzerda, *Lafayette in the Age of the American Revolution,* Vol. II, p. 11.

Chapter Thirty-Four: "So Superb a Man"

Hamilton reined his horse: Lender, *Fatal Sunday: George Washington, the Monmouth Campaign, and the Politics of Battle,* p. 294.

There, with Wayne urging: Busch, *Winter Quarters,* p. 170.

"A little skirmishing": "John Laurens Letter to Henry Laurens, 30 June 1778," in Simms, *The Army Correspondence of John Laurens 1777–1778,* p. 193.

Then, Washington's horse: Fischer, *Washington's Crossing,* p. 227.

"Will you fight?": Chernow, *Washington: A Life,* p. 343.

"His presence alone": Idzerda, *Lafayette in the Age of the American Revolution,* Vol. II, p. 11.

Citing Washington's "coolness": "Hamilton to Elias Boudinot, 5 July 1778," in Syrett, *The Papers of Alexander Hamilton,* Vol. 1, p. 512.

"The dust and smoke": Lockhart, *The Drillmaster of Valley Forge,* p. 162.

Darkness was falling: Martin, *Narrative of a Revolutionary Soldier,* p. 114.

According to the most reliable: Scheer and Rankin, *Rebels and Redcoats,* p. 335.

The Continentals buried: "To George Washington from Major General Philemon Dickinson, 28 June 1778," in *The Papers of George Washington,* Revolutionary War Series, Vol. 15, ed. Lengel, pp. 573–76.

In the hours to follow: Ibid., "General Orders, 30 June 1778," p. 590.

Though Monmouth was perhaps less dramatically timed: "From George Washington to John Augustine Washington, 4 July 1778, in *The Papers of George Washington,* Revolutionary War Series, Vol. 16, ed. Hoth, pp. 25–26.

In it he described: Ibid., "From George Washington to Henry Laurens, 1 July 1778," pp. 2–7.

"The passion caused by": https://en.wiki
pedia.org/wiki/A_Philosophical_Enquiry_
into_the_Origin_of_Our_Ideas_of_the_Sub
lime_and_Beautiful.

Epilogue

But it certainly represented: Winston Churchill, Speech at the Lord Mayor's Lun-
cheon, Mansion House, November 10,
1942.
As he wrote to the Virginia statesman: "From
George Washington to Brigadier General
Thomas Nelson, Jr., 20 August 1778," in
The Papers of George Washington, Revolu-
tionary War Series, Vol. 16, ed. Hoth,
pp. 340–42.
This coheres with the historian: Wills, *Cincin-
natus: George Washington and the Enlighten-
ment* (New York: Doubleday, 1984), p. 92.
But it was his valedictory speech: Washington's
"Farewell Address," September 19, 1796.
In a letter to John Laurens: "From George
Washington to John Laurens, 13 October
1780," National Archives, last modified
February 1, 2018.
Within days he was alternately: Chernow,
Washington: A Life, p. 345.
He then wrote to the commander in chief: Ibid.
Washington accused Lee: Ibid.
Since throwing his lot in with: http://www
.publicbookshelf.com/public_html/Our_

Country_vol_2/generalc_bbe.html.

As the Rev. William Howard Day: Cox, *Come All You Brave Soldiers,* p. v.

It is thanks to Waldo's journal: "Journal Entries of Albigence Waldo Regarding the Continental Army Moving to Valley Forge, 22 December 1777," in Waldo, *Account of the Ordeal at Valley Forge.*

"The sufferings of the Body": Ibid.

Regarding the signal: Martin, *Narrative of a Revolutionary Soldier,* p. 201.

Only a month earlier: Syrett, *The Papers of Alexander Hamilton,* Vol. III, p. 145.

Steuben's "Blue Book": "From George Washington to Major General Steuben, 26 February 1779," in *The Papers of George Washington,* Revolutionary War Series, Vol. 19, ed. Chase and Ferraro, pp. 271–73.

Even Bodle concedes: Bodle, *Valley Forge Winter,* p. 248.

"In the old days the Continentals": Buchanan, *The Road to Valley Forge,* p. 307.

George Washington, in his last official: "From George Washington to Friedrich Wilhelm Ludolf Gerhard Augustin, Baron [von] Steuben, 23 December 1783," in *The Papers of George Washington.*

"Acknowledging your great": Ibid.

Although he is most closely associated: Lockhart, *The Drillmaster of Valley Forge,* p. 167.

"America has joined": John H. George and

Paul Poller, *They Never Said It* (New York: Oxford University Press, 1990).

"We have made Italy": Charles, L. Killinger, *The History of Italy* (Westport, CT: Greenwood, 2002), p.1.

"With a heart filled": https://www.thenew american.com/culture/history/item/4765-george-washingtons-first-final-farewell.

Afterword

Tiring of the fishing: Diary entry, July 31, 1787, in Jackson and Twohig, *The Diaries of George Washington,* Vol. 5, p. 179.

Come spring he would: Bodle, *Valley Forge Winter,* p. 264.

Then he spurred: Ibid., p. 265.

ILLUSTRATION CREDITS

Part Titles

1. Courtesy of the Library of Congress
2. Courtesy of the Library of Congress
3. Courtesy of Independence National Historical Park

Photo Insert

1. Courtesy of the Library of Congress
2. Courtesy of the Library of Congress
3. Courtesy of Independence National Historical Park
4. Courtesy of the Library of Congress
5. Courtesy of the National Portrait Gallery, Smithsonian Institution
6. Courtesy of the Library of Congress
7. Courtesy of the Library of Congress
8. Courtesy of the Library of Congress
9. Courtesy of the Lilly Library, Indiana University
10. Courtesy of the Library of Congress

11. Courtesy of the Library of Congress
12. Courtesy of Independence National Historical Park
13. Courtesy of the Museum of the American Revolution
14. Courtesy of the Library of Congress
15. Courtesy of the Library of Congress
16. Courtesy of the Library of Congress
17. Courtesy of the Library of Congress
18. Courtesy of Independence National Historical Park
19. Courtesy of the Museum of the American Revolution
20. Courtesy of the Library of Congress
21. Courtesy of the Library of Congress
22. Courtesy of the Library of Congress
23. Courtesy of the Library of Congress
24. Courtesy of the Library of Congress
25. Courtesy of Valley Forge National Historical Park
26. Courtesy of Valley Forge National Historical Park
27. Courtesy of Yale University Art Gallery
28. Courtesy of Yale University Art Gallery
29. Courtesy of the Library of Congress
30. Courtesy of the Library of Congress
31. Courtesy of the Library of Congress
32. Courtesy of the Library of Congress
33. Courtesy of Valley Forge National Historical Park
34. Courtesy of the Mount Vernon Ladies' Association

35. Courtesy of the Library of Congress
36. Courtesy of the Library of Congress
37. Courtesy of the Library of Congress
38. Courtesy of the Library of Congress
39. Courtesy of the Library of Congress

ABOUT THE AUTHORS

Bob Drury and **Tom Clavin** are the #1 *New York Times* bestselling authors of *The Heart of Everything That Is, Halsey's Typhoon, Last Men Out, Lucky 666,* and *The Last Stand of Fox Company,* which won the Marine Corps Heritage Foundation's General Wallace M. Greene Jr. Award for nonfiction. They live in Manasquan, New Jersey, and Sag Harbor, New York, respectively.